Contemporary Issues on Governance, Conflict and Security in Africa

Adeoye O. Akinola

Contemporary Issues on Governance, Conflict and Security in Africa

palgrave
macmillan

Adeoye O. Akinola
Institute for Pan-African Thought and Conversation
University of Johannesburg
Johannesburg, South Africa

ISBN 978-3-031-29634-5   ISBN 978-3-031-29635-2 (eBook)
https://doi.org/10.1007/978-3-031-29635-2

© The Editor(s) (if applicable) and The Author(s), under exclusive license to Springer Nature Switzerland AG 2023

This work is subject to copyright. All rights are solely and exclusively licensed by the Publisher, whether the whole or part of the material is concerned, specifically the rights of translation, reprinting, reuse of illustrations, recitation, broadcasting, reproduction on microfilms or in any other physical way, and transmission or information storage and retrieval, electronic adaptation, computer software, or by similar or dissimilar methodology now known or hereafter developed.

The use of general descriptive names, registered names, trademarks, service marks, etc. in this publication does not imply, even in the absence of a specific statement, that such names are exempt from the relevant protective laws and regulations and therefore free for general use.

The publisher, the authors, and the editors are safe to assume that the advice and information in this book are believed to be true and accurate at the date of publication. Neither the publisher nor the authors or the editors give a warranty, expressed or implied, with respect to the material contained herein or for any errors or omissions that may have been made. The publisher remains neutral with regard to jurisdictional claims in published maps and institutional affiliations.

Cover illustration: © Alex Linch shutterstock.com

This Palgrave Macmillan imprint is published by the registered company Springer Nature Switzerland AG
The registered company address is: Gewerbestrasse 11, 6330 Cham, Switzerland

Preface

Motivation and Objectives

This book offers a holistic understanding of the convergence between governance, conflict and security in Africa. It adopts a political economy approach and qualitative research method, funded on unstructured interview and case studies, to unravel the governance and security questions in Africa. There are exhaustive studies on conventional threats to security in post-colonial Africa; however, there has been a dearth of rigorous research on other emerging threats to human security, which have the potency to aggravate Africa's insecurity and underdevelopment. While cases of armed insurrections and civil wars have reduced on the continent, diverse forms of violent conflicts have endangered the security of lives and property. What explains this trend? As well captured in the volume, the shrinking of many African states and the deepening of structural violence engendered new forms of violent conflict—terrorism, xenophobia, students-led violent protests, gender-based violence, youth-led dissent—and the resurgence of old conflicts, as seen in the new waves of coups in the Sahel and West Africa. Several African states continue to demonstrate their incapacity to ensure peace and security within their territorial delineations.

A resurgence of conflict generated by water and land impedes the quests for social stability, security and socio-economic sustainability in many parts of Africa. In the case of land, it manifests as both structural violence (a precondition for physical violence) and farm attacks as experienced in South Africa, where a high level of land-related inequality and physical violence persist. Despite the optimism associated with the 'Africa rising' conversation, conventional and contemporary threats to peace have stunted its developmental projects. Indeed, there is a strong connection between security and development. While Paul Coulier's insisted that economic consideration causes and perpetuates conflict, the literature identifies both economic and political variables—particularly the state and the political power system—as the main determinants of conflict.

Africa's shifting nature of conflict necessitates fresh conversation on exploring effective contextual techniques to ensure Africa's peace and security. Furthermore, the changing character of the security landscape reveals a rising gap between practice and classical thoughts on conflict, security and governance. Thus, the editor of the book, Oye Akinola, received support from the Institute of Pan-African Thought and Conversation (IPATC) at the University of Johannesburg, to host an author's workshop and brainstorm new trends on conflict and security and the imperativeness of proffering sustainable recommendations for policymaking. The authors in this volume attended and made paper presentations at the workshop, between 10 and 11 March 2022, at the Sheraton Hotel in Pretoria, South Africa.

As discussed during the workshop, many violent conflicts in Africa are occurring outside the purview of government and without government troops, which becomes alarming due to its volatility and difficulty in mediation and reconciliation. Unlike the past when terrorism was associated with ideological extremisms, contemporary forms of terrorism have been linked to religious fundamentalism. The fall of Libya and the global crusade against westernisation have led to the proliferation of armed conflicts in Africa. From the Sahel to the Horn of Africa, evidence of the state's failures and the resultant insecurity abound.

Therefore, the edited volume seeks to unpack how the interactions between the modern state, economy and society engender conflict. It is decisive to also focus on the victims of violent conflict and engage on the peculiarity of their vulnerabilities. Thus, it provides a robust engagement on some of the trends of conflict and insecurity that are becoming apparent in contemporary Africa. It also challenges the orthodox peace architecture on the continent and examines the changing demographics, economic and sociological factors that have implications for security. It provides deeper understanding of the nuances and new forms of conversation for addressing threats to African security, such as violent extremism, violent mass movements and underreported gender-based violence. The book is broad, multi-disciplinary and a knowledge pool for researchers, think-tank community and postgraduate students, and policy practitioners that are engaged in national and regional security and governance.

REALITY OF CONFLICT AND GOVERNANCE-GAP IN AFRICA

Generally, African states have experienced incessant threats to human security in various forms. In Nigeria, a United Nations Development Programme (UNDP) report recently revealed that attacks from the dreaded Boko Haram, including its splinter group—Islamic State West Africa Province (ISWAP) and Fulani herdsmen have resulted in 2.7 million internally displaced persons (IDPs) and 350,000 deaths. Besides the infiltration of Boko Haram's terrorism in Chad, the spillover effects of conflicts in its neighbouring countries—Cameroon, Libya, Sudan and Niger—have compounded Nigeria's quest for stability. According to the United Nations High Commissioner for Refugees (UNHCR), 237,000 refugees and 300,000 IDPs are living in Niger, which includes an additional 4000 refugees and 2000 newly displaced in 2021 due to attacks in the Tillabéri and Tahoua regions.

In June 2021, local armed men unleashed violence on a village—Solhan—in northeast Burkina Faso near the Nigerien border. This attack claimed 138 lives and 40 sustained injuries. By January 2022, the Burkinabè military struck and toppled the civilian government of President Roch Kaboré. The personalisation of political power has become one of the major reasons for military incursions into politics in West Africa and the Sahel. In Guinea, the military, and the populace, were frustrated by the tenure elongation of two successive post-independence leaders—President Sékou Touré and Lansana Conté—who stayed in power for 26 and 24 years, respectively.

Cameroon, which nearly went to war with Nigeria over border disputes, has become another concern. In 2016, what started as a protest by the two anglophone regions against marginalisation by the majority French-speaking government has turned the country into a war zone. The violent conflict between the central government and minority separatist groups has killed over 4000 people and displaced more than a million, including 66,899 refugees who fled to Nigeria. The spillover of Boko Haram's terrorism from Nigeria to Cameron has led to the killing of over 3000 people and displacement of 250,000 in northern Cameroon. The country has also played host to 441,000 refugees, mostly from Nigeria and the Central African Republic.

On 30 May 2021, about 60 people were killed during an attack—carried out by suspected Allied Democratic Forces (ADF)—in Ituri Province in the Democratic Republic of the Congo (DRC). The Ethiopian premier, Abiy Ahmed Ali, embarked on a military offensive in November 2020 to 'restore the rule of law' in Tigray by confronting the Tigray People's Liberation Front (TPLF), who had attacked a federal military base. Ahmed Ali, the winner of the Nobel Peace Prize 2019, continues with a crackdown on Tigray, and African leaders and the African Union (AU), that have initially 'refused' to respond effectively have now managed to broker a deal between the two warring sides.

The resource-part of Mozambique, Cabo Delgado Province, is also becoming a harbour for terrorism and lawlessness. This is too grave for regional security and too close for Pretoria's comfort. The regional body—the Southern African Development Community (SADC)—is currently exploring the best approach to curtail the threat that terrorism poses to regional security. SADC deployed a regional task force, under the SADC Mission in Mozambique (SAMIM), to support the country's effort at counterterrorism. The hitherto domestic Islamist insurgent group operating in the country's north-eastern Cabo Delgado Province drew global attention in March 2021, when they attacked Palma in the northern part of the country. According to the BBC, the attack killed many foreigners working on a $20 billion gas plant—the biggest single foreign investment in Africa.[1] More than 35,000 housing facilities have either been partially or totally destroyed at the start of the conflict,[2] and about 700,000 Mozambicans have now been displaced internally due to the ensuing reign of terror.

---

[1] See, https://www.bbc.com/news/world-africa-56886085.

[2] For more information on the conflict in Mozambique, see d'Orsi, Cristiano (2022). Catalogue of failures behind growing humanitarian crisis in northern Mozambique, https://theconversation.com/catalogue-of-failures-behind-growing-humanitarian-crisis-in-northern-mozambique-149343.

The Problematic

Despite slow efforts to silence the guns in Africa, there are cases of bloodletting, and it does not look as if the gun-wielding groups are retreating. What accounts for the expanding proliferation of conflicts? Colonial legacy? While this is close to the heart, the false promise of liberal democracy and capitalism systems have exposed the fragility of the disjointed elitist states that are dependent on global financial oligarchs, many of which are governed by greedy, corrupt and inept leaders. Democratisation in Africa, which is regarded as the antidote to both internal resurrections and external aggressions, has deepened poverty, structural violence, identity assertiveness and the politicisation of ethnic groups, as well as the privatisation of power by the ruling elites.

Indeed, the liberal peace architecture has recorded failures on several fronts in Africa. Proponents of this school of thought have continued to celebrate the democratic peace theory, based on the so-called resilience of political and representative institutions, as well as institutional constraints, within the broad discourse on effective internal mechanisms, which embrace peace, negotiation, accountability and reconciliation. The brand of democracy exported to Africa is lacking in these attributes. Any attempts by the citizens to discuss the nature of relations between themselves and the state, based on shared identity, common values and goals, have been resisted by Africa's ruling class, political entrepreneurs and upper-level bourgeoisie, who have personalised public goods, expanded the inequality gap and manipulated the political spaces. African societies have been militarised to the extent that citizens celebrated the incursions of the military in politics in West Africa and the Sahel. The term, 'military is an aberration', is becoming unpopular in the Sahel.

The AU, including regional organisations such as the Economic Community of West African States (ECOWAS), has its hands full, in attempting to restore order to troubled zones. While the institutional capacity of the AU is becoming worrying and apparent, other foreign powers are seizing the opportunity to consolidate their power and interests in Africa. The new 'scramble' for the soul of the Sahel and West Africa by France, China and Russia, including the existing military visibility of the United States (US), are reminders of imperial wars and colonialism. There have been allegations of mercenaries on African soil, and Russia continues to cut into Mali and Central Africa Republic (CAR). The US military, which is active in about 20 African countries, has continued to make its military footprint in Africa by investing $100 million in its armed MQ-9 Reaper drones base in Niger, with an annual maintenance cost of $30 million.[3] This became the largest 'airman-built' project in Air Force history and the largest base-building project ever undertaken by troops in US history. The AU should be worried. African states should be concerned, and Africans should begin to confront the foreign siege on the continent.

Johannesburg, South Africa
January 2023

Adeoye O. Akinola
Head: Research and Teaching,
and Head of Unit: African Union Studies

---

[3] See, Turse, Nick (2018) "The U.S. is building a drone base in Niger that will cost more than $280 million by 2024", *The Intercept*, 21 August; https://theintercept.com/2018/08/21/us-drone-base-niger-africa/.

Contents

1 Africa and the Scourge of Conflict and Insecurity   1
   Adeoye O. Akinola and Emmaculate Asige Liaga

2 African Conflict and the "Post-colonial" State   17
   Stephen Phiri

3 Climate Change and Emerging Conflict Between
   Herders and Farmers in Nasarawa and Plateau States,
   Nigeria   33
   Samuel K. Okunade and Habila S. Kohon

4 Grassroots Conflict Over Ecosystem Services Provided
   by the Inner Niger Delta: The Case of Mali   53
   Ratidzo C. Makombe

5 Conflict, Police Impunity and the Governance
   Question in Nigeria: Reflecting on the #EndSARS
   Protest   69
   Omololu Fagbadebo and Leke Oluwalogbon

6 Trapped in the Ivory Tower: Using Social Movement
   Theory to Analyse a 'Movement in Distress'   91
   Terri Maggott

7	Terrorism in Sub-Sahara Africa: Assessing its Economic and Social Implications Olumuyiwa Temitope Faluyi	109
8	Violent Conflict in the Sahel: Causes, Dynamics, and Actors Adeoye O. Akinola and Naledi Ramontja	125
9	The Resurgence of Military Coups in Africa: The Case of West Africa and the Sahel Gwinyai Regis Taruvinga	147
10	Media and Election Disputes in Nigeria N. Oluwafemi 'Femi' Mimiko and Harrison Adewale Idowu	159
11	Governance, Security and Development Nexus in Galkayo, Somalia: A New Approach to Explaining Somalia's Chronic Instability Abdullahi Mohammed Odowa	175
12	Ceasefire Arrangements as a Pre-condition for Independence in Southern Africa: Implications for Land Conflicts in Zimbabwe and South Africa Mzingaye Brilliant Xaba	191
13	The Security Sector in Zimbabwe's Diamond Governance (2006–2015) Tyanai Masiya	213
14	Ethnic Federalism, Exclusionary Self-Determination Rights and Conflict in Ethiopia: Consociational Democracy as an Alternative Approach to Peace and Security Seyoum Mesfin	227
15	Somaliland's Plural Justice System and Its Influence on Peacebuilding and Development Hamdi I. Abdulahi	249

16	Exploring the Impact of Women's Organisations in Peacebuilding in South Sudan: Post-independence Progress Tolulope Adeogun, Obianuju E. Okeke-Uzodike, and Abidemi A. Isola	273
17	Gender-Based Violence in South Africa: The Second Pandemic? Nompumelelo Ndawonde	287
18	A Reflection on Gender-Based Violence in Nigeria Bolanle Oluwakemi Eniola and Joseph I. Aremo	309
19	Food Security as a New Frontier of War: A Geo-Historical Perspective of Food Security and Armed Conflict in Sub-Saharan Africa Malaika Lesego Samora Mahlatsi	327
20	IGAD and the Quest for Economic and Security Regionalism Mohamed Farah Hersi	343

Index 363

CHAPTER 1

Africa and the Scourge of Conflict and Insecurity

Adeoye O. Akinola and Emmaculate Asige Liaga

INTRODUCTION

Africa has been characterised as a conflict zone since the turn of the twentieth century, and the continent experienced the highest number of armed conflicts in the world between 2015 and 2016 (PRIO, 2013). While conventional conflict such as civil war and communal clashes continue unabated, new forms of conflict have also become part of the African narrative. Indeed, conflict on the continent is assuming a shape and space that was not the norm in the two decades following the end of the Cold War. While conflict, violence and insecurity have been approached from the standpoint of states as the decisive actors, as argued by the securitisation school of thought, in Africa and beyond, it has also involved non-state actors and human security issues (see, Buzan et al.,

A. O. Akinola (✉) · E. A. Liaga
Institute for Pan-African Thought and Conversation, University of Johannesburg, Johannesburg, South Africa
e-mail: aoakinola@uj.ac.za

© The Author(s), under exclusive license to Springer Nature Switzerland AG 2023
A. O. Akinola, *Contemporary Issues on Governance, Conflict and Security in Africa*,
https://doi.org/10.1007/978-3-031-29635-2_1

1998). In many instances, non-state actors have taken up arms against other non-state actors, armed groups have fought other armed groups, and communal clashes have been characterised by socio-political and economic undertones. Religious terrorism and xenophobia are further forms of conflict in Africa. As such, conversations and discourses on conflict are shifting from simplistic rhetoric to embrace deeper, historical and non-exclusive understanding and approaches.

Despite various efforts by the state and non-state actors at the national, regional and continental levels, conflict and insecurity continue to haunt Africa. They have undermined social harmony and cut across faith movements, impeding sustainable development of the continent and its people. Failure to craft effective socio-economic interventions to combat poverty has aggravated conflict, as poverty deepens the vulnerability of a cross-section of the population, and the youth, in particular, regard violent conflict as a means of survival (Ismail & Olonisakin, 2021). This has hampered the attainment of peace in conflict zones, while hitherto peaceful societies such as those in the Sahel confront security challenges.

There is a rich body of literature on the nexus between governance, peace and security. Indeed, both the African Union (AU) Agenda 2063 and the United Nations' (UN) Sustainable Development Goals (SDGs) regard these three concepts as a precondition for sustainable development. A lack of peace and security has stymied the democratic consolidation of most governments in contemporary Africa. This negatively impacts not only the continent's ability to embrace effective governance, but also to achieve the "Africa We Want". The tenets of liberal democracy embraced by African elites have failed to achieve peace and security. A democratic state should be characterised by accountability and transparency, strong political structures, inclusivity, tolerance and justice, which are necessary to decrease violent conflict; however, the case of Africa is different.

The optimism that accompanied the waves of democracy that swept through post-colonial Africa from the early 1980s led to fewer conflicts a decade after the Cold War. During this period, around 11 of Africa's 54 countries were considered 'free' or democratic states (Lynch & Crawford, 2011). However, by the end of the 1980s democracy's inability to prevent conflict in Africa became apparent as civil war erupted in countries such as Liberia, Sierra Leone and Cote d'Ivoire. By 2017, ten countries, Nigeria, Somalia, Kenya, Sudan, Libya, Tunisia, DRC, Burundi, South Africa and South Sudan, were responsible for 70% of the conflict in Africa (Aremu, 2010). It should be noted that, in several of these countries, this took the form of protests and riots, with South Africa accounting for 16% of violent protests in 2017, followed by Nigeria, Kenya, Algeria and Tunisia.

Insecurity, and by extension violent conflict on the African continent, has evolved over time and became more complicated, complex and protracted, generally involving various actors at any given time and location. Many stakeholders in the African peace and security architecture have categorised these conflicts as core and peripheral: brutal and protracted, and less brutal and not protracted. There has been a tendency to ignore those regarded as minor conflicts such as xenophobia and violent protests, with a focus on civil war and ethnic conflict. In the past decade, terrorism and resource-based conflicts in Nigeria, Congo DRC and Mozambique have altered the nature of conflict due to the naked display of ruthlessness and the monumental destruction of lives and property. Furthermore, the herder-farmer conflicts that have rocked the Sahel have aggravated security threats in the region and caused far more damage than conventional warfare. In South Africa, xenophobia has resulted in around 100 deaths since the first outbreak of xenophobic violence in 2008. It has thus become more complex to categorise conflict into core and peripheral.

To engage the aforementioned emerging security threats and its complex link to governance deficit in Africa, the Institute for Pan-African Thought and Conversation (IPATC) at the University of Johannesburg, South Africa hosted a workshop from 10 to 11 March 2022. This chapter reflects on some of the important discussions on conflict and security trends on the continent. The workshop explored the historical and immediate causes of the conflicts and the manner in which neo-colonial African states have been structured that makes violent conflict inevitable. Issues of concern revolved around cases of conflict relapse, including the failure of ceasefire and peace agreements in countries like South Sudan and the protracted nature of the conflict in Congo DRC. The M-23 is cutting into the country, while resource-politics by the neighbouring countries are impeding sustainable peace in the resource-rich country. This chapter, therefore, provides an overview of Africa's security challenges and offers sustainable policy options to curtail lawlessness and armed conflict on the continent.

Contending Themes on Conflict and Insecurity in Africa

It is pertinent to highlight the contending concerns in relation to Africa's insecurity regime. This section presents a case-by-case analysis of these issues.

Youth, Dissent and Protest Action in Africa

The youth have both positively and negatively impacted the peace and development trajectory in Africa. Population growth has also yielded mixed results. While it could trigger development, Africa faces the herculean task of utilising the population for development purposes. Furthermore, given the extreme poverty that characterises society, the youth, in particular, have been at the receiving end of Africa's socio-economic crisis. Taking the continent as a whole, youth unemployment is estimated at 60%, while 34% of young Africans lived on less than $1.9/day, 59% on less than $3.2 /day; and 80 to 83% on less than $5.5 /day in 2019 (Phiri & Jones, 2022; UNCTAD, 2021). The UN projects that the global population will reach 10 billion by 2055, with 95% of the growth occurring in low- and middle-income countries. Africa is expected to contribute 57% of population growth (1.4 billion people). Currently, 60% of the continent's population is under the age of 25, making it the world's most youthful continent (Policy Commons, 2020). The youth will thus become the dominant force in Africa.

While research has shown that African youth exhibit low levels of civil and political participation, they have nonetheless been active participants in many conflicts across the continent. For instance, the youth were the backbone of the protests that led to the fall of Sudan's president Omar al-Bashir in April 2019. However, they remain largely excluded from political decision-making processes and bear the brunt of the country's economic hardships (Lovise, 2020). Libyan youth have been a major driver of conflict since 2011. The growing youth population and their increased activism should thus be of major concern to stakeholders involved in regional peace and development efforts.

In Nigeria, youth militancy has been exacerbated by allegations of police high-handedness and brutality. Given that they make up a substantial portion of the Nigerian population, the youth interact with uniformed police and the un-uniformed unit known as the Special Anti-Robbery

Squad (SARS) on a regular basis and, as in other parts of Africa, are among those most frequently arrested. The lack of space for public engagement for the many young people who graduated from university but have no employment prospects creates fertile ground for confrontations with law enforcement personnel.

This situation was exacerbated during the COVID-19 pandemic and the subsequent national lockdowns between 2020 and 2021 when the SARS' nefarious activities reached their peak. There were widespread allegations of police brutality and human rights violations in the course of enforcing the lockdown restrictions (Obaji, 2020). While the constitutional role of a police officer is to promote peace and security, and maintain law and order, the Nigerian police have resorted to extorting money from innocent civilians and crime rings for their personal benefit. In 2020, police brutality during the lockdown led to around 18 deaths (Arimie et al., 2021: 8). The youth in other African countries, including South Africa, suffered the same fate. Police brutality is a reflection of the government and the security system's authoritarian culture which is fuelled by corruption.

There is also a link between police brutality and larger issues of power. Osha (2020) argues that 'the colonial state established a police force as a means of solely enforcing its will and not to protect its subjects'. Thus, any form of resistance by civilians, even if legitimate, is usually met with brute force. The police are regarded as untransformed and as an instrument of post-colonial states to perpetuate domination and advance the interests of the elites. Such behaviour has become the foundation that defines the character of the state and by extension its security instruments. In 2021, the friction between the youth and the police threatened the peace and security of the most populous city in Nigeria and Africa, Lagos, when police opened fire on the youth during peaceful protests against SARS brutality and police complicity.

In South Africa, the power of the youth was recently felt during the #*Fees-must-fall* social movement led by university students in 2015. Unlike past student movements in Africa in general and South Africa in particular, which constituted a challenge to the status quo, #*Fees-must-fall* was restricted to the confines of the ivory tower. Nonetheless, this student uprising, which was the largest in the history of post-apartheid universities, not only resulted in the closure of institutions, but also degenerated into violent protests, accompanied by the destruction of property and disruption of order in surrounding areas. Universities became 'warzones', as locally manufactured bombs and firearms were used by students (Greeff et al., 2021: 83). The South African police adopted a 'zero tolerance' approach, crushing erring and innocent students alike (Greeff et al., 2021: 89).

While, on the face of it, #Fees-must-fall centred around demands for free education and curriculum transformation, at a deeper level, it constituted a critique of the commodification of education in South Africa, given its apartheid history. The ruling African National Congress[1] has abandoned its socialist or welfarist legacy which promised to empower black South Africans, particularly black students that have struggled to access quality education due to economic, social and racial inequality.

It is important to appreciate the complex networks of established student organisations that are in constant communication and contestation with one another. In several African countries, pursuit of knowledge in universities is rooted in practices and a culture of exclusion based on sexism, racism and exclusivity. These values translate into questionable epistemological foundations and trends as well as discrimination against black people and women. The post-apartheid government merged several higher education institutions in the interests of increasing funding, extending access to black people and implementing curriculum transformation. However, more than two decades later, universities remained largely untransformed and many are still structured along race and class lines.

The Security, Governance and Development Nexus

The links between governance, security and development have been revealed in many African countries such as Nigeria and the DRC, while the case of Somalia is cause for concern. The civil war that has been raging in Somalia since 1991 has brought the country to the brink of collapse. The prolonged conflict and emergence of the terrorist group, Harakat al-Shabaab al-Mujahideen, known as al-Shabaab, has rendered this a complex situation. While Somalia has managed to slowly make some progress in its security, economic and political landscapes since the formation of the Transitional Federal Government in 2004, the country, particularly the capital Mogadishu, remains insecure due to sporadic

---

[1] The ruling party since majority rule was attained in 1994.

terrorist attacks. With the adoption of the new provisional constitution, the country is on the road to recovery with annual growth of 2.9% in 2019 and 1.4% in 2020. International coalitions against terrorism have also yielded moderate success, with Al-Shabaab losing control of large urban settings in south and central Somalia.

However, challenges remain that jeopardise Somalia's efforts to become a peaceful, prosperous and fully sovereign state. Continued instability and conflict are directly linked to governance, security and development. The interaction between these concepts offers an appropriate lens to understand the contemporary challenges preventing the country from breaking the cycle of conflict and poverty. The government has been unable to facilitate legitimate constitutional reform, and the governance structure has failed to effectively address resource and power-sharing.

A lack of proper governance has an exponential effect on insecurity, economic development and political stability. For instance, in Galkayo City and the wider Mudug region, the lack of trading seaports means that local resources and exports are facilitated through Bossasso and Berbera ports far from the region. This accounts for the high cost of imported basic commodities.

The shortage of schools and poor-quality schooling in Somalia are believed to have forced many to migrate abroad, leading to a skills shortage with negative implications for the local economy. Weak capacity for internal revenue collection in some areas has exacerbated unemployment and resulted in dilapidated basic infrastructure, fanning the flames of discontent. The authorities are unable to cater for the basic needs of security personnel, create jobs for the restless and unemployed youth or implement successful disarmament and reintegration programmes for the armed clan militias.

A lack of constitutional reform plagues various countries like South Sudan, which after 10 adopted an interim constitution. However, there is a need to differentiate between a government with a constitution and constitutionalism, and one with a constitution, but without constitutionalism.

Somalia's neighbour, Somaliland, presents a different reality. Although no state recognises Somaliland's independence or sovereignty, it continues to function autonomously, with an active centralised government. The country has enjoyed peace and security since its disassociation from Somalia. It has been able to retain its traditional structures based on the clan governance arrangement, including a plural justice system. The multiple legal systems comprise the state justice system, Shariʿah and customary law. While the country has been able to maintain peace, concerted efforts have been made to address the inadequate judicial and policy frameworks that have restricted optimal performance of the state justice system. This is mainly due to the priority given to security and stability to the detriment of maintaining a strong judicial system and improving citizens' livelihoods.

The literature has also demonstrated the nexus between resource exploration and conflict. In countries such as Zimbabwe, mining has played a major role in insecurity. Rich in diamonds, Zimbabwe manifests the attributes of a resource curse, where the availability of mineral resources has led to a high level of political corruption and exploitation. Public office is seen as a potential cash cow for political and business elites. State security actors and the ruling elites have formed alliances that have negatively affected the legitimacy of the entire governance system, including the state bureaucracy and the security sector. The security sector supports the ruling elite's ambitions for power consolidation, while the government has opened up diamond deposits to looting and pilfering. It has become difficult to distinguish state security personnel from the ruling elite and citizens have not benefitted from the mineral resources. While citizens in resource-rich countries like Congo DRC, Nigeria and Zimbabwe regard such resources as sources of hope, the lack of effective governance has caused severe economic hardships and mismanagement of natural resources has been the major driver of violent conflict.

The convergence between security and governance dates back to the colonial period and remains deeply entrenched in post-colonial dispensations across Africa. While resources are fed into global capitalist value-chains, citizens suffer from poverty, abuse and environmental degradation. International capitalists, with the complicity of local capitalists and politicians, have politicised and commercialised societal resources and taken advantage of conflict environments.

Conflict and security issues in Africa should be located within post-Cold War dynamics, especially in Zimbabwe and South Africa. Land resources have become an instrument of patronage and corruption, with citizens relegated to helpless bystanders. While land expropriation without compensation was part of Southern African liberation movements' agenda, the world order leaned very favourably towards the West. Indeed, some of the South African military officials that were forced to the negotiating table and right-wing groups and institutions like the International Monetary Fund and World Bank were very influential during the land negotiations. Ceasefire agreements thus adopted the *willing buyer, willing seller* market-led approach. The capitalisation of land was further reinforced in 2019 when the US government cautioned its South African counterpart not to implement expropriation without compensation. Many black South Africans reacted negatively to such decisions, causing friction between the state and society, as well as the various political parties.

Military Coups and Terrorism in Africa

African governments' military spending was estimated at $43 billion in 2020 (Faria, 2021). On average, Africa accounts for around 2% of global military expenditure (Saleh, 2022). As at 2022, Algeria had the highest defence budget on the continent ($10 billion), followed by Nigeria ($5.9 billion) and Morocco ($5.4 billion) (Saleh, 2022). Despite these large amounts, violent conflict has become synonymous with Africa, while terrorism continues to inflict fear and terror across the continent. Since 2010, Africa has experienced unprecedented intra-state conflicts, with countries such as Nigeria, Mali, Algeria, Somalia and Burkina Faso unable to secure peace within their borders.

Terrorist groups are one of the most powerful non-state actors and are constantly increasing in number and force. Until 2021, Boko Haram, which emerged in Nigeria, was ranked third in the Global Terrorism Index, followed by terrorist groups in Iraq and Afghanistan. In addition to the loss of lives through their attacks, terror groups have caused large-scale human displacement, as thousands of people continue to flee their reigns of terror. For instance, in the northeast region of Nigeria where Boko Haram operates, about two million people have been displaced and are in need of humanitarian assistance. The agricultural sector has been negatively impacted by terrorism, with most farmers having fled and those who remain unable to access their farmland due to fear of being attacked and kidnapped. Around 100 Nigerian rice farmers were slaughtered in 2020. The multiplier effect has been food shortages in the areas controlled by the terrorist groups. The fishing and tourism industries in northern Nigeria have also been badly affected.

While terrorism has been on the rise in Africa, the past couple of years have also witnessed a wave of military coups in West Africa and the Sahel. Countries like Burkina Faso, Mali, Guinea and Sudan have been subjected to military insurgency, raising questions about these states' capacity to deepen democracy as well as the role played by the military in securing the state. In Mali and Burkina Faso, military insurgency has ridden on the back of transnational crimes such as local insurgency and terrorism. Governance failures and state fragility have also resulted in military incursions, as have presidents' attempts to extend their term of office (as was the case in Sudan). While the military has not stepped out of line in Southern Africa, terrorism is beginning to lay claim to the region through Mozambique. This highlights the spillover effect of protracted terrorism on the continent.

Despite the fact that military intervention has been condemned as an unconstitutional aberration, the military has at times seen itself as an agent of development and change. This thesis argues that the military should be seen as a saviour that intervenes to protect democracy. Constitutional governments in the Sahel have failed to deliver on effective governance and have stifled civil society groups and silenced citizens, reducing the likelihood of effective political opposition. For example, in Zimbabwe, Robert Mugabe clung to power for decades before being overthrown in a military coup. Sudan experienced a total of 17 military coups, of which six were successful. A careful look at institutions that support democracy reveals their inability to persist in times of strain. It is thus vital to revisit the discourse of democracy in a region where democratic norms and values have consistently been challenged due to democracy's failure to maintain the strong economic conditions necessary to improve the public good.

Security Reform, Border Disputes and the Post-Colonial State

Africa's border system was designed by the colonial powers at different points in time. However, the partitioning of Africa during the infamous 1884–1885 Berlin Conference laid the foundation for border demarcation. Several societies were merged under administrative units which became modern states, while societies of the same ethnic composition were separated. Thus, African borders were arbitrarily constructed to promote the colonial powers' exploitative interests. One of the perhaps unintended consequences is xenophobic conflict in many African countries. In South Africa, xenophobia has become a dire security concern that goes beyond an attack on foreigners, including questions on identity formation to expose one of the inadequacies of post-colonial Africa. The conflict between the local population and foreign nationals has threatened peace and harmony between heterogeneous populations in South Africa.

Why is the local population so hostile to non-locals? Firstly, people fight when they are deprived of something or when they are being discriminated against. While, as argued by the Marxist school of thought, this falls within broader societal divisions, xenophobia has reinforced the huge gaps between the suppliers and the absorber of labour. Secondly, xenophobia should be seen as a historical effect of the African colonial heritage: a heritage marked by control as well as divide and rule. Through indirect rule, societies were mobilised against each other for easy domination and control.

Several post-colonial African states have securitised xenophobia and used it as weapon during election campaigns. In South Africa, the ANC and other political parties have used xenophobic narratives to seek popular support from the predominantly young population, who buy the rhetoric that foreigners are responsible for the country's social and economic ills. As conceptualised by the Copenhagen school, political elites have succeeded in elevating this human issue to a security issue. Xenophobia was prevalent not only in South Africa but also in Ghana and Nigeria in the early 1980s. While there are differences in its manifestation from one country to another, South Africa's manifestation has been particularly violent. Xenophobia continues to challenge Africa's quest for regional integration and attainment of Pan-Africanism. Whatever lens is employed to view it, it is antithetical to African personhood, communalism and Pan-Africanism.

Women's Peace and Security in Africa

Women are the most vulnerable group in Africa. While they make up more than 50% of the continent's population, their participation in leadership remains minimal. Women occupy 25% of decision-making positions and constitute less than 40% of the labour force in developing countries (World Bank, 2022). According to the World Health Organisation (WHO), globally, one in three women experiences either intimate partner violence or non-partner sexual violence during their lifetime. Gender-based violence (GBV) is a public health emergency that has existed for many years and poses a significant threat to lives. On a global scale, around 38% of murders of women are committed by their partners and violence against women is estimated to cost countries about 3.7% of their GDP (World Bank, 2022). Constant references to GBV in media headlines have desensitised people to the gravity of the situation.

Violence against women is rooted in gender inequality, the abuse of power and harmful norms. Its nature and broad scope render it difficult to analyse. It can be sexual, physical, mental and economic and can include the threat of violence, coercion, manipulation and blackmail. It can also manifest through sexual violence by a spouse or intimate partner and includes child marriage and female genital mutilation. It is also important to note the difference between GBV and violence against women. The latter is an act of GBV that results in physical, sexual and psychological harm or suffering to women, including coercion or arbitrary deprivation of liberty. Therefore, the scope of GBV is wider than violence against women. Due to the high number of women and children experiencing such violence, males that suffer from GBV are not accorded as much attention.

Unequal power relations in African society, especially in terms of socioeconomic status, contribute to violence against women. It is important to understand the intersectionality of masculinity and femininity in a patriarchal gender order, and how patriarchal masculinity sustains gender inequality. It is critical to understand how social norms in a patriarchal society promote GBV. Norms such as sexual purity and family honour put women at a disadvantage and at risk of violence.

Climate Change, Conflict and Security in Africa

Climate change is directly linked to peace, conflict and security in Africa. Studies show that violent conflict results in climate change, and *vice-versa*, impacting the livelihoods of people in the area. Poor countries that already lack food are most likely to be most affected due to the impact on water, agriculture, infrastructure and health. Climate change and conflict not only affect the environment, but also cause social grievances (Barnett & Adger, 2007).

In the past few years, Nigeria has witnessed increased environmental degradation due to climate change, with negative impacts on livelihoods. Climate change has aggravated social destabilisation in the northern part of the country, where there is a recurrence of desertification. The northern region has been hardest hit by rising temperatures and declining rainfall in the past five decades.

In other parts of the continent sea levels continue to rise, causing flooding in countries like South Africa. In April 2022, the South African port city of Durban experienced devastating floods that destroyed property and infrastructure and claimed more than 300 lives (Nyoka, 2022). African societies have also been hard hit by drought caused by shrinking of Lake Chad and desertification that advanced rapidly into other parts of the northern region, especially the Middle Belt. Apart from forced migration and a humanitarian crisis, this has disrupted the lives of herders, who depended on a nomadic lifestyle as their only source of livelihood. Resource conflicts have erupted as a result of competition for pasture, land and water. Herders have clashed with farmers on numerous occasions, leading to the loss of lives and displacement. There is a sharp decline in the value of human lives across the farming communities in the affected northern states of Nigeria and Mali.

Women have also been caught up in this conflict, as many are farmers or farm workers. In Nigeria and other sub-Saharan African countries, women usually assist men in agricultural activities, such as planting and harvesting crops. Therefore, in pastoral societies, women grow crops while the men farm cattle. Climate change has, therefore, further disempowered women and rendered them vulnerable to hunger and starvation. The African Union has projected that about $12.6 billion is required to assist those in need (AU, 2022).

The wetlands that extend from Mali to Nigeria make an important contribution to the ecosystem for animals and also serve as a source of food security. They are also used for recreation purposes and as a source of water. Wetlands cover around 14,000 km^2 and constitute around 70% of agricultural land in the Inner Niger Delta of Mali. They produce about 50% of the national livestock and fishery and support the livelihoods of about half a million people. About 80% of Mali's population engages in agriculture that contributes 45% of the country's GDP. Conflict has affected agricultural productivity as 42% of the land is situated in the conflict zone.

Conclusion

This chapter situated conflict in Africa in contemporary contexts. It drew on the continent's colonial history for a holistic understanding of the trends, patterns and nature of conflict in Africa and depicted the nexus between governance and security. Furthermore, it exposed African states' fragility and their inability to address insecurity. The initial optimism that marked the attainment of independence and the waves of democratisation in the late 1980s and 1990s have been replaced by extreme pessimism. The decline in the quality of life is starkly apparent, and African elites seem unperturbed. While Africa is not the only continent experiencing violent conflict, the rate at which it is spilling over from one society or country to another as well as the depth of the violence and the protracted nature of African conflicts are cause for concern.

The chapter highlighted the various challenges confronting African states, including governance deficits, the colonial legacy, xenophobia, increased fragmentation of local armed groups in the Sahel, the proliferation of coups in the Sahel and West Africa, and the competing interests of foreign powers, such as France, China, Russia and Turkey in the Sahel. Other regions are also confronting internal insurgency, ethnic or communal conflict, political instability and terrorism. Africa's security actors need to reflect carefully on these threats and commit to finding sustainable solutions by implementing policies that eradicate structural violence, poverty, exclusive governance and institutional fragility.

There is an urgent need for a conscious shift from a state-centric approach to the allocation of communal resources and facilitation of peace processes. Civil society groups, think-tanks, communities, traditional authorities and the private sector should be involved in state-building and development. Regional organisations, particularly the AU, should be more committed to governance issues and resuscitate the early warning system to prevent the outbreak of violent conflict. Lastly, effective governance and human capacity development of the youth are important preconditions for peace and security in Africa.

References

African Union. (2022). *African Union humanitarian summit and pledging conference*. African Union. https://au.int/sites/default/files/newsevents/workingdocuments/40515-wd-HHS52399_E_Theme_2_Addressing_food_security_and_nutrition_challenges.pdf

Aremu, J. O. (2010). Conflicts in Africa: Meaning, causes, impact and solution. *African Research Review, 4*(4), 549–560.

Arimie, C., Eghaghe, A., & Omage, M. (2021). Policing and human violation in the Covid-19 lockdown in Nigeria: The role of the police in crisis intervention. *Journal of the Management Sciences, 57*(1), 1–16.

Barnett, J., & Adger, N. (2007). Climate Change, Human security and violent conflict. *Political Geography, 26*(6), 639–655.

Buzan, B., Weaver, O., & de Wilde, J. (1998). *Security: A new framework for analysis.* Lynne Rienner Publishers.

Faria, J. (2021). *Military expenditure in Africa 2000–2020.* https://www.statista.com/statistics/1244568/military-expenditure-in-africa/

Greeff, M., Mostert, K., Kahl, C., & Jonke, C. (2021). The #FeesMustFall protests in South Africa: Exploring first-year students' experiences at a peri-urban university campus. *South African Journal of Higher Education, 35*(4), 78–103.

Ismail, O., & Olonisakin, F. (2021). Why do youth participate in violence in Africa? A review of evidence. *Conflict, Security and Development, 21*(3), 371–399.

Lovise, A. (2020). *After the uprising: Including Sudanese youth.* https://www.cmi.no/publications/7420-after-the-uprising-including-sudanese-youth

Lynch, G., & Crawford, G. (2011). Democratization in Africa 1990–2010: An assessment. *Democratization, 18*(2), 275–310.

Nyoka, S. (2022). Durban floods: South Africa floods kill more than 300, 14 April. *BBC.* https://www.bbc.com/news/world-africa-61092334

Obaji, P. (2020, September 9). *Women 'abused' by police enforcing COVID-19 rules in Nigeria.* https://www.aljazeera.com/features/2020/9/9/women-abused-by-police-enforcing-covid-19-rules-in-nigeria

Osha, S. (2020, November 25). *#EndSARS: A brief history of police brutality in Nigeria.* https://www.africaportal.org/features/endsars-brief-history-police-brutality-nigeria/

Phiri, B., & Jones, M. (2022). Addressing youth unemployment in Africa. In *The Palgrave handbook of sustainable peace and security in Africa* (pp. 433–443). Palgrave Macmillan.

Policy Commons. (2020). *Africa's youth: Action needed now to support the continent's greatest asset.* https://policycommons.net/artifacts/1547958/africas-youth/2237706/

PRIO. (2013). *Conflict trends: Led by Siri Aas Rustad.* https://www.prio.org/projects/1631

Saleh, M. (2022). *Defense spending budget in Africa 2022, by country.* https://www.statista.com/statistics/1219612/defense-spending-budget-in-africa-by-country/

UNCTAD. (2021). Economic development in Africa Report 2021: Reaping the potential benefits of the African Continental Free Trade Area for inclusive growth. *UNCTAD/PRESS/PR/2021/046.* Internet source https://unctad.org/press-material/facts-and-figures-7

World Bank. (2022). *The World Bank in gender.* https://www.worldbank.org/en/topic/gender/overview

CHAPTER 2

African Conflict and the "Post-colonial" State

Stephen Phiri

INTRODUCTION

This chapter is presented in six sections. The first section focuses on conflict in general and African conflict in particular, while the second demonstrates that drawing on colonial history to explain African conflicts is not an excuse but a valid and genuine claim. Section three presents a brief overview of the African predicament to contextualise the argument. The fourth section outlines the architectural design of an African "modern" state drawing on Mahmood Mamdani's seminal work, *Citizens and Subjects* and his keynote address entitled Political Identity, Citizenship and Ethnicity in Post-colonial Africa, which he presented at the Arusha Conference in 2005. Section five uses the first chapter of Fanon's *The Wretched of the Earth* to describe an ideal post-colonial state, while section

S. Phiri (✉)
Johannesburg Institute for Advanced Study, University of Johannesburg, Johannesburg, South Africa
e-mail: sphiri@uj.ac.za

© The Author(s), under exclusive license to Springer Nature Switzerland AG 2023
A. O. Akinola, *Contemporary Issues on Governance, Conflict and Security in Africa*,
https://doi.org/10.1007/978-3-031-29635-2_2

six examines the post-colonial state using both Mamdani and Fanon's work. As part of the conclusion, I highlight the limitations of using Mamdani's work as the lens for understanding conflict in Africa.

Conflict is described by Coser (cited by Aremu, 2010) as a struggle over values and claims to "rare" status, power and resources. The objective of the conflicting parties is to injure or eliminate their opposition. Conflict can be violent or uncontrollable, dominant or recessive, and resolvable or insolvable (Aremu, 2010). In other words, conflict is not necessarily violent; however, 'unfolding events in world history suggest that most conflicts are violent, inflicting life-long injures on their victims apart from the monumental loss of lives' (Aremu, 2010: 551).

Conflict in Africa can be categorised into two broad groups, namely internal and international conflicts. The former 'is one in which the governmental authorities of a state are opposed by groups within that state seeking to overthrow those authorities with the force of arms' (Eminue, 2004: 15). International conflict takes place between two or more nations/states (Puchala, 1971 cited by Aremu, 2010). In addition to these two categories, Africa has witnessed the third type of conflict, which Aremu (2010) called internationalised internal armed conflict. This generally refers to civil war, but also involves 'varying degrees of external involvement. Examples of such include the conflicts in the Democratic Republic of Congo (DRC), Angola, and Sierra Leone' (Aremu, 2010: 551).

It is important to highlight that conflict is not restricted to Africa, as other parts of the world are also riddled with different kinds of conflict. Indeed, it is so widespread that some scholars (Azar, 1990; Deutsch, 1991; Otite, 1999; Zartman, 1991) have concluded that it is an inevitable aspect of human interaction. Nonetheless, Ajayi (2005: 143) highlights that, 'the regularity of conflicts in Africa has become one of the distinct characteristics of the continent'. Aremu concurs and adds that:

> The continent of Africa has been highly susceptible to intra and inter-state wars and conflicts. This has prompted the insinuation that Africa is the home of wars and instability. Most pathetic about these conflagrations is that they have defied any meaningful solution and their negative impacts have retarded growth and development in Africa while an end to them seems obscure. (2010: 549)

This chapter argues that the conflicts in Africa are not merely products of "normal" human interaction but can be attributed to European colonialism's profound and lasting impact on contemporary Africa's development. One of the legacies of the colonial period is the "artificial" creation of ethnic conflict, which I explore further in the coming sections. Some analysts of ethnic conflict have deployed a grievance-based model. This model is premised on the understanding of conflict as 'normal' human interaction as it emphasises 'economic, political, and social deprivation or discrimination as sources of ethnic strife… [but its] intuitive appeal…generate[s] little explanatory power with respect to ethnic conflict in Africa' (Blanton et al., 2001: 474).

Therefore, exclusive reliance on deprivation-based grievances as predictors of ethnic violence is inadequate empirically. It is also deficient theoretically. Collective action and social movement theories point out that widespread and deeply felt grievances are not likely to result in collective violence unless counter-elites and mobilising structures are available to persuade aggrieved individuals to participate in the collective action, convince them that others are likely to participate as well, and produce the rewards—both public goods and selective incentives—that participants demand in return for their support (Blanton et al., 2001: 474).

Hence, this chapter proposes that the colonial structural configuration that was "passed on to" post-colonial states is the source of prevailing conflict. The structural configuration of ethnic groups in a society is itself a part of the colonial legacy. In other words, African societies were restructured to suit colonial needs to the detriment of local people's structured livelihoods. This restructuring occurred in both rural (ethnicity—customary law) and urban (race—civil law) areas.

It Is Not an Excuse, but a Genuine Claim

The current problems associated with Africa cannot be exclusively attributed to colonial history which is the focus of this chapter. The post-colonial political leaders who took over from the colonists also contributed to this crisis. In as much as the historical discourse is central to my endeavour, I do not ignore the failures of those whose duty it was to try to resolve this impasse, but who ended up being caught up in and exacerbating prevailing conflictual incidents. Nonetheless, I argue that this historical viewpoint is one of the major perspectives from which African conflict can be understood.

Another argument that has been raised in relation to colonial history as a logical explanation for Africa's current predicament is that of "perpetual victimhood". Those who support this notion are not only the obvious distractors who seek to derail small decolonial gains by maintaining white privilege but include one of our own, Achille Mbembe. He seems to argue that we are stuck in the past; rather than allowing our wounds to heal and move on, we sit and lick them while lamenting past injustices (Mbembe, 2002).

For Mbembe, those who make constant reference to colonial history are "stuck" on the gross injustices of slavery, colonisation and apartheid, whose evil and violence resulted in Africans' alienation from themselves, and their material, and spiritual world (Sekyi-Otu, 2003). Mbembe favours a "progressive" post-colonial emancipatory mindset that embraces and takes advantage of the opportunities afforded by globalisation rather than wishing to go back or imagine what it was like to be an African or a black person before slavery, colonisation and apartheid. Sekyi Otu[1] responds to Mbembe in his paper, Fanon and the possibility of post-colonial critical imagination, where he argues that what Mbembe fails to recognise is that reference to the history of subjugation serves to highlight how,

> the effects of that history impose limits on being, action, and knowledge. By virtue of that very plaintive knowledge of limits, however, they signal the human refusal of abject captivity to their dominion. For they wonder aloud what the world and the drama of human life would look like, what promises and predicaments they might proffer, were they ever unshackled from the constraints of a particular time and place, a particular historical circumstance. A coherent historicism is predicated, has to be predicated, on a consciousness of the possibility of freedom, intimations of what the nature of things might have been. (Sekyi-Otu, 2003: n.p.)

How do we untie the shackles that bind us when we have little or no idea how they were secured? A critical understanding of the rationale of oppression and an uncompromising analysis of distorted historical accounts are necessary. I argue that historical inquiry is fundamental to such rigour. Such a search and demythologisation of colonial lies is not

---

[1] Professor Ato Sekyi Otu, a Ghanaian political philosopher best known for his work on Frantz Fanon and Ayi Kwei Armah.

an end in itself but a means and an irreplaceable foundation towards emancipation. It is also important to note that such questioning does not undermine the opportunities associated with globalisation. What it does is to avoid premature associations with "global dynamics", lest the colonial vicious circle is promoted because globalisation normally promotes strong, dominant cultures/identities.

A Brief Overview of the African Predicament

The crisis in which Africa finds itself is not a natural phenomenon, but one that was strategically designed out of insatiable greed based on European expansionism that fed on egoistic claims of a civilising mission. Onwutalobi Anthony-Claret states that modern/colonial African states are essentially European, not African because they were created to serve the needs of the former. The fundamental question in this chapter is, why is Africa riddled with unceasing conflict? There is a need to explain the complexity of African problems. Dube (2006) enlightens us on the possible source of the complexity of the African situation by pointing out that what distinguishes African problems from those in the rest of the world is Africa's status of marginality and exclusion. The continent exists at the periphery of the world in both an economic and political sense. However, this explains its economic status rather than its conflictual nature. Ongoing domination by those who colonised it, which is also raised by Dube, is only a partial explanation for conflict in Africa. In other words, Africa remains in a state of subordination in comparison with other regions in the world (Dube, 2006: 79). While Dube recognised the colonisers' major contribution to Africans' woes, he also highlighted that those who took over (nationalist leaders) should share the blame.

Dube used Berkeley's research on Africa to argue that the root cause of African problems can be traced to the continent's colonial history, and that African political leaders' tendency to oppress their own people can be understood against the backdrop of systemic colonial and institutional tyranny where the majority was dominated by the minority in a system of 'race-based tyrannies which relied upon institutionalized mechanisms of coercion and co-option that were inherently divisive' (Dube, 2006: 81).

The scramble for Africa was not based on European powers' need to secure African territories in order to carry out charity work, but was driven by insatiable greed and the fear of a possible clash among themselves. In order to fulfil their selfish and exploitative desires, they divided the states in accordance with the location of potential resources while completely ignoring the nature and function of existing African states. Those boundaries were drawn with little or no consideration to the actual distribution of indigenous ethno-cultural groups. With the demise of colonial rule, the former colonies, with their colonial borders essentially intact, were transformed into some of the most ethnically fragmented states in the world (Blanton et al., 2001: 473).

The colonial boundaries of the nineteenth century created political units that divided ethnic groups and, in some cases, even combined rival groups. The current boundaries of most African states were arbitrarily drawn without regard to ethnic and cultural affinities (Aremu, 2010). They influenced and controlled the means of production and what was produced. Senegal, Ivory Coast, Ghana, Nigeria and Zimbabwe that traditionally cultivated food for subsistence were forced to produce exports such as palm oil, rubber, cotton, cocoa, peanuts and tobacco for European markets (Gordon, 1996: 55–56). Malawi and Mozambique which had very few material resources were used as labour reservoirs.

Crowder (1970: 237) notes that, in order to disguise their economic interests and greed, the colonial powers 'salved their consciences by introducing arguments about their own inherent moral and racial superiority to the Africans'. In dividing Africa into states, they never bothered to understand existing cultures and nations. While, like any human society, Africa had its own problems and conflicts, this demarcation united enemies and divided extended families. Outsiders ordered a society to behave in a certain way without its consent. The fact that the colonies were designed to benefit the West or minority white people meant that the political structures that were put in place were also strategically designed to promote their economic and political interests.

The Colonial Architectural Design of an African "Modern" State

'Economic expropriation of the native' has been perceived as the greatest crime of colonialism (Mamdani, 2005: 2). This position was supported by Guyanese popular historian, Walter Rodney's seminal work, *How Europe Colonised Africa* that drew on political economy as the most reliable tool to analyse the colonial legacy. Mamdani (2005) argues that political economy or colonial markets/market-based identities do not adequately historicise colonial realities. He agrees with Blanton et al.

that 'deprivation-based grievances as predicators of ethnic violence is inadequate empirically' (2001: 474).

Mamdani and Blanton assert that variables which are the result of grievances may have the potential to spark ethnic conflict, but structural variables are effective predicators of grievances and mobilisation that create fertile ground for such conflict. Thus, Mamdani (2005) argues that an analysis based on political economy cannot adequately explain non-revolutionary political violence, whose identity is state-generated and divorced from both market and cultural-based identities. The colonial states need to be historicised as the legal institution responsible for creating political identities. Furthermore, race and ethnicity need to be understood not as biological or cultural constructs, respectively, but as constructs of the state's legal system.

Mamdani (2005) problematises the issue of colonial boundaries raised earlier. He notes that the symptoms of current African conflicts can be traced to the senseless colonial demarcation of borders:

> ... in dividing Africa among themselves, the colonial powers showed little regard for [existing] boundaries of "ethnic" groups. Each colony encompassed multiple "ethnic" groups within its newly imposed territorial boundaries, many "ethnic" nationalities were divided between two or more colonial entities. With independence these boundaries gained international legitimacy as borders of newly sovereign nation-states. (Mamdani, 2005)

Mamdani (2005) contends that all borders are essentially artificial because war and conquest have always been integral to state-building. A good example is the formation of the Zulu kingdom. According to Mamdani (2005), shifting power relations have always translated to shifting boundaries—each new boundary is declared more natural than the previous one. For him, the real problem with boundaries is the assumption that political boundaries are a product of culture; this also presupposes that the state should be a nation-state and that rediscovering/redrawing what is conceived as "natural" political boundaries will solve the political crisis of the post-colonial state. Mamdani (2005) asserts that the post-colonial state is not a product of shared common values that has evolved through consensus and mutual respect, but is the consequence of legality or laws prescribed by the state. These laws produce institutions that structure and determine citizen participation. The colonial state that birthed the post-colonial establishment distinguished between race and ethnicity. The former was not biological as generally perceived and the latter was not cultural; both were mere political identities.

Mamdani (2005) further argues that, according to the indirect rule imposed by the coloniser in Africa, only natives belonged to ethnic groups. This presupposes that the non-native had no ethnicity and could only be racially identified. Among those who were non-African/native and were identified by race there was a hierarchy, with "whites" at the pinnacle with others such as coloureds and Asians following (Mamdani, 2005). Race was perceived as a measure of one's civilised nature. Since natives were not classified as a race but within ethnic ranks, they were not considered as either civilised or belonging to civil society. In this sense, the colonial state divided the population into two categories, namely races and ethnicities. The former were governed by civil or European law, and the latter by customary law (Mamdani, 2005). Unlike races, ethnicities were not hierarchical but were horizontally demarcated. The distinction between race and ethnicities is not the same as that between the colonised and the coloniser. In as much as all natives were colonised, not all non-natives were colonisers (Mamdani, 2005).

There was no single customary law for all natives, but a horizontal distinction, in which each ethnic group had its own law and a native authority (Mamdani, 2005). The colonial regime imposed one of the chiefs as the native authority under indirect rule. 'The tribal leadership was either selectively reconstituted as the hierarchy of the local state or freshly imposed where none had existed, as in the so called "stateless societies"' (Mamdani, 2017/1996: 17). 'Not only did the chief have the right to pass laws and was the administrator in his area, he settled all disputes' (Mamdani, 2017/1996: 23). The remainder of the genuine chiefs were officially silenced. By "sanctifying" the authoritarian version of custom as genuine, the colonial powers constructed native customs as unchanging and singular. Furthermore, the native authorities were organised as despotic in a way that promoted colonial rule's objective of enabling a tiny white minority, mainly European, to rule over the indigenous majority—the native question. Indeed,

> customary local authority was reinforced and backed by central civil power. The British depended much more heavily upon local elites to manage the day-to-day affairs of the colony … Rather than colonize their African holdings with a large number of British citizens, the British government

preferred to leave in place indigenous local elites and simply coopt or coerce them into serving as agents of British rule ... Through this means, the British colonial state established a network of indigenous intermediaries who combined the useful authority derived from some customary title to office with the literate skills and exposure to basic administrative training that would make them serviceable auxiliaries of the would-be Weberian state. (Blanton et al., 2001: 479)

Also, 'Colonial despotism was highly decentralized' (Mamdani, 2017/1996: 23). The strategy of maintaining "different" customary laws for "different" ethnicities created minorities out of the native population so that they did not unite against the colonial master. It is important to note that Mamdani's account of indirect rule refers to the British colonial system. While civil law was organised on the basis of a specific function of power, customary law was based on a fusion of power, giving the chiefs unlimited, unchecked powers (Mamdani, 2005). In other words, customary authority was hinged on the customary "right" to use force to coerce subjects, with corporal punishment encouraged under some circumstances.

The language of rights claimed to set limits on power exercised through the law; however, the language of custom did not circumscribe power but enforced it in a way that was unchecked, rendering the rule of law impossible (Mamdani, 2005). The natives had no rights under civil law and were controlled by customary law. The colonial state was essentially what Mamdani (2005) called a bifurcated world—one divided into two, which Fanon dubbed the Manichaean world. The customary law associated with ethnicities falls under the part of the bifurcated world known as indirect rule. The other part fell under civil or European or civilised law that directly ruled the so-called "races" that constituted the hierarchy of civility. 'Direct rule was the form of urban civil power. It was about the exclusion of natives from civil freedoms guaranteed to citizens in the civil society' (Mamdani, 2017/1996: 18).

In the main, however, the colonial state was a double-sided affair. Its one side, the state that governed a racially defined citizenry, was bounded by the rule of law and an associated regime of rights. Its other side, the state that ruled over subjects, was a regime of extra-economic coercion and administratively driven justice (Mamdani, 2017/1996: 19). The nationalist struggle fought for Africans to be regarded as a race in order to be accepted in civil or civilised society. As noted earlier, it resorted to deracialisation and abandoned detribalisation.

An Ideal Conception of a Post-Colonial State

An ideal image of a post-colonial state was vividly described by Frantz Fanon in his seminal book *The Wretched of the Earth* in the first chapter, 'On Violence'. While this chapter is controversial due to its pronouncements on violence, it outlines the steps required to create a sustainable post-colonial African state. The keys words articulated by Fanon are "decolonisation" and "violence". The former is synonymous with decoloniality, and the latter needs to be understood in the context that Fanon was writing. The first paragraph sets the objective of its thesis by highlighting the relationship between decolonisation and violence in the process of going beyond colonial subjugation:

> National liberation, national renaissance, the restoration of nationhood to the people, commonwealth: whatever may be the heading used or the new formulas introduced, decolonisation is always a violent phenomenon. At whatever level we study it – relationships between individuals, new names for sports clubs, human admixture at cocktails parties, in the police, on the directing boards of national or private banks – decolonization is quite simply the replacing of a certain "species" of men [sic] by another "species" of men [sic]. Without any period of transition, there is a total, complete and absolute substitution. (Fanon, 2001/1967: 27)

He goes on to assert that a new state cannot be built from old ruins because 'the truth, the proof of success lies in a whole social structure being changed from the bottom up' (Fanon, 2001/1967: 27). For Fanon, the order of the world needs to be changed and he called this process a 'programme of complete disorder'. He encourages one to regard decolonisation as a historical process in which one should understand the movements which give it historical form and content. Decolonisation is not a fixed event but a process whose essential function is nourished by the situation that was meticulously designed by the coloniser. One of the main constituents that characterised the colonial logic of subjugation is violence, which the settler used to exploit the native. The oppressor understands the language of violence; it is this language that the native has to use to be free. It is important to note that Fanon did not conceive of violence as a solution to any oppressive situation, but as a necessary option in a world where alternative options no longer apply.

The decolonisation process can be characterised as a force that 'influences individuals and modifies them fundamentally...transforms spectators crushed with their inessentiality into privilege actors...it brings a natural rhythm into existence, introduced by new men [sic], and with it a new language and a new humanity' (Fanon, 2001/1967: 28). The context in which Fanon calls for decolonisation is a colonial world, which he calls a Manichean world, and which Mamdani calls a bifurcated world.

> This world is cut into compartments, this world cut in two is inhabited by two different species, the originality of the colonial context is that economic reality, inequality and the immense difference of ways of life never come to mask the human realities. When you examine at close quarters the colonial context, it is evident that what parcels out the world is to begin with the fact of belonging to a given race, a given species... at times this Manichean goes to its logical conclusion and dehumanizes the natives, or to speak plainly it turns him [sic] into an animal. (Fanon, 2001/1967: 30, 31, 32)

In other words, an ideal decolonised world cannot be a bifurcated or Manichean world. It has to be ruled by one law that is a product of a deracialised and detribalised society. It would seem that this chapter was written just before the first African states' transition to independence as Fanon's tone is optimistic. It is unfortunate that what Fanon anticipated did not transpire. Fanonian decolonisation is synonymous with decoloniality as it is not merely a transition but aims to build national consciousness, which Fanon defines as 'the all-embracing crystallization of the inner most hope of the whole people' (Fanon, 2001/1967: 119).

THE "POST-COLONIAL" STATE

Reforms and changes were part of the formation of a post-colonial state, even though they did not challenge the foundation of the colonial establishment. 'Even if there was a change in the title of functionaries, from chiefs to cadres, there was little change in the nature of power. If anything, the fist of colonial power that was the local state was tightened and strengthened' (Mamdani, 2017/1996: 26). The post-colonial government privileged a group of people whom they considered indigenous over those that they considered non-indigenous; in effect, turning the colonial world upside down without changing it (Mamdani, 2005). The independent African states afforded chosen natives a place at the top of the political world designed by the settler. In other words, even after the colonial powers had left, citizens were still defined by binary categories such as native or settler.

The question that Mamdani (2005) asks is, how does one address the past without reproducing it, especially in situations where a culture of entitlement is regarded as a form of justice, thereby making indigeneity the basis for entitlement. Such objective positioning ceases once one realises that some identities that one considers as cultural are in actual fact political identities that were strategically instituted by the state. While some customs remained untouched by the colonial regime and even fought against those structures that were colonially "sanctified", the overall customary system was colonially manipulated to appear unchangeable, fixed and authentic.

The bifurcated state that was created with colonialism was deracialised, but not democratised. If the two-pronged division that the colonial state enforced on the colonised—between ethnicities—was its dual legacy at independence, each of the two versions of the post-colonial state tended to soften one part the legacy while exacerbating the other. The limits of the conservative states[2] were obvious: they removed the sting of racism from a colonially fashioned stronghold but kept in place the native authority, which enforced the division between ethnicities (Mamdani, 2017/1996: 26).

On the other hand, radical states[3] joined the deracialisation process to the detribalisation one. Unfortunately, 'the deracialized and detribalized power they organized put a premium on administrative decision-making. In the name of detribalisation, they strengthened central control over local authorities' (Mamdani, 2017/1996: 26). As a result of these post-colonial changes, both systems reproduced a part of the dual legacy of the bifurcated state and in the process instituted their own versions of despotism.

The optimism that defined most of chapter one of *The Wretched of the Earth* is missing in chapter three. In Chapter 1, Fanon describes the colonial situation, not in despair, but in the hope of change that will be

---

[2] These African states opted to allow the hierarchy of local state apparatus, from chiefs to headman, to continue after independence.

[3] These states instituted a single customary law that transcended tribal boundaries as part of post-colonial changes.

achieved through violence (Phiri, 2021). The first paragraph of Chapter 3 states that those who assumed power were unprepared and lacked practical links to work effectively with the masses of the people. Fanon issues a fatalistic warning of the failure of the post-colonial state. His frustration is due to his belief that those who want to take over are not interested in fundamental change, but marginal reform of the colonial system as highlighted by Mamdani. For Fanon, these middle-class people or leaders seek to benefit from the colonial proceeds and become the custodians that maintain the colonial legacy on behalf of the mother country (Phiri, 2021). He laments:

> Before independence, the leaders generally embody the aspirations of the people for independence, political liberty and national dignity. But as soon as independence is declared, far from embodying in concrete form the needs of the people in what touches bread, land and the restoration of the country to the sacred hands of the people, the leader will reveal his inner purpose: to become the general president of that company of profiteers impatient for their returns which constitutes the national bourgeoisie. (Fanon, 2001/1967: 133)

Mamdani agrees with Fanon that the post-colonial African state is inherently a colonial creation. They refer to such states as 'weak' as they did not develop from the grassroots, but are an imposed colonial project; their influence thus lacks deep roots in African communities (Phiri, 2020). Many writers such as Enerst Wamba dia Wamba (1996), Ngugi Wa Thiongo (2005/1986) and Paul Gifford (1998) maintain that the post-colonial African state is profoundly influenced by imperialism and is essentially built on colonial ruins.

Fanon highlights a dialectical process that defines the failure of the post-colonial state. As noted above, the leaders who took over served as mere puppets of the system. Fanon (2001/1967: 122) uses the word 'intermediary' of the colonial regime to describe the national bourgeoisie. It is unfortunate that even those that genuinely wanted to serve beyond the colonial logic of rule failed because the very foundation of such a state is built on that logic. The colonial structures that were uncritically adopted in the transitional process are vulnerable to imperialist influence. They were created to serve the minority and enable easy manipulation of those in power. Similar to Mamdani's explanation of the failure of detribalisation and the effective introduction of indigeneity, Fanon points to inverted post-colonial oppression expressed in the form of tribalism, selfishness, unconscionable adherence to Western beliefs and xenophobia.

Conclusion

The structure of post-colonial states is inherently conflictual because it is a product of a colonial structure that is essentially volatile and unstable. Both Mamdani and Fanon are convinced that current conflicts associated with the post-colonial state are due to a compromised transition to independence. For Fanon, the colonial structures were merely reformed instead of being radically changed, while Mamdani asserts that the post-colonial leader deracialised but did not detribalise colonial structures. In this sense, conflict in Africa is the product of a failed transition process, which resulted in artificial changes that maintained the essential colonial logic of exclusion and discrimination.

Drawing on Fanon and Mamdani's arguments, it is illegitimate to call the current African "modern" state post-colonial as this presupposes that we have gone beyond colonialism. This chapter challenged this misnomer by renaming these states neo-colonial states because colonialism was not eliminated but redefined. The chapter drew extensively on Mamdani who bases his argument on the British colonial method of controlling the native population. Hence, his account cannot conclusively represent all African post-colonial states. Nonetheless, it is rendered credible due to the fact that the Britain colonised the largest number of African countries, followed by the French. However, Fanon's account of the post-colonial state is helpful since most colonial thinkers refer to his work.

References

Aremu, J. O. (2010). Conflicts in Africa: Meaning, causes, impact and solution. *African Research Review, 4*(4), 549–560.

Anthony-Claret, O. (2008, April). *The after Effects of European Colonialism*. Retrieved 10 November 2010. www.authorsden.com....Articles

Anthony-Claret, O. (2022). *Analysis of Africa*. Retrieved 26 February 2022. https://anthony-claretonwutalobi.com/analysis-of-africa

Azar, E. (1990). *The management of protracted social conflict: Theory and cases*. Gower Publications.

Berkeley, B. (2001). *The graves are not yet full: Race, tribe, and power in the heart of Africa*. Basic Book.

Blanton, R., Mason, T. D., & Athow, B. (2001). Colonial style and post-colonial ethnic conflict in Africa. *Journal of Peace Research, 38*(4), 473–491.

Crowder, M. (1970). The impact of colonialism. In J. N. Paden & W. S. Edward (Eds.), *The African experience Vol 1: Essays*. Northwestern University Press.

Deutsch, M. (1991). *Subjective features of conflict resolution: Psychological, social and cultural influences, new directions in conflict theory*. Raimo Varynsnes and Sage Publications.

Dube, J. G. (2006). *A socio-political agenda for the twenty-first century Zimbabwean Church*. The Edwin Mellen Press.

Eminue, O. (2004). Conflict resolution and management in Africa: A panorama of conceptual and theoretical issues. *African Journal of International Affairs and Development, 9*(1 and 2), 23–67.

Fanon, F. (2001/1967). *The wretched of the earth*. Penguin.

Gifford, P. (1998). *African christianity: Its public role*. London: Hurst & Co.

Gordon, D. L. (1996). African politics. In A. A. Gordon & D. L. Gordon (Eds.), *Understanding contemporary Africa* (2nd ed.). Lynne Rienner Publishers.

Mamdani, M. (2017/1996). *Citizen and subject: Contemporary Africa and the legacy of late colonialism*. David Philips.

Mamdani, M. (2005, December 12–15). *Political identity, citizenship and ethnicity in post-colonial Africa*. Keynote address at the Arusha Conference, New Frontiers of Social Policy.

Mbembe, A. (2002). African modes of self-writing (S. Rendall, Trans.). *Public Culture, 14*(1), 239–273.

Otite, O. (1999). On conflicts, their resolutions, transition and management. In O. Otite & I.O. Albert (Eds.), *Community conflicts in Nigeria: Management, resolution and transformation*. Spectrum Books Ltd.

Phiri, S. (2020). *Learning to be 'out of order': A life history of CLP and the development of its praxis* (Unpublished Doctoral Thesis). University of KwaZulu-Natal.

Phiri, S. (2021). South Africa and xenophobic violence: A critical analysis of the post-colonial state. In *Xenophobia, nativism and Pan-Africanism in 21st century Africa* (pp. 137–153). Springer.

Sekyi-Otu, A. (2003, September). *Fanon and the possibility of postcolonial critical imagination*. Paper prepared for the CODESRIA symposium on canonical works and continuing innovations in African Arts and Humanities, University of Ghana, Legon, Accra.

Wamba dia Wamba, E. (1996). Pan Africanism, democracy, social movements and mass struggle. *African Journal of Political Science, 1*(1), 9–20.

Wa Thiongo, N. (2005/1986). *Decolonising the mind: The politics of language in African literature*. East African Educational.

Zartman, W. (1991) (Ed.). *Resolving regional conflicts: International perspectives* (The Annals No. 518).

CHAPTER 3

Climate Change and Emerging Conflict Between Herders and Farmers in Nasarawa and Plateau States, Nigeria

Samuel K. Okunade and Habila S. Kohon

INTRODUCTION

In response to climate change, world leaders established the Conference of Parties (COP) (Ati et al., 2018). Different countries have hosted these conferences with the latest being held in Glasgow Scotland (COP 26) from 31 October to 12 November 2021.[1] Nigeria has been part of these discussions. Climate change is severely affecting the country, manifesting

---

[1] https://unfccc.int/process-and-meetings/conferences/glasgow-climate-change-conference.

S. K. Okunade (✉)
Institute for the Future of Knowledge, University of Johannesburg, Johannesburg, South Africa
e-mail: Samuel_okunade@yahoo.com

H. S. Kohon
University of KwaZulu-Natal, Durban, South Africa

© The Author(s), under exclusive license to Springer Nature Switzerland AG 2023
A. O. Akinola, *Contemporary Issues on Governance, Conflict and Security in Africa*,
https://doi.org/10.1007/978-3-031-29635-2_3

in drought, desertification, deforestation and soil erosion, displacement and insecurity in northern Nigeria (*Premium Times*, 29 August 2020). Environmental degradation has negatively affected people's livelihoods and triggered violence between Fulani herders (who are mainly Muslim) from the north, and farmers (who are predominantly Christian) in the south.

The farmer-herders conflict in Nigeria has become a further political interface between the dominantly Muslim north and predominantly Christian south with extremely destructive outcomes (International Crisis Group [ICG], 2017). Although it essentially involves Fulani herders and local farmers across the country, the crisis has been marked by political distrust between the various ethnic and religious entities (Iloanya & Ananti, 2018; Nwankwo, 2021). It is regarded as a political conflict due to Nigeria's political history. Akinyemi (2016) and Akerjiir (2018) trace these tensions to the post-independence period when the northern religious and political elites sought to hold on to the reins of power by asserting that political power resides in the north while economic power resides in the south, particularly the south-east. This led to the Nigerian civil war otherwise known as the Nigeria-Biafra war which was essentially a political power tussle between the north and the south-east that sought to gain political freedom (Adigun, 2019; Iloanya & Ananti, 2018).

Decades after the civil war, ill-sentiment persists due to the relegation of southern politicians, particularly those of eastern stock to the economic sector with little or no political recognition (Nwankwo, 2021). This is compounded by the Boko Haram insurgency that threatens national security and rumours of the complicity of the current president and his close aides who are predominantly Muslims of Fulani extraction from northern Nigeria (Iloanya & Ananti, 2018). These factors have influenced perceptions and management of the herders-farmers crisis, especially in the southern region where politicians and citizens believe that the encroachment by Fulani herders is an extension of the Boko Haram agenda to Islamise the country with the backing of the presidency (ICG, 2017; Iloanya & Ananti, 2018; Nwankwo, 2021).

However, climate change, especially unpredictable weather patterns, is regarded as the main cause of the herders-farmers conflict that has, therefore, been located within the broad discourse on resource conflict due to its focus on access to vegetation, water and land. In north-central Nigeria, especially Nasarawa and Plateau States, the violence has escalated to wanton destruction of lives and property worth millions of naira

(Ahmadu & Ayuba, 2018). The Fulani herders own a large number of herds and during the dry season they move more frequently from one place to another in search of pasture. Their animals are their main source of livelihood. In the process of their migration from the north to the south, crops are destroyed, and many farms are being turned into grazing areas. The once cordial relationship between Fulani herders and farmers has been destroyed and violence ensues between the two groups. Furthermore, the process has led to demographic shifts in some communities in Plateau State, which are reflected in the polarisation between settlements of Muslims and Christians (Nwangwu & Enyiazu, 2019). The conflict often escalates into religious strife since most of the farmers are Christian, while the Fulani herders are Muslim.

In a bid to address this issue, the Federal Government of Nigeria proposed the establishment of Rural Grazing Area (RUGA) settlements (Udegbunam, 2019). Under this arrangement, livestock farmers would be relocated to a designated area in an organised manner and provided with amenities, such as veterinary clinics, markets, schools, hospitals, good road networks and some manufacturing processing plants for animal products. However, the proposal was resisted in many quarters especially among farmers, who argued that cattle rearing is the business of the Fulani herders and that expropriating their farms for rearing purposes threatens their means of livelihood. After much criticism from the general public, and many farmers' associations such as the Rice Farmers Association of Nigeria (RIFAN) (Lawal, 2019), the plan was shelved, with the government noting that 'it was not consistent with the approved National Livestock Transformation Plan (NLTP)' (*Daily Trust*, 4 July 2019).

Drawing on desktop research, this study examined the herders-farmers conflict and the effects of climate change and such conflict on the economy and individual states.

The Nexus Between Climate Change, Forced Movement and Conflict

While there has been much discussion on climate change in past decades, its meaning is elusive. According to Johansson, 'climate change is a long-term change in the average weather patterns that have come to define Earth's local, regional and global climates' (Johansson, 2020: 1). Riedy (2016: 1) concurs that 'climate change is a change in either the average climate or climate variability that persists over an extended period, expressed in terms of expected temperature, rainfall and wind conditions based on historical observations'. The term is thus associated with variations in weather patterns over a period of time and its impact is different across different geographical locations. Scientists have identified the burning of fossil fuels as the main cause of climate change. Burning these fuels, which include oil and coal, releases greenhouse gases into the atmosphere, especially carbon dioxide (Woody, 2014). Other human activities that contribute to climate change include extensive mechanised agriculture, deforestation and industrial production. Adhikari et al. (2011: 18) explain that 'climate change may be due to natural processes or external forcing or to persistent anthropogenic changes in the composition of the atmosphere or land-use'. Thus, climate change refers to variations in weather patterns caused by a natural process or by human activities that have adverse effects on the environment in different geographical locations.

The impacts of climate change include flooding, excessive heat, drought and desertification (Brunner et al., 2014; Douglas & Hescox, 2016). Brunner et al. (2014: 16) lament that 'our planet is facing an acute ecocrisis and that its causes are overwhelmingly anthropogenic'. Stott notes that, of all 'the global threats that face our planet, this is the most serious' (Stott, 2010: 55–56). Holdridge (2019: 18) predicts that, 'Humanity may be heading towards a climate holocaust'. Thus, if not addressed, climate change is a threat to human existence.

Despite growing evidence of climate change's negative impacts on peoples' lives around the world, some scholars remain sceptical (Colvin et al., 2019; Kobayashi, 2019; Wang & Kim, 2018). Colvin et al. (2019) argue that the terms used to describe climate change or negative emissions have influenced the way it is perceived. This is to say, if a positive description or explanation were to be given, climate change would not be perceived as a negative phenomenon, with its attendant polarisation of political ideologies (Colvin et al., 2019: 3–4).

Maathai predicts that 'Africa will be hit hard by climate change' (Maathai, 2009: 11). Reports have pointed to increasingly low rainfall and erratic weather in East African countries, such as Kenya, Ethiopia and Somalia (All Africa, 2020), resulting in drought that has forced people from their homes.

In West Africa, especially Nigeria, climate change has impacted several communities. Rising sea levels in the south have caused excessive flooding while the north continues to experience drought due to the shrinking of Lake Chad, and rapid desertification (All Africa, 2020; Baba & Abeysinghe, 2017). This has resulted in Fulani herders moving towards the south. Their migration has also affected the central parts of the north (also known as the Middle Belt), where increased contestation for land has resulted in violent conflict (Abdi, 2020). According to All Africa (2020), 'the root of the conflict lies in the forced southern migration, owing to drought, of herdsmen from their traditional grazing grounds, mostly in the northeast of Nigeria', resulting in destruction of crops and the killing of cattle in what are thought to be reprisal attacks.

In response to climate change, the Nigerian government formulated a plan, *Building Nigeria's Response to Climate Change* (BNRCC). The policy document notes that climate change has resulted in variations in rainfall and temperatures (BNRCC, 2011: 4–6) and sets out various strategies to address this phenomenon. However, little effort has been exerted to curb the impact of climate change in the north, resulting in ongoing mass migration by Fulani herders to the southern region of the county (Amao et al., 2018; Chikaire et al., 2017) in order to sustain their livelihoods (Fulton & Nickels, 2017; McGregor, 2017).

Amusan et al. (2017) note that the Grazing Bill proposed by the National Assembly to prohibit open grazing and the establishment of ranches in some states met with stiff opposition (Kwaja & Ademola-Adelehin, 2017: 7). States that have passed laws regulating open grazing include Ekiti, Benue, Taraba and Edo (Crisis Group, 2017). However, this has increased tension between herders and farmers (ACAPS, 2017; Ahmed-Gamgum, 2018).

Anthony (2014: 62) observes that, 'As farmers take up more and more of the fertile river bank for farms, they come into direct conflict with other users, mostly the herders and fisher folks'. The land, therefore, becomes a source of contestation. Indeed, Babalola and Onapajo (2018) assert that Nigeria is a country under siege because of the intense violent conflict between Fulani herders and farmers. About 1.9 million people have been affected by climate change (Edeh & Ozor, 2020) and in 2016, the conflict between the farmers and Fulani herders was reported as 'costing Nigeria at least $14 billion in potential revenues annually' in the north-central region alone (*Premium Times*, 2016).

Climate Change vis-à-vis the Farmer/Herders Conflict in the Nasarawa and Plateau States of North-Central Nigeria

The farmers-herders conflict has triggered insecurity that cuts across regions and states. The herders have been accused of taking up arms against farmers whenever there are clashes. According to the ICG, these clashes claimed an annual average of 2,000 lives between 2010 and 2016 (ICG, 2017). Usman (2019) noted that, more recently, the number of casualties has ranged from 2,000 to 6,000. This exceeds the number of victims of the deadly Boko Haram insurgency in the northeast of the country. In recent years, clashes between farmers and herders have caused casualties not only in the northern region (Benue, Taraba, Nasarawa, Plateau, Adamawa, Niger, etc.), but also in the south (Oyo, Delta, Enugu, Imo, Rivers, Cross River, etc.) where scores of deaths and victims have been reported (Adigun, 2019; Chukwuemeka et al., 2018; Nwankwo, 2021), posing a major threat to security and safety.

While the violence associated with the conflict is felt across the country, the middle belt region[2] has been particularly hard hit (McDougal et al., 2015; Odoh & Chilaka, 2012), with communities suffering the destruction and loss of farm produce. Nasarawa and Plateau States have also witnessed a series of clashes between herders and farmers. An unspecified number of residents of Dogo Na Hauwa, Ratsat and Jeji communities in Jos South were killed by Fulani herders in 2010, 200 people, including Senator Gyang Dantong, were murdered in Matse and Kakuru villages by suspected Fulani herders in 2012, and ten people were killed and 100 houses were burnt in Riyan Local Government in Plateau State (Chukwuemeka et al., 2018). Thirty-two lives were lost in Nasarawa State in December 2009, with several farms and houses burnt following clashes between farmers and Fulani herders. In 2012, 16 people were killed and about 5,000 displaced following clashes between farmers and herders in the Kadarko community in Giza Local Council (ICG, 2017; McDougal et al., 2015; Okoli & Atelhe, 2014). The conflict in these states has been linked to the struggle for grazing and farming land occasioned by the non-designation of land for such purposes. As Odoh and Chilaka (2012) note, the earliest conflict between herders and farmers in Plateau State

---

[2] The Middle Belt refers to Nigeria's north-central states.

was the result of the lack of land for cattle breeders and their farming counterparts.

Okoli and Atelhe (2014) note that the drought that affected the Lake Chad region and other water bodies has resulted in a scramble for the little available water, particularly in the northern and middle belt region (Nwankwo, 2021). Inadequate water management policies and legislation and failure to address the security of herders and their cattle exacerbated the violence between farmers and herders in these states. The ICG reported that 'in the last six decades, over 350,000 sq km of the already arid region turned to desert or desert-like conditions, a phenomenon progressing southward at the rate of 0.6 km per year' (ICG, 2017). Similarly, Onyia (2015) noted that the northern region 'has been the hardest hit by the apparent rising air temperature and declining rainfall in Nigeria in the last five decades. It has also witnessed less than 10 inches rainfall within this period' (Onyia, 2015: 186) While this is taking place in the core northern regions of the country, the consequences have been felt in the Middle Belt and further south as herders and even farmers in some cases are forced to travel in search of pasture for their herds (McDougal et al., 2015). Subsistence farmers have also been hard hit by the shortage of water.

The influx of armed foreign individuals has exacerbated the situation in the middle belt region (Onyia, 2015). Odoh and Chilaka (2012) note that climate change and scarce natural resources have led to more clashes in Nasarawa State than the much talked about armed bandits. Although there are other reasons for the conflict between herders and farmers, the underlying cause of global climatic change has resulted in a struggle not for identities and politics as posited by some, but over the use of scarce resources (Chukwuemeka et al., 2018). In middle belt states like Nasarawa and Plateau, commentators have focused on the possible impact of terrorism on the farmer-herder clashes. Indeed, climatic change and changes in weather conditions have result in several clashes in these states.

The government's approach in Nasarawa and Plateau States has downplayed the issue of climate change, with attention focused on addressing the hostile behaviour and attitudes of the conflicting parties (Iloanya & Ananti, 2018). As Akinyemi (2016) argues, the conflict in the middle belt states calls for strategic management of scarce water resources in the country, especially in the northern region. However, both the federal and state governments have been largely myopic and reactionary and have focused on eliminating the threats posed by these clashes rather than the root cause (Adeniran, 2020). The implication is that the underlying cause is not addressed while efforts and resources invested in managing the security situation yield little (Chukwuemeka et al., 2018). Deep-seated ethnic distrust between indigenous and core northern Hausa-Fulani groups, especially in Plateau State, has also aggravated the conflict as when disputes arise, there is a tendency for them to assume an ethno-religious dimension. This results in government focusing on this dimension (Adigun, 2019).

Ignoring the overarching cause of this conflict in Nasarawa and Plateau States is a waste of vital resources. The federal government has launched a cattle ranching project across ten states, with an initial allocation of ₦6.25 billion per state (Njoku et al., 2021). Numerous commissions of enquiry have been established to mend relations between herders and farmers, but have failed to consider the root cause, i.e. scarcity and effective management of scarce water resources by key water users. Nwankwo (2021) notes that, stakeholders in the middle belt and southern region have resorted to peddling political rhetoric, accusing the northern elites of an Islamisation agenda[3] (Chukwuemeka et al., 2018; Nwankwo, 2021) rather than addressing the environmental issues that are at the core of the farmer-herder conflict. This affects their disposition towards northern nomads who annex farms and land of the Middle Belt and south. The misguided intervention by local farming communities in Nasarawa and Plateau States in the form of indigenous vigilante groups to fight off attacks on their communities and launch counter-attacks (Nwankwo, 2021) can be attributed to the failure of the state and federal governments to address the core environmental issues in the region.

Okoli and Atelhe's (2014) study on Nasarawa State observes that the clashes between farmers and herders in this state are clearly a resource-based conflict even though ethnic and religious dimensions have been drawn into the dispute. They add that both parties' failure to understand the role of environmental factors in enhancing the conflict has led to deep-rooted hostility and the displacement of thousands, especially in

---

[3] Popular belief in the north-central and southern states holds that the Fulani herders' encroachment on farming communities across the country is part of a larger Islamic jihad agenda to Islamise the country. This narrative has been fuelled by the political elites and the media in these regions that oppose Hausa-Fulani political hegemony in the country. This narrative has influenced political interventions and downplayed the need to find lasting solutions to the climate and water scarcity issues that are at the core of the clashes.

farming communities, leading to a vicious cycle of violence. Amusan et al. (2017) and Okwor's (2016) research points to similar trends in Plateau State. The role of climate change in altering global relations and interrelations has been well documented by scholars across the globe, but tends to be downplayed by governments and government institutions. According to Onyia (2015), governments' unwillingness to address these key issues stems from the assumption that climate change is a scientific myth fabricated by experts to promote their capitalist agenda. This position has been debunked by a large body of research, which shows that the rapid desertification of large water bodies in countries such as Nigeria has prompted the migration of farming communities (Nwankwo, 2021; Onyia, 2015).

Scholars have documented the migration of herders and their cattle from their natural abode in core northern states, such as Sokoto, Yobe, Bornu and Adamawa due to rapid desertification (Odoh & Chilaka, 2012; Usman, 2019). The literature shows that socio-political relations and the make-up of the middle belt states of Nasarawa and Plateau as well as the country's historical antecedents have rendered intervention in the violent clashes very complex (Iloanya & Ananti, 2018; Okoli & Atelhe, 2014). The use of the military and police has not helped to mend ill feelings between farmers and herders or address the growing impact of climate change. Furthermore, the security forces have been accused of taking sides, breeding more distrust (Para-Mallam & Hoomlong, 2013). Civil society and government organisations and agencies' interventions have focused on mending social relations between farmers and herders rather than addressing pressing agricultural needs. While Ogbozor et al. (2018) note that these interventions have improved farmer-herder relations in Nasarawa and Plateau States, the persistent effects of climate change that cause water scarcity render conflict inevitable.

Key northern elites' attempts to politicise the conflict in pursuit of personal interests (Adeniran, 2020) and the federal government's failure to provide a lasting solution to the effects of climate change are likely to result in ongoing conflict over agricultural resources. This calls for government at all levels to engage farming communities and Fulani herders as well as other stakeholders in productive dialogue aimed at deconstructing the Fulani jihad narrative and gaining the cooperation of north-central and southern states. It is also important to address the grazing routes and ranching issues. Failure to address the issue of the Islamic agenda could derail any efforts to respond to climate change and water scarcity. The ICG (2017) observes that the government's failure to provide modern technical and technological equipment to rural farmers and properly assign grazing routes negatively impact the situation. These are important strategies whose benefits will be reaped when ill feeling and suspicion on the part of both parties are addressed. Furthermore, the conflict between herders and farmers has been regarded as more of a religious matter than a national security threat. Nwankwo (2021) observed that religious bodies have received support from government and non-governmental organisations to launch interventions. However, this resulted in verbal altercations between two religious bodies, the Miyetti Allah Cattle Breeders Association of Nigeria (MACBAN) and the Christian Association of Nigeria (CAN) in the middle belt region.

The Impacts of Climate Change and the Farmer-Herders Conflict on Troubled Communities and States

The struggles between farmers and herders across the country have resulted in mass casualties and negatively impacted thousands of people in various ways (ICG, 2017). Amnesty International (2018) reports that they resulted in an estimated 3,641 deaths across the country between 2016 and 2018, while Mercy Corps calculated an estimated annual economic loss of $13.7 billion by the Nigerian government (ACAPS Thematic Report, 2017). For example, the Agatu crisis between herders and farmers in Benue State in 2016 resulted in an estimated loss of ₦65 million by the state government (ICG, 2017). According to Amusan et al. (2017), the clashes are an offshoot of global climate change and weather conditions that are altering agricultural and socio-economic conditions. Several farmlands and grazing lands as well as water bodies have been lost to desertification, drought and the like in Nigeria (Iloanya & Ananti, 2018). Muhammed et al. (2015) note that farmlands are farmers' private property while grazing is a private business. Encroachment of a private business on a private property without permission is a violation of personal and property rights; hence, erring herders and farmers ought to be prosecuted. However, this has not been possible due to various intertwined reasons, including politicisation of disputes by leaders who are themselves farmers or cattle owners (Muhammed et al., 2015). In other cases, religious intolerance and leaders' ethnocentrism influence how disputes are handled.

As noted previously, federal and state governments' interventions reveal a pattern of addressing the symptoms rather than the causes of these clashes, even though climate change has been recognised as the root cause (Adeniran, 2020; Akinyemi, 2016; Chukwuemeka et al., 2018; Nwankwo, 2021). In the core north where the change in climatic conditions has been most severe, desertification and drought have devastated states like Bornu, Yobe, Adamawa and Sokoto (Okwor, 2016), driving both herders and farmers to neighbouring states in the Middle Belt, such as Plateau, Benue and Taraba (Okwor, 2016). According to Skah and Lyammouri (2020), the severity of the drought is manifest in the shrinking of Lake Chad which serves as a source of water for four countries. They reported that the lake had dried up by up to 90% within a space of 30 years, necessitating the migration of border communities who depend on its water for survival. The shrinking of Lake Chad and reduced annual rainfall has also affected northern Nigeria because, unlike the southern region with its natural resources, it is fully dependent on agriculture and agricultural resources for survival and trade (Okwor, 2016). While the northern region experiences scarce annual rainfall and desertification of farms, the south (the tropical savannah) experiences excessive rain resulting in flooding as well as dry seasons annually. Furthermore, households in the majority of states in the northern part of the country practice either subsistence or commercial farming and therefore require water and fertile farmlands for survival. The threat occasioned by the change in climatic conditions in the region is, therefore, a direct threat to human security and survival in the north.

The lack of legislation to properly manage the migration patterns of farmers and herders in the core northern region to the middle belt and southern region has exacerbated the situation (ICG, 2017). Furthermore, as noted by Muhammed et al. (2015), the growing population in the southern and middle belt region has exerted pressure on available farmland and water bodies to meet food demand. It has resulted in a situation of survival of the fittest between herders and farmers (Iloanya & Ananti, 2018), where only the strong in possession of ammunition have triumphed. As Okwor (2016) also notes, the struggle for farm and grazing lands is basically an economic one; however, various stakeholders still treat the conflict as a political or religious issue. For communities like the Agatu in Benue State and others in Plateau and Nasarawa States where herders have wreaked havoc on farmlands, farm produce and even the lives of farmers, the immediate cause may not be readily identified as climate change but as inter-group rivalry (Conroy, 2014; Okoli & Atelhe, 2014). As Adeniran (2020) observes, although these clashes and accompanying destruction are indirectly caused by climate change, they are exacerbated by the politicisation of disputes by the federal and state governments, and poor management of the discord between farmers and herders in the country.

In the southern states, farmer-herder clashes have resulted in low agricultural output due to the incessant killing of farmers rather than a shortage of farmland or water (Akerjiir, 2018). Farmers in the southern states of Ebonyi, Delta and Edo States have been severely hit, such that female farmers are scared of going to their farms alone, while the youth and vigilantes have been attacked by herders (Akinyemi & Olaniyan, 2017). Iloanya and Ananti (2018) conclude that the effects of climate change have not been properly placed in context as several communities irrespective of region have recounted encounters between farmers and herders with high casualty rates that are sometimes not reported by the media. Hence, this study contextualises the existing conflict as rooted in climate change, but made worse by government's poor management and lack of regulation as well as by poor socio-political relations between the north and southern regions.

A recent clash between Fulani herders and local farming communities in Oyo State attests to the fact that the migration of herders from the north to the south has severe human security consequences (Akinyemi & Olaniyan, 2017; Amnesty International, 2018). Numerous properties were destroyed and scores of people were maimed, kidnapped and threatened by the incursion of northern herders, while commercial farmer, Mr Aborode, a PhD holder was murdered by suspected Fulani herders on his farm in Sarki (Taiwo-Hassan, 2021). These reports notwithstanding, all levels of government have focused on the symptoms rather than on climate change, which is the root cause of insecurity (ICG, 2017).

Okoli and Atelhe (2014) note that this climate change-induced conflict has further complicated Nigeria's unity and cohesion, as herders and farmers in the northern and southern regions have been further driven apart. It has largely been the result of herders taking over farmlands with little or no consideration for farmers' crops. As stated by Akinyemi and Olaniyan (2017), confrontations deteriorate into physical clashes, resulting in the loss of lives. In other cases, herders launch counter-attacks when farmers kill their cattle, attacking farming communities and destroying farms, homes and lives in the process (Akinyemi & Olaniyan, 2017; Muhammed et al., 2015).

Scholars have highlighted the fragility of Nigeria's unity due to the deep-rooted hostility and distrust that characterises inter-group relations (Akinyemi, 2016). The farmer-herders conflict and allegations that farmers and herders from the north are pursuing an Islamisation agenda in the south (Nwankwo, 2021) have further undermined unity The Fulani herders' cultural attachment to their cattle to the extent that they are prepared to die rather than witness their cattle suffer (Okoli & Atelhe, 2014) has caused them to resort to arms (Akinyemi & Olaniyan, 2017). National unity has been a goal since independence but several political antecedents hindered progress (Adigun, 2019; Okwor, 2016). Scholars (Amusan et al., 2017; Akerjiir, 2018; ICG, 2017; Iloanya & Ananti, 2018; Usman, 2019) note that the farmer-herder clashes in various states and farming communities are a relatively recent phenomenon as relatively peaceful interactions between these groups date back to pre- and post-colonial times. However, from the late 1990s to date, this interaction has assumed hostile, alarming proportions that threaten the delicate cohesion of the Nigerian nation (Akerjiir, 2018; Chukwuemeka et al., 2018; ICG, 2017).

The declining value of human lives is a further impact of climate change and resultant conflict among communities and states in Nigeria (Iloanya & Ananti, 2018). The security of farmers and farming communities, especially those far from city centres with no media reportage, has been severely undermined (Iloanya & Ananti, 2018). For the past decade, human rights and civil society organisations have highlighted the lack of human security due to vulnerability to attacks by either bandits or armed Fulani herders (Ekdahl, 2017). Thus, farming communities across the country are becoming uninhabitable (Ekdahl, 2017). Combined with the fact that several states in the northern region have been lost to desertification, drought and harsh weather conditions (Akinyemi, 2016; ICG, 2017), this has severe consequences for Nigeria's food production and agricultural sector. For example, Iloanya and Ananti (2018) note that large volumes of farm produce were lost during clashes between herders and farmers in Plateau and Benue States. While security in farming communities and states in the north-eastern part of the country has declined due to Boko Haram insurgency, the farmers-herders conflict complicated government's efforts to provide adequate protection.

Kwaja and Ademola-Adelehin (2018a) note that the deployment of military personnel to contain the farmer-herders conflict across the country has had the unintended effect of straining the relationship between these forces and civilians due to the unprofessionalism of security operatives. The negative impact of military intervention is primarily felt by the youth who are constantly harassed by military operatives in the name of curbing insecurity in troubled communities, especially in the north-central states (Onuoha & Okafor, 2019). This ranges from sexual abuses of females to physical abuse and exploitation of males accused of collaboration with armed bandits and armed local vigilantes securing their communities from herders' invasions (Kwaja & Ademola-Adelehin, 2018b; Sallek, 2018). Desertification, drought and harsh weather conditions have necessitated the deployment of soldiers to different parts of the country, threatening the human security of communities and national security (Amusan et al., 2017). While the military is portrayed as a neutral force, in Plateau, Nasarawa, Benue and other northern states (Iloanya & Ananti, 2018; Kwaja & Ademola-Adelehin, 2018), studies have revealed a pattern of bias, distrust and hostility towards residents (Akerjiir, 2018).

The response of the various states and the federal government has been more reactionary than anticipatory (Amusan et al., 2017). Although legislation is in place to address these conflicts, such as the 1964 National Grazing Reserves Act; National Agricultural Policy of 1988; 1978 Land Use Act; 2011 National Grazing Route and Reserve Commission Bill; 2015 Federal Government Comprehensive Livestock Development Plan; 2016 National Grazing Reserve (Establishment) Bill; and state-level legislation prohibiting open grazing, etc., its implementation has not been particularly effective (Akerjiir, 2018; Kwaja & Ademola-Adelehin, 2018a; Muhammed et al., 2015). As noted by Okoli and Atelhe (2014), climate change has been on the agenda since the 1990s, but the federal and state governments' policies have not reflected the expected level of preparedness, interventions and insight into the possibility of it causing conflict. Kwaja and Ademola-Adelehin (2018) highlight that this is evident in encroachment and destruction of grazing routes designated by the federal government as a strategy to manage herders' migration patterns.

Conroy (2014) notes that climate change has had real effects on livelihoods, social and economic life, and peace and stability. The livelihoods of many rural dwellers across Nigeria have been significantly affected by struggles over land resources. According to Adigun (2019), southern states such as Delta, Cross River, Kogi and Akwa Ibom have recorded deaths from clashes between herders and farmers and as a result of internal disputes between communities over land resources. The social order has been grossly distorted, with the agricultural and economic sectors in many states and communities negatively affected. Normal interactions among traders across regions have been impacted by the resurgence of herder-farmer clashes (Ekdahl, 2017; Okoli & Atelhe, 2014). Political stakeholders in the southern part of the country recently called for community members to boycott beef produced by Fulani herders (Onikepo, 2021; Sule, 2020) in protest against the clashes and killing of farmers, allegedly by herders. Lastly, Nigeria's security is threatened by constant conflicts and clashes among herders and farmers.

Conclusion and Recommendations

Climate change has not only resulted in conflict between farmers and the Fulani herders, but has also led to massive displacement, and the loss of lives and property in Nigeria's Nasarawa and Plateau States. The federal government's response has been inadequate and while state governments in the middle belt region have tried their best and sought the assistance of the federal government at different times, this has not been forthcoming. Indeed, top government officials in some states have been attacked, including the Governor of Benue who has been at the forefront of campaigning against Fulani herders' encroachment in the region.

It is crucial that the federal government take decisive steps to address this situation. Based on the analysis in this chapter, it is recommended that:

Government should be objective and committed in addressing this issue. It should bring all concerned stakeholders to the table to discuss the open grazing policy so that the violent conflict between Fulani herders and farmers can come to an end. The government should conduct awareness campaigns to educate Fulani herders about climate change and best practices in cattle rearing which do not disrupt the economic activities of others. This would reduce their movement in search of grazing. Every community should elect a committee that includes herders living in their communities to promote dialogue, build trust and promote peaceful coexistence. Some farmers should receive skills training in different trades to reduce competition for land.

REFERENCES

Abdi, H. (2020). *Chad is the country most vulnerable to climate change—Here's why.* https://www.independent.co.uk/environment/chad-is-the-country-most-vulnerable-to-climate-change-here-s-why-a7785246.html?fbclid=IwA R1JJd2Dm3LFQAfnGlKRDAleIvblRnqXWw08eQoYA1Ommiw732hdlgU TOSg. Accessed 7 February 2020.

ACAPS Thematic Report. (2017). *Farmer-Fulani Herder violence in Benue, Kaduna and Plateau States* (pp. 1–6).

Adeniran, A. I. (2020). Climatic factors in Nigeria's Farmer-Herder Conflict. *South Africa Institute of International Affairs Policy Briefing Climate Change and Migration* May 2020. SAIIA.

Adhikari, A., Shah, R., Sony Baral, S., & Khanal, R. (2011). *Terminologies used in climate change.* International Union for Conservation of Nature.

Adigun, O. W. (2019). A critical analysis of the relationship between climate change, land disputes, and the patterns of farmers/herdsmen's conflicts in Nigeria. *Canadian Social Science, 15*(3), 76–89. https://doi.org/10.3968/10967

Ahmadu, H. J. & Ayuba, H. (2018) The role of group solidarity in conflict between farmers and fulani pastoralists: A case study of northern Nigeria. *African Journal of Political Science and International Relations, 12*(3), 33–41.

Ahmed-Gamgum, W. A. (2018). Herdsmen and farmers conflict in Nigeria: Another dimension of insecurity. *Journal of Public Administration and Social Welfare Research, 3*(1), 35–62.

Akerjiir, A. S. (2018). *Increasing farmer-herder conflict in Nigeria: An assessment of the clashes between the Fulani Herdsmen and indigenous farmers in Ukpabi-Nimbo Community Enugu State (Nigeria)* (Unpublished Master's Thesis). International Development Studies, Wageningen University and Research.

Akinyemi, T. E. (2016). *Climate change, migration and resource contestations: A case study of North-South Migration in Nigeria* (Unpublished PhD thesis). School of Social Sciences, College of Humanities, University of KwaZulu-Natal.

Akinyemi, T. E., & Olaniyan, A. (2017). Nigeria: Climate war. Migratory adaptation and farmer-herder conflicts. *Conflict Studies Quarterly, 21,* 3–21. https://doi.org/10.24193/csq.21.1

All Africa. (2020). *How climate change contributes to insecurity in Nigeria, other African countries* (Online). https://www.premiumtimesng.com/news/top-news/377470-how-climate-change-contributes-to-insecurity-in-nigeria-other-african-countries.html. Accessed 15 February 2020.

Amao, O., Adeagbo, T. A., Olojede, M. O., Ogunleye, B. T., & Ogundoyin, C. O. (2018). Effects of Fulani herdsmen conflict on productivity of arable crop farmers in Ibarapa areas of Oyo State. *International Journal for Research in Social Science and Humanities, 4*(7), 1–12.

Amnesty International. (2018). *Harvest of death: Three years of bloody clashes between farmers and herders in Nigeria.* Amnesty International.

Amusan, L., Abegunde, O., & Akinyemi, T. E. (2017). Climate change, pastoral migration, resource governance and security: The grazing bill solution to farmer-herder conflict in Nigeria. *Environmental Economics, 8*(3), 35–45.

Anthony, A. O. (2014). A historical analysis of the migration, penetration and diffusion of the Fulani into the Middle Belt Region of Nigeria. *Journal of Humanities and Social Science (IOSR-JHSS), 19*(10), 54–62.

Ati, O. F., Agubamah, E., & Abaje, I. B. (2018). Global climate change policies and politics: Nigeria's response. *FUDMA Journal of Politics and International Affairs, 1*(1), 106–120.

Baba, I., & Abeysinghe, C. (2017). Farmers-herdsmen conflict in the North Central region of Nigeria: An analysis of cause and effect. *International Journal of Social Science and Humanities Research, 5*(3), 53–62.

Babalola, D., & Onapajo, H. (2018). *Nigeria, a country under Siege: Issues of conflict and its management.* Cambridge Scholars Publishing.

BNRCC. (2011). *Building Nigeria's response to climate change.* Federal Ministry of Environment Special Climate Change Unit.

Brunner, D. L., Butler, J. L., & Swoboda, A. J. (2014). *Introducing evangelical ecotheology: Foundations in scripture, theology, history, and praxis.* Baker Academic.

Chikaire, J. U., Onoh, P. A., & Echetama, J. A. (2017). Perceived causes of crop farmers and pastoralists' land use conflicts in South—East Agro—Ecological zone of Nigeria. *Nigerian Journal of Agriculture, Food and Environment, 13*(4), 7–15.

Chukwuemeka, E. E. O., Aloysius, A., & Eneh, M. I. (2018). Development implications of the perennial war between farmers and pastoralists: Which way Nigeria? *International Journal of Political Science (IJPS), 4*(2), 47–68. https://doi.org/10.20431/2454-9452.0402005

Colvin, R. M., Kemp, L., Talberg, A., De Castella, C., Downie, C., Friel, S., Grant, W. J., Howden, M., Jotzo, F., Markham, F., & Platow, M. J. (2019). Learning from the climate change debate to avoid polarisation on negative emissions. *Environmental Communication, 14*, 1–13.

Conroy, S. (2014). *Land conflict, climate change, and violence in Nigeria: Patterns, mapping, and evolution.* https://www.Land-Conflict-and-Climate-Patterns-in-Nigeria.pdf

Daily Trust. (2019). *Why Ruga project was suspended—Presidency.* https://www.dailytrust.com.ng/why-ruga-project-was-suspended-presidency.html. Accessed 28 September 2019.

Douglas, P., & Hescox, M. (2016). *Caring for creation: The evangelical's guide to climate change and a healthy environment.* Baker Books.

Edeh, E. I., & Ozor, L. (2020). *Nigeria strengthens capacity to address impact of climate change on health.* https://www.afro.who.int/news/nigeria-strengthens-capacity-address-impact-climate-change-health. Accessed 9 October 2021.

Ekdahl, K. (2017). *Climate change: The threat multiplier in pastoral conflicts: A case study on the pastoral conflicts in Nigeria.* Bachelor's thesis, Peace and Development Department, Linnaeus University.

Fulton, K., & Nickels, B. (2017, March 13). Africa's pastoralists: A new battle ground for terrorism (Online). *The Broker.* http://www.thebrokeronline.eu/Blogs/Sahel-Watch-a-living-analysis-of-the-conflict-in-Mali/Africa-s-pastoralists-A-new-battleground-for-terrorism. Accessed 9 September 2017.

Holdridge, D. W. (2019). *Climate change and the Bible.* Christian Faith Publishing Inc.

Iloanya, K. O., & Ananti, M. (2018). Marriage of inconvenience between herders and farmers in Nigeria: Can elephant and hippo tango? *International Journal of Pregnancy & Child Birth, 2*(6), 358–372.

ICG. (2017). *Herders against farmers: Nigeria's expanding deadly conflict.* https://www.crisisgroup.org/africa/west-africa/nigeria/252-herders-against-farmers-nigerias-expanding-deadlyconflict. Accessed 06 May 2023.

Johansson, A. (2020). *Weather, global warming and climate change.* https://climate.nasa.gov/resources/global-warming-vs-climate-change/. Accessed 20 April 2020.

Kobayashi, K. (2019). Effects of conflicting scientific arguments on belief change: Argument evaluation and expert consensus perception as mediators. *Wiley Journal of Applied Social Psychology, 48,* 177–187.

Kwaja, C. M. A., & Ademola-Adelehin, B. I. (2017). *The implication of the open grazing prohibition and ranches establishment law on farmer-herders relations in the Middle Belt of Nigeria.* Search for Common Ground.

Kwaja, C. M. A., & Ademola-Adelehin, B. I. (2018a). *Seeking security and stability: An analysis of security responses to farmer-herder conflict in the Middle Belt Region of Nigeria* (1st ed.). Search for Common Ground.

Kwaja, C. M. A., & Ademola-Adelehin, B. I. (2018b). *Responses to conflicts between farmers and herders in the Middle Belt of Nigeria: Mapping past efforts and opportunities for violence prevention.* Search for Common Ground.

Lawal, E. (2019). *Ruga policy is a bad idea.* https://tribuneonlineng.com/ruga-policy-is-a-bad-idea/. Accessed 28 September 2019.

Maathai, W. (2009). *The challenge for Africa.* Arrow Books.

McDougal, T., Hagerty, T., Inks, L., Ugo-Ike, C. L., Dowd, C., Conroy, S., & Ogabiela, D. (2015). The effect of farmer-pastoralist violence on income: New survey evidence from Nigeria's Middle Belt States. *The Economics of Peace and Security Journal, 10*(1). https://doi.org/10.15355/epsj.10.1.54

McGregor, A. (2017). The Fulani crisis: Communal violence and radicalization in the Sahel. *CTC Sentinel, 10*(2), 34–40.

Muhammed, I., Ismaila, A. B., & Umar, M. B. (2015). An assessment of farmer-pastoralist conflict in Nigeria using GIS. *International Journal of Engineering Science Invention, 4*(7), 23–33.

Njoku, L., Agbedo, O., Ogugbuaja, C., Wantu, J., Ahovi, I. A., & Idris, A. B. (2021, July 24). Herders-farmers clash: In search of lasting solution to age-conflict. *The Guardian.*

Nwankwo, C. F. (2021). Discursive construction of the farmer-pastoralist conflict in Nigeria. *Open Political Science, 4,* 136–146. https://doi.org/10.1515/openps-2021-0014

Nwangwu, C., & Enyiazu, C. (2019). Nomadic pastoralism and human security: Towards a collective action against herders-farmers crisis in Nigeria. *JCTN, 2*(1 & 2), 89–110.

Odoh, S. I., & Chilaka, F. C. (2012). Climate change and conflict in Nigeria: A theoretical and empirical examination of the worsening incidence of conflict between Fulani herdsmen and farmers in northern Nigeria. *Arabian Journal of Business and Management Review (OMAN Chapter), 2*(1), 110–124.

Ogbozor, E. N., Omale, D. J., & Umar, M. M. (2018, August). Building bridges between herders and farmers in Plateau, Nasarawa, and Kaduna States. *Final Evaluation Report of Peace Studies and Conflict Resolution Network (PSANDCRN).* SCG.

Okoli, A. C., & Atelhe, G. A. (2014). Nomads against natives: A political ecology of herder/farmer conflicts in Nasarawa State, Nigeria. *American International Journal of Contemporary Research, 4*(2), 76–88.

Okwor, D. (2016). *The political economy of the conflict between the farmers and Fulani herdsmen in the contemporary era of climate change in Nigeria.* Research Paper presented to the Institute of Social Studies, The Netherlands.

Onikepo, B. (2021, January 26). Issues in Akeredolu's 'Ultimatum'. *This Day.* Retrieved from thisdaylive.com

Onuoha, F. C., & Okafor, J. C. (2019). Deepening civil military relations in counterinsurgency operations in North East Nigeria. In D. E. Abdullahi & R. E. Olofin (Eds.), *Deepening Civil Military relations for effective peace-building and democratic governance in Nigeria.* CLEEN Foundation.

Onyia, C. (2015). Climate change and conflict in Nigeria: The Boko Haram challenge. *American International Journal of Social Science, 4*(2), 181–190.

Para-Mallam, O. J., & Hoomlong, K. (2013). *A critical investigation into the role of security sector agencies in the Jos conflict: Issues and strategies for institutional/security sector reform.* African Peacebuilding Network/Social Science Research Council Research Report.

Premium Times. (2016, 15th April). *Nigeria loses $14 billion annually to herdsmen-farmers clashes—Report.* Accessed from https://www.premiumtimesng.com/news/headlines/201829-nigeria-loses-14-billion-annually-herdsmenfarmers-clashes-report.html?tztc=1. Accessed 06 May 2023.

Premium Times. (2020, August). *Kano govt to plant 2m tree seedlings to control flooding, desert encroachment* (Online). https://www.premiumtimesng.com/regional/nwest/411484-kano-govt-to-plant-2m-tree-seedlings-to-control-flooding-desert-encroachment.html. Accessed 1 September 2020.

Riedy, C. (2016). Climate change. In G. Ritzer (Ed.), *Blackwell encyclopedia of sociology* (pp. 1–14). Blackwell.

Sallek, Y. M. (2018). *Military internal security operations in Plateau State, North Central Nigeria: Ameliorating or exacerbating insecurity?* (Unpublished PhD thesis). Faculty of Arts and Social Sciences, Stellenbosch University.

Skah, M., & Lyammouri, R. (2020). *The climate change-security nexus: Case study of the Lake Chad Basin.* Policy Center for the New South.

Stott, J. (2010). *The radical discipleship: Some neglected aspects of our calling.* InterVarsity Press.

Sule, P. E. (2020). Open grazing prohibitions and the politics of exclusivist identity in Nigeria. *African Review.* https://doi.org/10.1080/09744053.2020.1812041

Taiwo-Hassan, A. (2021, February 11). Investigation: Inside the Igangan abductions, killings that exposed Oyo's herder crisis. *Premium Times.*

Udegbunam, O. (2019). *Presidency lists benefits of 'Ruga settlements* (Online). https://www.premiumtimesng.com/news/headlines/338046-presidency-lists-benefits-of-ruga-settlements.html. Accessed 28 September 2019.

Usman, S. G. (2019). *Socio-ecological indices of farmer-herder conflicts: Implications for conflicts prevention in Northern Senatorial District of Kaduna State, Nigeria.* https://www._final_usman_research.pdf

Wang, J., & Kim, S. (2018). Analysis of the impact of values and perception on climate change skepticism and its implication for public policy. *MDPI, 6,* 1–28.

Woody, T. (2014). *What is climate change?* http://www.takepart.com/flashcards/what-is-climate-change/index.html. Accessed 20 April 2020.

CHAPTER 4

Grassroots Conflict Over Ecosystem Services Provided by the Inner Niger Delta: The Case of Mali

Ratidzo C. Makombe

INTRODUCTION

The resurgence of conflict in Africa, ranging from violence waged by terrorists to military coups and resource-driven conflict, has been cause for concern for the past ten years. Such conflict, which negatively impacts the continent's peace and security, is on the rise. These are several reasons for the resurgence of conflict in sub-Saharan Africa, while climate change represents an additional threat. This chapter focuses on the case of the Mopti region in Mali, where the Inner Niger Delta is located and where climate change is one of the drivers of conflict. Since 2015 there has been an increase in violent conflict over the ecosystem services provided by the

R. C. Makombe (✉)
Institute for Pan-African Thought and Conversation, University of Johannesburg, Johannesburg, South Africa
e-mail: ratidzom@uj.ac.za

© The Author(s), under exclusive license to Springer Nature Switzerland AG 2023
A. O. Akinola, *Contemporary Issues on Governance, Conflict and Security in Africa*,
https://doi.org/10.1007/978-3-031-29635-2_4

Inner Niger Delta. The conflict is cyclical in accordance with geographical seasons between farmers and herders. Farmers accuse herders of overstepping their prescribed boundaries during the seasonal livestock migration which destroys crops. For their part, herders accuse farmers of unlawfully increasing their agricultural land, hence, encroaching on their grazing pasture (Ursu, 2018).

Human autonomy and dominance of the earth and its resources have played a significant role in climate change, at times leading to conflict over scarce resources. Political ecology is defined as the complex relationship between nature and society through the lens of access to resources, its implications for the environment, and how it can sustainably support livelihoods (Watts, 2000). Lipietz defines political ecology as a human science and a social and political movement centred around social problems (2000). Post-structuralist scholars, Blackie and Brookfield, state that political ecology is concerned with the effects 'on people, as well as on their productive activities, of ongoing changes within society at local and global levels'. Thus, post-structural social theory on political ecology posits that the use of the environment/nature largely depends on the power dynamics among different stakeholders.

Within the post-structural school of thought, politics is understood within the boundaries of 'power relations (who gets what, when and how) that form and pervade interactions among individuals, which are informed by challenges and negotiations and are filled with symbolic and discursive meanings' (Paulson et al., 2005). Peet (1998) notes that, post-structuralism explains modern society as a system of power that takes the side of minority groups and values diversity over likeness. Watts identifies the specific characteristics that 'explain environmental conflicts, especially in the struggle over knowledge, power, and practice' and 'politics, justice and governance' (Robbins, 2012; Watts, 2000). In the 1980s, post-structuralism addressed access to land and natural resources, ecological degradation, social marginalisation, poverty and social justice. This conceptual framework is applied to explain the conflict nexus between herder and farmers over the Inner Niger Delta. This conflict has escalated over hundreds of years and is becoming bloodier. Post-structural political ecology is employed to understand disputes over the wetland in Mali and the lengths to which groups go to assert their dominance.

The chapter draws on post-structural political ecology to unpack this conflict. This concept, which offers theoretical understanding of the power dynamics that unfold over ecosystems within society, is used to examine the dynamics of the conflict over ecosystem services provided by the Inner Niger Delta. The chapter begins by briefly unpacking the concept of post-structural political ecology, followed by an overview of climate change, peace and security in Mali and an overview of the Inner Niger Delta. The dilemma of trade-offs between farmers and herders is explored in four main themes, namely (a) unsustainable livelihood conditions, (b) erratic migration patterns, (c) corruption and (d) armed actors. Using the lens of post-structural political ecology, these thematic areas enable an examination of women's role when faced with deteriorating livelihoods and offer insight into how statuary and customary laws have failed to intersect in the context of land rights and land ownership.

Climate Change, Peace and Security in Mali

Climate change is regarded as one of the most significant risks to peace and security. According to the United Nations (2022), 'climate change refers to long-term shifts in temperatures and weather patterns, these shifts may be natural, such as through variations in the solar cycle. However, from the 1800s, human activities have been the main driver of climate change, primarily due to burning fossil fuels like coal, oil and gas'. The earth is facing substantial increases in temperature, more extended droughts, increases in sea levels and increased frequency of storms, all of which affect the lives and livelihoods of the global population. The impacts of climate change are more significant in low-income states and conflict-ridden areas. They have exacerbated the economic, social and political drivers of insecurity, further exposing vulnerable people to multifaceted crises. This is the situation in which Mali finds itself. This section provides a detailed account of the state of peace and security in Mali in relation to climate change with a focus on the Inner Niger Delta.

Mali is a landlocked country that is thought to be among the most vulnerable to climate stress due to its socio-economic status, location and climate-sensitive economy. Climate change has altered the Malian landscape, with the northern desert experiencing very variable temperatures and extended dry seasons while the central Sahelian region is subjected to seasonal flooding. Mali's average annual temperature is 28.84 °C, with a 0.7 °C increase recorded from 1960 to 2015. It is projected that an additional 1.2 °C to 3.6 °C will be reached by 2060, mainly affecting the country's southwest, central and northern regions. The rate of recurrence of "hot days" has not changed drastically, however, the recurrence rate of "hot nights" has increased from December to February (World Bank, 2021). Furthermore, rainfall has decreased and droughts have become more frequent, particularly in the northern areas, resulting in increased migration. All these factors have led to increasingly violent conflicts since 2015 as the citizens of Mali fight for the fundamental right to water and to life.

Globally, there is increased pressure on freshwater resources due to an increase in population and rapid climate change. There is thus a need to improve the management of freshwater ecosystems to foster sustainability. Poverty and lack of access to water are linked and providing the poor with access to small quantities of water for individual and productive use can make a positive difference (Merrey et al., 2005).

Half of Mali's population lives below the poverty line, with two-thirds of the country located in the arid Sahara and the semiarid Sahel. Seventy-four percent of Malians are either pastoralists or farmers. Their livelihoods are thus vulnerable to the drought and rainfall variability typical of the Sahel region (World Bank, 2021). Political instability and uneven distribution of infrastructure add to Mali's vulnerability to climate stress. In addition, agricultural crop cycles have had a negative impact on herders whose livestock routes and migration patterns have had to change. Moreover, due to the fact that the government favours farmers over herders, herders have been segregated into areas where natural resources are scarce or severely depleted. There are no designated areas separating herders and farmers (Benjaminsen & Ba, 2018), increasing the risk of conflict which has taken on an ethnic/religious dynamic in the fight for natural resources. These conflicts resulted in more than 400 murders in 2018, with around 1,000 fatalities in 2019 (Brottem, 2021). Poor governance has contributed to growing inequality that has fed the conflict between different stakeholders over the ecosystem services provided by the Inner Niger Delta whose inhabitants suffer from livelihood insecurity, lack personal, food and economic insecurity, and suffer from religious insecurity.

Overview of the Inner Niger Delta

Mali's Mopti region is home to the Inner Niger Delta, covering four districts, namely Mopti, Djenné, Tenenkou and Youwarou. The wetland covers an area of $41,195 km^2$. This region has been recognised as one of national and international importance and was designated a Ramsar

Site in 2004 by Mali. It is the largest inland wetland in West Africa and supports exceptionally diverse, rich and complex ecosystems. The Inner Niger Delta comprises various wildlife resources and is protected as a listed area under the 1971 Ramsar Convention on Wetlands of International Importance. It also has rich agricultural land and highly nutritious dry-season pasture commonly known as *burgu* (*Echinochloa stagnina*). The Inner Niger Delta makes up around 70% of irrigable land in Mali, and throughout the dry season, it accommodates nearly 50% of national livestock and fisheries. According to Mahé (2021), the delta supports the livelihoods of about half a million rural and urban inhabitants.

Farmers and herders engage in a range of productive activities including farming, agropastoral, fisheries, farm fishing and transhumant herding (Rebelo et al., 2012). Millet is produced on sandy soils and rice is grown when the land is flooded, while local fisher people and transhumant groups follow the seasonal flooding. The herders and transhumant pastoralists move from the dryland areas into the delta to spend the dry season in the Inner Niger Delta, with many coming from Mauritania and Burkina Faso (Cotula & Cissé, 2006). This complex system of overlapping resource uses has meant that the delta is a crossroads for different ethnic groups and cultures.

The drastic changes in the climate of the region have had a negative impact on the Inner Niger Delta. Its ecosystem is shaped by seasonal cycles, with the hot, dry season running from April to June and the rainy season between June and September. As a result, a large area of land is covered by water between October and January. The size of this area varies from year to year, depending on rainfall, both in the area and, more importantly, upstream. According to USAID (2018), each year, the land area increases by an additional 25,000 to 30,000km^2 due to flooding during the rainy season. In the cold, dry season, the water gradually recedes along a southwest to a northwest line from January to March. It retreats into the riverbeds when the dry season ends, and floodplains revert to dusty lands (USAID, 2018).

Drivers of Conflict and Insecurity in the Inner Niger Delta

Mali experiences high demand for, but a limited supply of water for production and domestic use. Competition over natural resources is the root cause of several conflicts in the country. In addition, climate change led the government to declare that *bourgoutié* (plains where *bourgou* grows, which provides the best grazing during the dry season) should be converted into rice fields (WPS, 2019). This negatively impacted herd mobility, exacerbating land and agropastoral disputes between herders and farmers. There are also conflicts between herders and fisher people and between fisher people and farmers. These conflicts are intersectional and have taken root in communities in the Mopti region. For example, there are internal disputes among pastoralists over social and economic status centred on access to water resources. These disputes stem from (a) access to *bourgoutiérs* at what time and cost and who gets first access, and (b) how to divide the area with *bourgoutiérs* among fishermen and herders. These disputes have led to 700 deaths in Mali since 2010, with 2018 seeing the highest levels of violence (Brottem, 2021).

Ethnic divisions between herders and farmers divide the Fulani (or Peuls) from the Dogon (in non-flood zones) or Bambara (in flood zones). Lastly, conflicts around ponds involve Bozo fishing communities (WPS, 2019). In March 2019, an armed group of Dogon known to be traditional hunters attacked and killed 175 Fulani villagers in central Mali (Benjaminsen & Ba, 2021). Almost half the victims were children. However, the Dogon mainly identify as farmers and the Fulani as pastoralists; hence, this conflict fell into the traditional tensions between farmers and herders. In as much as this conflict dates back to the 1970s, what is significant is the increase in violence. According to Armed Conflict Locations and Event Data (ACLED) in 2019, 60% of deaths caused by violence occurred in the Dogon Escarpment and Plateau in central Mali near the Inner Niger Delta (International Crisis Group, 2020).

Climate change affects everyone; however, vulnerable groups are likely to be more severely affected. This is the case in the Mopti region, whereby climate change has impacted peace and security due to social, political and economic factors. In the Inner Niger Delta, four interrelated issues demonstrate the relationship between climate change, peace and security, namely unsustainable living conditions, erratic migration patterns, corruption and armed actors. This section explores these issues focusing on the conflict nexus between herders and farmers in the Inner Niger Delta. These issues also highlight issues relating to ethnicity, gender roles and land rights.

Unsustainable Living Conditions

Eighty percent of Mali's population engages in agricultural practices, accounting for 45% of the country's gross domestic product (GDP). However, approximately 42% of the land-use conflicts in Mali are between herders and farmers over access to and control over land and water resources, especially in the Inner Niger Delta (Jones-Casey & Knox, 2011). The agricultural sector is mainly based on rice, corn, millet and sorghum subsistence farming and includes the rearing of sheep, cows and goats, which contribute 10,8% of GDP (Jones-Casey & Knox, 2011).

Within the Inner Niger Delta, most businesses are small enterprises that sell produce from smallholder farmers and herders. These businesses are unsustainable as they are dependent on seasonal rainfall. This has undermined farming and herding to the extent that local peace and security are at risk. Moreover, such businesses cannot build resilience or become an economic force that warrants government subsidies. The Inner Niger Delta population is thus susceptible to climate shocks and lacks livelihood security. According to Mbaye (2020), climate change shocks on a natural resource-based economy without any means to sustain or cushion itself increase the risk of conflict when there are limited alternative means of survival. This is evident in the clashes between farmers and herders over water resources. The water table of the Inner Niger Delta has decreased due to intense upstream water usage as a result of drought and migration (Madgwick et al., 2017).

Forty percent of labour in the agricultural sector is provided by women through garden produce. However, less than 10% of these women own the land they work (McOmber, 2020). They are vulnerable to land grabbing and are often caught between herder and farmer disputes, constantly putting them out of work. Women are also involved in small businesses that sell produce they grow or harvest. This renders them vulnerable to the effects of climate change and conflict. While Mali has adopted legislation that promotes women empowerment and encourages them to own land, this has not had the desired effect. Diversification from farming, pastoralism and fishing to selling in the marketplace has not eased the conflict because women sell the goods they produce from these activities. Therefore, the cycle of conflict extends to the marketplace.

Erratic Migration Patterns

The correlation between migration and climate change has intensified over the past decade in the Sahel religion. Factors such as violence perpetrated in the name of jihadist extremism also cause migration. However, climate change is causing more insecurity in the region. Those working in vulnerable sectors, such as herders and farmers, are worst affected. Intensified climate change threatens livelihoods and sustainability. Interstate migration of herders in the Sahel region dates back to pre-colonial times. However, migration has increased and there have been changes in traditional migration patterns due to an unprecedented rise in sea levels, frequent droughts and water scarcity. This has fuelled violent conflict, with people fighting for survival.

Migrant herders have been affected by both short-term and long-term climate change such as the drying up of water sources and a limited supply of pasture for their livestock to graze on. Increased population pressure and limited resources for both farmers and fishers who are the host community has resulted in conflict, especially in the Inner Niger Delta. The influx of herders impinges on resources that are also required by the local population. According to the Norwegian Institute of International Affairs and Stockholm International Peace Research Institute (2021), 322,000 people had been displaced in Mali, 55% of whom were women as at January 2021 due to climate change, food insecurity and other factors. In 2012, the military coup led to the internal migration of herders from the Timbuku and Gao regions to central Mali and the Inner Niger Delta. This resulted in conflict between herders and local farmers. Overall, the migration crisis in Mali and its pressure on the Inner Niger Delta has caused insecurity in the Sahel region. This is evident in the escalating conflict in the Liptako-Gourma region, which has destabilised the Sahel region, with Niger and Burkina Faso pastoralists unable to migrate (Lyammouri, 2020). Erratic migration patterns due to climate change have significantly impacted the country's peace and security. Corrupt officials and poor policies to allocate land to herders and farmers have also contributed to instability in the Mopti region.

Corruption

The monetisation of African economies has had positive and negative impacts on the economics and politics of most countries. Corruption is at an all-time high, which has also impacted the climate change crisis that is looming in Mali. Access to financial resources has significantly shaped access to natural resources. This is evident in the monetarisation of resource access fees called *tolo* charged by the chiefs, also known as *jowro*. Land allocation for agricultural purposes became monetarised in the form of rental or sharecropping contracts and in communities where the chiefs owned land or claimed land management. This created a breeding ground for rent-seeking. The *Oxford English Dictionary* notes that rent-seeking occurs when one attempts to increase one's share of current wealth without generating any new forms of wealth. Before *tolo* was monetarised, people used to give a tribute as thanks; however, with the introduction of money, bribery has increased significantly, especially to secure one's livelihood through access to land. Conflicts then arise due to poverty and inability to access land.

Benjaminsen and Ba (2009) offer insight into administrative benefits that chiefs/*jowros* accrue from their informal power. In order to retain such power, they require support from officials within local government to manage pastures. They thus make payments to retain power over land allocation and in turn, obtain the money for such payments from herders and farmers faced with limited natural resources to survive. An annual conference is convened of countries surrounding the Niger Delta that decides on the dates and times that herders can enter the Delta. This arrangement is very profitable for the chiefs/*jowros* as herders and transhumant pay fees per head of livestock at several entry points. On the designated dates of entry, local government officials expect a share of the money made by the chiefs/*jowros*. In extreme cases, these officials claim all the payments. The chiefs/*jowros* comply as they retain control of land allocation (Turner, 2009).

The Mopti region suffers from weak governance which those in positions of power, such as chiefs, have taken advantage of. When Mali gained independence, national agricultural policies favoured sedentary farmers over nomadic herders and fishers, which restricts herders from accessing adequate land and water (Gaye, 2018). In the resource-rich Inner Niger Delta, smallholder farmers are vulnerable to exploitation by members of the elite who seek economic gains by expanding their agricultural production or making money from farmers who can afford to pay for access to more land.

One of the significant causes of conflict over land in the Inner Niger Delta is the large-scale conversion of *bourgoutié* pastures to rice fields that puts pastoral production under increased pressure. Given that livelihoods in Mali involve all three streams of economic survival, favouring one over the other causes conflict. Land conflict in the Niger Delta is exacerbated by rent-seeking, corruption at the local government level, excessive fees levied on herders for the use of pastures and the use of military force to protect farmers' access to land (Seter et al., 2018). These forms of corruption that favour farmers have led to herders joining armed groups (Benjaminsen & Ba, 2018).

Armed Actors

The frequent conflict in the Sahel region over natural resources has led to some stakeholders such as marginalised herders being exploited by radical armed groups like the Katiba Macina located in central Mali to gain support. To some extent, these armed groups have taken over the role of the Malian government at community level. They offer vulnerable groups economic incentives and essential goods such as food in exchange for their allegiance. The Fulani that have been subjected to social injustice and had their freedom of movement curtailed by central and local government due to their pastoral activities are being recruited at an alarming rate by radical groups (Hegazi et al., 2021; ICG, 2020) that have approached their leaders with the promise of restoring their honour and land rights (Ursu, 2018). At the central government level, armed groups are also capitalising on the vacuum in governance by mediating resource disputes and dictating the laws governing livestock migration.

In the Mopti region, radical armed groups occupied the power vacuum caused by the 2012 military coup, poor governance and the state's failure to protect civilians. These factors have resulted in an erosion of *ubuntu* among communities and small arms are easily accessible. Climate change has thus resulted in instability, unsustainable livelihood security and escalating conflict at community level, opening the door to local militias to gain support in return for access to natural resources (Human Rights Watch, 2017).

When a group of people decides to organise themselves as an armed force, counteraction will inevitably follow, hence the rise of multiple armed groups. These actors have overlapping interests, and in the case of the Inner Niger Delta, they are all fighting for limited natural resources. This is evident in the mobilisation of the Fulani and the Dozo who regard themselves as a 'self-defence militia' group (Human Rights Watch, 2017).

In response, the Fulani established the Alliance pour le Salut du Sahel in 2018, which they also identify as a self-defence group. This alliance is well-armed and operates in the Inner Niger Delta and on the borders of Burkina, Mali and Nigeria. It aims to foster the survival of their traditions as herders and to resist their marginalisation (Ursu, 2018).

According to Mbaye (2020) and Nagarajan (2020), the disputes over natural resources in the Mopti region are connected to national and regional conflict dynamics. The increase in community violence and the active presence of armed groups that aim to either exacerbate or end conflict in the region have made the situation difficult to resolve. There has been a significant increase in self-defence militia groups in central Mali, increasing the levels of violence between farming clans such as the Dogon and herding clans such as the Fulani. Increased access to small arms in the Sahel region has led to a rise in disputes and fatalities. ACLED data indicates that more than 2,000 fatalities occurred in this wave of violence from the beginning of 2019 to the first four months of 2020. Fulani villagers accounted for around 80% of these casualties, with Dogon hunters, government officials and soldiers making up the remainder (International Crisis Group, 2020).

Concluding Remarks

The conflict dynamics in the Inner Niger Delta reflect conflict trends in Africa. Struggles to secure livelihoods have escalated due to climate change. This chapter showed that peace and security in the Inner Niger Delta are increasingly at risk with a rise in fatalities during disputes over rights to land and water. While Mali's government has had a hand in causing the disputes between herders and farmers, climate change has made a greater contribution. If appropriate action is not taken, changes in migration patterns and increased pressure on resources will worsen over time.

The complexities of these conflicts render them extremely difficult to resolve as they involve multiple layers that have developed over the years. As a result, the African traditions of *ubuntu* are slowly disintegrating in the Mopti region. The most critical factor in addressing climate change is for all stakeholders, especially vulnerable groups, to work together. It is recommended that the Malian government craft and implement a grazing reserve policy to minimise conflict between herders and farmers. This would need to be revisited annually to account for factors, such as population growth and migration shocks. This is a superior alternative to allocating all the *bourgoutié* to farmers, as resources should be shared. A dedicated task team should drive this process as it will require ongoing research and forecasting.

Corruption in granting access to grazing land, ponds and water sources is exacerbating the conflict between herders and farmers. This is occurring at the local government level with the complicity of the traditional authorities. Mali's anti-corruption commission, the Supreme Audit Institution (Contrôle Général des Services Publics (CGSP)), should investigate the channels through which corruption is taking place and sanction the perpetrators. This will also serve as a lesson to opportunists who seek to exploit herders and farmers to gain access to grazing or farming land. Beyond this, the rule of law in Mali needs to be improved as corruption starts at the top of the "food chain". All perpetrators who are aiding corruption by exploiting the traditional *tolo* should face the might of the law.

The ethnic conflict between the Fulani and Dogon has resulted in jihadist armed actors taking sides and exacerbating the conflict. Multi-layered conflicts such as the one in Mali are not easy to resolve and different triggers result in people fighting along ethnic lines. The most effective way to resolve such conflict is through a Truth and Reconciliation Commission (TRC). Such commissions have been used by countries that have undergone mass violence and need restorative justice. Perpetrators and victims openly and willingly acknowledge incidents of violence. 'Such commissions provide a space for former enemies to bridge their differences. For the most part, they are designed to bring about processes of healing, processes that offer victims solace and reassurance that their trauma will not be repeated' (Facing History & Ourselves, 2022). African states that have used the TRC process include Ghana, Rwanda and South Africa, and there has been no reoccurrence of conflict along ethnic groups. It is important to note that climate change is a trigger for farmers and herders to attack one another along ethnic lines and these ethnic divisions are not caused by climate change. Hence, a TRC will assist in resolving ethnic conflict in Mali.

In conclusion, the conflict between herders and farmers over the ecosystem services provided by the Inner Niger Delta has been triggered by climate change. There are different layers to this conflict from the central government's poor decision-making to ethnic divisions. Climate change is upon the world, and it cannot be reversed; however, action can be taken to minimise conflict. Given that the state is not directly involved in this conflict, it is up to grassroots actors to end it and to lobby for improved policies in their region.

References

Benjaminsen, T. A., & Ba, B. (2009). Farmer–herder conflicts, pastoral marginalisation and corruption: A case study from the inland Niger delta of Mali. *Geographical Journal*, 175(1), 71–81.

Benjaminsen, T. A., & Ba, B. (2018). Farmer-herder conflicts, pastoral marginalisation and corruption: A case study from the Inland Niger Delta of Mali. *The Geographical Journal*, 174(1), 71–81.

Benjaminsen, T. A., & Ba, B. (2021). Fulani-Dogon killings in Mali: Farmer-herder conflicts as insurgency and counterinsurgency. *African Security*, 14(1), 4–26.

Brottem, L. (2021). *The growing complexity of farmer-herder conflict in West and Central Africa*. Africa Centre for Strategic Studies. https://africacenter.org/publication/growing-complexity-farmer-herder-conflict-west-central-africa/

Cotula, L., & Cissé, S. (2006). Changes in "customary" resource tenure systems in the inner Niger Delta, Mali. *The Journal of Legal Pluralism and Unofficial Law*, 38, 1–29.

Facing History and Ourselves. (2022). *Truth and reconciliation*. https://www.facinghistory.org/stolen-lives-indigenous-peoples-canada-and-indian-residential-schools/historical-background/truth-and-reconciliation

Gaye, S. B. (2018). *Conflicts between farmers and herders against a backdrop of asymmetric threats in Mali and Burkina Faso*. https://tinyurl.com/kc57xuc8

Hegazi, F., Krampe, F., & Smith, E. (2021). *Climate-related security risks and peacebuilding in Mali*. https://tinyurl.com/xuzb5kmb

Human Rights Watch. (2017). *Mali: Spate of killings by Armed Groups*. https://www.hrw.org/news/2017/04/05/mali-spate-killings-armed-groups

ICG. (2020). *The Central Sahel: Scene of new climate wars?* (Africa Briefing 154). https://www.crisisgroup.org/africa/sahel/b154-le-sahel-central-theatre-des-nouvelles-guerres-climatiques

International Alert. (2016). "They treat us all like Jihadists": Looking beyond violent extremism to building peace in Mali. *Policy Brief: December*. https://www.international-alert.org/publications/they-treat-us-all-like-jihadis/

International Crisis Group. (2020). *Stopping the communalization of violence in central Mali* (Report Number 293). https://www.crisisgroup.org/fr/africa/sahel/mali/293-enrayer-la-communautarisation-de-la-violence-au-centre-du-mali

Jones-Casey, K., & Knox, A. (2011). *Farmer-herder conflicts in Mali brief. Focus on land in Africa*.

Lipietz, A. (2000). Political ecology and the future of marxism. *Capitalism Nature Socialism, 11*(1), 69–85.
Lyammouri, R. (2020). *Mobility and conflict in Liptako-Gourma.* https://tinyurl.com/4hr2ms3c
Madgwick, F. J., Oakes, R., Pearce, F., & Tharme, R. (2017). *Watershocks: Wetlands and human migration in the Sahel.*
Mahé, G. (2021, June 15). *The inner Niger Delta, an exceptional natural environment,* News. https://www.initiativesrivers.org/actualites/gil-mahe-ird-the-inner-niger-delta-an-exceptional-natural-environment/
Mbaye, A. A. (2020). Climate change, livelihoods, and conflict in the Sahel. *Georgetown Journal of International Affairs, 21,* 12–20. https://tinyurl.com xfz4udwe
McOmber, C. (2020). *Women and climate change in the Sahel* (West African Papers 27). https://tinyurl.com/xntk7y3x
Merrey, D. J., Drechsel, P., de Vries, F. W. T., & Sally, H. (2005). Integrating "livelihoods" into integrated water resources management: Taking the integration paradigm to its logical next step for developing countries. *Regional Environmental Change, 5*(4), 197–204.
Nagarajan, C. (2020). *Climate-fragility risk brief: Mali.* https://tinyurl.com/3ef z3bcz
Paulson, S., Gezon, L. L., & Watts, M. (2005). Politics, ecologies, genealogies. In S. Paulson & L. L. Gezon (Eds.), *Political ecology across spaces, scale, and social groups.* Rutgers University Press.
Peet, R. (1998). *Modern geographical thoughts.* Blackwell Publishing.
Rebelo, L. M., Johnston, R., Hein, T., Weigelhofer, G., D'Haeyer, T., Kone, B., & Cools, J. (2013). Challenges to the integration of wetlands into IWRM: The case of the Inner Niger Delta (Mali) and the Lobau Floodplain (Austria). *Environmental Science & Policy, 34,* 58–68.
Robbins, P. (2012). *Political ecology: A critical introduction* (2nd ed.). Wiley.
Seter, H., Theisen, O. M., & Schilling, J. (2018). All about water and land? Resource-related conflicts in East and West Africa revisited. *GeoJournal, 83*(1), 169–187.
Turner, M. D. (2009). Capital on the move: The changing relation between livestock and labour in Mali, West Africa. *Geoforum, 40*(5), 746–755.
United Nations. (2022). *What is climate change?* https://www.un.org/en/climatechange/what-is-climate-change
Ursu, A. (2018). *Under the gun: Resource conflicts and embattled traditional authorities in Central Mali.* Institute of International Relations.
USAID. (2018). *Climate risk profile: Mali.* https://tinyurl.com/smx7f3sc
Water Peace and Security (WPS). (2019). *Challenges for Central Mali.* August 2019 Policy Brief.
Watts, M. (2000). Political ecology. In *A companion to economic geography* (pp. 257–274). Blackwell.

World Bank. (2021). *Climate change knowledge portal for development practitioners and policy makers. Country Mali.* https://climateknowledgeportal.worldbank.org/country/mali/climate-data-historical

CHAPTER 5

Conflict, Police Impunity and the Governance Question in Nigeria: Reflecting on the #EndSARS Protest

Omololu Fagbadebo and Leke Oluwalogbon

INTRODUCTION

The #EndSARS protests in Nigeria marked a watershed in the country's democratic history. A population known to be largely passive when it comes to public affairs, particularly elections, erupted in spontaneous protest against a long history of police impunity and poor governance. Previous protests in Nigeria include the Aba Women Riot (1929) and Egba women's revolt (1947) in response to the colonial government's

---

O. Fagbadebo (✉)
Department of Public Management, Law and Economics, Durban University of Technology, Pietermaritzburg, South Africa
e-mail: otomololu@yahoo.com

L. Oluwalogbon
Department of Political Science and Public Administration, Redeemer's University, Ede, Nigeria

© The Author(s), under exclusive license to Springer Nature Switzerland AG 2023
A. O. Akinola, *Contemporary Issues on Governance, Conflict and Security in Africa*,
https://doi.org/10.1007/978-3-031-29635-2_5

imposition of tax levies, with poor governance also cited in the latter case. Several labour protests also occurred in colonial and post-colonial times. Protests against military rule and associated issues included that against the Babangida government's (1989) Structural Adjustment Programme, the "Ali Must Go" students' protest (1978) and the 12 June protests against the Abacha regime (Adebowale, 2020). Since Nigeria's return to democratic rule, sporadic protests have occurred against the removal of the fuel subsidy, otherwise known as the Occupy Nigeria protest. The #BringBackOurGirls campaign agitated for the safe return of the more than 250 young Christian schoolgirls abducted from the Government Girls Secondary School in Chibok, Borno State in 2014.

However, the #EndSARS protest stands out for several reasons. Unlike most previous protests that could be described as fragmented, it cut across a large spectrum of Nigerian society. Although dominated by the youth, members of the older generation also participated. The protest also brought together people from diverse backgrounds, from professionals to artisans and the unemployed as the consequences of the Nigerian police's brutal force impact all sectors of society. Since the youth dominated the protests, optimal use was made of social media, hence the hashtag #EndSARS, which surpassed the likes of America's #BlackLivesMatter on Twitter. The protest also transcended international boundaries, as Nigerians in the diaspora and international figures lent their voices to the cause (Uwazuruike, 2020).

The most significant factor that made the protest stand out from the pack was Nigeria's governance crisis, manifested in police impunity. Though democratic in outlook, the Nigerian state has proven incapable, on the one hand, of delivering public goods to the teeming population (Yagboyaju & Akinola, 2019) and, on the other, of recognising the challenges that threaten the state's survival and mitigating their effects. Examples of the latter include the protracted insurgency in the northeastern part of the country, the herder-farmer conflicts that dot almost the entire landscape, and armed banditry (Okoi & Iwara, 2021). In 2018, Nigeria was ranked 123rd out of 137 countries on the reliability of police services.

Police impunity as a manifestation of poor governance is a global phenomenon. In the United States (US), it spurred the launch of Black Lives Matter and this Flag movement (Ebiede, 2020). In South Africa, 440 people died as a result of police action between 2018 and 2019 (Feltham & Rupiah, 2021) and 5,524 cases of police brutality were reported to the South African Independent Police Investigative Directorate (IPID) between 2019 and 2020.

A survey by the Socio-Economic Rights and Accountability Project (SERAP) revealed that the police were the most corrupt public institution in Nigeria (*The Guardian*, 27 March 2019). It further revealed that Nigerians had to pay a bribe 'in 54 percent of interactions with the police', and 'there is a 63 percent probability that an average Nigerian would be asked to pay a bribe each time he or she interacted with the police' (cf. *The Guardian*, 27 March 2019). The 2016 World Internal Security and Police Index (WISPI) ranked the Nigeria Police Force as the worst in the world. The index measured allocation and utilisation of resources for, and threats to internal security. The 2019 Global Police Index ranked Nigeria among the countries with an average-performing police force (Global Police Index, 2019). This is a manifestation of the state's failure to uphold its traditional responsibility.

The State and Security

Security has remained a primary societal concern since Thomas Hobbes' conceptualisation of the Leviathan as a symbol of the state in his theory of the social contract of the state. Hobbes argued that, in the state of nature, human beings live in perpetual fear of violence and death due to the absence of an overarching authority to address conflicts of interest and the proclivity to self-defence in an anarchic society (Lakitsch, 2021; Villarreal, 2020). He described life in the state of nature as characterised by the 'war of every man against every man' due to constant violence and competition, rendering life 'solitary, poor, nasty, brutish, and short' (Villarreal, 2020: 20). Hence, his concept of a Leviathan that would take responsibility to mitigate conflict and associated violence.

Like his fellow social contract theorists, such as John Locke and Jean Jaques Rousseau, Hobbes identified the need for the state, the Leviathan, to rise to the occasion by providing security for citizens in exchange for their freedom in the state of nature. In other words, the primary responsibility of the state is protection and promotion of the security of citizens and society at large. This contractual agreement evolves from citizens' willingness to surrender their freedom to the state that would serve as an arbiter, constantly reconciling competing interests and forces capable of jeopardising citizens' security.

The modern state derived its relevance and purpose from the ideas of these early political thinkers. Subsequently, the concept of security became more encompassing. Central to the role of the modern state is the guarantee of citizen's security against physical harm and danger and their ability to secure their means of livelihood through effective governance (Howe, 2013). Governance connotes 'a process through which collective good and goods (including security) are generated, or their production facilitated so that all are better off than they would be acting individually' (Howe, 2013: 13). This implies a collective concern, championed by the state with the support of citizens to promote 'security and development' (Howe, 2013: 13). Thus, the modern conception of security transcends the resolution of conflictual interests and prevention of war to include poverty eradication and effective public service delivery.

Governance requires cooperation between the state and citizens. This is usually characterised by public participation, adherence to the rule of law, transparency, accountability, government legitimacy and responsiveness, effective and efficient public service delivery and security (Keping, 2018). The rule of law plays a vital role in ensuring good governance. This encompasses the transparent exercise of the power of the state, with government officials and agents of the state held accountable. Adherence to state rules and regulations set out in legislative frameworks guides the conduct of both the government and the governed. Central to this chapter is the exercise of policing power in regulating conflictual interests and the promoting citizens' security.

POLICING AND VIOLENT CONFLICT: A CONCEPTUAL EXPLORATION

Every state has policing structures and mechanisms, with measures to combat domestic violence and conflicts. As part of its responsibility, the leadership of the modern state prioritises domestic protection. Thus, the policing structure is designed to activate the ancient responsibility of the state to promote and protect citizens' security (Agbiboa, 2015). In other words, the police comprise a security unit that is the gatekeeper and custodian of citizen's security and safety. Hence, the paraphernalia of the office accord every police personnel the status of a symbol of the state:

Police officers, as gatekeepers of the criminal justice system, hold almost exclusive authority—by way of citations, arrests, and even physical force—to enforce and regulate the law. And they have increasingly been asked to do this in situations that involve societal problems that would be better resolved in the community—problems like homelessness, mental illness, and substance use. (Neusteter et al., 2019: 2)

This power of enforcement, exercised by the state through the police, is central to the Hobbesian conceptualisation of the state. With the police as the gatekeeper, enforcement of law and order is a direct action to guarantee citizen's security irrespective of their status. Since, in the Hobbesian conception, citizens have relinquished their freedom and power of self-defence to the state, it behoves the relevant authority to exercise the power of the state in a manner that demonstrates the government's commitment to its responsibility.

Across societies, the establishment of policing units is based on the realisation that mitigation of conflicting interests with the framework of the law is essential to advance citizens' interests. In advanced democracies, the police, as an organic component of the state, symbolise orderliness, peace and security (Sherman, 2018; United Nations, 2011). The evolution of the police service defines its operational characteristics.

The Historical Trajectory of Nigerian Policing

Modern policing in Nigeria has its origins in the colonial era. Different policing structures were established in towns in 1820 (Onoja, 2013; Otu, 2004). In 1861, the Lagos Colony established a 30-member Consular Guard and in 1896, the colonial government established the Lagos Police. The Hausa Constabulary, a 1,200-member armed paramilitary unit, was formally established in the north in 1879 and the Niger Coast Protectorate established the Niger Coast Constabulary in Calabar in 1894. In 1888, the Royal Niger Company (RNC) established its police unit, the Royal Niger Company Constabulary (RNCC) located in Lokoja. The RNCC later became the Northern Nigeria Police (NNP). Although the Northern and the Southern Protectorates were amalgamated in 1914, the various police formations only became a unified police unit in 1930 that was named the Nigeria Police Force (NPF). The primary role of the colonial police 'was to stifle dissent to colonial rule' (Nwanze, 2014). It thus served as an 'occupation force to suppress the indigenous Nigerian peoples as the colonizers exploited their resources to develop their own countries' (Soniyi, 2020).

In the early days of its existence, the Nigerian police force focused on crime investigation and control (Onoja, 2013). Nevertheless, the repressive culture that grounded the formation of the force as a colonial tool has remained an integral characteristic (Alemika, 1993). The colonial police in Nigeria were dreaded by citizens. As Alemika (1993: 187) has noted, the brutality, oppression, repression and corruption associated with the Nigerian police were rooted in the country's 'legacy of political authoritarianism and social exploitation'. Thus, the colonial police and other security agencies and their Nigerian successors were state instruments that were used 'in a way that stifles democracy and impedes social justice' (Alemika, 1993: 187). Given the lack of accurate and transparent guidelines, the police have remained an instrument of oppression and intimidation under successive military and civilian governments.

The NPF's statutory duties set out in Sect. 4 of the Police Act of 1990 are to prevent and detect crime, apprehend offenders, preserve law and order, protect lives and property, enforce laws and regulations and participate in military duties as a peace-keeping force within and outside the country. Thus, the police are an arm of the government that activates the state's primary and most essential role. Nevertheless, it is not insulated from corruption and abuse of power.

Police Corruption in Nigeria

Corruption is a common phenomenon in the modern state that represents an obstacle to good governance. Scholars note that it stifles growth and development (Lewis, 2017; Cooray & Schneider, 2018; Fagbadebo, 2019). Corruption, in whatever form, is simply abuse of public trust for personal or private gain (World Bank, 2021). Roebuck and Barker (1974: 423) define police corruption 'as deviant, dishonest, improper, unethical, or criminal behavior by a police officer' that aims to advance personal interests. Hope expands on this conceptualisation and defines police corruption as:

> any action or omission, a promise of any action or omission, or any attempt of action or omission committed by a police officer or a group of police officers characterized by the police officer's misuse of the official position

and motivated in significant part with the achievement of personal/private or organizational gain or advantage. (Hope, 2018: 85)

Police corruption is a symptom of a governance crisis. Hope (2018: 84) explains that when corruption becomes endemic in law enforcement agencies, especially the police, it is a manifestation of 'a systemic failure of governance wherein the principal institutions responsible for ensuring police governance, the observance of ethics and integrity standards, and enforcing the rule of law are compromised and may themselves be infected with corrupt individuals and syndicates'.

> The result is that a chain environment of personal and collective impunity prevails and police corruption is, therefore, both perceived and real as running rampant. That, in turn, has considerable negative impacts on justice or security sector development and performance and is a challenge to nation-building, to the maintenance of public order and the rule of law, and to support the legitimacy of the state. (Hope, 2018: 84)

The above describes both the policing institution and its activities.

Over the years, there have been numerous reports of corruption and deviant behaviour in policing institutions and structures. Roadblocks are a common means of police corruption in Nigeria (Human Rights Watch, 2010).

> On a daily basis throughout Nigeria, drivers of taxis, minibuses, and motorcycles, as well as private motorists are subjected to routine extortion under threat of arrest, detention, and physical injury after being obliged to stop at official or semi-official police roadblocks. These checkpoints, ostensibly put in place to combat rampant and rising crime, have in practice become a lucrative criminal venture for the police. (Human Rights Watch, 2010)

Indeed, Human Rights Watch (2010) noted that police roadblocks are "standardised toll" points where police extort money from commuters and drivers. At each checkpoint, especially in Lagos, police on duty employ 'a creative system in which drivers are given a password, based on an identifying mark on their vehicles—such as a number on their license plate—to identify which drivers had already paid the daily "toll"' (Human Rights Watch, 2010).

From Civility to Impunity: The Nigeria Police Force's Scorecard

A basic duty of any democratic government is to safeguard citizens' life and property. Section 14(2)(b) of the 1999 Constitution of the Federal Republic of Nigeria states that 'the security and welfare of the people shall be the primary purpose of government'. A policing system is required to enforce the intent of the law. The police have powers to prevent crime, protect citizens' lives and property, preserve law and order and arrest offenders. Furthermore, the police detect crime and detain criminals, perform military duties within and outside Nigeria, and enforce laws and regulations. Other duties include identification of persons, searching belongings and prosecution of criminal cases.

The Nigerian police have become synonymous with high-handedness that has culminated in gross violations of human rights (Uwazuruike, 2020). There seems to be a penchant for violation of the most basic right—the right to life. This manifests in the form of extrajudicial killings and other random, unprovoked killings, often described as accidental discharges by trigger-happy police officers. The Open Society Justice Initiative (OSJI) found that extrajudicial executions were a regular occurrence in the discharge of policing duties in Nigeria. It was estimated that 10,000 people were killed by the Nigerian police from 2000 to 2007 (Human Rights Watch, 2007). While most extrajudicial killings are done in secret, some officers have become so brazen that they perform them in broad daylight (Folarin, 2019).

Torture has also been adopted to extract confessions from detainees, and many police formations have designated offices and personnel to oversee such (OSJI, 2010). This takes the form of physical and sexual assaults on detainees, including inflicting pain using guns, machetes and other weapons, causing bodily and psychological trauma (Amnesty International, 2016). Violation of liberty, privacy and the right to family life are other means by which the police have held the Nigerian citizenry hostage. On average, it takes around three years and ten months for a detainee to be arraigned before a court of competent jurisdiction. Pre-trial detention is a gimmick that allows officers to hold anyone they want for as long as they want (Uwazuruike, 2020).

The WISPI measures the police and other security providers' ability to effectively tackle internal security matters across 127 countries. It ranks states in four dimensions of internal security, viz., capacity, process, legitimacy and outcomes. Capacity relates to the level of resources available to achieve internal security, such as the number of police officers and military officers per 100,000 citizens and the ratio of prisoners to official prison capacity. Process considers how effectively those resources have been deployed. Its indicators include control of corruption, the effectiveness of the criminal justice system, payment of bribes to police, which is measured by the percentage of respondents who offered a bribe to a police officer in the past, and underreporting, measured by the ratio of police-reported thefts to survey reported thefts.

Legitimacy measures the extent to which the public affirms the police and other internal security providers. It focuses on the due process of the law and the rights of the accused, the percentage of respondents who have confidence in the local police, the extent to which police officers and the military do not use public office for private gain and the government's use of force against its citizens. Lastly, outcomes assess the real-time threats to internal security measured by homicides per 100,000 people and the percentage of citizens who are victims of violent crimes. It is also measured by the number of deaths, injuries and incidents of terrorism and citizens' perceptions of safety when walking alone at night (WISPI, 2016).

Sub-Saharan Africa was ranked the worst-performing region, with Nigeria leading seven other countries. Capacity was the most noticeable deficit in poorly performing sub-Saharan African countries. The number of police officers and other security agents within the region is below the global average, while it has an average prison occupancy rate of 166%, well above the global average (WISPI, 2016).

Nigeria's rating was abysmally poor across all four dimensions, with the worst scores in process and outcomes. Overall, Nigeria was ranked lowest among 127 states on the WISPI, scoring 0.255, while Botswana and Rwanda were sub-Saharan Africa's best performers, with the former ranked 47th with 0.685 and the latter 50th with a score of 0.683. The report noted that Nigeria had 219 police officers for every 100,000 citizens, far below the global average of 300 and sub-Saharan Africa's average of 268. It also noted that 81% of Nigerian respondents in the Global Corruption Barometer admitted to paying a bribe to a police officer in the previous year. Furthermore, the Rule of Law index found that police officials and other security personnel are likely to use their public positions for private gain (WISPI, 2016).

SARS, Brutality and the Crime Prevention Philosophy in Nigeria

The SARS was an elite unit of the Nigerian Police that was established in 1992 to combat rising cases of armed robbery and banditry in Lagos, the nation's former capital. As a unit designed to fight high-level crime, SARS became a notorious force that was dreaded by citizens. Simeon Danladi Midenda, a police officer reputed to have fought crime in Benin, was deployed to Lagos to lead a crack team of officers to combat the armed gangs that were terrorising densely populated metropolitan Lagos. The members of this squad did not operate as conventional police, but worked undercover, with no public display of arms, uniforms and vehicles.

> In the early days of the unit, combat-ready SARS officers operated undercover in plain clothes and plain vehicles without any security or government insignia and did not carry arms in public. Their main job was to monitor radio communications and facilitate successful arrests of criminals and armed robbers. (Malumfashi, 2020)

The SARS' initial operations were limited to Lagos. Its initial success created an image of an effective anti-crime mechanism and ten years after its establishment, the SARS became a unit of the Nigeria Police that was extended to other states.

> Its mandate was to arrest, investigate, and prosecute suspected armed robbers, murderers, kidnappers, hired assassins, and other violent criminals. The unit quickly began to set up roadblocks and extort money. The SARS officers started to carry weapons in public and over time were implicated in extrajudicial killings, torture, arbitrary arrests, and unlawful detention. (Amnesty International, 2021)

However, as the unit grew in popularity, it soon became an instrument of oppression and extortion. Public outcry against the use of force that resulted in a series of extrajudicial killings promoted a government investigation aimed at reformulating its operations. Local and international civil society organisations also investigated complaints against SARS operatives and human rights violations. The pressure intensified when it was discovered that members of the squad were killing citizens at will with no evidence that any crime had been committed (Amnesty International, 2009). Amnesty International (2021) reported frequent disappearances of citizens arrested by police, many of whom were killed at will, and that 'many families were looking for their loved ones in police stations and detention centers'. In 2013, the bodies of 35 citizens who disappeared after being arrested by the SARS were discovered in a river in Anambra State (Amnesty International, 2021). Before that, six men arrested by the SARS in Port Harcourt had disappeared from the unit's custody in 2010. Indeed, Human Rights Watch (2010) noted that members of the Nigeria Police were 'more as predators than protectors' of citizens.

> Police corruption not only leads to these very serious human rights abuses that are generally carried out by rank-and-file police officers, but it also undermines the rule of law in Nigeria. For many Nigerians, the police have come to be viewed more as predators than as protectors. (Human Rights Watch, 2010)

A report by Amnesty International (2016) documented ongoing abuse and violation of human rights by the SARS. It noted the extent to which the squad had become a money-spinning outfit through extortion, corruption and other criminal activities. The SARS Abuja detention centres were singled out for their disregard for human dignity.

Arbitrary arrest and detention are one of the tactics to extort money from innocent but vulnerable citizens. In its 2010 report, Human Rights Watch noted:

> Once a person is arrested by the police and refuses, or is unable, to pay the money demanded, they are often detained until they negotiate an amount for their release. In many cases, this unlawful detention may last for days or even weeks. Those who do not pay face threats, beatings, sexual assault, torture, or even death. Extended periods of detention leave victims and their friends and family vulnerable to repeated threats and demands for bribes. (Human Rights Watch, 2010)

It was against this backdrop that the #EndSARS campaign surfaced on social media. Victims, who were lucky to be alive, and family members of those who lost their lives to the brute force of the SARS, documented their ordeals. As Amnesty International (2021) reported, the popular social media movement drew the attention of the Nigerian government as well as the international community. Nevertheless, the government remained docile in dealing with the monster of corruption and the brutal application of force to intimidate and oppress Nigerian citizens.

Incontrovertible documentation of atrocities sparked demands for genuine reforms that would reposition the unit to its original purpose. The government had previously proposed certain measures, but these were not implemented. Instead, SARS grew wings and became an entrenched unit in the NPF to the extent that all measures to contain its operation were rebuffed. For instance, in 2017 when the youth initially launched protests the SARS unit and demanded police reforms, the police high command at the time announced that the unit had been banned from stop and search operations. However, this was not enforced, and its officers continued their nefarious activities. In 2018, Acting President Professor Yemi Osinbajo set up a Commission of Inquiry to investigate atrocities allegedly perpetrated by the SARS. While he acknowledged that atrocities had occurred, no one was held accountable. The findings of the Commission were not made available to the public and all the Acting President's directives were reversed (Adetayo, 2018).

> Following persistent complaints and reports on the activities of the Special Anti-Robbery Squad that border on allegations of human rights violations, Acting President Yemi Osinbajo, SAN, has directed the Inspector General of Police to, with immediate effect, overhaul the management and activities of SARS and ensure that any unit that will emerge from the process will be intelligence-driven and restricted to the prevention and detection of armed robbery and kidnapping, and apprehension of offenders linked to the stated offences, and nothing more. (cf. Adetayo, 2018)

Rather than a general overhaul of the squad, as ordered by the Acting President, the Inspector General of Police (IGP) merely renamed it the Federal Special Anti-Robbery Squad (FSARS) (Erunke, 2018). The abuse continued unabated, with deafening public outcry. The FSARS was later disbanded and reverted to the SARS.

#EndSARS: The Governance Crisis in Nigeria

The spontaneous protest by Nigerian youth against police brutality on 8 October 2020 was a symbolic representation of public displeasure at longstanding police brutality in the country. Popularly known as the #EndSARS protest, public outrage against the SARS' brutal oppression of citizens reached a crescendo with the release of video and audio-visual content of its officers harassing and brutalising innocent people. Policing in Nigeria has been characterised by the infliction of brutal force. Since the description of the federal government's response to the declaration of Biafra on 6 July 1967, as a "police action", the culture of civility in policing in Nigeria has been replaced by the application of force.

#EndSARS first emerged in 2017 to demand police reforms. However, its resurgence in October 2020 had more impacts, the most significant of which was the disbandment of the notorious SARS unit. The protesters also made further demands that were captured in #5for5. These included the immediate release of all detained protesters, justice for deceased victims of police brutality and compensation for their families. They also demanded an independent inquiry to investigate and prosecute reports of police misconduct, psychological evaluation of all members of the disbanded SARS unit and their retraining before redeployment. Lastly, the movement demanded that police officers' remuneration be increased to motivate them to protect citizen's lives and property (Ejiofor, 2020).

Nigerians expected that the advent of civilian rule in 1999 would halt the incessant brutality by security agencies that characterised military rule. Instead, the brutality intensified. Between 2011 and 2021, extrajudicial killings by Nigerian security agencies claimed the lives of 13,241 citizens (Nwannekanma et al., 2021).

The SARS' activities were characterised by fraudulent activities and cover-ups. For example, Eric Okwaji was arrested because he complained that SARS officers parked their vehicle, blocking the pavement outside his residence in Lagos (*Premium Times*, 11 May 2021). His father, Mr Laurence Macaulay, searched for him for days, but when he located him, he could not afford the N400,000 demanded by the SARS officer to secure his son's release. Eventually, the SARS announced that he was implicated in an armed robbery, and his whereabouts have remained unknown since 2014.

> Last October, as years of SARS-related brutality, reached their peak, provoking protests nationwide and garnering global attention for Nigeria, the anguish of aggrieved families hit close to home. One of such families, Mr. Macaulay and his household continue to live in perpetual anxiety, not knowing where their beloved Eric is, or even whether he is alive or not. (*Premium Times*, 11 May 2021)

A journalist, Kofi Bartels, recounted his ordeal at the hands of SARS officers in Port Harcourt: 'They took turns to slap, punch and kick me while

I was struggling with a swollen knee. At least six officers, one at a time' (cf. Malumfashi, 2020). He was covering an incident where SARS officers took turns to beat a citizen on the road. Another victim described how SARS officers pulled over their car on their way from her university graduation. In her accounts to the media, Philomena Celestine said,

> My four-year-old niece was in the vehicle but they cocked their guns at our car and drove my brothers into the bush where they harassed them for over 30 minutes, and accused them of being cybercriminals. They could see my graduation gown but that did not deter them. My sister was trembling and crying in fear (cf. Malumfashi, 2020).

Media commentators and writers have noted the prevalent culture of corruption in the country's law enforcement agencies, 'with officers extorting people over the years, often violently and without consequence' (Paquette, 2021).

The SARS as an Albatross: Corruption in Law Enforcement

At no time in history has the Nigerian public positively appraised the country's law enforcement agencies. Fear and dread occasioned using force in policing since the colonial era have reinforced the need for citizens to surrender to this oppression. While the worst criminals enjoy police protection, innocent citizens are victims of extortion, detention without trial based on false accusations, arrest, torture and extrajudicial killings.

In 1986, a notorious armed robber, Lawrence Anini enjoyed protection provided by a Chief Superintendent of Police, George Iyamu (Marenin, 1987). Upon his arrest, Anini disclosed that he owed the success and near invincibility of his deadly operations to Iyamu's collaboration and support. Aside from supplying sophisticated weapons for his operations, Anini disclosed that the police chief had his own deadly armed robbery gang (Marenin, 1987). Due to his privileged position as an agent of the state, Iyamu had access to information that could have led to Anini's arrest. However, he chose to work against the public interest by suppressing information 'given by citizens concerning his whereabouts' (Marenin, 1987: 262). He even organised the killing of a senior police officer who was deployed to assist in apprehending the notorious armed robber. Iyamu was subsequently arrested and killed along with Anini and his gang.

More recently, a former SARS leader in Lagos, Deputy Commissioner of Police (DCP) Abba Kyari, was indicted for being a member of a drug-smuggling cartel (*The Guardian*, 14 February 2022; Princewill, 2022). Once regarded as a "super cop" based on his "successes" in apprehending criminal elements, Kyari was indicted for being 'part of an international drug ring and was involved in a 25 kg cocaine deal' (Princewill, 2022). Nigeria's National Drug Law Enforcement Agency (NDLEA) declared him wanted in the belief 'that DCP Kyari is a member of a drug cartel that operates the Brazil-Ethiopia-Nigeria illicit drug pipeline, and he needs to answer questions' (Princewill, 2022).

> The Nigeria Police Force has arrested DCP Abba Kyari and four other police officers for their involvement in an alleged case of criminal conspiracy, discreditable, unethical, and unprofessional conduct, official corruption and tampering with exhibits in a case of illicit drug trafficking involving a perpetual transnational drug cartel. The arrest of the officers was sequel to pieces of information received from the leadership of the National Drug Law Enforcement Agency (NDLEA) on 10th February 2022 (Nigeria Police Force, 2022).

The police press release indicated that prior to his arrest, the Inspector General of Police had ordered an investigation of the allegations (Nigeria Police Force, 2022). The findings confirmed that the arrested officers were involved in the crime. According to the press release signed by the spokesperson for the NPF, CSP Olumuyiwa Adejobi,

> the findings of the in-house investigation ordered by the Inspector General of Police established reasonable grounds for strong suspicion that the IRT officers involved in the operation could have been involved in some underhand and unprofessional dealings as well as official corruption which compromised ethical standards in their dealings with the suspects and exhibits recovered. (Nigeria Police Force, 2022)

The NPF subsequently announced the arrest of Abba Kyari and the other officers indicted in the crime, Sunday Ubuah, Bawa James, John Umoru, Simon Agrigba and John Nuhu, all high-ranking NPF officers (Nigeria Police Force, 2022). Kyari's involvement in this crime occurred while he was on suspension as the officer in charge of the Intelligence Response

Team (IRT) of the force headquarters in Abuja. It was based on a report by the US Federal Bureau of Investigation (FBI) that accused him of aiding and abetting Ramon Abbas, an internet fraudster who confessed to having participated in cybercrime activities and money laundering (Busari & Princewill, 2021; Princewill, 2022).

The IGP ordered his suspension 'to create an enabling environment for the NPF Special Investigation Panel to carry out its investigations into the weighty allegations against DCP Abba Kyari without interference' (Nigeria Police Force, 2021). Abbas alleged that he used Kyari to arrange the arrest of his co-fraudster and outsmarted him in a fraudulent deal (Busari & Princewill, 2021). According to the report, Abbas claimed that Kyari took 'a bribe last year to arrest a man who betrayed his cybercrime syndicate' (Paquette, 2021). The FBI was able to establish Kyari's involvement and the amount of money paid to his accounts as a reward. The FBI report included conversations between Kyari and Abbas that implicated the "super cop" (Paquette, 2021).

These and other incidents have eroded public confidence in the NPF. Extortion, at what have become police toll points, has become an everyday occurrence. Commuters are at the mercy of police extortionists that often occupy major roads in the name of security. Nigerian citizens dread anything that involves the police because innocent people are likely to end up in detention if they on not have the money to bribe the police.

No one in Nigeria will argue that Nigeria is heavily challenged by internal security as we are hostages to terrorists, armed robbers, bandits, herdsmen militias, militants, kidnappers, economic saboteurs (pipeline vandals), cultists, human traffickers, ritualists, election robbers and every kind of law-breaking (*Vanguard*, 13 February 2020).

The African Capacity Building Foundation (ACBF) report (2007) noted that Nigeria was among the countries whose citizens regarded the police as the least useful law enforcement institution capable of combating corruption.

Human Rights Watch summarised the characteristic features of the NPF thus:

> Extortion, embezzlement, and other corrupt practices by Nigeria's police undermine the fundamental human rights of Nigerians in two key ways. First, the most direct effect of police corruption on ordinary citizens stems from the myriad human rights abuses committed by police officers in the process of extorting money. These abuses range from arbitrary arrest

and unlawful detention to threats and acts of violence, including physical and sexual assault, torture, and even extrajudicial killings. (Human Rights Watch, 2010)

Conclusion

Law enforcement in Nigeria has remained a mirage. Indeed, the NPF is enmeshed in state politics, with a centralised command structure. Over the years, this warped structure's efficiency and performance has declined. Given its long history of an instrument of state oppression, the NPF has been unable to promote security. As Human Rights Watch has noted, it is a predator rather than a protector of Nigerian citizens' lives.

Nigeria is experiencing one of its worst phases of domestic insecurity. Banditry, kidnapping, armed robbery and ritual killings, among various other security challenges and the police's inability and/or lack of will to confront and apprehend the perpetrators are the manifestations of the policing system's institutional weaknesses. Corruption and other unethical conduct have weakened the law enforcement system's commitment to transparency and accountability. The consequence is the erosion of its legitimacy as the lack of public trust grows. The #EndSARS protest demonstrated this public resentment and the festering crisis of governance that has undermined the country's public sector.

Comprehensive, pragmatic reforms are required to reposition police systems and management in Nigeria and restore the public's trust. Public awareness campaigns on the roles and responsibilities of the police are also required. An apolitical police force that is committed to promoting security is necessary to instil public confidence.

References

Adetayo, O. (2018, August 14). Osinbajo orders IGP to overhaul SARS. *The Punch*. Retrieved from https://punchng.com/osinbajo-orders-igp-to-re-organise-sars/

Adebowale, O. (2020). *History of protests in Nigeria: Reactions and consequences*. Retrieved on 14 October 2020 from https://guardian.ng/life/history-of-protests-in-nigeria-reactions-and-consequences-2/

Agbiboa, D. E. (2015). Protectors or predators? The embedded problem of police corruption and deviance in Nigeria. *Administration & Society, 47*(3), 244–281.

Alemika, E. E. O. (1993). Colonialism, State and policing in Nigeria. *Crime, Law and Social Change, 20*(3), 187–219.

Amnesty International. (2016). *Nigeria: 'You have signed your death warrant': Torture and other ill treatment in the special anti-robbery squad (SARS)*. Retrieved from https://policehumanrightsresources.org/you-have-signed-your-death-warrant-torture-and-other-ill-treatment-in-the-special-anti-robbery-squad

Amnesty International. (2009). *Killing at will: Extrajudicial executions and other unlawful killings by the police in Nigeria*. Retrieved from https://www.amnesty.org/en/documents/afr44/038/2009/en/

Amnesty International. (2021). *#Endsars movement: From Twitter to Nigerian streets*. Retrieved from https://www.amnesty.org/en/latest/campaigns/2021/02/nigeria-end-impunity-for-police-violence-by-sars-endsars/

BBC News Africa. (2017, December 4). *Nigeria's #ENDSARS campaign at police brutality video*. Retrieved from https://www.bbc.com/news/world-africa-42225314

Busari, S., & Princewill, N. (2021, July 30). *FBI investigating Nigeria's 'super cop' in Instagram influencer HushPuppi fraud case*. CNN. Retrieved from https://edition.cnn.com/2021/07/30/africa/kyari-hushuppi-investigated-fbi-intl/index.html

Cooray, A., & Schneider, F. (2018). Does corruption throw sand into or grease the wheels of financial sector development? *Public Choice, 177*, 111–133. https://doi.org/10.1007/s11127-018-0592-7

Ebiede, T. M (2020). *The massive protests in Nigeria, explained*. Retrieved from https://www.washingtonpost.com/politics/2020/10/26/massive-protests-nigeria-explained/ on 16 October 2021.

Eck, K. (2018). The origins of policing institutions. *Journal of Peace Research, 55*(2), 147–160.

Ejiofor, P. F. (2020, December 22). Looting as Catharsis: #EndSARS and the Crisis of Governance in Nigeria 4(4). *The Republic*. Retrieved from https://republic.com.ng/december-20-january-21/looting-as-catharsis/ on 16 October 2021.

Erunke, J. (2018, August 14). Acting on Osinbajo's order, IGP overhauls, renames SARS FSARS. *Vanguard*. Retrieved from https://www.vanguardngr.com/2018/08/acting-on-buharis-order-igp-overhauls-renames-sars-fsars/

Feltham, L., & Rupiah, K. (2021, April 25). When violence is policy: How do we curb police brutality? *Mail&Guardian*. Available at https://mg.co.za/politics/2021-04-25-when-violence-is-policy-how-do-we-curb-police-brutality/

Folarin, S. (2019). *Policemen shoot dead suspected phone thieves in lagos*. Retrieved from https://punchng.com/sars-operatives-shoot-dead-suspected-phone-thieves-in-lagos/ on 18 October 2021

Global Police Index. (2019).

Hope, K. R. (2018). Police corruption and the security challenge in Kenya. *African Security, 11*(1), 84–108.
Howe, B. (2013). *The protection and promotion of human security in East Asia.* Critical Studies of the Asia Pacific Series. Palgrave Macmillan.
Human Rights Watch. (2007). Nigeria: Investigate Widespread Killings by Police. Retrieved from https://www.hrw.org/news/2007/11/18/nigeria-investigate-widespread-killings-police on 18 October 2021.
Human Rights Watch. (2010). *Everyone's in on the game: Corruption and human rights abuses by the Nigeria Police Force.* Retrieved from https://www.hrw.org/report/2010/08/17/everyones-game/corruption-and-human-rights-abuses-nigeria-police-force
Kadıoglu, U. (2021 January 27). Police Brutality in Nigeria and the #EndSARS Movement. *Harvard International Review.* Retrieved from https://hir.harvard.edu/police-brutality-in-nigeria-and-the-endsars-movement/
Keping, Y. (2018). Governance and good governance: A new framework for political analysis. *Fudan Journal of Humanities and Social Sciences, 11,* 1–8. https://doi.org/10.1007/s40647-017-0197-4
Lakitsch, M. (2021). Hobbes in the anthropocene: Reconsidering the state of nature in its relevance for governing. *Alternatives: Global, Local, Political, 46*(1), 3–16.
Lewis, J. (2017). Social impacts of corruption upon community resilience and poverty. *Jàmbá: Journal of Disaster Risk Studies, 9*(1), a391. https://doi.org/10.4102/jamba.v9i1.391
Malumfashi, S. (2020, October 22). *Nigeria's SARS: A brief history of the Special Anti-Robbery Squad.* Aljazeera. Retrieved from https://www.aljazeera.com/features/2020/10/22/sars-a-brief-history-of-a-rogue-unit
Marenin, O. (1987). The Anini Saga: Armed robbery and the reproduction of ideology in Nigeria. *The Journal of Modern African Studies, 25*(2), 259–281.
Neusteter, S. R., Subramanian, R., Trone, J., Khogali, M., & Reed, C. (2019). *Gatekeepers: The role of police in ending mass incarceration.* Vera Institute of Justice.
Nigeria Police Force. (2021, August 1). *Press release: FBI indictment—IGP recommends suspension of DCP Abba Kyari.*
Nigeria Police Force. (2022, Februsry 14). *Press release: Police arrest DCP Abba Kyari, 4 other Police Officers for Allegations of Tampering with Narcotic Exhibits, Official Corruption and Sundry Unprofessional Infractions.*
Nwannekanma, B., Nwokoro, S., Musa, W., & Omolaoye, S. (2021, November 30). 13,241 Nigerians unlawfully killed by security forces in 10 years. *The Guardian.* Retrieved from https://guardian.ng/news/13241-nigerians-unlawfully-killed-by-security-forces-in-10-years/

Nwanze, C. (2014, April 21). *A history of Nigeria's police service. Africa is a country*. Retrieved from https://africasacountry.com/2014/04/historyclass-nigerias-police

Okoi, O., & Iwara, M. (2021). *The failure of governance in Nigeria: An epistocratic challenge*. Retrieved from https://gjia.georgetown.edu/2021/04/12/the-failure-of-governance-in-nigeria-an-epistocratic-challenge/ on 16 October 2021.

Otu, N. (2004). The development and growth of the Nigeria Police Force from a social context perspective. *The Police Journal: Theory, Practice and Principles, 77*(1), 19–31.

Onoja, A. (2013). A re-appraisal of the historiography of the police in Nigeria during the colonial period. *Journal of the Historical Society of Nigeria, 22*, 1–32.

OSJI. (2010). Criminal force torture, abuse, and extrajudicial killings by the Nigeria police force. Open Society Institute.

Paquette, D. (2021, July 30). He is known as Nigeria's 'super cop'. The FBI says he supported a cybercrime ring. *The Washington Post*. Retrieved from https://www.washingtonpost.com/world/2021/07/30/nigeria-fraud-super-cop-hushpuppi-abba-kyari/

Premium Times. (2021, May 11). #MySARSStory: Abba Kyari, where is Eric Okwaji? Retrieved from https://www.premiumtimesng.com/news/more-news/460825-mysarsstory-abba-kyari-where-is-eric-okwaji.html

Princewill, N. (2022, February 14). *Nigeria hero 'supercop' wanted for part in cocaine smuggling cartel*. CNN. Retrieved from https://edition.cnn.com/2022/02/14/africa/nigeria-supercop-declared-wanted-intl/index.html

Retief, R., & Green, S. (2015). Some challenges in policing domestic violence. *Social Work, 1*(1), 134–147.

Roebuck, J. B., & Barker, T. (1974). A typology of police corruption. *Social Problems, 21*(3), 423–437.

Sherman, L. W. (2018). Policing domestic violence 1967–2017. *Criminology & Public Policy, 17*(2), 453–465.

Soniyi, T. (2020, November 15). History of policing in Nigeria. *ThisDay*. Retrieved from https://www.thisdaylive.com/index.php/2020/11/15/history-of-policing-in-nigeria/

The Guardian (2022, 14 February). Police arrest Abba Kyari. Retrieved from https://guardian.ng/news/police-arrests-abba-kyari/

The Guardian. (2019, 27 March). Police most corrupt institution in Nigeria, survey reveals. Retrieved from https://guardian.ng/news/police-most-corrupt-institution-in-nigeria-survey-reveals/

World Bank. (2021). *Combating corruption*. Retrieved from https://www.worldbank.org/en/topic/governance/brief/anti-corruption

United Nations. (2011). *Handbook on police accountability, oversight and integrity.* United Nations.

Uwazuruike, A. R. (2020). #EndSARS: The movement against police brutality in Nigeria. *Harvard Human Rights Journal.* Retrieved from https://harvardhrj.com/2020/11/endsars-the-movement-against-police-brutality-in-nigeria/ on 16 October 2021.

Vanguard. (2020, February 13). Our police world ranking. Retrieved from https://www.vanguardngr.com/2020/02/our-police-world-ranking/

Villarreal, B. D. (2020). A critique of Hobbes's state of nature. *Philologia, 12*(1), 20–24.

World Internal Security and Police Index (WISPI). (2016).

World Internal Security and Police Index (WISPI). (2019).

Yagboyaju, D .A., & Akinola, A. O. (2019, July-September 1–10). *Nigerian state and the crisis of governance: A critical exposition.* Sage Open. https://doi.org/10.1177/2158244019865810

CHAPTER 6

Trapped in the Ivory Tower: Using Social Movement Theory to Analyse a 'Movement in Distress'

Terri Maggott

INTRODUCTION

In 2015 and 2016, university students at South African universities participated in what became known as the FMF movement, which students—and to some extent, workers and sympathetic academics—organised around the broad demand for free, decolonised, quality education. Fees Must Fall has sparked research interest among prominent scholar-activists and researchers (Booysen, 2016; Naidoo, 2016) who have promoted and criticised the movement's aims, methods and victories. It could be argued that while it was the largest (black-led) student movement in South Africa since the 1976 Uprisings, the extent to which FMF was able to have a

---

T. Maggott (✉)
Department of Sociology, University of Johannesburg, Johannesburg, South Africa
e-mail: terrim@uj.ac.za

© The Author(s), under exclusive license to Springer Nature Switzerland AG 2023
A. O. Akinola, *Contemporary Issues on Governance, Conflict and Security in Africa*,
https://doi.org/10.1007/978-3-031-29635-2_6

meaningful impact beyond campus walls is debatable given its often weak and unsustainable links with other social, education and political movements. The movement was critical in bringing about change in South African higher education in terms of Africanising curricula and pedagogies. However, in terms of development and social change, its broader impact on South African and African society is arguably limited.

This chapter argues that the limitations of FMF lie within the structure of society itself, given the elite and at times exclusive location of the university as a social institution and the way it responded to the protests through severe repression and militarisation of campuses. After the heat of the 2015–2016 protests, FMF was not able to forge meaningful, lasting links with other sectors of the South African 'Left' (including organised labour and youth movements)—not due to any fault on its part, but to, firstly, the difficulties of organising in social settings (campuses) where staff, students and workers are isolated from one another in nuanced ways; and secondly, the lonely position of the ivory tower, perched high above and separate from society upon its two-pronged pedestal of epistemic prestige and social status, while simultaneously influencing social policy, values and ideals. The chapter draws on social movement theories, namely resource mobilisation and political process, as well as previous research conducted by the author during her postgraduate studies (Maggott, 2019) which have been supplemented with further reading and research on the student movement/s in South Africa. It contributes to scholarship by problematising the idea that student movements are at the forefront of radical societal change.

Student protest movements have historically played a pivotal role in anticolonial struggles in Africa. For example, from as early as the 1950s, students and youth were instrumental in mobilising for an independent Tanzania free from colonial domination. In Nigeria, the 1960s saw the development of student activism as part of the broader anticolonial movement for a free Nigeria. Students in South African and southern African universities organised boycotts, solidarity campaigns and programmes of civil disobedience to demand an end to racial segregation and white supremacy throughout the apartheid era. Post-independence and with the onset of structural adjustment policies in the 1980s and 1990s, students continued to play important roles in resisting colonial impositions in higher education and beyond. For example, in Uganda in 1980, university students formed the Makerere Student Guild that established itself among the social forces organising to resist the effects of liberalisation, privatisation and the austerity spawned by these programmes. Similarly, in 1988, students at the University of Zimbabwe organised 'The Great Demo' in Harare to campaign for a multi-party democratic system. This rich history of student activism can be understood as not only part of the struggle for the decolonisation of Africa but also within the broader global political current of ant-capitalist struggle in which FMF itself is historically embedded.

Fees Must Fall—a national social movement in South African higher education institutions (HEIs) in 2015 and 2016 (and, to a lesser extent, 2017)—has been described as the largest, black-led student movement since the education uprisings of 1976 (Gillespie & Naidoo, 2019). The movement was the culmination of a series of actions against a pending fee increase for the year 2015 and broader critique of the material hardships experienced by black, poor students. Under this broad banner as well as the social media hashtag #Feesmustfall, students also called for the decolonisation of a society struggling to emerge from the grips of apartheid's racial capitalism. Within a context of widespread unemployment and increasing inequalities, in 2015, students in Cape Town marched to parliament to demand an address from the Minister of the Department of Higher Education, Science and Innovation Blade Nzimande. Students in Gauteng descended on the Union Buildings in Pretoria to demand an address from the president of the country himself, resulting in a violent response from riot police and private security.

In both 2015 and 2016, students managed to successfully shut down the daily workings of campus life at almost all universities nationally, preventing completion of some examinations. In some cases, universities deployed private security companies and, in many instances, police riot squads. As the latter part of the name implies, 'must fall' implies that the *status quo* is not working and must go. Historical cracks in the interwoven superstructure of capitalism, patriarchy and white supremacy in post-apartheid South Africa were exposed during this rupture in time (Motimele, 2019). In line with but distinct from the Rhodes Must Fall (RMF) movement, the 'must fall' aspect of FMF took on less of a literal demand for the destruction of a statue of Cecil John Rhodes at the University of Cape Town (UCT) and demanded the decommodification of education and a more immediate lowering of already expensive fees.

A Campus-Based Movement

Understood in relation to South African universities' increasing management as corporations, with students treated as customers and academics subject to the demands of working in large bureaucracies (Godsell & Chikane, 2016), FMF was also a rupture in neoliberal time which is measured in clear outputs and deliverables, since it disrupted business as usual at several campuses (Motimele, 2019). As hinted at above, FMF called for the decolonisation of universities as historical sites of elitist, racist, male-dominated, Eurocentric knowledge production, locating it within the broader history of efforts to decolonise Africa dating back to colonial times (Ngwane, 2017). One can—but only to some extent—understand FMF in the broader context of student politics, particularly RMF at UCT and the RU Reference List[1] at Rhodes University in the Eastern Cape. These moments of protest and agency were key ideological tenets in the national FMF movement frame, and the context is useful for locating the roots of the revolution (Godsell & Chikane, 2016). However, grouping together these distinct movements occludes their different life trajectories from gestation and beyond: RMF came to a clear end when the statue of Cecil John Rhodes was removed from the UCT campus, while FMF somewhat fizzled out, but with bursts of protest activity from 2017 to 2021.

While it is not possible to completely detangle the many inputs, pathways to and people involved in this national movement, a tension exists in the literature on FMF, with many scholars arguing for a collapsing of the boundaries between RMF and FMF and a centring of historically white universities such as UCT or the University of the Witwatersrand (Wits) in the movement (see, e.g., Sempijja & Letlhogile, 2020; von Holdt & Naidoo, 2019). However, Malebela (in Langa et al., 2017) foregrounds the protests that occurred at a previously black institution, the University of Limpopo (UL), to show the ways in which previously white universities such as UCT and Wits have come to dominate accounts of FMF. Malebela (in Langa et al., 2017) argues that the struggle for 'free education' had been taken on by students since the late 1990s and resulted in many being given access to National Student Financial Aid Scheme

---

[1] The Rhodes University (RU) Reference List was a list of students identified as alleged rapists on the campus in Grahamstown, South Africa. The protests were centred on taking action against alleged rapists who continued to attend classes with impunity.

(NSFAS) bursaries in recent years—a major success. In 2015, students at UL (Turfloop) were protesting in support of a different set of demands, including a better quality curriculum, better qualified teaching staff and the resources to compete with graduates at previously white institutions, namely Wits and UCT (Malebela in Langa et al., 2017: 109). This shows that FMF constituted a broad set of collective but nuanced demands that varied across campuses and overlapped and diverged according to specific contexts.

However, these debates highlight disagreements about how to carefully think through these charged moments of rupture in time and the nature of contemporary—perhaps pre-COVID is a better categorisation—student politics in South Africa, which, coupled with retrospect, allow space for reflection on what the movement achieved. From the beginning, FMF claimed to be a non-hierarchical structure facilitated by a strong social media base (von Holdt & Naidoo, 2019). However, as time wore on, the clear dominance of political parties such as the African National Congress (ANC) aligned Progressive Youth Alliance (PYA) and the Economic Freedom Fighters' (EFF) Student Command (EFFSC) in the movement eroded the mass democratic nature of moments in the 2015 and 2016 protests. Indeed, FMF called into question the mountain of failures committed by the ANC and the collapse of its farce of a 'rainbow nation'. The political culture in post-apartheid South African student politics is dominated by party-aligned student organisations—a consequence of the collapse of civil society and the dominance of ANC-aligned structures from the mid-1990s. However, the magic of FMF lay in its ability to appeal to many groups of students across political affiliation (or lack of), class, gender and sexuality. In a sense, one can, therefore, argue that FMF successfully experimented with new, fresh forms of organising and mobilising (Heffernan & Nieftagodien, 2016). It did so mainly through disruptive repertoires of protest and cleverly interrupting the business of campus, shutting down its day-to-day operations (this latter point is discussed in more detail in the theoretical section below).

A major victory for FMF was the zero-increase concession announced by government in late 2015 which led universities to strategise new funding models. The Department of Higher Education and Training (DHET) set the cap for fees at a startling 16% for 2016, a hike which many so-called middle-class families feared they would not be able to cope with. Due to prolonged protests and disruptions to learning, the DHET later conceded to students' demands and announced that there would be no fee increase for 2016. A moment of victory was celebrated and students left campuses for the 2015 summer break in high hopes. However, when they returned in 2016, many experienced financial obstacles to registration, including debt from previous years and difficulty in raising registration and accommodation fees (Motimele, 2019).

A perhaps more latent victory came in the form of curriculum change. Students demanded a university education that is not only free from commodification in the form of exorbitant tuition fees, but also from Euro-American frames of knowledge; an education that speaks to their material realities as young Africans. They argued that this calls for total decolonisation of society as we know it and evoked various Marxist, Leninist and Fanonian theories to critique the lingering coloniality of life in post-apartheid South Africa (Gillespie & Naidoo, 2019). In response, universities made moves to include more black, African and women scholars on course reading lists, and a strong research agenda for decolonisation was developed at several universities. For example, at UCT and the University of South Africa (UNISA), leading scholars on decolonisation have gained global recognition, and funding has increased for postgraduate students researching this issue (Ngwane, 2017). While its other successes, whether in the short or longer term, may be difficult to quantify or qualify, FMF was a watershed moment in South African higher education in curriculum and research development.

Indeed, the movement stretched the epistemic limits of some of the debates surrounding the texture and scope of 'decolonisation', with some arguing for a more radical dismantling of colonial systems of race, class and gender, and others favouring a more conservative agenda framed around the more palatable notion of transformation or incremental change (Ngwane, 2017). It is beyond the scope of this chapter to define the orientations of either, but the discrepancy is noted because what preceded these debates were strong critiques offered by students themselves of respected professors: students forced the academy to take a serious look at the colonial mess it was implicit in sustaining. Disciplines such as Engineering, Philosophy and Psychology were forced to reconfigure their paradigms and methods during their annual conferences—even if superficially—because their students were demanding such a change, which evokes the agentive power of collective action in institutions of higher learning, particularly universities to facilitate emancipatory change.

Another longer-term impact of FMF on South African HEIs is an unintended consequence. As universities struggled to find ways to limit the success of FMF shutdowns and thus keep the business of learning going, they started introducing 'blended' modules with online and contact components. This enabled them to circumvent the disruptions caused by shutdowns and, in turn, depoliticise campuses which FMF had constituted as sites of struggle and collective action (Gillespie & Naidoo, 2019). Given the impact of COVID-19 on contact learning and the rapid move to online teaching and learning (T&L) by universities, in some ways and unintendedly, FMF provided universities with a chance for practice-run for a far longer shutdown (in March 2020). For the purposes of this chapter, however, what is noteworthy is that FMF facilitated changes in T&L at HEIs and clearly displayed the potential of collective student agency to drive change in their institutions.

Repression and Decline

While FMF protestors often made collective decisions to abandon their party-political affiliations, in its young life and aftermath, party divides have deepened. It could be argued that student political life, even at the University of the Western Cape (UWC), historically the home of the Left, is now largely constituted through indirect membership of one of the dominant political parties via their student wings. For example, the ANC is affiliated to various student and youth structures through the PYA including the South African Students' Congress (SASCO), the Young Communist League and the ANC Youth League; the remnants of the once-mighty Pan-Africanist Congress (PAC) is the mother of its more vibrant student wing, the Pan-Africanist Student Movement of Azania (PASMA); and the young but formidable EFF gave birth to its Student Command in early 2015. Serious attempts were made by independent groups such as the Trans Collective at UCT and the Differently Abled Students Organisation at UWC to influence these rigid forms of leadership. However, what prevailed in the frenzy of the harsh repression meted out by university management was an environment that discouraged—indeed punished—radical activism, and political student parties were able to capitalise on this vacuum.

University management responded to FMF in harsh and subtle ways. At the University of Johannesburg (UJ) and UWC, biometric systems to gain entry to campuses were installed during or after the 2016 protests.

In 2018, Wits followed suit, citing security reasons. Campuses have since been securitised in other ways, including hiring private security companies such as Fidelity—the group that owns the ADT Security Company. During campus raids, individual student leaders were often singled out, arrested and subjected to lengthy legal proceedings. Police became a standard feature on campuses as early as 2015, despite calls from civil society to prevent them from entering essentially public institutions. Sempijja and Letlhogile (2020) view FMF through the security-development nexus and argue that the 'de-securitisation of university spaces will open the way for constructive dialogue on the delivery of education service to … students…'. By securitising and militarising spaces of learning, debate and expression, university management shut down spaces to address serious concerns raised by students relating to broader concerns but also more material ones such as accommodation, food security and policy change. Repression stifled the movement. Student leaders were expelled, suspended or in some cases legally banned from ever participating in student leadership, whether political or other (Maggott, 2019).

Sempijja and Letlhogile (2020) and others also argue that the protests were powerful enough to not only disrupt and shut down campuses, but to paralyse the whole country. Protests occurred at all 25 South African universities and many but not all were shut down. Those that were tried tirelessly to get academic calendars back online (Motimele, 2019). Through their organisations and working groups, students were able to build relationships with workers and worker organisations (although the forms of politics and collective decision-making were markedly different from those practised in traditional trade unions [von Holdt & Naidoo, 2019]). Godsell and Chikane (2016) highlight the ways in which students and workers collectively and radically reimagined a decolonised university free from exploitation. However, there is not enough evidence to suggest that these links have been able to sustain any real change in universities or the broader society after FMF. These relations are unpacked in more detail below. For now, I to turn to a discussion on which lens is most useful when thinking through what FMF was and what it brought about in HEIs as well as in the broader 'movement landscape' within which it is located and ultimately shaped (von Holdt & Naidoo, 2019).

Fees Must Fall shook the government and influenced governance structures in South African universities (Booysen, 2016). This seems to be agreed among commentators who have analysed the movement in various ways. For example, Everatt (in Booysen, 2016) adopts a historical view, examining the history of protest in South Africa and its collective agency to begin the dismantling of apartheid. Similarly, Hewett, Mukadah, Kouakou and Zandamela (in Booysen, 2016) argue that understanding the history of student protest in Africa enables a more careful examination of the case of student protests in South Africa—among the last African states to achieve 'independence', while Satgar (in (Booysen, 2016) highlights how a class lens reveals the workings of class formation for students of an aspirant middle class and their relations with precarious workers.

Sempijja and Letlhogile (2020) use arguments framed around the security-development nexus to link FMF to human (in)security and increased securitisation of campuses to the insecurity of T&L at universities. Scholars and others have described FMF as part of a broader social movement and, indeed, social movement history. Besides a conference paper by Ngwane (2017)—and to some extent the work of von Holdt and Naidoo (2019)—I could find no analysis of FMF framed within the broad schools of social movement theory, which I address in the following section with a view to exploring how FMF, as a result of the neoliberal university within which it is now trapped, underwent change as a movement. The application of the theories uncovers more questions than answers, which are posed in the concluding section.

Using Social Movement Theory to Analyse FMF and 'Post-FMF'

A social movement is a collective grouping of individuals and organisations framed around a set of demands, identities or values over a sustained period of time. An accepted definition developed by Tilly (1984: 7) describes a social movement as 'a sustained series of interactions between powerholders and persons successfully claiming to speak on behalf of a constituency lacking formal representation, during the course of which those persons make publicly-visible demands for changes in the distribution or exercise of power, and back those demands with public demonstrations of support'. For Tarrow (1998 in Ngwane, 2017: 1), a social movement organisation (SMO), which is part of a broader movement, 'is characterised by the direct participation of constituents in action and an orientation that makes claims on authorities'. The distinction is useful because it allows a broader analysis of the political components that constituted the broader FMF movement. As noted earlier, various student parties, alliances and independent collectives constituted the broad movement. Interestingly, it started off as a self-identified leaderless or horizontal movement in an attempt to retain its mass base and democratic style of collective decision-making.

To unveil the nuances of these political processes, I now turn to the application of the two mainstream schools of social movement theory, providing a discussion along the way on the life and containment of FMF within the neoliberal university. Rather than focusing on the rational actor models proposed by researchers before the 1960s in Euro-America, this section uses collective action theories, namely resource mobilisation and political process, to discuss how FMF is, in many ways, confined to highly securitised campuses. Unlike those who argue that student movements are at the forefront of revolutions (Sempijja & Letlhogile, 2020), I propose that FMF and the movement for free education have been trapped within a specific realm of political reality (i.e. the neoliberal university) that is only minimally connected to the broader South African movement landscape, particularly organised labour and unions. The argument is also perhaps applicable to the rest of Africa, but the focus here is on the case of FMF in South Africa.

Resource Mobilisation Theory

Developed in response to the strategies adopted by various actors in the New Left Movement in the US in the early 1970s, resource mobilisation theory focuses on how collectives mobilise certain resources such as activist networks, donations and the media, mainly TV and radio (Martin, 2015). Whereas earlier researchers used notions of rationality to question why people come together to oppose their realities, resource mobilisation theory argues that it is more rational for them to get involved in movements than not, using the evidence of educated, middle class and white groups and individuals who, for example, donated to and sympathised with black organisations such as the Black Panthers (Martin, 2015). Resources are needed to sustain movements and SMOs so that they can successfully turn their demands into collective action.

Social media was a major resource for the various SMOs and leaders in FMF (von Holdt & Naidoo, 2019: 177). Students were able to advertise mass meetings and protests, and solicit public sympathy for the movement using video footage and photos of, for example, the repression they faced as unarmed students. Indeed, student activists worked to produce a movement archive through the use of media, especially social media. In addition to this media archive, students at Wits also produced a Fallist Diary that captured student experiences from their particular vantage point. The advent of smartphones has meant that students have easy access not only to information (e.g. about important meetings organised by other students) but also to a resource that can enhance public support. This has been instrumental in countering some media narratives that position students as violent and lawless.

Resource mobilisation theory also tells us that beneficiaries of SMOs are not necessarily the people donating to it. Malebela (in Langa et al., 2017) provides accounts of students receiving donations from outside parties, whether from sympathetic parents and academics, local church groups or international solidarity online. Donations included food, medical supplies and, in a less material sense, solidarity from other sectors of universities, including sympathetic academics and workers. As for any political movement, solidarity from the larger society is an important resource to mobilise for and with, and FMF garnered solidarity in South Africa, Africa and internationally. Students were the main beneficiaries of the movement, but the broader society will also benefit from students' efforts to, for example, Africanise university curricula, making it more relevant to the realities of African students. However, students were also the major victims of FMF, given the harsh repression they often faced, which was the subject of numerous media headlines. In many ways, they were able to channel public outrage generated by the media into support for the movement in the form of resources to sustain FMF's trajectory.

Finally, resource mobilisation theory is also concerned with how and by whom SMOs are staffed and the ways in which movements and SMOs ultimately seeks to sustain themselves. The applicability of this to FMF is questionable, given that it did not host any national conferences or elect any national structures. It was a self-proclaimed, flat structure without any particular political affiliation, nor was it accountable to any donors. For von Holdt and Naidoo (2019), this experiment with horizontality is what differentiates FMF from other post-apartheid movements. They use the concept of a movement landscape to situate FMF within a broader political terrain in which mobilisations increasingly both criticise the ANC and divert from the party's organisational and ideological positions. This is useful because it demonstrates FMF's power in shaping popular protests and forms of organisation in South African social movements. However, the extent to which FMF diverted from historical forms of mobilising is limited given the dominance of political parties, such as the ANC and the EFF, since the latter is arguably a perpetuation of ANC styles of organisation and, to some extent, ideology (i.e. Marxist-Leninist). The students who managed the day-to-day operations of SMOs affiliated to FMF are an underexplored group and further research is needed on this aspect of movement work. Resource mobilisation could be a good theoretical tool on which to draw when analysing the staffing aspect of FMF SMOs.

Political Process Models

This aspect of movement theory is useful to explore how movements emerge and the broader political and economic conditions that give rise to them (Martin, 2015). Here, movements came to be understood as sets of political processes and of interest were questions around the conditions likely to facilitate collective action. In 2015, one of the common conditions facing students was increasing strain with regard to high tuition fees. When the minister made the announcement that fees would increase by as much as 12% in 2016, this provided the impetus for groups such as student representative councils (SRCs), and student political parties and societies to make the collective call to disrupt the oppressive, frustrating reality of being a student in South Africa. Students were radicalised into realising the personal nature of being black and poor in institutions grounded in white male elitism, and the political process which underpinned this is not separate from the larger forces at play. Viewed this way, the announcement of a fee increase in October 2015 is important, but perhaps of more significance is the broader reality of financial exclusion that students faced on the one hand and cultural exclusion on the other, especially in previously white institutions such as UCT and Wits.

Central to this theory are concepts such as the political opportunity structure, meaning the shape and texture of the political landscape at the time. Coming off the back of RMF, students saw what collective action could achieve when they came together to demand change, and this sense of confidence, coupled with collective frustration about being black and poor in elite institutions, resulted in the biggest student protests since 1976 (Naidoo, 2016). Unlike during apartheid, the 2015/2016 students existed within a culture (at least in theory) of participation and freedom to question the *status quo*. However, universities had been undergoing a process of restructuring, largely due to a decrease in public funding and increasing neoliberalism. The role of student organising diminishes as market forces dictate *inter alia* tuition fees, university operations and funding for certain disciplines. Indeed, for Godsell and Chikane (2016), the trend towards neoliberalism meant that the logic of managerialism found footing in the academy, resulting in frustration with an education that spoke more to the needs of the labour market than to fundamentally changing society through education and learning.

In addition to larger societal forces, the mobilising structures—or collective vehicles through which people initially mobilise and begin to engage in sustained collective action (McAdam, 2017)—played critical roles in the gestation of the movement. These included the various communication networks on social media (hashtags) and on and across campuses, the various SMOs, some formal (e.g. SASCO), some student societies (e.g. the Differently Abled Students Organisation at UWC), and others less established and relatively independent (e.g. Aluta, an independent party at UWC). These actors and the ways in which they were able to mobilise groups of unorganised students laid the foundations for a growing movement. While the movement would not have mushroomed without the agency of such mobilising structures, these same structures—in addition to repression metered out by the state and university management teams—arguably assisted in the decline of FMF, given that their party interests often conflicted with those of the movement. For example, in the 2015 wave of protests, the ANC-aligned PYA called for students to abandon protest and to return to classes following the zero per cent increase announced by the minister.

Finally, as the theory teaches, the framing processes involved in FMF emerged from students' immediate and more long-term solutions to their problems and facilitated the call to convince other students to mobilise and take action. Political processes also include movements' protest cycles. Commentators have noted the sporadic and spontaneous nature of FMF protests, and how they tend to die down over the December-January break (Maggott, 2019). Connected to this are the repertoires of protest, usually contentious, that movements employed. As noted earlier, FMF made use of shutdowns that were organised and carried out by groups of students who would disrupt classes, conduct teach-ins and/or occupy and rename strategic buildings for days on end (von Holdt & Naidoo, 2019). Mass protests at Parliament and the Union Buildings were also key moments in the history of FMF.

Entrapment and 'Post-FMF'

To sustain the movement, FMF SMOs organised various protests, held numerous meetings and encouraged debate on campus. Students and workers met and developed relationships and more formal groups. For example, the protest on 6 October 2016 was the culmination of a coming together of workers, student groups who made up various working groups under the banner of FMF and (some) academics. The context of serious securitisation, (alleged) spies within the movement and efforts by the management teams to return to maintain academic order and stability, coupled with a broader reality that many students were alienated from FMF in its aftermath, ideologically and socially, were major sources of concern. The university is a microcosm of society in which hegemonic values, such as 'excellence', 'hard work' and 'getting ahead' have been internalised by the general public and young people entering institutions. When violence escalated during times of protest, management teams and the media sometimes portrayed FMF as a minority group of radical students who burned buildings and resources. This resulted in rifts between many of the SMOs and student groups often fought each other online in public view (Maggott, 2019). In the context of securitisation, students were also afraid to jeopardise their primary university goal of graduating by associating with the radicalised FMF.

As the state, through its police, and private security companies defended the ivory towers, essentially bastions of profit and profiteering (Godsell & Chikane, 2016), the student movement of FMF was demobilised, with its activities decreasing rapidly during 2017. The security forces changed the mood on campuses, and this securitisation is responsible for crushing important links that students, workers and academics fought hard for. The use of court interdicts to prohibit gatherings by students and the insourcing of workers but with terrible conditions also contributed to the decline of the energy of FMF. I have not seen the term 'post-Fees Must Fall' used, but it might be worth using to describe the period from 2017 onwards because it implies that FMF not only ended, but was contained, trapped by security forces within the walls of learning, unable to sustain serious links with the various trade union movements and the broader 'South African Left'. This counters arguments that position students as driving forces of radical change in society (Sempijja & Lethlogile, 2020).

Fees Must Fall was a movement but it was also a moment in time that ruptured the fabric of neoliberal reality (Motimele, 2019), a snapshot of what collective action can become; a moment cut short by the heavy-handedness of university security forces. However, these were moments of powerful solidarity between labour and students. One could argue that because collective action was so violently repressed, and because this essentially entrapped FMF within this context, the movement for free education needs rescuing from the ivory tower by Left-leaning forces, workers and sympathetic academics. Fees Must Fall played a significant role in shaping research agendas and reminding the current political elite—who participated in the anti-apartheid movement—that a counter-frame of resistance is emerging from the new generation of young leaders. Students often engaged in heated debates with older politicians, academics and intellectuals about the limits of the two-stage theory of the so-called national democratic revolution (Gillespie & Naidoo, 2019). These debates placed students squarely in the continued struggle to decolonise society and shaped decolonial research in several institutions (Ngwane, 2017).

Conclusion

This chapter employed resource mobilisation theory and the political process model of social movement theory to show how FMF has become entrapped within the ivory tower of learning. While scholars have argued that student movements have been at the forefront of revolutionary change, it argued that student movements can become trapped or contained within the increasingly neoliberal university whose interests lie in continuing with the business of learning. Harsh repression meted out by university management teams against FMF in the form of court interdicts and securitisation of campuses meant that the movement was cut short. While there have been protests on university campuses since 2017, none have inspired the national, mass action that FMF did in 2015 and 2016, and it can be thought of as a movement in distress in need of urgent rescue by other radical sections of society, such as organised labour and other, non-campus, youth formations. Part of the reason for this entrapment within the ivory tower lies in the neoliberal structure of the university as a social institution, one that has been corporatised, evident in its insistence on harshly repressing rather than addressing radical student concerns. This repression has severed the important links that students forged with workers and trade unions.

As Desiree Lewis argues, 'another university is possible'. This chapter applied social movement theory to some of the political processes that made up the broad FMF movement, which raised further questions, such as: What resources, besides the media, were available to FMF SMOs and alliances, and how do these interact within the new political opportunity structure that limits freedom of expression, association and movement on securitised campuses? What do these issues, along with the difficulties brought on by the COVID-19 pandemic, mean for student organising and the role of students in emancipatory action? Lastly, what do the restrictions of the neoliberal university and its economy of knowledge production mean for radical student activism in South Africa and more generally? FMF demonstrated the agentive power of coming together to demand change, and the students of today can and should draw some of the lessons learnt during and after FMF. What is needed is a reinvigoration of student-worker alliances that destabilise the current hegemonic order of South African universities.

REFERENCES

Booysen, S. (Ed.). (2016). *Fees Must Fall: Student revolt, decolonisation and governance in South Africa*. Wits University Press.

Gillespie, K., & Naidoo, L. A. (2019). Between the Cold War and the Fire: The student movement, anti-assimilation, and the question of the future in South Africa. *South Atlantic Quarterly, 118*(1), 226–239.

Godsell, G., & Chikane, R. (2016). The roots of the revolution. In S. Booysen (Ed.), *Fees Must Fall: Student revolt, decolonisation and governance in South Africa* (pp. 54–73). Wits University Press.

Heffernan, A., & Nieftagodien, N. (2016). *Students Must Rise: Youth struggle in South Africa before and beyond Soweto '76*. Wits University Press.

Langa, M., Ndelu, S., Edwin, Y., & Vilakazi, M. (2017). *#Hashtag: An analysis of the #FeesMustFall movement at South African Universities*. Centre for the Study of Violence and Reconciliation (CSVR).

Maggott, T. (2019). *Contested feminisms, masculinism and gender relations in the economic freedom fighters student command: a view from the branch* (Masters dissertation). University of Johannesburg.

Martin, G. (2015). *Understanding social movements*. Routledge.

McAdam, D. (2017). Social movement theory and the prospects for climate change activism in the United States. *Annual Review of Political Science, 20*, 189–208.

Motimele, M. (2019). The rupture of neoliberal time as the foundation for emancipatory epistemologies. *South Atlantic Quarterly, 118*, 205–214.

Naidoo, L. (2016). Contemporary student politics in South Africa: The rise of the black-led student movements of #RhodesMustFall and #FeesMustFall in 2015. *Students Must Rise: Youth struggle in South Africa before and beyond Soweto '76* (pp. 180–190). Wits University Press.

Ngwane, T. (2017). *Decolonisation and the 2015 Student Movement in South Africa: A political assessment*. Centre for Social Change Annual Symposium. Cullinan.

Sempijja, N., & Letlhogile, R. (2020). Security-development nexus and the securitization of university spaces in the #FeesMustFall protests in South Africa 2016–2018. *Africa Review, 13*, 1–21.

Tilly, C. (1984). Social movements as historically specific clusters of political performances. *Berkeley Journal of Sociology, 38*(1993–1994), 1–30.

von Holdt, K., & Naidoo, P. (2019). Mapping movement landscapes in South Africa. *Globalizations, 16*(2), 170–185.

CHAPTER 7

Terrorism in Sub-Sahara Africa: Assessing its Economic and Social Implications

Olumuyiwa Temitope Faluyi

INTRODUCTION

Global anti-Islamic solidarity like the Soviet invasion of Afghanistan in 1979, the Bosnian war of 1992, Russia's invasion of Chechnya in 1994 and 1999, the US-led Gulf War of 1991, the invasion of Afghanistan and Iraq in 2001 and 2003, respectively, and the Danish cartoon issue in relation to Prophet Muhammed in 2006, among others (Thurston, 2018) sparked intense resentment among Muslims. This marginally snowballed into the formation of extreme Islamic groups that have adopted terrorism to wreak havoc in different parts of Africa. Their activities pose a severe threat to security on the continent as their attacks traverse more than one country. They include among others, al-Shabab in Somalia, al-Qaeda in the Islamic Maghreb, Boko Haram, Islamic State in West Africa Province

O. T. Faluyi (✉)
Institute for Pan-African Thought and Conversation,
University of Johannesburg, Johannesburg, South Africa
e-mail: muyiwafaluyi@gmail.com

© The Author(s), under exclusive license to Springer Nature Switzerland AG 2023
A. O. Akinola, *Contemporary Issues on Governance, Conflict and Security in Africa*,
https://doi.org/10.1007/978-3-031-29635-2_7

(ISWAP), Ansar Dine in Mali, the Movement for the Unity and Jihad in West Africa, *Ahlu Sunnah Wal Jammah* (ASWJ) and the Support Group for Islam and Muslims. Others include the Islamic State in the Greater Sahara, Tripoli Province, Barqa Province and Fezzan Province of the Islamic State, Islamic State-Democratic Republic of the Congo (IS-DRC) and the Islamic State Central Africa Province (ISCAP).

Sub-Saharan Africa was selected as terrorist activities are geographically grouped, with sub-Saharan African countries grouped together while North Africa is grouped with the Middle East (Institute for Economics & Peace, 2020). Hence, for the purposes of this chapter, sub-Saharan Africa represents the continent. The chapter focuses on Boko Haram/ISWAP in Nigeria and ASWJ in Mozambique. Boko Haram was selected as it mainly operates in Nigeria, which the Global Terrorism Index ranked third for terrorist activity behind Afghanistan and Iraq for some years (Institute for Economics & Peace, 2020). While Boko Haram operates in Nigeria, Niger, Cameroon and Chad, this chapter focuses on its activities in Nigeria, where it mainly operates in the North East. ASWJ was chosen because attacks by an Islamist extremist group in the Southern African sub-region were rare until October 2017. The group has unleashed terror in Mozambique and Tanzania, but the chapter focuses on its operations in the former where it has carried out the most attacks. ASWJ is active in Cabo Delgado in North East Mozambique and its activities and Boko Haram/ISWAP's have had adverse social and economic consequences for the governments, communities, institutions and individuals. They have led to the loss of lives, hostage taking, destruction of property and displacement of millions.

This chapter is presented in seven parts. The introduction sketches a background on terrorism in Africa and explains the choice of Nigeria and Mozambique. The second part conceptualises terrorism, while the third examines the reasons for terrorism in these countries. Section four highlights terrorism's economic and social effects, while the fifth and sixth sections focus on these effects in Nigeria and Mozambique, respectively. The last section presents a conclusion and offers pragmatic recommendations to stem the tide of terrorism and fill the social and economic lacunae it has created.

Conceptual View of Terrorism

In the post-Cold War era, interstate wars have been displaced by civil wars, and recently, the activities of non-state actors such as intra-state ethnic conflicts, guerrilla groups, resistance movements and terrorist organisations (Heywood, 2011). Terrorist organisations have engaged in battles with governments within states and internationally. Some acts of terror by armed groups "announced" the start of global attacks. For instance, al-Qaeda has been linked to the 1993 attack on the World Trade Centre, the 1996 bombing of the Khobar Towers in Saudi Arabia, the bombing of the United States embassies in Tanzania and Kenya in 1998, the 2000 attack on the *USS Cole*, the 2004 train bombings in Madrid and the 2005 London bombings (Heywood, 2011). In most of these cases, the perpetrators were non-state actors outside the affected countries, probably in collaboration with local accomplices.

Terrorism in Africa has taken a form where the perpetrators are citizens and non-citizens of the countries under attack. The common denominator among these groups is that their threats and attacks pass a message to the government and citizens that their agendas should be respected and accepted. This is encapsulated in the Institute for Economics and Peace's definition of terrorism as 'the threatened or actual use of illegal force and violence by a non-state actor to attain a political, economic, religious, or social goal through fear, coercion, or intimidation' (Institute for Economics & Peace, 2020: 6). This captures the activities of Boko Haram/ISWAP and ASWJ and explains why they are referred to here as terrorist organisations.

Reasons for Terrorism in Nigeria and Mozambique

Boko Haram emerged as a small religious group in North East Nigeria in 1995, with Mohammed Yusuf appointed as its leader in 2002. It engaged in open preaching from 2001 to 2009 before turning to violence (Thurston, 2018). The group has been given different names, including *Ahlulsunna wal'jama'ah hijra, Yusufiyya* movement, Nigerian Taliban, *Jama'atu Ahlis Sunna Lidda'awati Wal-Jihad* and other names. Residents of Maiduguri named it Boko Haram, which means "Western education is forbidden".

Salaam (2012: 156–157) identifies the following factors responsible for Boko Haram's emergence and why it resorted to terrorism, some of which relate to Nigeria and some that are peculiar to the North East region:

> poverty and social injustice; illiteracy and the educational disparities between the northern and southern regions; ingrained cultures of corruption; the lack of professional law enforcement capacity; the availability of illegal weapons; the intelligence failure or inability of the security network to prevent and end conflicts; the sublime structure of the Nigerian government, especially in leadership posting and resource distribution; and the porous borders and socioeconomic ties across borders.

These factors also account for the group's survival.

Poverty is more prevalent in Northern Nigeria than in the South. The North's poor economic state is aggravated by desertification, drought and competition from the international textile industry (Solomon, 2021). The average poverty level in the North East is 70.7%, which is second to that of the North West (National Bureau of Statistics, 2018). Similar conditions exist in the regions in the countries in the Chad Basin that have been targeted by Boko Haram (Desinova, 2021; Solomon, 2021; Thurston, 2018). It has also been speculated that Boko Haram and ISWAP woo members with financial incentives (Desinova, 2021). This makes it easy to recruit the youth.

Northern Nigeria's historical preference for Islam over Western education is also significant. Colonialism and postcolonial experiences subjugated Islam and its emirs to the political class, and there was a perceived need to protect Islam from the Western education system that is believed to corrupt it (Thurston, 2018). Boko Haram leaders that grew up in this environment aim to Islamise the country through Sharia law and clamp down on infidels and those who oppose the implementation of Sharia law (Thurston, 2018). This aligns with the submission that in West Africa, terrorists aim to combat social inequality (especially corruption) and globalisation which they regard as tools of the West (Institute for Economics & Peace, 2020). Thus, education, ideological and religious factors as well as corruption come into play.

Religious and cultural similarities in the Lake Chad region and the porous borders between countries are also influential factors. Boko Haram leaders are from Nigeria, and Nigerians and some foreigners serve as its foot soldiers (Thurston, 2018). The Kanuri language is also crucial in recruitment as it is spoken in the border towns of Nigeria and Cameroon (Desinova, 2021). It was easy for people to travel from neighbouring countries to listen to the teachings of Mohammed Yusuf. Porous borders have also enabled small arms to be smuggled (Faluyi et al., 2019). There were rumours that following Muammar Gaddafi's assassination, the Libyan armoury was looted and these weapons found their way southwards, boosting Boko Haram's arsenal (Thurston, 2018). The group also took arms and ammunition from the military bases it overran (Wuyep, 2015) and it was alleged that Nigerian soldiers sold it arms (Thurston, 2018). These highlight Boko Haram/ISWAP's use of economic, social and political tools to pursue their religious agendas.

Different reasons are advanced for the emergence of ASWJ. Okunade et al. (2021) posit that poverty and inequality were the major causes, with religion used as a means to express these grievances. One account has it that ASWJ grew from an Islamist sect in 2007 and gradually turned to violence over the period of a decade (Demuynck & Weijenberg, 2021). Another speculates that ASWJ was influenced by Aboud Rogo Mohammed, a Kenyan Islamic cleric, because it started as a religious sect in 2015, but later switched to guerrilla tactics (Neethling, 2021). However, there is consensus that the group adopted violence in October 2017. Its radical approach has also been linked to the influence of Mozambican students who studied in Saudi Arabia, Egypt and Sudan (Morier-Genoud, 2020). ASWJ seeks to impose Sharia law (Islamic law) in Cabo Delgado and also rejects the state's education and health systems and laws (Neethling, 2021). Aside from religious affinities, economic factors made the religious bandwagon attractive.

Demuynck and Weijenberg (2021) submit that violent extremism thrives in Cabo Delgado because the province is one of the poorest in the country and has a predominantly Muslim population that feels neglected by the majority Christian ruling elite in Maputo, the capital city in the South. The members of ASWJ are Mozambicans, socio-economically disadvantaged young men with no formal education and employment, and young people from neighbouring countries in similar situations who migrate to Northern Mozambique to join the group (Neethling, 2021). Cabo Delgado has the largest number of people in the country aged five to 25 who never attended school (Matsinhe & Valoi, 2019). While it is rich in natural gas and produces 80% of the world's rubies (Els & Chelin, 2021), this has not transformed ordinary citizens' economic status; indeed, they were evicted from their homes in order to build infrastructure for exploration, allegedly with the complicity of corrupt Front for the Liberation of Mozambique officials (Neethling, 2021). In 2014/2015, the average poverty rate in the Northern region (which comprises the provinces of Cabo Delgado, Nampula, Niassa and Zambezi) was 54.75%, far higher than the average in other regions (Alden & Chichava, 2020). Service delivery in Cabo Delgado is poor and the province has the highest poverty and illiteracy rates in Mozambique (Els & Chelin, 2021; Matsinhe & Valoi, 2019).

Funding has also been a significant factor in Boko Haram/ISWAP and ASWJ's survival. Boko Haram imposed a levy of N100 on its members when Mohammed Yusuf was alive, received financial support from al-Qaeda (Onuoha, 2014) and made a profit by selling fish (Thurston, 2018). The group has also received ransoms in exchange for some of its kidnap victims (Arvin, 2021). Cabo Delgado is known for heroin and human trafficking, and smuggling of ivory, rubies, timber and gemstones (Neethling, 2021) and it is speculated that ASWJ capitalises on the country's porous borders to smuggle these commodities to generate funds (Alden & Chichava, 2020). These also have economic implications for the countries and citizens where these groups operate.

Apart from similarities in religious ideology, ASWJ and Boko Haram have both established themselves in poorly governed, poverty-stricken areas of the countries in which they operate (Neethling, 2021). The Nigerian and Mozambican governments' use of force, such as the murder of Mohammed Yusuf and Buji Foi, a Boko Haram member and former commissioner in Borno in response to the 2009 uprising (Faluyi et al., 2019) and extrajudicial killing of ASWJ members and civilians suspected of collaborating with them (Demuynck & Weijenberg, 2021) hardened their resolve.

Boko Haram and ASWJ have affiliations with the Islamic State (IS) (Botha, 2021). Allied Democratic Forces aligned to the Islamic State that formed the IS-DRC fused with ASWJ in Mozambique to form ISCAP (Botha, 2021). The ASWJ does not claim responsibility for its actions, but ISCAP has done so for 27 attacks, highlighting possible links between IS and ASWJ (Fabricius, 2020). Boko Haram's ties with the IS led to the emergence of ISWAP.

Economic and Social Impact

In 2019, the economic impact of terrorism in sub-Saharan Africa was estimated at US$12.5 billion, while the global impact was US$26.4 billion (Institute for Economics & Peace, 2020). Its economic impact encompasses direct and indirect costs, including deaths, injuries, damage to property and Gross Domestic Product losses (Institute for Economics & Peace, 2020). Direct costs involve expenditure incurred by victims, the government and perpetrators, while indirect costs accrue from loss of future income, and physical and psychological trauma (Institute for Economics & Peace, 2020).

Social impact means how a government or group's activities, policies, programmes and/or decisions affect society or how it is organised. Hence, economic issues affect social issues and vice versa.

Social and Economic Implications of Boko Haram/ISWAP's Activities

Under the leadership of Abubakar Shekau, Boko Haram pledged allegiance to IS in March 2015, which led to its formal integration as ISWAP (Institute for Economics & Peace, 2020). However, in 2016 the IS, which was not satisfied with Shekau's leadership, replaced him with Abu Musab al-Barnawi. Shekau rejected the new leader, which led to the group splitting into two factions (Institute for Economics & Peace, 2020: 101). The Shekau faction reverted to *Jama'atu Ahlis Sunna Lidda'awati Wal-Jihad*, while the al-Barnawi faction stuck with ISWAP (Institute for Economics & Peace, 2020). ISWAP, which is now operating separately from Boko Haram, is against the killing of Muslims. This chapter refers to the group as one, and in some parts, it is referred to Boko Haram/ISWAP.

Boko Haram/ISWAP has attacked government buildings, schools, military and police formations, villages and towns. It has been involved in kidnappings, the use of improvised explosive devices, assassinations and forceful conscription. Attacks by ISWAP and Boko Haram have been most effective in North East Nigeria, where about two million people have been displaced and around ten million require humanitarian assistance (US Department of State, 2021). Boko Haram attacks civilians and state agents, whereas ISWAP mainly focuses its attacks on the state and security forces, but also kidnaps civilians (US Department of State, 2021).

Between 2015 and 2019, ISWAP was responsible for about two-thirds of deaths, with the remainder caused by *Jama'atu Ahlis Sunna Lidda'awati wal-Jihad* (Institute for Economics & Peace, 2020).

Farming is a major occupation in Northern Nigeria and Boko Haram's activities have disrupted the agricultural sector (Faluyi et al., 2019). Most of those that plant cannot harvest their crops, and harvested crops are among the items looted in villages (Lipp, n.d.). Some farmers have paid the ultimate price. On 28 November 2020, Boko Haram killed more than 100 rice farmers in Jere Local Government, Borno State (US Department of State, 2021). Its usurpation of the fishing business in Baga from the locals (Thurston, 2018) was another setback to agriculture. The resultant hunger and loss of income from selling agricultural products have aggravated poverty in the North East. While the government and international partners have launched initiatives to revive agriculture in this region (Faluyi et al., 2019), funds devoted to this effort would have been better used to boost agriculture or build infrastructure.

The Sambisa forest, which is a game reserve, is a Boko Haram stronghold. It is a habitat to animals like elephants, leopards, lions, hyenas, baboons, monkeys, porcupine, hare and gazelle, as well as different species of birds, among others (Azeez, 2018; Mbaya & Malgwi, 2010). Local and foreign tourists are no longer able to access the area, negatively impacting income that would otherwise have been generated, as well as local and foreign investment. When businesses cease operation, the government loses tax revenue and locals lose jobs. Bonding among families and friends that comes with visiting recreational sites has also been destroyed.

In 2017, staff from the University of Maiduguri that collaborates with the Nigerian National Petroleum Corporation, who were conducting an oil exploration research trip in the Chad Basin were kidnapped by suspected Boko Haram members, with one losing his life (Eboh, 2018). Potential oil revenue is thus lost due to terrorist activities. If oil had been discovered there, the project would also have attracted investment from multinational corporations that would have created direct and indirect employment for locals.

In December 2020 Boko Haram killed 20 people and abducted 12 in attacks on villages in Borno and Adamawa States. Churches, schools and police stations were burnt and hospital pharmacies and shops were looted (US Department of State, 2021). Rebuilding these public buildings will cost money, and local citizens have been deprived of the social benefits they offered. The destruction of bridges also has negative consequences. In 2014 Boko Haram destroyed the Madafuma bridge linking the 185 km Biu-Damboa-Maiduguri federal road (Marama, 2014). The movement of people and goods was affected, adversely impacting the commercial sector and socially isolating ordinary citizens.

Boko Haram has also targeted schools for kidnappings (Thurston, 2018). The major examples include the kidnapping of schoolboys in Buni Yadi, Yobe State, in February 2014, schoolgirls in Chibok in April 2014 in Borno State and incidents involving ISWAP in February 2018 in Dapchi, Yobe State which led to the kidnapping of schoolgirls (International Crisis Group, 2018). Teachers have also been attacked, and schools have been forced to suspend operations several times. Payment of ransoms for kidnap victims has taken a toll on the government purse and the families of those kidnapped. Kidnapped victims were also psychologically traumatised, with kidnapped girls made *sex slaves* or forcefully married to terrorists (Thurston, 2018).

Families whose breadwinners are killed by Boko Haram/ISWAP suffer economic and social hardship (Thurston, 2018). The killings may also cause religious divisions. ISWAP is not in support of killing Muslims, which may cause some resentment among Christians. For instance, in 2019, ISWAP released a video showing the showing the public execution of 11 Christians in retaliation for the death of ISIS leader Abu Bakr al-Baghdadi (US Department of State, 2021).

It has been reported that Boko Haram/ISWAP has been imposing taxes on individuals and livestock since 2015 (Campbell, 2018; Ogundipe, 2018; Opejobi, 2022). The group's control of some territories has made this easy. It also collects taxes on major highways (Opejobi, 2022). The hijacking of government's prerogative suggests that the government has failed in its duty to citizens. While these have the effect of further impoverishing local citizens, it also enables the terrorists to earn locals' trust because they are not attacked once they pay taxes. The military has also been accused of unlawful arrest of citizens, claiming they are Boko Haram and forcing family members to part with money to bail them out (Thurston, 2018). The result could well reduce confidence in the government and more recruits for the terrorist groups.

The security budget was misappropriated, and it was alleged that corrupt military officers were the main perpetrators (Thurston, 2018). Military officers, civilians and a former National Security Adviser are on trial in connection with a $2 billion arms deal. Soldiers protested in Maiduguri on 25 March 2021 over unpaid allowances, and obsolete equipment (Omilana, 2021). In 2016, it was alleged that some soldiers were selling ammunition and weapons to Boko Haram (Thurston, 2018). All these instances highlight the level of corruption in the military. Indeed, it is possible that some military officers might not want to put an end to terrorism in the county due to the personal gains they stand to lose. However, such practices continue to drain the national purse and reduce funds for development. The social implication is that soldiers fighting the terrorists who are poorly paid and lack sophisticated weapons may suffer from reduced morale and become easy prey to Boko Haram/ISWAP that commands more sophisticated weapons. Citizens are negatively affected because they feel that they will be more vulnerable if military personnel are vulnerable.

The displacement caused by Boko Haram/ISWAP has led to the establishment of internally displaced persons (IDPs) camps, which have also attracted humanitarian agencies. The displaced are robbed of their livelihoods (Thurston, 2018). Cases of rape have been reported in the camps, with security agents identified as perpetrators in some instances (*Premium Times*, August 27, 2017). Camps have also been attacked. A suicide bomber attacked the IDP camp in Dikwa, Borno State in February 2016 (Thurston, 2018). On 18 August 2020, the ISWAP launched an attack on security forces assigned to protect 500 IDPs in Kukawa, Borno State and more than 100 people were abducted (US Department of State, 2021). In 2019, ISWAP attacked a convoy of Action Against Hunger (AAH) and Nigerian health ministry officials in North East Nigeria (US Department of State, 2021). An AAH driver was killed and five hostages were taken, four of whom ISWAP later claimed to have killed (US Department of State, 2021). Such incidents not only cause psychological and social distress among those displaced, but also discourage aid workers from coming to the region.

Social and Economic Implications of the ASWJ's Activities

The ASWJ attacks military outposts and police stations, villages, banks, hotels, oil and gas installations and employees of foreign companies, among others. The group has also beheaded villagers. There have been a reported 697 violent attacks in Cabo Delgado Province and 2,393 deaths since 2017, and the violence associated with the group led to the internal displacement of more than 500,000 people (US Department of State, 2021).

Cabo Delgado is the headquarters for multinational oil and gas companies involved in Mozambique's offshore liquefied natural gas projects (Neethling, 2021). While most ASWJ members do not have the skills required to be employed by these companies, this has not prevented them from demanding jobs (Hanlon, 2018). The group's original members were less educated young men who did not want to become farmers. They are thus aggrieved that the gas stations employ workers from outside the region (Hanlon, 2018). Furthermore, people were forcefully removed from their ancestral lands to make way for ruby mines. The manner people were displaced from their land is so harsh. People were sent off their lands by vigilantes backed by the police (Els & Chelin, 2021) who threatened and tortured the locals, and their houses were burnt, with some buried alive (Els & Chelin, 2021). They were thus deprived of mining and farming rights (they were not given other land to farm) in these areas, although the mining companies built houses for them (Els & Chelin, 2021). The manner of displacement and the fact that they were not employed by the mining companies sparked a violent reaction by ASWJ. Its attack on a convoy of workers of oil company, Anadarko led to the suspension of the construction of a liquefied natural gas plant in Cabo Delgado (Neethling, 2021). On 25 March 2021, a four-day assault was launched on the town of Palma, with shops, banks, military barracks, and the Amarula Hotel targeted, and dozens of people killed (Neethling, 2021).

These attacks will no doubt disrupt the mining companies' operations, with negative effects on their bottom line and the tax the government generates from them. The attacks created insecurity, and some local communities were displaced, negatively impacting development and farming in the region (Neethling, 2021) and exacerbating poverty. Food security is also likely to be threatened.

ISCAP took over the port of Mocímboa da Praia in the North of Mozambique in September 2020, with the intention of declaring a caliphate after taking over the town (Institute for Economics & Peace, 2020). Local inhabitants suffered high levels of insecurity, and their confidence in the government declined. Economic activities in the port were also disrupted, once again negatively impacting government revenue.

Political campaigns, which are an integral part of the electoral process, have also been restricted in some parts of Cabo Delgado due to the activities of ASWJ (Human Rights Watch, 2020). Political participation is a social right and political campaigns are essential platforms for the electorate to hold politicians accountable.

Conclusion and Recommendations

This chapter explored the economic and social effects of the activities of Boko Haram/ISWAP and ASWJ. While the origins of these groups lie in religious ideologies, the catalyst for their support is economic and social disparities. Their activities have economic and social impacts on both the government and society at large. These have decimated trust in government, worsened citizens' socio-economic status and undermined social cohesion and the morale of the military. Failure to address these consequences could bolster Boko Haram/ISWAP, and ASWJ's membership and new terrorist groups may emerge.

Poverty alleviation programmes by government and civil society organisations are recommended to tackle the root causes of terrorism, as well as de-radicalisation programmes to mitigate religious extremism and hatred of Western education. Western education will impart skills that will make it easier for locals to find jobs, which in turn could change their extremist tendencies. Government also needs to provide infrastructure and impose tariffs on imported goods to enable local industries to thrive. Modern equipment should be acquired to monitor movement inside and outside the affected countries. Corruption should be eradicated at all levels in order to reduce popular discontent and the grievances of the armed forces. Lastly, terrorists should face the full might of the law and reintegration programmes should be established to enable them to become productive members of society.

References

Alden, C., & Chichava, S. (2020). Cabo Delgado and the rise of militant islam: Another Niger delta in the making. *South African Institute of International Affairs Policy Briefing, 221,* 1–10.

Arvin, J. (2021). *How Kidnap-for-ransom became the "most industry business in Nigeria"*. Accessed from https://www.vox.com/22596198/students-nigeria-profit-kidnapping on 20 February 2022.

Azeez, O. (2018, Spring). Once upon a game reserve: Sambisa and the tragedy of a forested landscape. *Environment and Society Portal, Arcadia, 2.* Rachel Carson Center for Environment and Society. https://doi.org/10.5282/rcc/8176

Botha, A. (2021). Assessing the status and addressing violent extremism in East Africa. In G. Segell, S. Kostelyanets, & H. Solomon (Eds.), *Terrorism in Africa: New trends and frontiers* (pp. 62–76). Institute for African Studies of the Russian Academy of Sciences, University of Haifa.

Campbell, J. (2018). *Boko Haram faction reportedly collecting "taxes" in Northeast Nigeria.* Accessed from https://www.cfr.org/blog/boko-haram-faction-reportedly-collecting-taxes-northeast-nigeria on 20 February 2022.

Demuynck, M., & Weijenberg, G. (2021). *The upcoming SADC intervention: A new way ahead to combat terrorism in Mozambique?* Accessed from https://icct.nl/publication/the-upcoming-sadc-intervention-a-new-way-ahead-to-combat-terrorism-in-mozambique/ on 16 February 2022.

Desinova, T. S. (2021). Islamic radicalism in cameroon: Origins and prospects of further gains. In G. Segell, S. Kostelyanets, & H. Solomon (Eds.), *Terrorism in Africa: New trends and frontiers* (pp. 48–61). Institute for African Studies of the Russian Academy of Sciences, University of Haifa.

Eboh, M. (2018). *UniMaid defies Terrorists, to resume oil exploration with NNPC.* Accessed from https://www.vanguardngr.com/2018/03/unimaid-defies-terrorists-resume-oil-exploration-nnpc/ on 20 February 2022.

Els, W., & Chelin, R. (2021). Mozambique, Cabo Delgado Insurgency: Extraordinary mineral resources and liquid natural gas, a blessing that may be a curse are we missing the point? In G. Segell, S. Kostelyanets, & H. Solomon (Eds.), *Terrorism in Africa: New trends and frontiers* (pp. 106–114). Institute for African Studies of the Russian Academy of Sciences, University of Haifa.

Fabricius, P. (2020, January 10). *Is Islamic State taking charge of Mozambique's Jihadist insurgency?* Institute for Security Studies. Accessed from https://issafrica.org/iss-today/isislamic-state-taking-charge-of-mozambiques-jihadist-insurgency on 12 June 2020.

Faluyi, O. T., Khan, S., & Akinola, A. O. (2019). *Boko Haram's terrorism and the Nigerian State. Federalism, politics and policies.* Advances in African Economic, Social and Political Development. Springer Nature.

Hanlon, J. (2018). *Mozambique's insurgency: A new Boko Haram or youth demanding an end to marginalisation?* Accessed from https://eprints.lse.ac.uk/90103/1/africaatlse-2018-06-19-mozambiques-insurgency-a-new-boko-haram-or.pdf on 20 February 2022.

Heywood, A. (2011). *Global politics.* Palgrave Macmillan.

Human Rights Watch. (2020). World report 2020. Events of 2019.

Institute for Economics and Peace. (2020, November). *Global terrorism index 2020: Measuring the impact of terrorism*. Sydney.
International Crisis Group. (2018, April 13). Preventing Boko Haram adductions of school children in Nigeria. (Briefing No. 137/Africa). Accessed from https://www.crisisgroup.org/africa/west-africa/nigeria/b137-preventing-boko-haram-abductions-schoolchildren-nigeria on 20 February 2022.
Lipp, C. (n.d). *Boko Haram causes hunger crisis in the Lake Chad Basin*. Accessed from https://borgenproject.org/hunger-crisis-in-the-lake-chad-basin/ on 20 February2022.
Marama, N. (2014). *Boko Haram destroys bridge linking Maiduguri-Damaturu-Biu*. Accessed from https://www.vanguardngr.com/2014/07/boko-haram-destroys-bridge-linking-maiduguri-damaturu-biu-rd/ on 20 February 2022.
Matsinhe, D. M., Valoi, E. (2019, October). *The genesis of insurgency in Northern Mozambique*. Institute for Security Studies. Southern Africa Report 27. Accessed from https://media.africaportal.org/documents/The_Genesis_of_insurgency_in_N_Moz.pdf on 12 June 2020.
Mbaya, Y. P., & Malgwi, H. (2010). Species list and status of mammals and birds in Sambisa game reserve, Borno State, Nigeria. *Journal of Research in Forestry, Wildlife and Environment, 2*(1), 135–140.
Morier-Genoud, E. (2020). The Jihadi insurgency in Mozambique: Origins, nature and beginning. *Journal of Eastern African Studies, 14*(3), 396–412.
National Bureau of Statistics. (2018). *Computation of human development indices for the UNDP Nigeria Human Development Report (2016)*.
Neethling, T. (2021). Extremism and insecurity in Northern Mozambique: Why be concerned? In G. Segell, S. Kostelyanets, & H. Solomon (Eds.), *Terrorism in Africa: New trends and frontiers* (pp. 91–105). Institute for African Studies of the Russian Academy of Sciences, University of Haifa.
Okunade, S. K., Faluyi, O. T., & Matambo, E. (2021). Evolving patterns of insurgency in Southern and West Africa: Refocusing the Boko Haram lens on Mozambique. *African Security Review, 30*(4), 434–450.
Ogundipe, S. (2018). *Boko Haram now collecting taxes from Nigerians in Borno, Yobe- report*. Accessed from https://www.premiumtimesng.com/news/headlines/266636-boko-haram-now-collecting-taxes-from-nigerians-in-borno-yobe-report.html on 20 February 2022.
Omilana, T. (2021). *Soldiers protest over unpaid allowances, obsolete equipment*. Accessed from https://guardian.ng/news/soldiers-protest-over-unpaid-allowances-obsolete-equipment/ on 20 February 2022.
Onuoha, F.C. (2014). Boko Haram and the evolving Salafi Jihadist threat in Nigeria. In M. Montclos (Ed.), *Boko Haram: Islamism, politics, security and the state in Nigeria* (pp. 158–191). African Studies Centre.

Opejobi, S. (2022). Boko Haram, ISWAP Openly Celebrating Marriages, Collecting Taxes Without Confrontation- Zulum. Accessed from https://dailypost.ng/2022/01/12/boko-haram-iswap-openly-celebrating-marriages-collecting-taxes-without-confrontation-zulum on 20 February 2022.

Premium Times. (2017, August 27). Rapists on rampage in Borno IDP camp, victims say. Accessed from http://www.premiumtimesng.com/regional/nnorth-east/241692-rapists-on-rampage-in-borno-idp-camp-victims-say.html on 1 December 2017.

Thurston, A. (2018). *Boko Haram. The history of an African Jihadist movement*. Princeton University Press.

Salaam, A. O. (2012). Boko Haram: Beyond religious fanaticism. *Journal of Policing, Intelligence and Counter Terrorism, 7*(2), 147–162.

Solomon, H. (2021). Terrorism, counter-terrorism and the need to problematise the state in the Sahel. In G. Segell, S. Kostelyanets, & H. Solomon (Eds.), *Terrorism in Africa: New trends and frontiers* (pp. 36–47). Institute for African Studies of the Russian Academy of Sciences, University of Haifa.

US Department of State. (2021). *Country reports on terrorism 2020*.

Wuyep, A. (2015). *Terrorism in Nigeria—Revisiting Nigeria's socio-political approach to counterterrorism and counterinsurgency* (Unpublished MA Thesis Fort Leavenworth). Kansas.

CHAPTER 8

Violent Conflict in the Sahel: Causes, Dynamics, and Actors

Adeoye O. Akinola and Naledi Ramontja

INTRODUCTION

The Sahel is a semiarid region of Africa extending from Senegal eastward to Sudan—or from the Atlantic Ocean to the Red Sea. While "Africa has become the region hardest hit by terrorism" in 2021 (Ledererun, 2021), the Sahel region has remained the epicentre of conflicts in Africa dominated by a combination of protest movements, coups d'états, jihadist insurgencies, local armed conflicts, including herders-farmers conflict, and illegal trafficking of drugs and weapons. Out of the ten countries that make up the Sahel, countries like Nigeria, Burkina Faso, Chad, Guinea, Mali, Sudan and Cameroon are involved in diverse conflicts,

---

A. O. Akinola (✉) · N. Ramontja
Institute for Pan-African Thought and Conversation,
University of Johannesburg, Johannesburg, South Africa
e-mail: aoakinola@uj.ac.za

N. Ramontja
e-mail: naledir@uj.ac.za

© The Author(s), under exclusive license to Springer Nature
Switzerland AG 2023
A. O. Akinola, *Contemporary Issues on Governance,
Conflict and Security in Africa*,
https://doi.org/10.1007/978-3-031-29635-2_8

which prove that the region is still prone to insecurity and political instabilities (Walther, 2017). Despite the efforts of state and non-states to curtail the violent conflicts, including the presence of international troops, the number of casualties has increased substantially, raising the threats to aggravate the political and economic crisis that has confronted the region.

The fall of Libya and the violent conflict that ensued partly account for the insecurity of the Sahel since 2011. Following the transfer of weapons, ammunition and armed fighters from Libya into Mali, a dormant Tuareg rebellion was strengthened. In Nigeria, Boko Haram's reign of terror has gotten out of hand, and Cameroon is under the siege of secessionist conflict that has killed thousands and threatened its nationhood and aggravated the regional insecurity. Between January 2019 and December 2021, West Africa experienced the highest cases of terrorist attacks on the continent. During this period, about 2,602 attacks occurred, leading to 10,899 deaths (ACSRT, 2022). Since the outbreak of conflict in Mali in 2012, leading to the deployment of more than 4,000 French-led peacekeeping troops, the country has not enjoyed peace. The violence has escalated and reached its climax in March 2019 when a Dogon armed group attacked and massacred about 160 Fulani, including children and women; while in January 2021, religious fundamentalists killed over 100 defenceless people in Tillabéri, Niger, close to the border with Burkina Faso and Mali (Pye, 2021: 4). In Burkina Faso, hundreds of civilians died during terrorist attacks (in the eastern region) in the first three months of 2021, and about 15 civilians, initially kidnapped were thereafter killed in Seytenga, located in the northern part of the country; and by April, 70 people were killed, including more than 30 civilians (UNSC, 2021: 5). Rather than being curtailed, the insurgent groups in the Sahel are consolidating. In June 2022, 89 people were massacred in the northern village of Seytenga, one of the worst attacks in the history of the country (Aljazeera, 2022).

Other Sahel countries have also had their shares of the consequences of the militarisation of the zone. In Nigeria, a United Nations Development Programme (UNDP) report recently revealed that attacks from the dreaded Boko Haram, including its splinter group—Islamic State West Africa Province, and Fulani herdsmen have resulted in 2.7 million internally displaced persons (IDPs) and 350 000 deaths (Akinola, 2021). Apart from Boko Haram's acts of terror in Chad, the spillover effects of conflicts in its neighbouring countries—Cameroon, Libya, Sudan and Niger—have complicated the country's efforts at peace and security. In

February 2021, Boko Haram attacked polling stations and killed electoral officials during a run-off presidential election in Bankilare, Niger (UNSC, 2021: 6). According to the UN High Commissioner for Refugees, 237 000 refugees and 300 000 IDPs were in Niger, which included an additional 4 000 refugees and 2,000 newly displaced in 2021 due to attacks in the Tillabéri and Tahoua regions (Akinola, 2021).

Besides terrorism and ethnic or religious conflict, other illicit activities including oil bunkering, human, drugs, and firearms trafficking, migrant smuggling, organised crime, money laundering, transfer of counterfeited goods and looting of natural resources, have become a feature of the Sahel. The environment of conflict, with insecurity and political instability in form of coup d'état, has concertedly undermined any prospects for instigating sustainable development and redressing the loss of lives through conflict, poverty and famine. Many of the actors, with divergent interests such as exploration of mineral resources and arms sales, have politicised the conflict; thus, scrambling for the soul of the Sahel.

Through the adoption of desktop research due to the availability of relevant literature and official documents, including vital reports in newspapers, this article examines the root and immediate causes of the instability in the Sahel region and identifies the interests of the actors involved in the Saheli-conflicts. It also analyses the patterns of violence in the region, drawing from a historical context. The next section unpacks the strategies which have been implemented by the states and external actors to combat conflict in the Sahel and concludes.

THE SAHEL: AN OVERVIEW

The change in the security environment in the Sahel since the 1960s is a reflection of the situation in other parts of Africa, characterised by an increase in violent conflicts perpetrated by state and non-state actors. Since the middle and early 1960s, following the independence of many Sahel states such as Sudan, DRC (formerly Zaire) and Nigeria, the geopolitics of Sahel was initially characterised by stability and peaceful co-existence. Although there were several coups d'état in the region that ushered in authoritarian regimes in Nigeria, Chad, Mali, Niger and Sudan, the relationships between the newly independent states were relatively peaceful and there were few cases of local armed groups. Nevertheless, the DRC experienced a proxy Cold War in 1960–1965, orchestrated by the United States and the Soviet Union (now Russia). The deposit of

Uranium in the DRC was a decisive factor in turning the DRC into a battlefield. Northern Mali experienced its first Tuareg rebellion (1962–1964) during Modibo Keïta's government (Walther, 2017), and Nigeria experienced a civil war between 1967 and 1970.

The biggest challenge to Mali's stability since independence has been the nefarious activities of insurgent groups, particularly by the Tuareg people also known as 'The Blue Men of the Desert'. The group is characterised by its unorthodox practices of Islamic religious beliefs and nomadic pastoral culture (Keita & Henk, 1998). Besides the thousands of Tuaregs in Niger and Burkina Faso, about 620 000 Tuaregs are in Mali (Keita & Henk, 1998). While radical Islamists have taken control of the main cities in northern Mali and displaced the Tuareg armed group, diverse criminal groups and the Islamic fundamentalist continue to impose their own version of sharia law and judicial system on the northern part of Mali (Briscoe, 2014).

The region is ethnically diverse, with several ethnic groups contending with the others, while armed Islamist groups also dominate several parts of the region. The Tuareg ethnic group is dominant in Mali, Niger, Burkina Faso and other West African states; Bambara, who are farmers, are predominant in the Fulani part of Mali; Mossi constitutes the largest ethnic group in Burkina Faso; Dogon are dominant in Mali and Burkina Faso; and Daoussahak groups, called the pastoralists are dominant in Niger. In the case of terrorist groupings, Boko Haram holds sway in Nigeria and some parts of Niger; the Islamic State in the Greater Sahara (ISGS) operations run across Northern Mali, Niger and Burkina Faso; Al-Qaeda in the Islamic Maghreb and its affiliated groups such as Ansarul Islam are operating largely in Burkina Faso (Pye, 2021). Indeed, Burkina Faso has become the most violent country in the Sahel, leading to the forced displacement of more than 1.9 million people (Aljazeera, 2022).

The period, 1975–1990, was marked by two major regional conflicts that affected the region (Keita & Henk, 1998): in the far western region of the Sahel, the Western Sahara crisis involved Morocco and Mauritania, where the Popular Front for the Liberation of Saguia el-Hamra clashed against Río de Oro. In the East, Libya and Chad clashed over the desert area of the Aouzou Strip following its invasion by Libyan forces. In 2012 Mali collapsed in the face of a military coup and uprising by the Jihadist and Taureg rebellion groups, sparking violent and intercommunal conflicts. This led to the invitation of France to assist in terms of rescuing Mali from disintegration. France launched *Operation Barkhane,* and other international peacekeeping operations such as the United Nations Multidimensional Integrated Stabilization Mission in Mali (MINUSMA), and the G-5 Sahel Force, emerged. The G-5, a multilateral force established in 2017 to curtail terrorism and fundamentalist extremism, was a joint effort of five countries: Burkina Faso, Chad, Mali, Mauritania and Niger. In recent years, the conflict has spread to neighbouring Niger and Burkina Faso, sparking ethnic tensions (Pye, 2021). The Tuareg militants have long desired their own independent state, Azawad (comprising the Timbuktu, Gao and Kidal regions of Mali), with several uprisings in 1962, 1990 and 2007 (Pye, 2021).

The current conflicts in the Sahel cannot be reduced to its multifaceted terror groups only. Rather, there are a variety of factors and actors that have contributed to the complex situation of instability that affects the entire Sahel region. The Sahel is characterised by low human development, including inadequate health care facilities, poor education, high rate of unemployment, low life expectancy rates and high birth rates. In Chad, the population continues to grow "at the rapid pace of 3 percent per year, as Chad has one of the highest fertility rates in the world: 6.4 children per woman" (OCHA, 2020). Despite its vast wealth in mineral resources, mining in Mali; Oil and Gas in Nigeria and Cameroon, uranium in Niger, and oil in Chad, the Sahel remains vulnerable to political and economic instabilities which contribute to the underlying issues of human security. For instance, in Burkina Faso, 40.1 percent of the people live below the poverty line. The country ranks 185 out of 188 states on the Human Development Index (HDI), and 144 out of 157 countries on the World Bank's new Human Capital Index (HCI). There is extreme inequality between urban and rural areas. Indeed, 90% of the poor reside in the villages, and less than 5% of the poorest households are connected to the national electricity grid.

In a context already marked by fragility and vulnerability, the rise and expansion of Al-Qaeda in the Islamic Maghreb (AQIM) from Mali to other countries, and the increase in the number of armed and radicalised groups have further contributed to instability and violence in the region. In February 2016, AQIM and Al-Mourabitoun, two groups that until then had mostly operated in neighbouring Mali, claimed responsibility for the attack that occurred at the Splendid Hotel and Cappuccino café-bar in the centre of Ouagadougou (the headquarter of Burkina Faso), which claimed the lives of 30 people. The situation is exacerbated by the illegal trafficking of drugs, cigarettes and humans (Baudias et al., 2021).

These activities hinder economic development and expanded the zone of lawlessness in a region where states struggle to impose their authority and suffer from a lack of capacity and an uneven territorial presence (Baudias. et al., 2021). In Burkina Faso, 60% of the territory is only controlled by the state, leaving 40 percent in the domain of non-state armed groups that have turned the country into a theatre of war (Aljazeera, 2022).

Root Causes of Conflict and Insecurity

Since the 2012 uprising in Northern Mali, the situation has gone from bad to worse—where armed groups have multiplied and emerged in areas where they never did—sparking violence from the northern parts of Mali and Nigeria to more central parts, with spillover effects on neighbouring countries like Niger and Burkina Faso (Walther, 2017).

In order to understand the Sahel and, more broadly, the growing instabilities in the region, it is necessary to unpack the root causes of the conflicts in the region, before delving into the proliferation of coups, evolution of terrorist organisations and the roles of external actors, including regional and other international organisations. Violent conflicts in the Sahel are a result of tensions over land, territories and access to governmental power and resources (Walther, 2017). Conflicts in relation to the government concern disagreements over the type of political system, the change of government structures, regime consolidation or transitions, and conflicts over territory relate to contestations over the status of a territory, a case for secession or granting of autonomy to a group (Walther, 2017). There have also been conflicts over land and its produce, which have accounted for the farmers/herders clashes, with dire consequences such as the destruction of farmlands and loss of lives in countries such as Nigeria and Mali.

In Mali, state fragility and governance crisis, high levels of poverty, and unemployment, climate change as well as socio-economic and political inequality, have made it easy for armed groups such as the ISGS and the AQIM to mobilise for new recruits in areas that had long been abandoned by the government and left to fend for themselves. AQIM had about 800 members in the Sahel in 2012 (Rao, 2014: 10) and has since that time expanded. These armed conflicts are a result of unresolved issues that plague the region and sadly, the political elites and several armed groups and its members have benefitted from profits generated from crimes including smuggling of Moroccan cannabis resin and cocaine and kidnapping for ransom. Individuals and networks involved in these activities have converted their wealth into political influence, and the military, on the hand, has used their holds on the instruments of force to convert their military power into political powers.

One of the major challenges in the Sahel is ineffective border control, which is linked with the zone's distinct geopolitical landscape. Islamist terror groups and organised criminal groups operate across the porous borders of the Sahel without restrictions. This has worsened the militarisation of the zone, as arms and ammunition are transferred easily from one country to the other. Thus, there is a clear link between organised crime and insecurity in the region, as contestations and local conflict categorised under organised crimes significantly played an important role in the outbreaks of protracted conflicts in Mali (Lacher, 2012). In Mauritania following the end of President Maaouya Ould Sid'Ahmed Taya's rule (1984–2005), the country experienced increased levels of complex and intertwined conflicts.

In general, "Key drivers of conflict are Islamist terrorist movements and the risk of radicalisation; the often divided and belligerent Mauritanian military; domestic protests similar to the Arab Spring protests; trafficking and kidnapping; and wider social, economic and political tensions" (Rao, 2014: 4). The businessmen, political elites and security personnel were all actively involved in crimes such as smuggling weapons (Lacher, 2012). Ould Taya's rule relied heavily on an alliance among the Smacid, Ouled Bou Sba and Rgeybat tribes, to facilitate smuggling and other illicit activities (Lacher, 2012). Between 2007 and 2008, the son of former Mauritanian President Sidi Mohamed Ould Haidallah and other influential people were arrested on drug charges. The country has become one of the routes for trafficking drugs, arms and cigarettes from South America to Europe (Rao, 2014).

The proximity of the Sahel to other conflict zone has also played a role in the vulnerability of the Sahel to violent conflict. The Sahel shares a border with Libya (Chad on the South, Niger on the Southeast), which became a conflict zone after the fall of Tripoli in 2011. Libya is Africa's gateway to Europe. Thus, arms are smuggled through Libya into the Sahel, moving from one conflict zone to another. Apart from arms, several warlords and fighters that were displaced in Libya cross into the Sahel, reinforcing the links between terrorist organisations such as Boko Haram,

Tuareg armed groups, and Al-Qaeda, including the expansion of transnational organised crimes such as drug and human trafficking (Walther, 2017).

Though Boko Haram's activities started before 2009, the dreaded terrorist group became violent after the extra political murder of its leader, Yusuf Mohammed, by the Nigerian police force after his arrest and detention because of the group's involvement in violence in Maiduguri, northern Nigeria (Faluyi et al., 2019: 5). The group made headlines in April 2014, with the kidnap of 276 predominantly female students (between 16 to 18 years old) from the Government Girls Secondary School in Chibok in the Borno State of Nigeria. This created local and international outrages and a global campaign called *#BringBackOurGirls*, which jolted the Nigerian government into taking Boko Haram more seriously. It particularly drew the attention of international media such as *CNN* (Abubakar & Levs, 2014). Indeed, the group "has challenged the strength of the armed forces and shaken Nigeria's security framework" (Faluyi et al., 2019: 1). While emphasis has been placed on the number of casualties, there has been less focus on the financial value of the property the group has destroyed. For instance, the damage to property caused by Boko Haram in 2014 was estimated at more than US$40 million (Faluyi et al., 2019: 5). Boko Haram's gradual expansion out of northern Nigeria, its traditional operation area, has led to terrorist activities in countries that border northern Nigeria like Chad, Niger and Cameroon (Walther, 2017).

Apart from Boko Haram's terrorism, Nigeria has also faced threats from several other armed groups such as the Oodua People's Congress, the Arewa People's Congress, the Movement for the Actualization of the Sovereign State of Biafra (MASSOB) as well as the Indigenous People of Biafra (IPOB), the Niger Delta Volunteer Force, Egbesu Boys, Movement for the Survival of Ogoni People (MOSOP) and Ijaw National Congress. At the base of their agitations are issues of misgovernance, state weaknesses, dislocated fiscal relations, exclusive governance and structural violence. The violent nature of these groups, of which many such as IPOB and MASSOB, are pushing for secession from the federal government.

Not only in the highlighted case studies, but the entire countries that make up the Sahel—Chad, Cameroun, Nigeria, Niger, Burkina Faso, The Gambia, Guinea, Mali, Mauritania, Senegal and Sudan—have similar characteristics: weak leadership, socio-economic and political crisis, high rate of poverty and insecurities. Between 2018 and June 2022, the military overthrew the civilian administration in Mali, Burkina Faso, Sudan, Chad and Guinea, further plunging the countries into political instability and insecurity. The threats of suspensions from regional organisations and the imposition of sanctions on some of the countries, where the military has sacked civilian administrations, have also driven the countries into further economic challenges and political isolations.

THE SAHEL: REGIONALISATION OF CONFLICT

The rise of extremist groups in the Sahel such as the Al-Qaeda in the Islamic Maghreb and Boko Haram, with international affiliations and the spillover effects of the attacks on other countries, have imposed a responsibility on regional and international actors to intervene. Due to border porosity in the zone, arms and fighters are easily transferred across the state's borders. The Sahelian states affected most by the Jihadist threats are Mali, Chad, Mauritania and Burkina Faso—members of the G5 states. The violent conflicts happening in the region are both inter- and intra-state conflicts, involving insurgencies against the state and society, such as the cases of terrorism in northern Nigeria and Mali, including the conflict between Burkina Faso and Mali in the 1990s. In Mali, intrastate conflicts are also manifested between the Fulani and Bambara communities, with spillover effects in the neighbouring Segou region of Mali (Nsaibia & Duhamel, 2021).

In 2019, the Sahel recorded the highest state-based conflicts in Africa. Many of these are related to the rise and expansion of Islamic states (IS), while 13 of them were fought over territories. Cameroon and Burkina Faso also experienced the involvement of external actors in their domestic conflicts. In the same year, a number of peace agreements and ceasefires were achieved. Many of the Sahelian contemporary conflicts are driven by crime, which has led to an increase in the levels of insecurity in the whole region (Marc et al., 2015:17). As the epicentre of the violent conflicts in the Sahel, Mali continues to be fragile due to the inter-jihadist violence between the Jama'at Nasr al-Islam wal Muslimin (JNIM)—operating in the country as well as Burkina Faso and Niger—and the ISGS continued to destabilise the country (ACLED, 2021). In 2021, the ISGS was responsible for 66% of the entire deaths from organised political violence in Niger. However, as compared to Mali and Burkina Faso, Niger has fewer local armed groups but faced a major challenge posed by terror groups such as Boko Haram in Lake Chad and the insurgencies in the Northern and the south-western Tillaberi (ACLED, 2021).

The Roles of International Actors

As a fallout of the Libya crisis in 2011, the terrorist attacks across northern Mali led by the Tuareg, after capturing Northern Mali and about 150 kilometres from the Malian capital, the turmoil within the army, and the growing of armed local groups, led the newly sworn-in-Malian President, Dioncounda Traoré, to invite France for help in January 2013. In response, France President Francois Hollande sent French initially dispatched 2, 500 troops to assist the 3,000-strong African force, and the Malian military to push back the insurgency groups and establish Malian authority over central Mali and larger parts of the northern part (Aljazeera, 2013; Pye, 2021). As part of the international efforts to restore national integrity in Mali, the UN and former President Blaise Compaoré, acting as the ECOWAS mediator, negotiated a ceasefire and preliminary peace agreement on June 2013 between the transitional Malian Government, the National Movement for the Liberation of Azawad (NMLA) and the High Council for the Unity of Azawad (Baudais. et al., 2021). The agreement opposed the separation of Azaward and aimed at facilitating presidential and legislative elections as a means to end the hostilities and preserve the ceasefire (Baudais et al., 2021). The implementation of the agreement was to be monitored by a joint technical security commission and supervised by the United Nations Multidimentional Integrated Stabilisation Mission in Mali (MINUSMA) with the assistance of Operation Serval (Pye, 2021).

The intervention of international troops eventually opened up the Sahel to different major global powers such as France, China, Russia and even Turkey—all of them with key interests in the region's huge deposit of mineral resources. The recent exit of France from the Sahel has created immense opportunities for other global powers to expand their interests in the Sahel. Russia has been regarded as one of them, with suppliers of arms to several countries in the Sahel, and there have been reports of the presence of the Russian military, acting as mercenaries, in the region. For the past decade, Western governments have focused heavily on AQIM's presence in the Sahel, providing technical assistance in an attempt to strengthen the capacity of the security sectors and justice systems to combat the group (Lacher, 2012). France troops that were deployed under the cover, *Opération Sérval* in 2013 were supported by the United States and European air cover (Pye, 2021).

In a bid to increase the offensive against the Malian armed groups in 2014, *Opération Barkhane* was established by France with the deployment of 5100 military personnel to help the G5 deal with counter-terrorism operations in the region (Pye, 2021). Other EU member states such as Denmark, Swedish, Estonia, German and Czech contributed to the EUTM Mali and EUCAP Sahel Civilian mission, as part of the EU strategy for the Sahel and the Sahel Regional Action Plan 2015–2020. The EU was the first foreign actor to develop a Strategy for Security and Development in the region (PSC, 2014). The foreign power continued to provide technical support and training to strengthen the military of member states of the Sahel region and also in support of *Opération Barkhane*, including the training of 15 000 Malian forces. The UN is also instrumental in counter-terrorism operations in the Sahel, playing a major peacekeeping and humanitarian role through the MINUSMA, while the African Union Mission for Mali and the Sahel (MISAHEL) aimed at securing the region for the enhancement of economic growth and sustainable peace (PSC, 2014).

The economic and political instabilities in the Sahel have a direct effect on France. The jihadist organisations fuel forced migration across the region. Like any other former colonial power, France has economic and political interests in the Sahel: there are many French nationals, including several French companies, in the region. France and its allies were also wary of the possibility that the region could become a Jihadist region, a terrorist zone and a training ground for terrorism (Baudais et al., 2021).

Europe's strategic approach to the Sahel conflict is aimed at addressing terrorism and Africa/EU migration, without addressing the root causes of the conflicts. There has also been neglect of intercommunal conflict, which continues to pose threats to the region. Just as terrorism spilled over from Nigeria and Libya into the region, communal clashes in central Mali eventually spread into Burkina Faso and Niger. Disputes over land between the Fulani and Mossi (the largest ethnic group) in Burkina Faso, and between Fulani, Tuareg and Daoussahak people in Niger, have become intensified (Pye, 2021). Lack of effective governance, structural violence and accountability have accounted for the outbreak and protracted nature of intercommunal conflicts in the zone (Pye, 2021).

In 2015, the Algiers peace accord aimed at protecting civilians against mass atrocities, ensuring government authority was operational in central Mali, with the expectation of creating an enabling environment of peace and security. Despite this, the region soon relapsed into conflict. The

French-led military operation and the Task Force, *Operation Takuba*, found a way to weaken the ISGS and brought a provisional end to violence in the North. It shifted its focus to the JNIM in October 2020, inflicting a significant number of casualties on the group. However, the group continued to wage a multi-front war and maintain operations in the Sahel. As they continue to attack strategic locations in 2021, key battles were lost by France and G5 forces, particularly in Konna and in Aguelhok, where sporadic attacks were recorded in April 2021 (Nsaibia & Duhamel, 2021). A joint operation conducted by 1,500 French, 900 Burkinabé, 850 Malian and 150 Nigerien soldiers, from 2 January to 3 February, weakened the militants' grip on parts of northern Mali and facilitated the reopening of the road from Gao to Hombori (UNSC, 2021: 6).

France has invested in the Sahel, both politically by supporting the African Peace and Security Architecture and militarily through different military operations like Operation Serval in 2013 and *Operation Barkhane* in 2014. The United States supports the region through capacity building and strategic security cooperation, together with the Sahel Region Capacity Building Working Group of the Global Counterterrorism Forum (GCTF). This framework, under the joint leadership of Turkey and the US, has tried to increase the capacity of the police and the judicial system, to enhance border security, to strengthen the fight against Islamic extremism and the financing of terrorist groups. Lastly, the action taken by other countries, such as Switzerland and the United Kingdom (UK), can be seen in their appointment of Special Envoys for the Sahel (PSC, 2014).

Indeed, the international actors have been very active in the Sahel, while they have recorded successes, particularly in combating insurgencies at the initial stage, their presence in the Sahel has also compromised the region's socio-political and security landscape. France, the major Western player in the Sahel with a political and commercial interest in the Francophone region, being the former colonial power, success in launching the anti-terrorist project has been mired with controversies. Malian Prime Minister, Choguel Kokalla Maiga, has accused France of complicity in the deteriorating state of Malian security due to the constant manner in which Paris continued to violate the military pact it had with Mali (Dinc & Donmez, 2022).

The military onslaught against the armed groups, led by the French, the G-5 forces and Takuba, the European military task force, in the Sahel has led to the transformation of the conflicts. The "renewed engagement in local conflicts has allowed jihadist militant groups to enlarge their scope of action, reassert their influence, remobilize, and gain resources to rebuild" (Nsaibia & Duhamel, 2021). The Islamist fundamentalists became more enraged to resist the offensives because of Paris' support of the Benghazi's separatist movements of 2011 and the eventual murder of the Libyan leader, Moumad Ghaddafi, by the French-led military operation. Kokalla Maiga reinforced the fact that the "security jam" by international actors in the region, including the 15, 209 UN peacekeeping forces, has not yielded peace and security; instead, armed attacks have increased, and the region is engulfed by the waves of political instability (Dinc & Donmez, 2022).

Humanitarian Crisis in the Sahel

Since the rise of terrorist groups of in the Sahel, most of the states considered as conflict zones such as Mali have become more securitised and militarised. The militarisation of the zone has a negative impact on elements of human security such as human rights, provision of social amenities and social protection. Some of the consequences of conflicts is the gruesome killings and displacements of civilians. As experienced in the Sahel, and elsewhere in Africa, "conflict disrupts rural livelihoods including agricultural and pastoral activities, transport and marketing among the affected communities. It has led to access constraints impeding the delivery of timely humanitarian assistance and development of sustainable livelihood-support assistance further aggravating the needs of the communities that are in most cases dealing with multi-layered shocks" (AU, 2022: 2).

In Niger, a series of large-scale killings perpetrated by the Islamic State in the Greater Sahara (ISGS) targeting civilians of Djerma and Tuareg ethnicity resulted in most of the deaths (Nsaibia & Duhamel, 2021). The number of people killed by ISGS accounted for 66% of all deaths from organised political violence in Niger in 2021, and an estimated 79% of the fatalities from violence targeted civilians (Nsaibia & Duhamel, 2021). According to these authors, the violence perpetrated by ISGS against Nigerians was triggered by several factors including retaliation tactics as many villages opposed the ISGS. For instance, in February 2020, a cross-section of people in Kaourakeri village ganged up against the ISGS; while in December 2020, villagers in Mogodyougou killed some ISGS tax collectors, in response, ISGD attacked the communities and killed many people. In Burkina Faso, the deadliest attack since the insurgency began occurred in June 2021 with a massacre in Solhan town, killing about 160 people (Nsaibia & Duhamel, 2021).

Attacks against civilians in the Sahel have been on regular intervals. While the armed groups have been responsible for the insecurity in the region, government security apparatus have also been using their access to arms to terrorise the people. According to Pye (2021), between January and May 2021, more civilians were killed by the government security forces than by the Islamic fundamentalists in Mali and Burkina Faso. States' acts of terror against their citizens have created hostilities between communities and the state, turning communities to Islamist forces for protection against state forces that have the legitimate responsibility of protecting the state and its entire population. For instance, in Mali, the attacks on the Fulani community by state forces turned the Fulani community into Jihadist groups for protection (Nsaibia & Duhamel, 2021). Apart from national security personnel, international troops such as the French Operation Barkhane, and the G5 Force, have been accused of human rights violations against locals (Nsaibia & Duhamel, 2021). The abuses varied from sexual assault, rape, and molestation of women and children, including deliberate attacks on civilians, particularly during operations. In Niger, two people were killed and 18 wounded after a French military convoy heading to Mali was blocked by protestors angry at the failure of French forces.

The challenges confronting the Sahel go beyond security, issues of corruption by the governments have triggered anger from the citizens, thereby becoming an instrument used by the Jihadist armed groups and other local militia operating in the region (Pye, 2021). Countries like Nigeria and Chad are particularly notorious for high levels of corruption. According to the 2020 Corruption Perceptions Index, out of 179 countries involved, Chad ranked 160, and Nigeria occupied the 149 most corrupt countries (Amnesty International 2020). Corruption makes effective governance difficult, diverts national income into private pockets and slows down the 'engine' of sustainable development. It distorts societal moral standards and social relations. Indeed, there is a strong link between political corruption and drug trafficking, and the Sahel has become a transit route for all kinds of trafficking, ranging from drugs to humans (Thurston, 2012). Government officials receive bribes at border posts and corrupt state security agencies, including immigration officials, continue to protect those involved in these illicit trades.

Food insecurity is another underlying human security issue exacerbated by climate change and violent conflicts over land and resources. The agricultural sector is a key driver of the economy in the region (Cooper, 2018). The region is rich in subsistence crops such as sorghum, millet, rice, cassava and their cash crops include cotton, generating employment opportunities for approximately 15 million people (Cooper, 2018). The dire climatic conditions have aggravated food insecurity and worsened the levels of human displacement in the zone.

According to the United Nations High Commission for Refugees (UNHCR), 2.5 million Sahelian people have been internally displaced since 2013. The highest number of IDPs is recorded in Burkina Faso, with more than 1.5 million by 2021: this is the highest since (UNHCR, 2021). As of 2021 more than 400 000 people have been displaced in Mali. In 2021, Niger recorded a 53% rise in IDPs from 2020 (UNHCR, 2021). In March 2021, between 20 000 and 30 000 civilians were forced to flee because of concurrent attacks in Bohoma, a village in Lac province of Chad, joining the 208 000 internally displaced persons (IDPs) and 13 900 refugees in the province (Akinola, 2021). The humanitarian situation in the Sahel has deteriorated; the COVID-19 pandemic, poverty and the effects of climate change all contribute to human insecurity, the most affected being women and children.

Humanitarian responses in the Sahel have been very militarised and politicised, creating gridlock for interventions. The local, national and international donor agencies and NGOs have been exposed to danger in their attempts to assist people in the conflict zones. The education sector has been negatively impacted by the incessant conflict in the region with about 5,000 schools non-active (AU, 2022). In 2019, 4.3 million people in Chad were affected by humanitarian crises and desperate for assistance, about 46.7% of the citizens were living below the poverty level, and 3.3 million were food insecure (OCHA, 2020). Of the 157 countries ranked in the 2019 global Human Capital Index, Chad occupied the last position, with 6.3 million Chadians living in extreme poverty. According to the AU, the funding for the Regional Refugee Response Plans for African refugee crises in the last five years was below 50 percent (AU, 2022: 5). This has been reflected in the dire humanitarian crisis experienced across Africa, including the Sahel.

Conflict: The Roles of Regional Organisation

There are a number of African-led interventions in the Sahel conflicts. The ongoing Malian conflict is a catalyst for numerous regional initiatives and strategies designed to promote peace, security, governance and development in the Sahel region. The African Union (AU), Economic Community of West African States (ECOWAS), and the G-5 Sahel have played a significant mediatory role in the bid to restore peace and order in the Sahel. For instance, the G5 alliance was specifically established to confront armed conflicts in the region, through the coordination of several initiatives aimed at promoting peace in the Sahel. as the initiative also aimed at finding inclusive governance solutions within each Sahel state which address the needs of the respective state, particularly in protecting civilians from terror (Walther, 2017). As applicable to all violent conflicts, civilians pay a high price and are always the most vulnerable during conflicts. Regional organisations tend to only act when the conflict has degenerated into a dire humanitarian crisis, and at that point, there would have been thousands of civilian casualties. This is where the effectiveness of the AU's early warning system is usually called into question.

There are a number of African-led interventions conducted by the AU and ECOWAS in Sahel countries such as Burkina Faso, Guinea, and Mali. In the case of Mali, the African-led International Support Mission to Mali (AFISMA), has played a role in combating insurgencies. In 2014, after the military had removed President Blaise Compaore of Burkina Faso and installed Lieutenant Colonel Isaac Zida as the interim leader, the military tried to defy the two weeks ultimatum given to the military to return power to the civilian administration and conduct an election within a year. Yacoub Zida initially dismissed the regional organisations' threats, but he later resigned from office in a power bargaining act that later saw him appointed as the Prime Minister by his successor, President Michel Kafando. Both former President of Nigeria, Goodluck Jonathan, and ex-ECOWAS boss, IBN Chambas have led peace missions to the Sahel on numerous occasions. ECOWAS has gone further to suspend Mali from the regional bloc and imposed sanctions on the country, including the members of the military regime. This has not argued well with many, who have accused the regional organisations of double standards, as other countries with similar military takeovers such as Guinea Bissau only got restricted sanctions, while the Colonel Paul Henri Damiba-led

Burkina Faso has also been suspended but no sanction was imposed by ECOWAS (VOA, 2022). The AU has been less active in response to the coups, while the UN has carefully been muted over the growing military interventions in the Sahel. Though many military regimes have cited poor governance, exclusive politics, poverty and rising insecurity as the reasons for the democratic reversals. However, the military has not fared better as cases of attacks continue, and no serious attempts have been made towards economic growth or democratisation. Despite all the multilateral interventions in the Sahel under several tags such as *Operation Serval*, *Operation Barkhane*, MINUSMA and MISAHEL, the region remains under the weight of precarious security challenges that continue to destabilise the region's economies and endanger human lives.

What is the implication of these to regional stability? Post-colonial Africa has played host to different types of violent conflicts, but the rate of the proliferation of armed conflict in the Sahel is of particular attention. Of more concern has been the abject destruction of lives and property, including the dilapidated state infrastructures. This has mandated the governments to spend more on the military, which limits funding for social infrastructures and the development of important sectors such as education, health and housing (see Akinola & Uzodike, 2015). This has also deepened the socio-economic crisis in a region already stretched by governance deficits. The effect of the conflict on the agricultural sector is particularly enormous. Farmers have been killed and farms destroyed, and many have fled the crisis zone and joined the already over-populated refugee camps in several areas in the Sahel. This engendered food insecurity and drove the region into possible famine in countries like Burkina Faso and part of Mali. Government incomes have also been reduced due to the inability to generate tax in conflict-affected areas. Several international donor organisations have left and the few ones around are struggling to implement programmes in an environment of warfare, political instability and humanitarian crisis.

Conclusion

The article has located the armed conflict in the Sahel in both historical and contemporary discourses and examined the root causes of the conflict. It has also used case study analysis to establish the deepening of socio-economic and political crises in the Sahel. The study exposes the divergent pattern of conflict and the motivation for violence, which ranges from struggles for political power and regime consolidation to personal gain, and the lust for ethnic and religious hegemony. Democratisation in Africa, which is seen as the antidote to both internal resurrections and external aggressions, has deepened poverty, structural violence, identity assertiveness and the politicisation of ethnic groups. Poverty remains closely associated with conflict. Democracy has actually failed in the Sahel; thus, the rate of democratic decline remains highly staggering. While the military, like that of Mali, claimed to have intervened to protect democracy and restore order, military intervention—as proven across Africa—does not have the 'magic touch' to address the underlying problems, which have subjected the region to extreme poverty and low human development, have triggered, conflict and violence in the Sahel.

The weakness of states' authority, or its absence, as the case may be, has led to the outbreak of conflict and its protracted nature. The expansionist character of conflict and threats experienced in the region due to border porosity have made border control to combat trafficking, a regional security concern. To stem the tide, the national and regional partners must begin to have a serious reflection on information exchanges and joint surveillance measures. The region remains highly vulnerable and violent conflicts have deepened in the face of the exit of France and the reconfiguration of power dynamics in the region. Longstanding disputes make the Sahel a fatal ground for armed militia and a haven for jihadist groups to establish operations in public spaces and areas that are outside governments' control and authority. As reinforced in the main text, there are many communities in the Sahel that have been totally cut off from the government, lacking any physical representation of government. The armed groups have seized this opportunity to freely operate in these spaces and established. This calls for more responsibilities on the part of governments to implement responsive and effective governance in the Sahel.

In Africa, the political elites live differently and are unmoved by the interests of the masses. States' sensitivity to the plights of the citizens could curtail insurgencies and massive hostilities directed at states in the region. This could limit the high number of IDPs and the staggering number of people that require humanitarian assistance. There is a need for the government, in partnership with the private sectors and civil society actors to address several underlying issues such as food and human insecurity, particularly the lack of basic necessities of life such as water and basic infrastructures. As strongly reinforced by Pye (2021), a focus on good governance will be a key strategic approach to ending conflict and instability in the Sahel, and the EU-Africa strategy should be integrated governance and good governance strategies (Pye, 2021). Pye's recommendations are built on the approach that encourages reconciliation and building strong relationships between the governments, civil society and communities. While the need for partnership is not misplaced, African governments have generally been less proactive in driving their own developmental process, surrendering the initiative to foreign actors. It was high time for African elites to take lead in the future direction of their countries. Indeed, foreign actors may assist, but they should not occupy the driving seat in the drafting and implementation of policies on development, including efforts at peacemaking and peacebuilding.

Indeed, a lack of governance and accountability accounts for the military incursions in politics across the region and also contributes to an increase in the conflicts in the Sahel. African governments are noted for their poor conflict prevention and management. This is where the regional bodies, particularly the AU should use the platform of the early warning system to forewarn and promptly act to address both root and immediate causes of conflict. Other preventative measures such as negotiations and timely mediation can be employed to douse attention and evade the outbreak of law and order.

In cases where the actors were unable to peacefully resolve issues and took to arms, regional organisations should implement the responsibility to protect (R2P) clause in the Charter of the AU and protect the civilian population—who would be at the risk of humanitarian disaster—and enforce peace and security in the troubled zones. As shown in the study, insecurity and violent conflict in one state could easily spill over into another. Thus, the faster such conflict is curtailed, the more secured the region is. One of the recurrent causes of conflict, ethnic hostility, results from exclusive governance. While this is linked to the colonial legacy, African leaders should endeavour to jettison the temptation to mobilise ethnic sentiments for political gains. Ethnic groups are not the problem, the challenge comes from the politicisation of the groups. African leaders should see opportunities in African diversity and explore its benefits for the good of everyone.

REFERENCES

Abubakar, A., & Levs, J. (2014, May 6). 'I will sell them,' Boko Haram leader says of kidnapped Nigerian girls. CNN. https://edition.cnn.com/2014/05/05/world/africa/nigeria-abducted-girls/index.html

African Centre for the Study and Research on Terrorism (ACSRT). (2022). *Coups d'état and Political Instability in the Western Sahel: Implications for the Fight against Terrorism and Violent Extremism*. AU/PAPS/ACSRT/PP/002 Policy Paper. https://reliefweb.int/report/world/coups-detat-and-political-instability-sahel-implications-fight-against-terrorism-and-violent-extremism-april-2022

Akinola, A. O. (2021, September 9). Poverty is the driving force behind conflicts in Africa. *IOL*. https://www.iol.co.za/news/politics/opinion/poverty-is-the-driving-force-behind-conflicts-in-africa-8aaf2c69-f418-4a5e-b5f5-3c98e0ba9737

Akinola, A. O., & Uzodike, U. O. (2014). The threat of 'Boko Haram' terrorism and Niger delta militancy to security and development in Africa: From myth to reality. *Ghandi Marg, 35*(3), 391–417.

Aljazeera. (2013, August 13). *Timeline: Mali since independence*. https://www.aljazeera.com/news/2013/8/13/timeline-mali-since-independence.

Aljazeera. (2022, June 18). *State controls just 60 percent of Burkina Faso: ECOWAS mediator*. https://www.aljazeera.com/news/2022/6/18/state-controls-only-60-percent-of-burkina-faso-mediator

Amnesty International. (2022). *Corruption perceptions index 2020*. https://www.transparency.org/en/cpi/2020/index/cod

AU. (2022). African Union Humanitarian Summit and Pledging Conference," Addis Ababa: African Union. https://au.int/sites/default/files/newsevents/workingdocuments/40515-wd-HHS52399_E_Theme_2_Addressing_food_security_and_nutrition_challenges.pdf

Ayoob, M. (2003). *The Third World Security Predicament: State Making, regional conflict and international system*. Oxford University Press.

Baudias V., Bouegrous, A., & O'dreiscoll, D. (2021). *Conflict mediation and peacebuilding in the Sahel: The role of Maghreb countries in an African framework*. Stockholm International Peace Research Institute.

Briscoe, I. (2014). *Crime after Jihad: Armed groups, the state and illicit business in post-conflict Mali*. https://globalinitiative.net/wp-content/uploads/2018/01/Clingendael_Crime-after-Jihad.pdf

Cilliers, J. (2003). Terrorism and Africa. *African Security Review, 12*(4), 91–103.

Cooper, R. (2018). *Natural Resources Management Strategies in the Sahel*. https://assets.publishing.service.gov.uk/media/5c6acc2340f0b61a196aa83a/453_Sahel_Natural_Resources_Management.pdf

Dinc, B., & Donmez, U. (2022). Exclusive interview: Malian premier says France responsible for Mali's security situation, economic woes. *Anadolu Agency*, 20

February, https://www.aa.com.tr/en/africa/exclusive-interview-malian-premier-says-france-responsible-for-mali-s-security-situation-economic-woes/2495064

Faluyi, O., Khan, S., & Akinola, A. O. (2019). *Boko Haram's terrorism and the Nigerian state: Federalism*. Springer International Publishing.

Keita, K., & Henk, D. (1998). *Conflict and conflict resolution in the Sahel: The Tuareg insurgency in Mali*. Strategic Studies Institute. US Army War College. http://www.jstor.com/stable/resrep11304

Lacher, W. (2012). *Organized Crime and Conflict in the Sahel- Sahara region*. https://www.swp-berlin.org/publications/products/fachpublikationen/sahel_sahara_2012_lac.pdf

Ledererun, Edith M. (2021, July 24) UN experts: Africa became hardest hit by terrorism this year. https://apnews.com/article/middle-east-africa-health-coronavirus-pandemic-united-nations-16cecaf2e97ed54dc5116f760a31f4db

Lucky I., Enwo-Irem, I. N., Ani, U. S. & Eke, J. U. (2021). *AU-ECOWAS Intervention in Burkina Faso Political Conflict in 2014*. https://doi.org/10.31920/2050-4306/2021/10n3a5

Nsaibia, H., & Duhamel, J. (2021). Sahel 2021: Communal wars, broken ceasefires, and shifting frontlines. *The Armed Conflict Location & Event Data Project (ACLED)*. https://acleddata.com/2021/06/17/sahel-2021-communal-wars-broken-ceasefires-and-shifting-frontlines/

OCHA (2020). Chad—Country profile (September 2019). https://www.humanitarianresponse.info/en/operations/chad/document/chad-country-profile-september-2019

Peace and Security Council (PSC). (2014). Peace and security council report. *Institute for Security Studies, 58*; https://issafrica.s3.amazonaws.com/site/uploads/PSCMay_14Eng.pdf

Pye, Katherine (2021) The Sahel Europe's forever war? Brussels: Centre for European Reform.

Rao, S. (2014). *Conflict analysis of Mauritania*. GSDRC, University of Birmingham.

RFI. (2021). *Two killed, 18 wounded as protestors in Niger clash with French military convoy*. https://www.rfi.fr/en/africa/20211128-two-killed-18-wounded-as-protestors-in-niger-clash-with-french-military-convoy-sahel-barkhane

Thurston, A. (2012, September 24). *For corruption, few places worse than the Sahel*. https://theglobalobservatory.org/2012/09/for-corruption-few-places-worse-than-the-sahel/

UNHCR. (2021). Decade of Sahel conflict leaves 2.5 million people displaced. https://www.unhcr.org/news/briefing/2022/1/61e137ac4/decade-sahel-conflict-leaves-25-million-people-displaced.html

UNSC. (2021). "Report of the Secretary-General on the activities of the United Nations Office for West Africa and the Sahel", S/2021/612, https://digitallibrary.un.org/record/3930688#record-files-collapse-header

Voice of America (VOA). (2022, February 21). *ECOWAS Suspends Burkina Faso's membership.* https://www.voanews.com/a/ecowas-suspends-burkina-faso-s-membership-/6417087.html

Walther, O. (2017). *Wars and conflicts in the Sahara-Sahel* (West African Papers, N°10). OECD.

CHAPTER 9

The Resurgence of Military Coups in Africa: The Case of West Africa and the Sahel

Gwinyai Regis Taruvinga

INTRODUCTION

Military interventions on the African continent have been widely debated within the academic realm. It was expected that, following the process of democratisation that swept across Africa in the 1950s, events such as *coup d'états* would be few and far between. When Ghana attained independence from colonial rule in 1957, the belief of many was that the continent would move towards a successful period of democratic freedom; however, this did not transpire instead the early period of independence on the African continent was marred by several events that resulted in democratic reversals. Military coups on the African continent are not a new phenomenon. Countries such as Togo in 1963 and Nigeria in 1966 experienced military coups which were proof of the challenges that the

G. R. Taruvinga (✉)
Wits Humanities Graduate Centre, University of the Witwatersrand, Johannesburg, South Africa
e-mail: Gwinyai.Taruvinga@wits.ac.za

© The Author(s), under exclusive license to Springer Nature Switzerland AG 2023
A. O. Akinola, *Contemporary Issues on Governance, Conflict and Security in Africa*,
https://doi.org/10.1007/978-3-031-29635-2_9

African continent faced with the democratisation processes which many hoped would have been successful African continent.

West Africa and the Sahel have experienced military interventions due to deteriorating economic conditions, extractive institutions and incumbent leaders' abuse of power. Concerning economic conditions, it has been reported that in Mali, for example, previous governments had failed to successfully develop the country economically which culminated in the military coups that occurred in 2020. The International Monetary Fund (IMF) noted that the citizenry in the country grew tired of the government's inability to fight corruption and fight terrorism thus creating conditions that would make a coup inevitable (IMF, 2021). As this chapter will allude to, conditions within a country such as lack of employment or poor economic conditions can cause deficits in the populace's expectations. In many cases, this allows groups such as military entities to intervene as the case study of this chapter will show.

This chapter examines the resurgence of military *coup d'états* within this region and argues that the failure by African countries, in this case, countries in the Western Sahel, have failed to adhere to democratic principles and this has allowed environments in these countries to be conducive for military coups to take place. West Africa and the Sahel have experienced more coups than other regions. This chapter further examines the resurgence of military coups in this region and explores the root causes and emerging realities that have made military regimes attractive during this epoch. It acknowledges that socio-economic factors and political instability motivate military interventions, but also argues that regional bodies should adopt stronger measures to promote adherence to democratic principles.

The chapter discusses an overview of *coup d'états* within the African continent. This aspect is important as it sheds light on how coups have been a regular occurrence on the continent for time immemorial. In addition to this, chapter further applies this general perspective to West Africa and the Sahel and subsequently link this notion to the resurgence of military coups in the region.

Military Coups in Africa

Several African countries, including Nigeria and Ghana, gained independence from colonial rule in the late 1950s and early 1960s. It was expected that African countries would follow the trajectory of their

Western counterparts and adopt democracy as an ideology. Samuel Huntington framed the famous term *third wave of democracy* which spoke to a new era of democratic rule. While there are various definitions of democracy, a common definition, especially in the African context, involves elections, governance and a peaceful change in government.

Huntington (1991) notes that modern democracy is 'a democracy of the nation-state' which is strongly linked to sovereignty and a community of people in one nation. In essence, democracy is associated with a country's ability to oversee how it is governed without interference from external forces. This was important within the African context as colonial governments created systems that marginalised the majority at the expense of the minority. This was evident especially in countries like Rwanda where the exit of the colonial government resulted in unrest among local citizens. The Rwandan case can be understood through the 1994 genocide between the Hutu and the Tutsi groups. The end of colonial rule, therefore, aimed to serve as a catalyst for an inclusive form of rule. However, this was not the case as military coups became the norm in many countries.

Military coups violate the norms of democracy as the leader who assumes power due to a coup gains power through unjust means. Several reasons have been advanced for military coups, including debilitating economic conditions and the government's failure to adhere to democratic principles (Onwumechili, 1998). Military interventions are regarded by their perpetrators as a means to rectify governments' errors.

While there is no consensus on why coups were common in Africa following independence, it is clear that democracy was under threat in many regions. Democracies in countries such as Burundi, the Republic of Congo (Brazzaville), Nigeria and Sierra Leone were all threatened at some point by military interventions (Onwumechili, 1998), negatively impacting the democratisation processes. For example, democratisation only lasted a few months in Burundi, while it was "stillborn" in Nigeria (Onwumechili, 1998). Historical analysis of military coups shows that democracy was under threat from the powerful military from an early stage.

One of the earliest coups occurred in Sudan in November 1958. Led by Lieutenant General Ahmed Abboud and Major General Wahhab, the coup was motivated by the army's belief that the Sudanese civilian government had failed to turn the country's economic fortunes around (Onwumechili, 1998). This case speaks to how the military intervenes in the name of altering a country's trajectory. It is estimated that by 1975, 20 of the continent's 41 states were under the control of military or civil-military groups (Decalo, 1990). While this demonstrates the military's strength in some African countries, it also highlights the threat posed to the democratisation process.

Various theories have been advanced to understand why coups occur. The *development thesis* posits that coups occur because the military intervene on behalf of citizens who are unable to challenge the government (Onwumechili, 1998). In this case, the military serves as a nationally organised group that purports to represent citizens' interests. This theory is associated with the military intervention in Zimbabwe in November 2017. The military claimed that it intervened because the lives of Zimbabweans had become extremely difficult, especially on the economic front, under President Robert Mugabe (Tendi, 2020). The Zimbabwe National Army (ZNA) thus used Zimbabwe's economic fortunes to end Mugabe's rule.

From a historical perspective, the *development thesis* played an important role in previous coups in Africa. Economic woes resulted in coups in the following countries:

Ghana—In 1966, General Ankrah cited the government of Dr Kwame Nkrumah's failure to address economic issues and the steep rise in the cost of living as the reason for the coup.

In Liberia, Sergeant Samuel Doe led a coup in 1980 that was driven by the belief that the Tolbert government had overseen unequal distribution of the nation's economic resources (Onwumechili, 1998).

In these cases, the army intervened due to poor economic conditions. In Ghana, it was believed that under Nkrumah's rule, the economy of the country was below par. Under his tenure, Nkrumah was accused of mismanaging the economy even though the country was deemed by many to be wealthy (Welch, 1968). Nkrumah's perceived mismanagement of the economy by the Ghanaian army provided an opportunity for the army to forcibly remove him from the presidency of Ghana. One of the challenges Ghana faced from an economic perspective are best summed up by the famous phrase "*seek ye first the political kingdom and all things will be added to it*". Due to Ghana's engagement with the International Monetary Fund (IMF), the country would be at loggerheads with institutions that deviated from Nkrumah's political and economic beliefs—which led to a poorly run economy (Tignor, 2016). The state of the economy would be key to the army forcibly removing him.

While many would argue that military coups violate democratic principles, it should be noted that coups have also occurred due to a perceived lack of democracy by the government in the eyes of the military. An example of this would be the November 2017 military intervention that resulted in the ouster of the late Robert Mugabe. The coup announcer noted that one of the key reasons the military was intervening in the country was to address a situation that had the potential to result in anarchy within the country (Tendi, 2017). The argument by the army was that under the leadership of Mugabe there was a threat that the country could fall into anarchy as the economy was not performing accordingly. The army felt that an intervention would arrest the perceived poor governance as perceived by the military.

Other reasons for military intervention can be linked to the *guardian perspective,* which notes that the military is responsible for maintaining peace within a country and is obliged to intervene when an incumbent leader refuses to cede power after losing an election. The army intervenes to uphold the principles of democracy enshrined within the country's constitution (Onwumechili, 1998). It is thus regarded as justified in staging a coup. Further reasons cited by coup leaders relate to the lack of law and order within a country, and unlawful acts on the part of the government (Onwumechili, 1998). Again, the army's interference would be regarded as justified under such circumstances.

Some military coups in Africa have occurred due to ethnic divisions. For example, in Nigeria the failed coups in February 1976 and April 1990 were believed to be linked to ethnic tensions. The former was led by Lieutenant Colonel Buka Suka Dimka (middle belt region) with the aim of reinstating General Yakubu Gowon[1] who had been deposed in 1975 by soldiers of northern Hausa extraction (Onwumechili, 1998). Lastly, military coups have occurred due to personal ambition. The coup that led to General Idi Amin Dada's reign in Uganda is one such example. It is believed that he did not have the intention of ruling Uganda but staged a coup due to fears that Milton Obote would remove him from his position as the head of the Ugandan Army (Onwumechili, 1998). In such a scenario as this one, it would appear that General Idi Amin was

---

[1] General Gowon was from Nigeria's middle belt region.

ill-prepared to govern as his ascendancy to power was driven by power retention, this might have had ramifications on his tenure as leader of Uganda. General Amin's tenure shows what transpires in the event that a military figure abuses power to attain leadership in a country.

West Africa and Sahel Military Interventions

Although military coups have long dominated the narrative within Africa, West Africa and the Sahel have experienced more than other regions. In recent times, coups have occurred in Chad, Mali, Guinea and Sudan (Mwai, 2022). It is argued that poor living conditions were a major cause of military interventions. In 2020 for example, Mali's economy went through a recession due to the impacts of the COVID-19 pandemic, poor agricultural outputs and socio-political crises (World Bank, 2022). In addition to this, the WB, in 2019, stated that the poverty level in the country was 42.3% and this was concentrated in rural areas (World Bank, 2022). These figures from Mali show the standard of living in the country was dire and this could be seen as a factor that has led to military interventions within the country. Moreover, in Africa, where many countries suffer from poor economic conditions, a coup is often a harbinger of more military interventions (Mwai, 2022). This could explain why West Africa and the Sahel have experienced several coups.

Sudan has witnessed a total of 17 military coups, of which six were successful (Mwai, 2022), giving substance to the argument that one coup leads to another. Following months of protest by citizens, Omar al-Bashir was removed from power in 2019. The irony is that al-Bashir himself assumed leadership through a military coup in 1989 (Mwai, 2022). This renders the adage "a coup begets another coup" a reality in understanding the cycle of coups in West Africa and the Sahel. In Sudan, the army also intervened on the back of protests by the citizenry. In many cases, popular uprisings driven by people at a grassroots level are successful if the army gives its stamp of approval (Mwai, 2022), as armies in these regions are highly influential.

Nigeria's post-colonial history is littered with military coups. In the years following independence, eight military coups occurred between January 1966 and General Sani Abacha's takeover in 1993 (Mwai, 2022). Several reasons can be attributed to these military coups such as ethnic hostilities and the failure of nationalist movements to fully implement their agenda within a post-colonial setup. The Nigerian can be strongly linked to the challenges that were faced by countries that had gained independence (Huntington, 1991). The end of colonialism, as mentioned earlier, was meant to promote democracy but instead several democratic reversals were as in this case.

In 2020, the Malian army launched a coup to overthrow President Ibrahim Boubacar Keita which was received well by the citizenry. The army promised to bring about political change but instead proved to embody the very tendencies it had purported to stand against (Haidara, 2021). The army using societal ills to intervene only to further its agenda has also been a recurring theme. Nine months after the 2020 Malian coup, another coup was staged, with some authors describing it as a 'coup within a coup' (Haidara, 2021). The 2020 coup resulted in Mali being suspended from ECOWAS as well as the imposition of economic sanctions which targeted some individual military elites, highlighting the importance of regional bodies in upholding the principles of democracy.

The coup in Mali has significant ramifications for the fight against other threats confronting the region. It has been noted that it was a major threat to the fight against terrorism, particularly Jihadism, which was expected to flourish due to weak political leadership in the region (Edu-Afful, 2021). The coup went against the norms and principles that underpin the 2001 ECOWAS protocols on democracy and good governance which speak strongly against military intervention (Edu-Afful, 2021), as well as the principles espoused by the AU and neighbouring countries. It was also feared that the Malian coup would set a precedent for the region. Neighbouring countries such as Burkina Faso, Chad and Sudan also experienced military coups which many linked to events in Mali. As noted earlier, Jihadi groups would benefit greatly from an unstable Mali (Edu-Afful, 2021) and the coup in that country could enable other radical groups within the region to regroup, presenting a major security threat, since many of the states in the region are deemed to be weak. In June 2021, 160 lives were lost to terrorist attacks in the village of Solhan in Burkina Faso, and attacks were also reported in central Mali (Edu-Afful, 2021). This is a clear indication that military interventions can have impacts that affect countries in the wider region.

Burkina Faso's coup was the fourth in 18 months in the West African and Sahel region. Coups also occurred in Chad and twice in Mali, once again demonstrating their domino effects on other countries. Some military coups also have their roots in historical events. The coup in Burkina Faso can be traced back to 1966. Prominent leaders such as Thomas

Sankara assumed leadership of the country through military coups but were also removed from power using the same method (Thurston, 2022). The main beneficiary of military coups in Burkina Faso was Blaise Compaore who was eventually overthrown by a popular uprising in 2014 (Thurston, 2022). These historical events have no doubt contributed to current events within the country. Security all but collapsed due to the coups and it has been argued that Sahelian jihadists have taken advantage of this instability (Thurston, 2022). While jihadists played some part in the challenges in Burkina Faso and Mali, it is important to focus on the role played by military coups in creating instability.

A Resurgence of Military Coups?

The resurgence of military coups in the West African region has occurred despite the AU and ECOWAS speaking out against such interventions. The lack of democracy in some West African countries is a major cause. When democracy, which is meant to safeguard countries from coups, fails, coups are a likely consequence.

Coup leaders often argue that they aim to restore democracy. However, military regimes on the African continent have performed worse than civilian governments (Akinola, 2021) and rarely result in positive progress. The Malian case comes to mind, as one coup almost immediately led to another one solidifying the standpoint that in some cases military coups are proof of a lack of progress as a governance mechanism. The African continent's model of democracy is based on that of the Western world. However, freedom of speech, a hallmark of this model that enables citizens to critique the state is often frowned upon or met with heavy resistance by the state apparatus (Akinola, 2021). This disjuncture between the citizenry and the state has contributed greatly to the resurgence of military coups in the West African region.

To fully understand the resurgence of military coups in this region, it is important to analyse previous events. Africa has experienced more military interventions than any other continent. Nigeria experienced eight military coups between 1966 and 1993, and Burundi 11, while Sierra Leone experienced three coups between 1967 and 1968 and five between 1992 and 1997. Ghana has witnessed eight coups, with Kwame Nkrumah being removed as a result of the 1966 military intervention (Mwai, 2022). Military coups are, therefore, not a new phenomenon within Africa. In

2017, 13 coups were recorded globally, with all but one (Myanmar) on the African continent (Mwai, 2022).

Between 1960 and 1969, the continent witnessed 26 successful military coups, with 18 successful ones from 1970 to 1979 and 16 between 1990 and 1999 (Mwai, 2022). This highlights the challenges experienced by democracy. In the current decade, there have been successful coups in Chad, Mali, Guinea and Sudan while there were failed attempts in Niger and Sudan (Mwai, 2022). The current decade has seen a rise in military attempts which again proves that the continent continues to struggle with the role of the military, especially in the West African region.

In addition to the challenge of implementing democratic principles, it has been noted that the lack of unity in the international community has contributed to the rise in military interventions. United Nations (UN) Secretary-General, Antonio Guterres, noted that this is reflected in the reaction to military coups (Mwai, 2022). Although regional bodies such as ECOWAS have condemned coups the rest of the international community tends to shy away from castigating military regimes. Bodies such as the UN did not speak against the Malian coup which violates the norms of the institution. The involvement of countries such as France and Russia, who are permanent members of the Security Council, might be one of the reasons why the UN did not speak out against the military intervention that occurred in Mali. The resultant culture of impunity by the international community through organisations such as the UN results in more coups, as witnessed in the West African and Sahel regions (Mwai, 2022).

The living conditions in some of the countries in West Africa and the Sahel have also contributed to the resurgence of military coups. Poverty and poor economic conditions coupled with a lack of democracy cause frustration among the populace that the military often takes advantage of (Mwai, 2002). The resurgence of military coups also highlights the lack of regional responses from various African institutions. Although bodies such as the AU and ECOWAS have been clear in their condemnation of coups, in many cases they have failed to condemn constitutional amendments (Ani, 2021). This is important in understanding the resurgence of military coups in the West African region because, as in the case of Guinea, such amendments lead to unrest as leaders attempt to solidify their tenure as president in violation of the constitution.

In Guinea, the AU and ECOWAS failed to condemn President Conde's action in amending the constitution to extend his tenure. This violated Article 23(5) of the AU Charter on Democracy, Elections and

Governance (Ani, 2021). Citizens responded by engaging in protest action. Such scenarios often create power vacuums that the military exploits to stage coups. It is, therefore, important for regional bodies to apply the same energy that is used to condemn coups to castigate leaders who subvert the will of the people by abusing the constitution. The resurgence of coups in West Africa can also be attributed to weak national institutions. As noted in the case of Guinea, some African leaders have used this situation to solidify their position (Munshi & Schipani, 2021). The Guinea example shows what transpires when power is centralised in the hands of an individual, this eventually leads to unrest which is the breeding ground for military interventions.

Conclusion

This chapter analysed the factors that have contributed to the resurgence of military coups in Africa, with a focus on West Africa and the Sahel. These include dire economic straits, weak institutions and a perceived lack of democracy. Democracy entails that political leaders should uphold and abide by the constitution and when leaders fail to do so, citizens stage protests as seen in Guinea and other West African countries. Armies often step in to fill in the gap when an elected government fails to meet the needs of the populace. This chapter drew on examples of various countries such as Guinea and Mali where the military intervened when a civilian government was incapacitated.

One of the key factors that have resulted in the resurgence of coups has been the levels of poverty in West African countries. Many coup conspirators have stated that they aimed to address such challenges; however, little change ensued after they seized power. Thus, one of the biggest challenges is that the leaders of military coups do not honour their promises to change the fortunes of the citizenry.

It is also important to highlight that institutions are fundamental to the governance of any country. When institutions are captured and abused by leaders, there are significant ramifications. As seen in countries like Guinea, regional bodies such as the AU and ECOWAS need to do more to condemn violations of democratic principles to ensure that the environment in West Africa, and indeed Africa, is not conducive to military interventions.

References

Akinola, A. O. (2021). *The sudden proliferation of coups in West Africa and the Sahel bodes ill for the democratic project in Africa.* https://www.dailymaverick.co.za/article/2021-10-06-the-sudden-proliferation-of-coups-in-west-africa-and-the-sahel-bodes-ill-for-the-democratic-project-in-africa/

Ani, N. C. (2021). *Coup resurgence in Africa: The pitfalls of a regional response.* https://www.accord.org.za/analysis/coup-resurgence-in-africa-the-pitfalls-of-a-regional-response/

Decalo, S. (1990). *Coups and army rule in Africa: Motivations and constraints.* Yale University Press.

Edu-Afful, F. (2021). *Implications of Mali's latest coup for Sahel and West Africa.* https://www.accord.org.za/analysis/implications-of-malis-latest-coup-for-sahel-and-west-africa/

Haidara, B. (2021). *Inside Mali's coup within a coup.* https://theconversation.com/inside-malis-coup-within-a-coup-161621

Huntington, S. P. (1991). *The third wave: Democratization in the late twentieth century.* Norman.

IMF. (2021). IMF Executive Board Concludes Second and Third Review Under the Extended Credit Facility Arrangement for Mali. https://elibrary.imf.org/view/journals/002/2021/067/article-A002-en.xml

Munshi, N., & Schipani, A. (2021). *'Failure of democracy': Why are coups on the rise in Africa?* https://www.ft.com/content/a669c8e3-a744-445c-b613-9ff83059c90c

Mwai, P. (2022). Are military takeovers on the rise in Africa? https://www.bbc.com/news/world-africa-46783600

Onwumechili, C. (1998). *African democratization and military coups.* Greenwood Publishing Group.

Tendi, M. (2020). The motivations and dynamics of Zimbabwe's 2017 military coup. *African Affairs, 119*(474), 39–67. https://academic.oup.com/afraf/article/119/474/39/5607894

Thurston, J. A. (2022). *After a fourth coup in West Africa, it's time to rethink international response.* https://theconversation.com/after-a-fourth-coup-in-west-africa-its-time-to-rethink-international-response-175991

Tignor, R. (2016). *Ghana: Lessons from Nkrumah's fallout with his economic advisor.* https://theconversation.com/ghana-lessons-from-nkrumahs-fallout-with-his-economic-adviser-53233

Welch, C. (1968). Ghana: The Politics of Military Withdrawal. *Current History, 54*(318), 95–100. https://www.jstor.org/stable/45311838

World Bank. (2022). *The World Bank in Mali.* https://www.worldbank.org/en/country/mali/overview

CHAPTER 10

Media and Election Disputes in Nigeria

N. Oluwafemi 'Femi' Mimiko and Harrison Adewale Idowu

INTRODUCTION

It is a truism that as human society became more complicated and increasingly differentiated, direct democracy became increasingly impracticable in the Greek city states. This provided the context for the transition from direct to representative democracy, with the latter predicated on periodic elections to choose those who rule on behalf of the *demos*. Elections are thus a mechanism that is consequent of the need to reflect the defining principle of popular participation in governance which defined democracy when human society was less complex. This accounts for the primacy of elections in modern liberal democracies and explains why free, fair and transparent elections have become a measure of the robustness of democracy in any country (Idowu & Mimiko, 2020; Mimiko, 2017). Thus,

N. O. 'Femi' Mimiko (✉) · H. A. Idowu
Obafemi Awolowo University, Ile-Ife, Nigeria
e-mail: nomimiko@oauife.edu.ng

H. A. Idowu
Adekunle Ajasin University, Akungba-Akoko, Nigeria

© The Author(s), under exclusive license to Springer Nature Switzerland AG 2023
A. O. Akinola, *Contemporary Issues on Governance, Conflict and Security in Africa*,
https://doi.org/10.1007/978-3-031-29635-2_10

elections not only legitimise the government that is their by-product, but the democratic system as a whole. They are one of the democratic institutions that have endured and they enhance social stability in that they guarantee acquisition of power within a regulated context broadly subscribed to by the citizenry of a polity. Indeed, studies have shown that the integrity of elections is fundamental to a peaceful transfer of power in democratic societies (Idowu & Mimiko, 2020).

Nonetheless, elections alone do not equate democracy (Mimiko, 2007). It is for this reason that conceptualisations of democracy highlight core principles rather than institutional frameworks (Ake, 2000; Dahl, 1971, 1989; Mimiko, 2017). Irrespective of the institutional forms by which it is manifested, a conventional democratic system must be constructed on a platform of popular participation in governance, public accountability, majority rule and respect for minority rights. While transparent elections are a condition for democracy in modern times, they are not a sufficient condition. Democracy is a holistic process, a bouquet as it were of several elements that underscore the fact that it is at best a journey rather than a destination. Yet, as has been demonstrated at different times in different places, elections can make or mar an otherwise well-structured democratisation agenda. This has been the experience in Nigeria where mismanagement of national elections served as the trigger for the collapse of democratisation programmes in 1966, 1983 and 1993.

By their very nature, elections involve mass action by the adult population as candidates or voters. The electoral process, in all its complexity and multidimensionality, needs to be widely and effectively communicated through the mass media. Thus, the media is central to the electoral process in any country. Nigeria's 1999 Constitution (as amended) gives effect to this reality in Section 22:

> The press, radio, television and other agencies of the mass media shall at all times be free to uphold the fundamental objectives contained in this Chapter and uphold the responsibility and accountability of the Government to the people. (Federal Republic of Nigeria, 1999: 27)

As noted in this document, a critical measure of the effectiveness of the mass media in a democracy is its ability to hold government to account. However, informal platforms of engagement, like the town crier (the traditional communication platform) and in more contemporary times, the ubiquitous "okada" (commercial motorcycle) riders tend to be marginalised and neglected in contemporary discussions on the media's impact on the electoral process. In rural areas, where they are more clearly defined or differentiated, they lack the infrastructure required for the operation of the more formal media; nonetheless, they continue to serve the neglected poor. Less formal media outlets are a veritable tool to share information, and in the process, canalise the hopes, aspirations, fears and frustrations of the segments of the citizenry that patronise them, including the voting population.

While mapping such media outlets is beyond the scope of this chapter, it should be undertaken to reveal their influence on the nation's electoral process. What is certain is that the sensibilities of the often-taken-for-granted citizens who patronise the informal media play a critical role in determining whether electoral disputes are peaceful and peaceable or conflictual and violent. Disputes are endemic to electoral systems across the world and formal processes exist to resolve them. The public space is by nature a contested terrain. Disputes over elections tend to be few and far between in polities with long established democratic practice and tested institutions such as the United States (US) that enjoy effective election management systems. Beyond Florida in 1996, and Ohio in 2000, disputes in US presidential elections are rare. Only, the 2016 and 2020 elections stand apart in modern US history in bearing the imprimatur of conflict, sustained controversy and bickering that was deep enough to warrant the extant narrative of democratic reversal in the country.

However, in less institutionalised terrains the entire electoral process including administration of the voters' roll, balloting, counting of ballots, declaration of results and the transfer of power (or lack of it) are veritable arenas of conflict. The extent to which they are managed peaceably depends to a large extent on the media's orientation with regard to elections that is itself a consequence of the character of the media, and the broader socio-political context within which it operates. Against this backdrop, it is apposite to examine the nature of the Nigerian media, and its impact on the country's electoral process. Given the media's overriding influence in shaping perceptions, this chapter also examines how this influence is exercised in relation to electoral disputes in Nigeria, such that they do not degenerate into violence. In this regard, we focus on the role of the media in the 2019 general elections.

The chapter draws on the political economy framework as it enables a robust analysis of the complex interaction of political and social elements in deconstructing the relationship between the media and electoral disputes in Nigeria. Complementing this is the social responsibility (media) theory, which posits that the media in its totality, but especially in the manner in which its mandate is executed, constitutes the fountain of social responsibility. It is therefore obliged to report truthfully in a manner that promotes social stability (Oboh, 2015: 72–83) and the public good.

The Nature of the Nigerian Media

The mass media in Nigeria evolved in the context of the anti-colonial struggle, with its ownership structure largely dominated by the pioneering elites of the decolonisation struggle. It was therefore confrontational, and revolutionary in nature, even though its audience tended to be restricted to the small elite. It was, however, not particularly ideologically situated, as the overriding aim was to rid the country of the British colonists rather than a desire to substitute their political economy with something markedly different. Indeed, what eventually played out was the inheritance of the colonial structures by a new class of educated elite, which had no compelling desire to deviate from same as they served their purpose of dominating the post-colonial state and society. This neo-colonial formation has proven to be enduring, defined by a local economy that is anchored on the global economy in the same way that it was under colonialism. Nigeria remains a supplier of primary products and a net importer of finished goods, a situation that has been further consolidated under globalisation, effectively the current phase of global capitalism. The political system remains largely restricted and is only open to a very small percentage of the population, which is leveraged to occupy leadership positions on a consistent, and sustained, if ineffectual basis.

Consolidation of power in the central government consequent upon military rule also resulted in the takeover of regional and/or private media organisations and the establishment of others with a view to consolidating the central government as the locus of influence vis-à-vis the information disseminated to citizens. The wave of privatisation in the media industry in the late 1980s and early 1990s also resulted in a number of private print and electronic media organisations being granted licences. The terrain is now largely dominated by private enterprises, with the ownership structure of Nigerian media having turned full circle, returning to where it started from in the pre-independence era. The implications for the electoral process are addressed later in this chapter. Suffice to note that in comparative terms, there are no indications that the public media outlets have done any better than the private ones. Indeed, the population has more confidence in the private than the public media. A random opinion survey in the Ile-Ife and Edun Abon communities in Osun State that covered Nigeria's southwestern elite and rural populations, respectively, found that private media organisations tend to be regarded as more objective, truthful, informative and entertaining than publicly-owned ones.

Social media is a more recent arrival on the Nigerian media scene. While its impact on the country's electoral process is yet to be fully interrogated, it was a critical player in electioneering and the election of 2015. Social media has democratised mass communication in Nigeria; however, there is a need for some control of its usage in order to ensure that it promotes rather than hinders the democratisation agenda. The ungoverned space which social media represents is akin to what the United Nations Research Institute for Social Development (UNRISD) refers to, in a different context, as the exercise of power without responsibility (UNRISD, 1995). This does not bode well for the electoral system or the country's fledgling democracy.

Media Engagement with the Electoral Process in Nigeria

The Nigerian state is highly centralised, dominant and overbearing, leaving only a constricted space for individuals and constituencies outside the domain of power to engage in political or economic processes. State capture has ensured its privatisation to promote the narrow agenda of primitive accumulation by the dominant faction in the ruling elite. In the words of the Peace and Security Network (2014), it is a state that 'is marked by extreme social exclusion and violent division'. This provokes frustration and aggression among those on the lowest rung of the social ladder while members of the ruling elite that are excluded from the corridors of power, albeit temporarily, resort to desperate attempts to penetrate this enclave in order to pursue their private interests. Indeed, for such elements, this is the overriding reason for engaging in the electoral process. As McLoughlin and Bouchat (2013: 39) note, 'Economic gains from holding office are the primary motivation of politics in Nigeria'. This equates to what Joseph (2014) refers to as prebendalism and is at variance with the situation obtained where there is a large, well-structured private sector to which free entry is broadly guaranteed. The state is thus the locus of survival.

The nature of the Nigerian state provides the recipe for electoral disputes, especially for politicians for whom exclusion from the arena of power is an existential threat. This explains the desperation and intolerance that are the hallmark of Nigerian political practitioners. The poorer segment of the population is often mobilised as foot soldiers in this war of attrition that is based on existing fault lines, even when they stand to gain little or nothing from the resolution of such conflicts. Elections are viewed as a 'do or die' affair (Obasanjo, cited in *Leadership* newspaper (Online), 2 September 2017); and one in which the 'monkey and baboon will soak in blood' (Buhari, cited in *Vanguard* (Online), 15 May 2012). It is interesting that the election management authorities made no effort to sanction individuals who engaged in such electioneering rhetoric. The decision to swiftly and firmly hold such divisive individuals to account is one hallmark of a truly independent election management body. Such incendiary and divisive comments and calls to arms laid the basis for the genocide in Rwanda in 1994; post-election crises in Kenya, and Cote d'Ivoire in the 2000s; state collapse in Somalia, and large-scale violence in Algeria in the 1980s and 1990s.

Poor election management lies at the heart of the difficulties experienced in resolving post-election crises. Mismanagement of elections leaves any reasonable opposition element with no option but to conclude that victory has wittingly or otherwise (through acts of omission or commission) been awarded to a party that should not have won. This is often a function of a combination of corruption, compromise and incompetence. Orji and Iwuamadi's (2015) study on the 2015 election identified the reform measures adopted by the Independent National Electoral Commission (INEC) as being responsible for what they described as 'the most credible election in Nigeria's history', a claim that is nevertheless debatable. These included the adoption of biometric technology to administer the voters' roll; the public display of results at voting stations; increased deployment of party agents at voting stations; and 'expanded feedback channels' that increased trust in the process. They also noted that 'national and international' actors 'supported the electoral process with strong conflict mitigation measures, including risk analysis, preventive mediation, and peace messaging' (Idowu & Mimiko, 2020; Orji & Iwuamadi, 2015). However, the single most important reason for the relative peace in the 2015 election, and the peaceful transition was former president, Goodluck Jonathan's willingness to concede defeat even before the results of the elections were made public (Mimiko, 2015, 2018). As we noted elsewhere,

> Perhaps more importantly, many would argue that the results of the 2015 elections were not uncontentious because the elections were free and fair. Rather, the elections were not contentious because critical players chose to accept the results. To then give the impression that 2015 was not just a free and fair election, but the very first in the history of democratic engagement in the country is again, quite ominous. (Mimiko, 2015)

President Jonathan's concession of defeat was a critical step that demobilised individuals that were already prepared for violence. The 'strong conflict mitigation measures' would not have amounted to much if the sitting president had refused to concede, as was the case in Cote d'Ivoire under Laurent Gbagbo (Idowu & Mimiko, 2020).

The extent of the malfeasances that occurred in 2015 could not be established as President Jonathan and his Peoples Democratic Party (PDP) chose not to litigate. However, images of underage voting especially in areas considered the stronghold of opposition candidate, Muhammadu Buhari, suggest that the election could have been more effectively delivered. As Orji and Iwuamadi (2015) noted, the INEC's inability to ensure that the 3.3 million internally displaced persons (IDP) voted; the abandonment of the constituency delimitation project that the 1999 Constitution had made mandatory; and inefficient distribution of the permanent voter's card (PVC) call the electoral body's planning and technical ability into question.

It should be noted, however, that ineffective election management is not the only cause of disputes around elections. Citizens' perceptions of the integrity of the electoral process are also important (Idowu & Mimiko, 2020: 190). If people hold negative perceptions, no matter how well elections are run, they are likely to conclude that they were rigged. This is due to the massive disconnect between the state and the citizenry and a lack of trust in the state that is not dispelled by assurances that the election management agency is independent and autonomous. As the Peace and Security Network (2014) noted,

Past electoral violence in Nigeria has been fueled by acts or rumors of electoral fraud and the perception that authorities have a partisan bias. Media outlets are often seen as partisan and lack objectivity and credible platforms to counter rumors.

Complementing this is the campaign rhetoric that has come to define Nigeria's electoral process. When a sitting government boastfully declares in Yoruba that '*E dibo funwa, eedibo fun wa, ati wole unopoosi*! (our victory is assured even when you are not voting for us), this has grave implications for stability in a fragile state like Nigeria. Proclamations like 'no vacancy in the Government House' (Jaafar, 2018; Onoyume & Ahon, 2019); 'if we are rigged out, we would form an alternative government,' etc. (Ochereome, 2014) breed tension in the run-up to and after elections. A victory secured in the context of such incendiary campaigns stands the chance of being tainted and challenged.

While the role of the media in all of the foregoing issues looms large, its ability to shape perceptions and thereby influence the direction of post-election activities is of critical importance. A key element is the ownership of media organisations. Most of Nigeria's leading electronic media organisations are owned by politicians, with the result that their employees feel obliged to view elections through partisan lenses that favour their proprietors. Except for Channels TV, virtually all other television stations of note, including African Independent Television (AIT), Silverbird, etc., are wholly or substantially owned by key political operatives. For their part, public media organisations have an unstated obligation to not report from an angle that is unfavourable to the government of the day. Indeed, reportage is deemed appropriate only when it is favourable to such institutional promoters. In such situations, the editorial bent and reportage are brazenly partisan, often without any effort to give air time to the opposition.

Oboh (2015) asserts that 'media institutions are established to facilitate the socio-economic and political development of the society' (Oboh, 2015). However, concentration of ownership tends to bestow power on certain individuals that, if not responsibly exercised, could be injurious to society as they have the ability to shape and determine public opinion. It is for this reason that many countries have adopted anti-trust legislation. This logic informs Section 16 (2) (c) of Nigeria's 1999 Constitution, which states that:

'The State shall direct its policy towards ensuring ... that the economic system is not operated in such a manner as to permit the concentration of wealth or the means of production and exchange in the hands of few individuals or of a group'.

It is sheer naivety to assume that these media organisations were established for the public good and it is difficult to distinguish their goals from the political aspirations of their politician-owners, which do not necessarily cohere with the public interest. The Nigerian media industry also suffers from a general lack of professionalism. Popular wisdom would have it that many Nigerian journalists are willing to write any story as long as the "brown envelope" is forthcoming. A perusal of daily newspapers revealed that the same reports are replicated across newspapers, with journalists making no effort to rephrase or add to them before filing them with their editors. This highlights the need for improved training.

The challenge of false equivalency (Clinton, 2017) also shapes the nature of media engagement during elections in Nigeria. This occurs when a negative development about a candidate or party is reported, but to create the impression of balanced reporting, a reporter fishes for a negative issue, or invents one where none exists, in relation to the opposing candidate or party. In seeking to achieve this balance, innocuous issues can be inflated to become scandals. This theoretical weakness needs to be addressed. The scope of coverage is also important. Most traditional media organisations are based in cities and their impact on election disputes is thus greater in urban areas.

Media Engagement with the Electoral Process and Electoral Disputes in Nigeria

Egbela's (2014) checklist of expectations of the media vis-à-vis management of conflict attendant upon elections in Nigeria includes 'strict observance of the ethics of the profession,' objectivity, commitment to the truth, accuracy, fairness and honesty in reportage, and avoidance of 'reward and gratification' by journalists in the course of doing their job. Others are 'avoidance of sensational or sensationalization of electoral reports,' promotion of voter education, and helping to set an agenda for the election. As noted by the Peace and Security Network (2014), 'reporting around elections should be sensitive to conflict dynamics so that reporting does not intensify tensions that already exist'.

An independent media is a sine qua non for credible discharge of the mandate to support social stability and the public good. While the conceptualisation of the "public good" will always remain contested, every society has underlying or overarching values, which all are expected to subscribe to. In the Nigerian context, broad consensus has emerged on the values of democratic governance, an effective public sector, stability and harmonious inter-ethnic and inter-religious relations. The same is true of the social goals defined in Chapter II of the 1999 Constitution (as amended) on the Fundamental Objectives and Directive Principles of State Policy. These values remain entrenched even when disputations arise or nuances exist and every media organisation should subscribe to them. Using them as the lens to determine a media organisation's editorial orientation would thus equate to working for the public good to enhance social stability.

The concept of media independence should not be limited to press freedom and editorial autonomy for publicly-owned media organisations, but should also encompass regulations that prohibit ownership concentration and ensure compliance with a code of conduct. However, Nigerian news organisations that choose the path of mischief face few sanctions. The main regulatory body, the Nigerian Broadcasting Commission (NBC), has tended to look away when media organisations are influenced by powerful personalities to air incendiary broadcasts.

It would seem that the issue of "responsible conduct" on the part of the media, and its critical importance to the democratisation process is not lost on President Buhari, who remarked in his inauguration speech on 29 May 2016, that his government would pursue this issue. We analysed his pronouncements as follows:

> Although delivered in a very innocuous manner, PMB's warning to the media in that Speech is ominous. According to him, the media must begin 'to exercise its considerable powers with responsibility and patriotism'. While I agree with the general outline of that, especially given the level to which otherwise serious media agencies degenerated in the last election, it is not for the President, especially one that has a history of media intolerance, to decree. Pray, who decides the boundaries of responsibility and patriotism? I doubt if it is Mr. President. The lot should perhaps fall on the judiciary to rein in the media. Immediately the executive arm begins to covet this role, as PMB would seem to be doing, it amounts to '... handshake beyond the elbow'. Recall that it took the intervention of his Party against what looked like PMB's move against AIT soon after the election

for him to drop his move against that media organisation. The new President obviously did not realise that he was not doing AIT or indeed any media agency any favour by opening his activities and himself for reportage. It is simply a constitutional duty and anything at variance with that would amount to a violation of the Constitution. It is understandable that in the frenzy for change everywhere, our media practitioners have not bothered to pay attention to this latent danger to free press. Yet, the danger signs are there for those who care to look more closely and somberly. (Mimiko, 2016)

The media must make it a point of duty to encourage politicians and their parties to be appropriately focused on issues. Proper dissemination of constructive ideas to the public should be its primary responsibility. The pre-election debate by the Nigerian Election Debate Group is noteworthy in this respect. Abstaining from such platforms, or engagement of any kind, should be a thing of the past. Indeed, legislation should be adopted before the next round of elections to make participation in such debates mandatory for every candidate—or at least those in executive positions. The media should serve as a watchdog that steers political parties away from breaking their own rules when they nominate election candidates, and indeed, in their general conduct. Much of the tension that undermines the electoral process begins at the level of primary elections to nominate candidates for elective positions.

The media should encourage discussion on the superiority of recourse to the judiciary, rather than self-help, in the event of electoral disputes. By and large, the Nigerian judiciary has acquitted itself creditably in terms of election litigation, making it worthy of some degree of trust by citizens. For example, in the 2007 elections, the election of nine governors and 21 legislators was annulled across the country by the judiciary out of a total of 1,185 petitions. The media should thus encourage political actors to approach the courts rather than resorting to street violence. Involving the judiciary would also increase the integrity of the electoral system (Joseph & McLoughlin, 2019).

It is of the utmost importance for the media to exercise restraint and resist pressure to announce results other than those certified at the polling stations. Releasing conflicting figures after an election is usually a turning point that transforms tension into violence. This again speaks to the role of social media. Many users of social media platforms use networks in irresponsible ways. The use of such channels to disseminate hate speech, and fake news in a polity that is as fragile as Nigeria leaves much to be desired. Managing such pressure is a challenge that confronts the country during every election. We argue that some modicum of *regulation* (and not necessarily *control*) is required to promote disciplined use of social media.

As noted by the Peace and Security Network (2014: 1–12), the media must at all times 'be sensitive to conflict dynamics so that reporting does not intensify tensions that already exist'. How this feeds into the extant Nigerian situation defined by divisions and violence on a scale never before seen in the country deserves closer examination. The first step is to come to terms with the tenuous nature of the country, which McLoughlin and Bouchat (2013: 41–42) describe thus:

> Nigeria already possesses the characteristics of a shatter belt, the fracturing of a region under persistent stress from external forces. Parochial interests created by religious, cultural, ethnic, economic, regional, and political secessionist tendencies, … are endemic in Nigeria. Under such stresses, Nigerian unity may fail. Should Nigeria's leaders mismanage the political economy and reinforce centrifugal forces in Nigeria, the breaks to create autonomous regions or independent countries would likely occur along its previously identified fault lines. Having already experienced one brutal Civil War, Nigeria is at risk for a recurrence of conflict or dissolution, especially since some of the underpinning motivations of the war remain unresolved.

Appreciation of this structural weakness should compel responsible conduct among the elite, including the media. Addressing 'some of the underpinning motivations' of the Civil War would involve some devolution of powers to ethnic nationalities or the federating units in a manner consistent with the nuances and principles of federalism to which the country officially subscribes. It is in this context that the narrative on restructuring should be mainstreamed and implemented.

Conclusion

The media has a critical role to play in the run-up to, during and after future elections in Nigeria in order to douse electoral disputes. However, its partisan orientation, the fact that ownership is concentrated in the hands of a few active political players, and the weakness of the regulatory regime suggest that the media is not capable of discharging the responsibility expected of it. Furthermore, the fractious nature of the key political parties, which mars nomination of candidates for key positions; growing tension; perpetuation of mindless violence by itinerant herdsmen and *Boko Haram* insurgents, and "bandits", especially in the Middle Belt, north east and north west of the country, respectively; the acute economic pressure to which the mass of citizens has been subjected; and endemic corruption promise to make the 2023 election cycle more divisive than Nigeria has ever witnessed.

Taken in tandem with abuse of social media during elections; the possibility of foreign interference in the electoral process, especially in relation to the posting of fake results; militancy and growing support for extremist movements; and the progressive undermining of calls for the restructuring of the federal system, this raises serious concerns that the elections could trigger a national implosion.

A more rigorous media regulatory regime is required, as well as enforcement of the code of conduct. This should take cognisance of the need to address ownership concentration. A framework also needs to be developed for swift responses to infractions on social media, including fake news, hate speech, hacked accounts/pages and cloning of telephone numbers. Existing social networks for the most disadvantaged groups in the society need to be expanded. Rigorous training should be put in place for journalists across media organisations, especially those that report on elections. The election management body must be focused to deliver free, fair and transparent elections in all the off-cycle elections preceding the 2023 general elections. The social capital of civil society should be fully leveraged, including sensitising it to the task of monitoring the media. All these strategies would refocus and reposition the media to report on the electoral process in a manner that reduces electoral disputes to the minimum and ensures that, where they do occur, they are swiftly addressed to avoid full-blown violence.

References

Ake, C. (2000). *The feasibility of democracy in Africa* (pp. 649–655). CODESRIA.
Clinton, H. (2017). *What happened*. Simon and Schuster.
Dahl, R. (1971). *Polyarchy: Participation and opposition*. Yale University Press.
Dahl, R. (1989). *Democracy and its critics*. Yale University Press.
Egbela, S. (2014, December 15). Role of media in managing conflicts. *Observer*. https://www.nigerianobserver.com

Federal Republic of Nigeria. (1999). *Constitution of the Federal Republic of Nigeria 1999.* https://publicofficialsfinancialdisclosure.worldbank.org/sites/fdl/files/assets/law-library-files/Nigeria_Constitution_1999_en.pdf

Idowu, H. A., & Mimiko, N. O. (2020). Enabling factors for peaceful political power alternation and democratic consolidation in Ghana and Nigeria. *Taiwan Journal of Democracy, 16*(1), 161–195.

Jaafar, J. (2018, August 12). 2019: No vacancy in Lagos government house, lawmaker tells PDP. *Daily Nigerian.* https://dailynigerian.com/2019-no-vacancy-lagos-government-house-lawmaker-tells-pdp

Joseph, O., & McLoughlin, F. (2019). *Electoral justice system assessment guide.* International Institute for Democracy and Electoral Assistance. https://www.idea.int/publications/catalogue/electoral-justice-system-assessment-guide

Joseph, R. A. (Ed.). (2014). *Democracy and prebendal politics in Nigeria: The rise and fall of the Second Republic.* Cambridge University Press.

Leadership Newspaper (Online). (2017, September 2). *Political disaster: Tale of do-or-die politics in Nigeria.* http://www.leadership.ng/2017/09/02/political-disaster-tale-die-politics-nigeria/

McLoughlin, G., & Bouchat, C. J. (2013). *Nigerian unity: In the balance.* Strategic Studies, and U.S. Army War College Press.

Mimiko, N. O. (2007). Party formation and electoral contests in Nigeria: The Labour Party and the 2007 election in Ondo State. *Journal of African Elections, 6*(2), 114–133.

Mimiko, N. O. (2015, July 7). Of inauguration speech and ominous signs. *Vanguard.* https://www.vanguardngr.com/2015/06/of-inauguration-speech-and-ominous-signs/

Mimiko, N. O. (2016, July 3). Buhari and a template for real change. *The Guardian.* https://m.guardian.ng/features/buhari-and-a-template-for-real-change/amp/

Mimiko, N. O. (2017). *Democradura: Essays on Nigeria's limited democracy.* Carolina Academic Press.

Mimiko, N. O. (2018, March 22). Trump, Tillerson and the restructuring agenda. *Nigerian Tribune* (Online). http://www.tribuneonlineng.com/trump-tillerson-and-the-restructuring-agenda/

Oboh, G. E. (2015). Reflecting on Nigerian media, elections, and African democracy. *American International Journal of Social Science, 4*(3), 72–83.

Ochereome, N. (2014, December 18). Threats of a parallel government. *Vanguard Nigeria.* https://www.vanguardngr.com/2014/12/threats-parallel-government/

Onoyume, J., & Ahon, F. (2019, February 10). 2019: No vacancy in Asaba government house—Gbagi, Urhobo Group. *Vanguard Nigeria.* https://www.vanguardngr.com/2019/02/2019-no-vacancy-in-asaba-government-house-gbagi-urhobo-group/

Orji, N., & Iwuamadi, K. C. (2015). *Conflict mitigation in Nigeria's 2015 elections: Lessons in democratic development*. https://www.nsrp-nigeria.org/wp-content/uploads/Conference-Paper-by-Kelechi-Iwuamadi.pdf

Peace and Security Network. (2014). *Nigeria elections and violence: Synthesis of the national picture and regional dynamics and recommendations for action*. Peace and Security Network.

United Nations Research Institute for Social Development. (1995). *State of disarray: The social effects of globalization*. Earthscan.

Vanguard. (2012, May 15). *2015 will be bloody if…Buhari*. http://www.vanguardngr.com/2012/05/2015-ll-be-bloody-if-buhari

CHAPTER 11

Governance, Security and Development Nexus in Galkayo, Somalia: A New Approach to Explaining Somalia's Chronic Instability

Abdullahi Mohammed Odowa

INTRODUCTION

Following two years of negotiations in Kenya facilitated by the Inter-Governmental Authority on Development (IGAD), Somali stakeholders agreed to form a Transitional Federal Government (TFG) and formally adopted the Transitional Federal Charter (TFC) in November 2004. Seventeen years after the formation of the TFG, Somalia has made slow but remarkable progress in its political, economic and security landscapes.

On the political front, the country has witnessed significant progress since 2004, including (a) the adoption of a new provisional constitution

A. M. Odowa (✉)
Ambassador of the Federal Republic of Somalia to the State of Kuwait, Kuwait City, Kuwait
e-mail: abdullahi.odowa12@gmail.com

© The Author(s), under exclusive license to Springer Nature Switzerland AG 2023
A. O. Akinola, *Contemporary Issues on Governance, Conflict and Security in Africa*,
https://doi.org/10.1007/978-3-031-29635-2_11

on 1 August 2012, which led to the official end of the transitional government and paved the way for the establishment of the current Federal Government. These developments and preparations for the 2012 national election involved prolonged political wrangling (a transitional roadmap) between the transitional leadership and other vital Somali stakeholders (Hammond, 2013) and (b) relatively successful negotiated federalism that resulted in the formation of four new Federal Member States (FMS) to bring the total to five[1] (2013–2016), the formation of the Upper House of Parliament (54 members), negotiation and implementation of several regional and federal electoral processes, and ongoing national consultations on constitutional review led by the Ministry of Constitutional Affairs. While some observers criticised Somalia's post-transitional political processes as hasty, elite-driven and foreign-influenced (ICG, 2018; Mushtaq, 2019), it cannot be denied that, in sharp contrast to the preceding decade that was marked by warlordism, heavy, widespread armed conflict and massive displacement, these are commendable steps that could lead to a more stable and legitimate polity in the country.

Somalia's economy, which is mainly dependent on livestock exports, remittances and foreign aid continued to recover with annual growth of 2.9% in 2019 and 1.4% in 2020 (ADBG, 2021). On 25 March 2020, the International Monetary Fund (IMF) and the World Bank announced that the country qualified for a debt relief package under the Highly Indebted Poor Countries (HIPC) Initiative. According to the IMF:

> Debt relief will help Somalia make lasting change for its people by allowing its debt to be irrevocably reduced from US$5.2 billion at the end of 2018 to US$557 million in net present value terms (NPV) once it reaches the HIPC Completion Point in about three years (2020).

The international creditors' decision to write off a significant portion of the national debt came in response to a series of economic reforms under successive IMF Staff Monitored Programs.

Furthermore, Somalia's private sector continued to make strides. Partially financed by diaspora remittances, telecommunications and financial institutions continue to dominate this sector. For example, Somali moved from 29 to 8th position in telecommunications rankings among

---

[1] The new FMSs are Jubbaland, Southwest, Galmudug and Hirshabelle. Furthermore, Puntland was established in 1998 before the adoption of the federal system.

African countries. A dozen or so telecommunication firms offer affordable mobile phone and internet services that are not available in many other parts of Africa. There are an estimated 25 mainlines per 1,000 persons, and local availability of telephone lines (tele-density) outpaces those in neighbouring countries and is three times that of adjacent Ethiopia (Mohamed et al., 2019). A growing number of remittance companies have been established in the country to smooth the flow of the estimated US$1.4 billion dispatched by Somali diaspora to their families and friends each year, which represents 23% of Gross Domestic Product (GDP) (World Bank, 2016).

From a security perspective, there are noticeable differences from ten years ago, when the Al-Shabaab militant group controlled large swathes of south and central Somalia, including the capital Mogadishu, pirates controlled the seas and widespread armed conflict and warlordism were common (ICG, 2016). Since 2011, the African Union Mission in Somalia (AMISOM) and the Somali army have driven Al-Shabaab militants out of Mogadishu and the militant group has lost significant territorial strongholds. Al-Shabaab's decline and fewer attacks by the group in Mogadishu and other major urban centres during the 2021 election season compared to previous national elections could be linked to the improved capacity and effectiveness of some of Somalia's new federal units and the National Intelligence and Security Agency (NISA) as well as external military pressure including drone strikes that have eliminated some of the group's influential leaders.

Despite these significant political, economic and security developments, many challenges remain that hinder Somalia from becoming a peaceful, prosperous and fully sovereign state. The political context remains profoundly fractured and tense. The political leadership's failure to finalise the provisional constitution means that the significant political questions of how power and resources will be shared between and among national government and federal member states remained unanswered, stoking tension between these parties (ICG, 2018). As the International Crisis Group (2021) rightly argues, reconciliation and regular engagement between the federal government and federal member states is a prerequisite for finalising the provisional constitution, defeating Al-Shabaab insurgency and enhancing Somalia's governance (ICG, 2021).

Failure to extend governance and state authority beyond a few urban centres continues to undermine state-society relations and the authorities' ability to mobilise the resources required to run the state (Odowa,

2021a). National election cycles continue to be a source of violence and political tension, with the ongoing (2021/2022) presidential and parliamentary elections arguably being the most contested in the country's recent history (Elmi, 2021). The federal and regional political leadership's failure to agree on an election road map before 8 February 2020, when the current President's term of office ended, and the subsequent parliamentary decision to extend the executive and parliament's terms by two years on 14 April 2021, triggered the worst violence in Mogadishu's recent history (Walsh & Mohamed, 2021).

Notwithstanding improved economic performance and interim debt relief, Somalia confronts challenges in transitioning to modern, sustainable economic markets. The lack of productive economic activities, governance deficits and vulnerability to shocks (such as drought, floods and locust plagues) undermine meaningful economic recovery. For example, 'a projected growth of 3.2% in 2020 was interrupted by triple crisis of COVID-19 (coronavirus), locust's infestation and floods which caused the economy to contract by 1.5%' (World Bank, 2021). At the same time, it is estimated that 71% of Somalis will live below the global poverty line in 2022 and 2023 (World Bank, 2021). Seven out of ten Somalis currently survive on less than $2 per day and it is likely that the impact of the COVID-19 pandemic could exacerbate this situation (ADBG, 2021). Despite limited improvements in public financial management under the HIPC Initiative, corruption remains a massive problem, with Somalia rated the most corrupt country in the world by Transparency International.

Al-Shabaab remains a threat as it controls large parts of rural areas in south-central Somalia and supply routes between some towns. Despite the setbacks discussed above, it continues to conduct assassinations and suicide attacks in major cities, including Mogadishu (ICG, 2018). The UN mandate for the AMISOM expired on 31 December 2021, and the parties concerned, including donor countries, the African Union (AU), troop-contributing countries and the Somali government had yet to agree on its future. It should, however, be noted that while AMISOM was very instrumental in removing Al-Shabaab from major cities and protecting federal institutions, it has made little progress against insurgency in recent years (ICG, 2021).

This chapter argues that Somalia is a very different country from what it was in 2004 when the TFG was formed; therefore, commonly cited explanations for the persistence of Somali crises, namely culture, leadership crises and failed external interventions, might not be adequate to capture post-transitional challenges. An examination of the governance, security and development nexus could offer a better explanation for the contemporary challenges preventing the country from breaking the cycle of conflict and poverty. The chapter draws on the field research for my doctoral dissertation in July and August 2020 in Galkayo, complemented by relevant secondary data to show how a complex web of threats and patterns of vulnerability related to the interplay between governance failures, insecurity and underdevelopment is slowing progress towards a more stable, prosperous and fully functioning sovereign Somali state.

Why Galkayo Matters

The city of Galkayo is the capital of the Mudug region of Somalia, with a total estimated population of 137,000. Galkayo and the broader region of Mudug have political, economic and security significance. Politically, Galkayo is the only city in Somalia in which two federal member states (Puntland and Galmudug) operate, with each claiming ownership of the city. Consequently, the city is divided into north and south, with Puntland controlling the former and Galmudug the latter (HIPS, 2016). Not only Galkayo but the entire Mudug region is divided along clan and administrative lines, as its five districts are also divided between the Puntland and Galmudug authorities. Burtinle and Galdogob fall under Puntland; Hobyo and Harardheere under Galmudug, and Galkayo is divided between the two. The Mudug region has produced some prominent Somali politicians, including, but not limited to, Abdulla Isse, the chairperson of the Somali Youth League (SYL), and the first Somali Prime Minister prior to independence; Mohamed Farah Aidid, chairperson of the United Somali Congress (USC); Abdirashid Ali Sharmake, the first Prime Minister and second elected President of the Republic of Somalia; the second Prime Minister Abdirisaq Haji Hussein; Omar Abdi Rashid (who served twice as Prime Minister, first in 2009 and again in 2014) and Abdiwali Gas who became Prime Minister in 2011.

Due to its strategic location at the junction between the northern and southern parts of the country, Galkayo is the commercial centre for vegetables and crops from the neighbouring Hiiran region, and livestock herds, in which the region is rich, that are traded in the northern regions, as well as imported goods in transit from the ports of Berbera and

Bossasso to the southern regions. The city has been a security hotspot since colonial times due to hostility and political rivalry between the Hawiye and Darood clans. The collapse of the central government in 1991, and the subsequent formation of clan-based federal systems, which resulted in the formation of Puntland and Galmudug Federal Member States exacerbated this situation (HIPS, 2016).

During the civilian (1960–1969) and military (1969–1991) governments, Galkayo had a single district administration, and crime within the city was under control. However, the military's divide-and-rule tactics and ongoing competition for water and pasture in the countryside created deep rifts between neighbouring clans and sub-clans in the region. The convergence of governance deficits, widespread insecurity and underdevelopment has created a massive humanitarian crisis in Galkayo city and the broader region of Mudug.

Insecurity

Traditional security threats in the form of sporadic clashes between pastoralist communities over ownership of and access to water and pasture and new threats induced by state collapse in 1991 created a chronically insecure environment in Galkayo. Since much of the insecurity in the city and the wider region is shaped and re-shaped by past events, its sources are discussed under five sub-headings: the pre-colonial era, colonial era, civilian government, the military regime and post-state collapse.

Pre-colonial era: Like the rest of Somalia, the pre-colonial history of Galkayo and surrounding districts in the Mudug region was characterised by: (a) Somali clans' expansion from the coastal areas to the hinterland, displacing non-Somali tribes towards the west and south. As a result, the name Galkayo is believed to derive from the combination of two Somali words "Galla" and "Kacayo", which implies that the "Galla", a tribe found in Ethiopia, was driven out (Odowa, 2021b: 117) and (b) inter-clan conflicts, mainly between the Hawiye and Darod competing for scarce water and pasture for their livestock (PDRC, 2021: 6). In terms of the indigenous system of governance in the region, Sultan Yusuf Ali Kenadid of Honyo (Obbia) is believed to have been the first leader to establish some form of governance regime in Hobyo, and he later extended his jurisdiction to include Galkayo, Jerriban, Garaad Galladi, El-Dheer and Dusa-Mareeb (Issa-Salwa, 1996).

Colonial era: Following the arrival of the Italian colonial forces in Somalia, the Sultan negotiated with the Italian colonial administration and signed two treaties which, among other things, stipulated that Italian troops in the Italian Somaliland Protectorate would protect but not interfere with the internal affairs of the Sultanate (Issa-Salwa, 1996).

The British forces in British Somaliland decided to eliminate the threat posed by the Daraawiish—an anti-colonial local resistance movement led by Sayid Mahamed Abdulle Hassan (Mullah)—who was reported to be hiding in the Galadi district in northwest Galkayo (Jardine, 1923). According to General Manning's plan, the British forces, in close collaboration with Italian and Abyssinian forces (present Ethiopia), would attack the Daraawiish from three sides; the east coast of Hobyo in order to prevent the Daraawiish from retreating to the area surrounding the River Shebeli; from the west to occupy Tog Fafan valley, and from the north (Jardine, 1923). However, Sultan Yusuf Ali Kenadid of Hobyo objected to British forces landing at Hobyo (Obbia), which caused the Italians to exile him and his son to Eritrea (Issa-Salwa, 1996: 32). The Sultan's forces rebelled against the Italians, who were ultimately forced to install his son, Ali Yusuf, as the new Sultan in May 1903 (Jardine, 1923). The first clash between Italian forces and forces loyal to Sultan Yusuf Ali took place in Hobyo in 1903.

The second major confrontation in the Mudug region took place in 1908 between forces loyal to the Sultan Ali Yusuf of Hobyo and Daraawiish forces who sought to capture water points at Mudug valley and annexe the vast areas under their control (OCVP, 2011: 14). Unable to defeat Daraawiish resistance militarily, the British opted to make peace with Sayid Mahamed and asked the Italians, who had maintained communication channels with the Sayid Mahamed, to mediate (Issa-Salwa, 1996: 32). Following lengthy negotiations, a provisional peace agreement was signed by the representatives of the Daraawiish forces and the British on 5 March 1905. Among other things, the parties agreed to release Sultan Yusuf Ali Kenadid of Hobyo (Obbia). He and his son were deposed and imprisoned by the Italians after refusing to allow British forces to disembark at Hobyo to attack the Daraawiish forces from the east (Issa-Salwa, 1996: 32).

Following the rise of Benito Mussolini and his fascist party in October 1922, Somalis were exposed to discrimination and subjugation. Cessere De Vecchi, one of the founders of the fascist party, was sent to govern

Somalia and quickly disarmed the Somalis using violence and imprisonment (Bulhan, 2008: 47). Having subdued the Biyamaal and Wa'daan rebellions in the Banaadir and Shabelle provinces, it was time to invade Hobyo. As a pretext for the attack, and perhaps to overturn the protection treaties with the Sultanate of Hobyo, the Governor of Italian Somaliland De Vecchi ordered Sultan Yusuf Ali of Hobyo to disarm. The Sultan refused as this was in breach of the protectorate agreements of 1888 and 1895 (Issa-Salwa, 1996: 41). Once, the process of dismantling the Sultanate was complete and Sultan Yusuf Ali surrendered to the Italians; a local colonial administration was formed under the leadership of Trivulzia as the new Hobyo Commissioner. However, the defeated Sultanate's military forces reorganised, and under the commandership of Omar, Samatar launched a deadly rebellion against the Italian forces in the region (Issa-Salwa, 1996: 41). While these forces were preparing to retaliate and take back the town of El-Buu, they were ambushed and sustained heavy casualties. A second ambush by the same group was far deadlier and operational commander Lieutenant-Colonel Splendorelli and several of his staff was killed while travelling between Bud and Buula Barde (Issa-Salwa, 1996: 41).

As the prospects of militarily subduing the rebellion became more and more complex, the Italian government adopted a divide-and-rule strategy and fostered animosity between the people of the Mudug region by buying the loyalty of some (Issa-Salwa, 1996: 41). While this led to the gradual demise of the rebellion, the mistrust and enmity planted by the Italians continue to wound the people in the region. According to the OCVP (2011), the first waves of inter-clan hostilities occurred in the region at this time, including the Hodoed (1943), Dibiro (1950), Caado-Kibir (1952), CaagaDuubat (1953) and TeendhoBalo (1958) conflicts. In response, the Italian administration declared an imaginary security line (or clan border known as the Tomaselli Line) between the Hawiye that dominated south Galkayo and the Darod in the north. The boundary, which aimed to prevent the clans from trespassing on each other's grazing land, has failed to put an end to inter-clan conflicts (HIPS, 2016: 3).

Civilian government (1960–1969): During the nine years of democratic rule in Somalia, apart from a few localised rural conflicts, the city of Galkayo and the larger Mudug region enjoyed relative stability and communal integration. As I have discussed elsewhere (Odowa, 2021b: 128–129), the three main factors that accounted for the cessation of large-scale inter-clan conflicts in the city and surrounding districts were: (a) The robust nationalist agenda that emerged in the years leading up to independence that fostered unity and undermined the divisive clan agenda; (b) hopes that the vibrant multi-party democracy that existed in post-colonial Somalia would lead to the creation of a Somali nation-state encompassing all Somali people in the Horn of Africa, hence, re-establishing the "Greater Somalia" that the European colonisers destroyed and (c) given that most senior leaders of the civilian governments were from the region, it appeared that civilian leaders were not interested in politicising local grievances and competition between neighbouring clans.

Military regime (1969–1990): Growing dissatisfaction among the military led to a group of military officers, mainly from the Majeerteen clan, staging an unsuccessful coup against Siyad Barre's military regime on 9 April 1978 (Issa-Salwa, 1996: 87). The coup's mastermind, indigene of Galkayo city, Colonel Abdullahi Yusuf Ahmed, escaped to Nairobi and later Ethiopia, where he formed the first armed opposition group, the Somali Salvation Democratic Front (SSDF), on 8 February 1979. However, the leader of the failed coup, Colonel Mohamed Sheikh Osman 'Irro' and other prominent actors were captured, sentenced to death by the National Security Court, and executed on 26 October 1978 (Issa-Salwa, 1996: 87). As Issa-Salwa (1996) argues, the military regime was of the view that the attempted coup and the formation of the SSDF were orchestrated by the Majeerteen, prompting the Barre regime to launch a war against the entire Majeerteen people in the Mudug, Nugaal and Bari regions. This marked a turning point in the Mudug conflict and state-society relations in Somalia.

The security forces and the military were granted extensive powers to bring the rebellion under control. When the SSDF started to launch military operations across the Ethiopia-Somali border, the government tightened security control of the entire Majeerteenia territory, including Galkayo city. Students were jailed and prosecuted, schools and hospitals in the Mudug and other regions under the control of the Majeerteen clan were closed or destroyed, and land mines were planted around strategic towns. An old trade route in the Bari region was also targeted, with around 20 commercial boats seized and all forms of trade with the neighbouring Arabian Peninsula blocked (Issa-Salwa, 1996: 88–89).

As Adam (1992: 13) argues, the government's strategy of using national law enforcement agencies to target specific clans and opposition leaders to mobilise members of their clans has poisoned clan relations and triggered clan-based warfare in the country. Adam (1992:

17) notes that: 'From 1978–1980 onwards, Siyaad actively began to poison clan relations, instigating conflicts indirectly, providing arms and funds to protagonists, and then publicly dispatching his cabinet ministers to mediate such a conflict'.

The government offensive against Majeerteen in the 1970s and 1980s impacted the security of Galkayo and the wider Mudug region in two ways. First, the military regime's instigation of conflict between neighbouring clans contributed to the politicisation and militarisation of clan politics in Somalia. In the process, it undermined the social fabric that held the Somali people together. Second, urban and nomadic populations from Galkayo and the wider Mudug region abandoned their grazing land and water sources and moved to Ethiopia to escape government persecution.

Post-state collapse (1991-present): In addition to traditional security threats emanating from conflict over control and ownership of grazing land and water sources as well as the poisoned inter-clan relations that were manipulated and aggravated by the Italians and later by the military regime of Siyad Barre, state collapse in 1991 introduced new security challenges to the population of the city of Galkayo.

The Hawiye dominated the USC, overran the remaining regime forces in Mogadishu, and on 27 January 1991, forced President Siyad Barre to flee first to his hometown of Garbaharey, and later to Nigeria, where he died on 2 January 1995. Unfortunately, the offensive against the regime quickly turned into clan warfare—mainly an inter-clan war between the Hawiye and Darod—which led to massive displacement in south and central Somalia and massacres in some areas of the country (Issa-Salwa, 1996). The Mudug region and Galkayo city were badly affected by these new waves of clan revenge wars and insecurity introduced by state failure. While competition for grazing land and critical water points intensified in the surrounding rural areas, in the city, the Hawiye and Darod continued to fight for control of significant resources and power. In the process, the city changed hands, creating anarchy and chronic insecurity. Since most of the top leaders of General Mohamed Farrah Aidid's faction of the USC belonged to the Haber Gidir of Mudug and Galgadud, including Aidid himself, who was from Galkayo city, they sought to consolidate their power in Mudug, particularly the disputed city of Galkayo. In February 1991, heavily armed Hawiye forces moved from Mogadishu and attacked the city of Galkayo, killing an estimated 2,500 mainly Darod inhabitants and wounding many more. This also resulted in massive destruction of property and human displacement (Salad, 2011: 15). The peace agreement signed in June 1993 between local stakeholders in Galkayo restrained inter-clan conflict until recently, when the newly introduced federal system of governance sparked new waves of conflict in the city (PDRC, 2021).

Governance Deficiencies

With the introduction of the federal state system in Somalia following the formation of the TFC in November 2004, clan-based mini-states were created, including the Puntland and Galmudug Federal Member States. Both administrations claimed ownership and the right to govern Galkayo. Consequently, since 2015 when Galmudug State was officially established, the city has been governed by two competing administrations. In the Galmudug controlled north the Governor and District Council comprise 27 councillors nominated by the clan elders. The councillors elect the District Mayor and Deputy.

Similarly, in the Puntland administered north, governors and 37 councillors selected by the clan elders elect the Mayor and Deputy from among their number. There are thus two Governors, two sets of Councillors and two Mayors and Deputy Mayors with little collaboration (OCVP, 2011). The lack of a single authority that is responsible for the administration and development of the city as a whole has led to divisions and rivalry and created a political vacuum and ongoing tension between the two communities (OCVP, 2011). For example, on 22 November 2015, conflict broke out between Puntland and Galmudug forces and their associated clans in Galkayo, costing the lives of 20 people, wounding another 120 and displacing an estimated 90,000 locals (OCHA, 2015). Less than a year later, on 7 October 2016, another violent conflict erupted in the city, leaving at least 45 people dead and 162 injured, with more than 85,000 internally displaced people settling in nearby villages (UN, 2016). Poor collaboration between the two administrations stymies efforts to address cross-border issues. Al-Shabaab is exploiting the governance deficit in the city to increase its terrorist attacks against residents, leading to the death of more than eight civilians since January 2020 (PDRC, 2021: 13). The two administrations that claim control of the city are also unable to agree on provision of essential public services. Indeed, the construction and use of airstrips, roads, police stations and livestock markets led to deadly clashes in 2015 and 2016 (PDRC, 2021). The governing structures of the two administrations are in an embryonic stage, and minimal capacity and inefficient revenue collection by the local authorities has led to many public services being privatised (OCVP, 2011). The local authorities are detached from the day-to-day life of the city's residents; a recent report noted that close to 40% of the population was not aware of the existence of the local council, let along receiving services.

Economic Underdevelopment

State collapse and the subsequent chaos negatively impacted the already poorly performing Somali economy. Critical public infrastructure was looted or seized by warlords, and conflicts have also damaged public sector institutions, leading to the loss of economic and social services provided by these institutions. Many members of the skilled urban population have fled the country, resulting in skills shortages in both the private and public sectors (Mubarak, 1997: 2030).

Furthermore, dependence on the climate-sensitive rural economy—livestock, agriculture and fisheries—and weak public institutions and insecurity have undermined the government's ability to collect domestic revenue (Menkhaus, 2003). This means that it can only support very basic government operations and often relies on external assistance to survive (World Bank, 2016: x).

Despite its strategic geographical location, which links the movement of people and goods from the north to the south and vice versa, the city of Galkayo and the broader central regions of Somalia continue to suffer from natural and human made calamities. Recurring drought, climate change and deforestation of scarce forests continue to destabilise livelihoods and economic recovery (GNY, 2011: 13). The region was also neglected by the colonial and successive Somali governments from 1960 to 1991. There is thus no significant infrastructure or economic development projects in the region (GNY, 2011: 14). For example, there are no functioning trading seaports on the vast coastline of the central regions, and two small airstrips in the south and north of Galkayo serve the population of the city and the entire Mudug region (A participant in the focus group interview with members of Galmudug local authority, south Galkayo, 19 July 2020). The only tarred road that passes through the central regions of Somalia, including the city of Galkayo that was built by the military regime in the late 1970s, has disintegrated due to a lack of maintenance and heavy traffic, increasing the cost of transport between major cities in the central regions (In-depth interview with a local taxi driver, north Galkayo, 5 August 2020). The lack of basic infrastructure and economic development coupled with weak governance means that the local authorities are forced to operate with meagre revenue (Odowa, 2021b: 242).

The Governance, Security and Development Nexus in Galkayo

This chapter points to a significant nexus between governance, security and development in Galkayo and the wider Mudug region. For example, the lack of trading seaports in the region means that local resources and exports, including livestock, are exported through Bossaso and Berbera, far from the region. The Galkayo authorities are therefore missing out on significant local revenue that could be used to create jobs for the large population of unemployed youth, provide essential public services and pay the salaries of local security agencies. The high cost of imported essential commodities—food, construction material and textiles—is also linked to the lack of seaports and transportation costs from Bossaso or Mogadishu (In-depth interview with businessperson, north Galkayo, 6 August 2020). The shortage of schools in the city is forcing families to migrate to major cities in the other regions, including Garowe, Bossaso and Mogadishu. At the same time, wealthier families move to overseas countries to educate their children, depriving the city's local economy of revenue and skills (In-depth interview with Women's Group Chairperson, south Galkayo, 22 July 2020). Uneducated or poorly educated youth are a significant source of insecurity in the city as they are involved in crimes such as rape, street theft, house burglaries and the drug trade (Odowa, 2021b: 158).

Weak capacity for internal revenue collection among the Puntland and Galmudug administrations exacerbates poverty and economic plunder by both formal and informal actors as the authorities are unable to cover the basic needs of their security personnel or create jobs for unemployed youth (In-depth interview with a member of local clan militia, south Galkayo, 20 July 2020). This nexus of underdevelopment, weak governance and insecurity is particularly stark in the Galmudug-administered part of the city. There is no tax collection system and the local authority struggles to fund basic government operations, including security. Consequently, various state efforts aimed at disarming and reintegrating armed clan-based militia into state security institutions have failed, mainly due to a lack of financial resources (In-depth interview with a member of local clan militia, south Galkayo, 20 July 2020). Further complicating the problem, the local authorities' inability to provide essential public goods and perceived chronic corruption within public institutions is causing tax resistance among the public, increasing governance deficits and insecurity in the city (In-depth interview with the Police Commissioner of south Mudug Region/Galkayo, 19 July 2020).

Conclusion

This chapter has demonstrated that a complex triple trap of underdevelopment, insecurity and weak governance is halting state-building efforts in Somalia despite significant political, economic and security progress since the formation of the TFG in 2004. The lack of basic economic and social infrastructure in Galkayo and the wider Mudug region has created widespread poverty, unemployment and insecurity. As the economic bases of both authorities in the city shrink due to weak local revenue collection, they are unable to create jobs for unemployed youth, provide essential public services—including security, health, education and water—and ensure decent, regular salaries for their employees, including security personnel. These economic challenges are also causing insecurity in the city as unemployed youth and underpaid/unpaid security forces turn to economic crimes, including theft, street robbery, bribery and illegal roadblocks. Unable to respond to the numerous social and economic challenges facing the local population, the local authorities are reduced to one of the many social actors competing for power and resources and thus become less legitimate in the eyes of residents. Widespread development and governance failures, misuse of power and meagre public revenue and crime have led to a complex cycle of poverty and conflict in Galkayo. This implies that programme or policy interventions and prescriptions that do not reflect this complex web of causation between governance, security and development, and how this nexus shapes and re-shapes state-building efforts in post-state collapse Somalia will arguably not deliver tangible results. Instead, evidence-led policies and programmes that adopt a holistic approach to the contemporary economic, security and governance challenges facing Somalia are recommended.

REFERENCES

Adam, H. M. (1992, July). Somalia: Militarism, warlodism or democracy? *Review of African Political Economy, 54*, 11–26.
African Development Bank Group. (2021). *Somalia's economic outlook*. Retrieved November 19, 2021, from https://www.afdb.org/en/countries-east-africa-somalia/somalia-economic-outlook
Bulhan, A. H. (2008). *Politics of Cain: One hundred years of crises in Somali politics and society*. Tayosan International Publishing.
Elmi, A. A. (2021). The way out of Somalia's political impasse. *Aljazeera*. Retrieved November 23, 2021, from https://www.aljazeera.com/opinions/2021/2/25/the-way-out-of-somalias-political-impasse
GNY. (2011). *Assessment report 2011: Phase 1—Peace and reconciliation joint-together action for Galmudug, Himan and Heb, Galgaduud and Hiiran Regions, Somalia*. GSA, Norsom and YME report.
Hammond, L. (2013). Somalia rising: Things are starting to change for the world's longest failed state. *Journal of Eastern African Studies, 7*(1), 183–193.
Heritage Institute for Policy Studies. (2016). *Galkayo conflict: Drivers, contributors and potential solutions*. Mogadishu, HIPS.
International Crisis Group. (2016). *Somalia's Al-Shabaab down but far from out*. Commentary/Africa. Retrieved 21 November 2021, from https://www.crisisgroup.org/africa/horn-africa/somalia/somalia-s-al-shabaab-down-far-out
International Crisis Group. (2018). *Somalia's current security and stability status*. US Congressional Testimony. Retrieved 18 November 2021, from https://www.crisisgroup.org/somalias-current-security-and-stability-status
International Crisis Group. (2021). *Reforming the AU mission in Somalia* (Briefing No. 176/Africa). Retrieved 21 November 2021, from https://www.crisisgroup.org/africa/horn-africa/somalia/b176-reforming-au-mission-somalia
Issa-Salwa, A. M. (1996). *The collapse of the Somali state: The impact of the colonial legacy*. HAAN Associates.
Jardine, J. D. (1923). *The mad Mullah of Somaliland*. Herbert Jenkins Limited.
Menkhaus, K. (2003). *Somalia: A situation analysis and trend assessment*. https://www.refworld.org/pdfid/3f7c235f4.pdf
Mohamed, M. M., Isak, N. N., & Roble, D. H. (2019). Private sector developments in Somalia: Analysis on some major sectors. *International Journal of Economics, Commerce and Management, VII, 12*, 938–951.
Mubarak, A. J. (1997). The "hidden hand" behind the resilience of the stateless economy of Somalia. *World Development, 25*(12), 2027–2041.
Mushtaq, N. (2019). State-building amidst conflict: The urgency of local reconciliation. In *War and peace in Somalia: National grievances, local conflict and Al-Shabaab*. Oxford University Press.

Observatory of Conflict and Violence Prevention. (2011). *Safety and security district baseline report: Galkayo*. OCVP.

Observatory of Conflict and Violence Prevention. (2013–2017). *District conflict and security assessments*. Retrieved 1 February 2020, from http://www.ocvp.org/ocvp5/index.php/publications/dcsa

OCHA. (2015). *Somalia: Flash update humanitarian impact of fighting in Gaalkayo*. Retrieved 20 November 2020, from https://reliefweb.int/report/somalia/somalia-flash-update-humanitarian-impact-fighting-gaalkacyo-8-december-2015

Odowa, A. M. (2021a). Sate-society relations and state capacity in Somalia. In K. Omeje (Ed.), *The governance, security and development nexus* (pp. 273–293). Palgrave Macmillan.

Odowa, A. M. (2021b). *Negotiating security governance in Galkayo, Somalia* (Unpublished doctoral dissertation United Nations Mandated University for Peace in Costa Rica).

PDRC. (2021). *Re-assessment of the social, peace and security situation in Galkayo*. Retrieved 28 November 2021, from https://pdrcsomalia.org/wp-content/uploads/2019/09/Galkayo-Re-assessment-Report.pdf

Salad, O. (2011). *Assessment report 2011: Phase 1-Peace and Reconciliation Joint-Together Action for Galmudug, Himan and Heb, Galmudug and Hiiran Regions of Somalia*. YME/NorSom/GSA.

United Nations. (2016). *Displacement continues amid recurrent classes in north-central Somalia—UN*. Retrieved 20 November 2020, from https://news.un.org/en/story/2016/11/545182-displacement-continues-amid-recurrent-clashes-north-central-somalia-un#.WD-YvjJh3R0

Walsh, D., & Mohamed, H. (2021). Gunfire erupted in Mogadishu as Somalia's political feud turns violent. *The New York Times*. Retrieved 23 November 2021, from https://www.nytimes.com/2021/04/25/world/africa/somalia-fighting.html

World Bank. (2016). *World Bank makes progress to support remittance flows to Somalia*. Retrieved 19 November 2021, from https://www.worldbank.org/en/news/press-release/2016/06/10/world-bank-makes-progress-to-support-remittance-flows-to-somalia

World Bank. (2021). *Somalia overview*. Retrieved 23 November 2021, from https://www.worldbank.org/en/country/somalia/overview#1

CHAPTER 12

Ceasefire Arrangements as a Pre-condition for Independence in Southern Africa: Implications for Land Conflicts in Zimbabwe and South Africa

Mzingaye Brilliant Xaba

INTRODUCTION

I have asked Secretary of State @MikePompeo to closely study the South African land and farm seizures and expropriations and the large scale killing of farmers. South African government is now seizing land from white farmers. (Kekana, 2018)[1]

---

[1] A controversial tweet by then United States (US) president Donald Trump in 2018. At the time, the ruling African National Congress (ANC) had adopted "expropriation without compensation" at its 2017 Conference, and there was much left-leaning and politicised talk about expropriation, to the extent that right wing groups lobbied the US government to exert pressure on the ANC to abandon talk of it.

M. B. Xaba (✉)
Institute for Pan-African Thought and Conversation,
University of Johannesburg, Johannesburg, South Africa
e-mail: mzingayexaba89@gmail.com

This chapter discusses the unending land conflicts in southern Africa, with reference to Zimbabwe and South Africa. It argues, firstly, that the African development discourse is still stuck in colonial narratives, which has constrained meaningful land reforms in southern Africa and thus caused prolonged land conflicts. Contemporary African conflicts and security issues thus cannot be properly explained without an examination of the Cold War and post-Cold War dynamics. Secondly, the chapter highlights powerful outsiders' role in destabilising African countries. It asserts that African political elites have failed to adequately address land issues due to shortcomings such as greed, corruption, maladministration, nepotism and malfeasance. Furthermore, the ceasefire negotiations that were imposed on liberation movements due to Western countries' fear of left-leaning policies such as nationalisation and expropriation without compensation that would abolish their control of African resources stymied comprehensive land reform.

The ceasefire arrangements were a series of neoliberal conditionalities that were imposed on African liberation leaders by Western countries to prevent them from achieving independence through military conquest. At the time, many African countries tended to gravitate towards socialist policies as they were funded by the United Republic of Soviet Union (USSR). The Western powers feared that African liberation movements were likely to implement left-leaning (socialist) policies upon attaining independence through military conquest. Ceasefire arrangements were crafted to avoid land reforms that would upset the interests of neoliberal global white capitalists in Africa, and more to the point, extended coloniality. Historical evidence shows that following World War II (WWII), the Western powers sought to destabilise socialist states, to create 'evidence' that socialist/left-leaning development is not achievable (Perkins, 2005; Xaba, 2020). Thus, the fear of expropriation without compensation is based on fear of the rise of socialist or left-leaning ideas in southern Africa, or what the Western powers termed the "communist threat". Basically, a "communist threat" was the potential rise of communism or socialism after the end of World War II, which the United States saw as their threat in their attempt to spread capitalism throughout the world (Perkins, 2005, 2016).

Land narratives in southern Africa remain dominated by neoliberal, Eurocentric/Western/colonial concepts of commodification of land, food sustenance, private ownership, food security and commercial productivity (Tafira & Ndlovu-Gatsheni, 2017). These marginalised more people-centred approaches. As illustrated in this chapter, colonialism is an unfinished project, and African states remain weak, artificial and submissive to the dictates of neoliberalism and white interests, with the costs borne by African communities. Ghana's first post-independence president, Kwame Nkrumah, famously argued that neocolonialism manifests in the form of political independence with full recognition of a country's sovereignty; yet, its economic and political order are shaped by powerful former colonisers through a range of sophisticated means (Nkrumah, 1965).

Therefore, when former US president, Donald Trump, tweeted in 2018 against South Africa's attempt to adopt "expropriation without compensation" to give effect to land reform (Kekana, 2018), he was expressing developed countries' sense of entitlement to meddle in the politics and affairs of African countries, and more to the point, these countries' imperialist intention to impose neoliberal land policies. Ordinarily, successful "expropriation without compensation" would lead to broader socialist experiments such as nationalisation that many leaders of developing countries have always gravitated towards since the early years of independence, which could derail global white interests (Meredith, 2011; Perkins, 2005; Xaba, 2020). Given that the Zimbabwean government was harshly punished by the Western powers, the European Union and other powerful countries for experimenting with "expropriation without compensation" (Xaba, 2020), the South African government has been hesitant to adopt left-wing land policies for fear of upsetting the markets and to preserve the young democracy (Ntsebeza, 2018). Indeed, the 2019 South African Presidential Advisory Panel on Land Reform and Agriculture stated that a blanket "expropriation without compensation" would be unconstitutional, although noting conditions and scenarios where it could be possible.

While it should be acknowledged that effective land reforms in southern Africa is hamstrung by the corruption of political elites, nepotism and a lack of political will on the part of ruling parties, any serious attempt to tackle this issue will be limited by the interests of global white capitalists. Socialist-leaning leaders who sought to uplift citizens' lives by adopting left-leaning policies have been unceremoniously removed from power by Western countries using nefarious means (Perkins, 2005, 2016; Williams, 2021). This chapter situates African leaders' failure to articulate home-grown land policies in the historical roots of colonialism and neocolonialism, with negative impacts on society, the economy and the state.

As shown in this chapter, the slow pace of land reform in South Africa has resulted in the *politicisation, racialisation* and *elitisisation* of land reform. Debates on land reform have been captured by politicians, albeit in a polarised manner. Left-leaning politicians in and outside the ruling African National Congress (ANC) have proclaimed that they are pro-poor and support "expropriation without compensation", while right-wing elements raise the spectre of the impact on the economy (Xaba, 2021) and champion a market-based approach. The land discourse has also been captured by Zimbabwe's ruling elite. The post-2000 land repossession has emboldened the ruling Zimbabwe African National Union-Patriotic Front (ZANU PF) and closed the democratic space.

The chapter begins by setting the context of the Cold War and its impact on politics and development in developing countries. This is followed by a discussion on neoliberalism's impact on land reform and the implications for society, the economy and the state.

Contextualising the Cold War's Impact on African Affairs

African politics has long been shaped by developments and politics in developed countries that themselves are driven by the interests of global white capitalists. This is especially true of the period between the end of World War II (1945) and the end of the Cold War (1991). Given that the socialist Soviet Union was highly instrumental in funding and supporting African liberation movements, its weakening and ultimate fall was a huge blow to African liberation movements (Meredith, 2011; Terreblanche, 2012).

For Africa, independence ushered in political rather than economic freedom (Mupambwa & Xaba, 2019), as African politics is still largely controlled by the former colonisers through a range of sophisticated socio-economic and political processes. Due to colonialism and post-independence governments' inability to address historical imbalances in land ownership and poor access to land and land inequality remain the main cause of land conflicts on the continent (Akinola, 2019: 76, 2021).

When World War II ended, colonial empires were no longer morally, militarily and economically justifiable. Furthermore, it had become increasingly difficult to contain liberation struggles in Africa. Thus, the Europeans moved with varying speed to grant their colonies independence, albeit attached to unscrupulous conditions (Cooper, 2015; Mazrui, 1982; Meredith, 2011; Shipway, 2008).

As Young (2012: 12) notes, granting independence was 'not simply a matter of forward-looking statesmanship [sic]' but was driven by growing resistance to colonialism in Africa and the cost of containing liberation wars. After a long struggle for independence, negotiated settlements became the focal point of the Cold War between Soviet Union-led communism and American-led capitalism (Cousins, 2019) in the scramble for Africa.

In southern Africa, liberation movements were weakened by the fall of the Soviet Union and were cajoled into accepting neoliberal political independence and neoliberal constitutions that left the economy, the land and natural resources in the hands of the white propertied class (Meredith, 2011; Terreblanche, 2012). Africa became an ideological battlefield between left-wing communism/socialism and right-wing capitalism. In the end, the US under Ronald Reagan, who assumed office in 1981, and the United Kingdom (UK) under Margret Thatcher, who came to power in 1979, shrewdly outwitted the Soviet Union's attempts to spread socialism/communism, leading to neoliberal compromises in ceasefire settlements in Africa (Meredith, 2011; Terreblanche, 2012). The neoliberal dogma set out in ceasefire arrangements did not enable African countries to be their authentic selves following independence. Thus, colonialism did not end at the ceasefire tables and the eventual granting of independence. Rather, coloniality changed shape.

In Francophone Africa, especially West Africa, the Colonial Conference held in Brazzaville on 30 January 1944, which was the precursor to the 14 French colonies' independence, prioritised the 'incorporation of the African mass into the French world' (McNamara, 1989: 51). In the context of rising anti-colonialism movements in Africa, France's defeat at Dien Bien Phu in Vietnam in 1954 and the Algerian civil war in North Africa, France could not afford violent confrontation in Francophone Africa (Fanon, 1963: 55; Mazrui, 1982; McNamara, 1989: 70; Shipway, 2008). By 1960, France had acceded to pressure and granted African countries independence, albeit with continued close ties to France and other conditions (McNamara, 1989: 87–91). France has retained a close colonial relationship with its former colonies, including control of the military and their currencies (Venkatachalam & Niang, 2017).

The impact of such settlements on land reform and related politics in southern Africa was the adoption and implementation of the "willing buyer, willing seller" approach to avoid expropriation or nationalisation. Clauses in the imposed constitutions continued to protect white property while promising land redistribution. This resulted in the subjugation of black communities' voices on the land issue, promotion of the commercial agriculture model to the detriment of small-scale farming, the commodification of African land with white farmers retaining control, and neoliberal policies which dismantled farmer support systems (Tafira & Ndlovu-Gatsheni, 2017).

Right-wing actors have created the impression that only markets can deliver constitutional and orderly land reforms, while left-wing instruments such as nationalisation and "expropriation without compensation" have been described as unworkable, disastrous, unconstitutional and chaotic. For instance, there has been a desperate attempt by right-wing stakeholders, especially through the media, to use the radical Zimbabwean fast-track land reform approach as a scare tactic to deflect left-leaning (expropriation) ideals in South Africa. Although sanctions were defended on the basis that they protect Zimbabweans' interests, Western, European and American powers' greatest fear was that if the fast-track land reform programme were successful, it would have inspired broader socialist/left-leaning models of development, which threaten the colonial interests of the West (Mupambwa & Xaba, 2019; Xaba, 2020).

Independence Without Independence: A Decolonial Reflection

Decolonialist scholar, Edward Said rejects the orientalist view of othering by Western nations based on their belief that non-Western people are primitive and need to be controlled. For Said, neocolonialism persists in the imposition of the former colonisers' culture and languages and the subjugation of non-Western cultures and languages as inferior (Hamadi, 2014). The late socialist and Pan-Africanist leader from Burkina Faso, Thomas Sankara noted that, following independence, a 'western imperialist camp' comprised of former colonial countries destabilised any attempts by African countries to gain meaningful political and economic independence (Jaffre, 2018).

On an official visit to Paris, then president of Gabon, Leon M'ba, remarked that 'Gabon is independent, but between Gabon and France nothing has changed; everything goes on as before' (Fanon, 1963: 52–53). For Ramon Grosfoguel, a decoloniality scholar, the removal of direct colonial administration did not end coloniality; global coloniality persisted (Grosfoguel, 2007, 2011).

In southern Africa, the UK and US shrewdly cajoled the leaders of liberation movements into negotiated ceasefire agreements (Meredith, 2011; Terreblanche, 2012) to craft sham independence. Given that many African countries had gravitated towards socialism after attaining independence, these negotiations were an attempt to contain left-leaning or socialist policies such as "expropriation without compensation" or nationalisation. Tired of fighting, living in the bush and the lack of military support due to the fall of Soviet Union, liberation movements were forced to make many neoliberal compromises via their countries' constitutions. In his last bitter years, Frantz Fanon wrote that Africa had achieved 'false decolonisation' through independence because real power remained in the hands of white 'foreigners' and their 'agents' among the ruling African elite (Meredith, 2011: 147). Thus, African countries were given independence, but could not be independent.

How Did Ceasefire Arrangements Compromise People-Centred Land Reform?

Zimbabwe and South Africa are fitting examples of how global politics shaped the policies of freedom fighters after independence, specifically in relation to land reforms. The history of the white regime and land dispossession in Zimbabwe is well documented, as well as how black people fought that regime (Nmoma, 2008). Amidst the liberation war which started in the 1960s, the Commonwealth heads of state and government resolved that the UK should start 'decolonising' the-then Rhodesia. Eventually, the two liberation leaders Joshua Nkomo and Robert Mugabe and other smaller parties were forced into the Lancaster House Agreement in 1979 (Bratton, 2014: 47–48; Nmoma, 2008).

At the Lancaster House negotiations in 1979, the-then leader of Rhodesia, Ian Smith, set a precondition that, following independence, the black majority government could not seize white farmers' properties for a minimum of ten years, under Section 16 of the Constitution (Compagnon, 2011: 167; Kriger, 2003: 41–42; Nmoma, 2008). Thus, contrary to the liberation movements leaders' aspirations to expropriate land without compensation as it was grabbed from black people without compensation, the Lancaster House Agreement mandated that land for land reform would be acquired via the market-based "willing buyer willing seller" approach. Given that the new government lacked the funds to purchase and develop land, and that donors were reluctant to support land reform (Bratton, 2014: 52, 57) the British and American governments promised some funding.

The Lancaster House Agreement also barred the black government from amending the Constitution for the first ten years of independence, except by unanimous vote of the House of Assembly and a two-thirds majority in the Senate. Bearing in mind that whites were granted 20 seats in Parliament, they effectively controlled constitutional amendments. Therefore, the state was restricted to using the market-based approach to land redistribution (Kriger, 2003: 41–42).

In South Africa, from the time of the arrival of Dutch settlers in 1652, successive white governments subjugated and dispossessed black people of their land. The ANC was formed in 1912 and land was at the core of the struggle against the white settler regimes. The global neoliberal political and economic order influenced land reform policies and their implementation in South Africa. For instance, although, as expressed in its Freedom Charter, the ANC was largely communist and socialist from its formation until the 1950s, by the 1990s, it had been forced to abandon its socialist orientation, especially policies such as nationalisation due to the influence of neoliberal Western institutions such as the World Bank (WB) and the International Monetary Fund (IMF) (Hall, 2010: 20). Pro-capitalist forces, particularly private capitalism and neoliberalism, have dominated the global economy since the 1980s (Ntsebeza, 2007: 126).

South Africa's liberation and entrenchment of neoliberal polices after 1994 should be understood in the context of the post-World War II rise of American-led neoliberalism. According to Terreblanche (2012: 2), the post-1994 political economic system is a '...neo-colonial satellite of the American-led neoliberal global empire that systematically excludes the poorest part of the population from participating in the global economy'. The election of Ronald Reagan as US president in 1981 represented the triumph of neoliberalism, with socialism and communism severely discredited. The US managed to force the Soviet Union to cease funding liberation movements in proxy liberation wars as it feared that outright military victory on the part of the freedom fighters would boost socialism's influence in Africa. As a result, the ANC and other liberation movements were left in limbo. The Soviet Union put pressure on the ANC to negotiate with the apartheid regime, while the US and Thatcher-led UK pressured the apartheid government to negotiate with the liberation movement. South African corporations, especially the mining giants, also cajoled the ANC into submitting to their neoliberal dictates. Collectively, this led to the ANC surrendering its socialist orientation and making many compromises during the negotiations (Ibid.).

Contrary to the declarations of the socialist-leaning Freedom Charter of 1955, land would now be privatised as a market commodity and exchanged under the "willing buyer willing seller" principle, while communities could claim ancestral land via a legalistic approach called "land restitution". The approach agreed to by the Convention for a Democratic South Africa (CODESA), neoliberal institutions (Bretton Woods institutions), the IMF and the WB championed market-based land reform and the South African Constitution's property clause was designed to protect white property while at the same time promising to redress land dispossession (Ntsebeza, 2018).

Terreblanche (2012: 65, 73) argues that during the negotiations, the American pressure group presented subtle threats to the ANC that highlighted the US' ability to ruin the South African economy if the ANC rejected neoliberal dogma. In other words, the post-apartheid ANC did not have the power to shape policies; policies were dictated. Eventually, the American pressure group succeeded in cajoling the ANC into accepting neoliberal globalism and market fundamentalism '…so that South Africa could become a neocolonial satellite of the American-led neoliberal empire' (Terreblanche, 2012: 73). Trump's attempt in 2018 to bully the South African government into rejecting "expropriation without compensation" (Kekana, 2018) to thwart increasing left-wing politics on land reform therefore came as no surprise.

Compromised Independence, Land Politics and the Dilemma of Land Reform

Respected South African land researcher, Ruth Hall describes independence in southern Africa as 'compromised independence' because it arose from negotiations, with no outright winners or a revolution, and the white minority class's property rights at the centre of the transitional arrangements Africa (eNCA, 2018). Thus, while African countries were independent, they were not free from colonial control. There is a need for them to free themselves from this colonial control to become authentic

Africans in terms of shaping their own policies to own their destinies. It is widely known that when whites came to Africa, they grabbed the continent's resources and human capital for labour to develop capitalism, which led to landlessness, semi-proletarianisation, and the emergence of fragile, yet resilient, peasant groups (Moyo, 2004: 2).

Land reform in southern Africa remains "unfinished business" largely because of the compromises made by liberation movements to favour neoliberalism, forced by the Western powers on the eve of independence (Lee & Colvard, 2003: xi). At the time of the transition to democracy in 1994, South African white farmers, who numbered about 60,000, owned almost 86% of farmland, and 68% of the total surface area (Moyo, 2000, cited in Murisa & Helliker, 2011: 9). Racially skewed land ownership patterns and access to land show that the legacy of colonialism and apartheid has remained relatively intact in this country (Hendricks et al., 2013: 1).

In Zimbabwe, before the fast-track programme, about 4,500 white commercial farmers controlled around 31% of the land, and approximately 42% of agricultural land under freehold, while around a million black subsistence farmers controlled about 41% of the country's surface area (Moyo, 2005, cited in Murisa & Helliker, 2011: 9).

Neoliberalism, Markets and the Land Question

Given that I situate land reform in the Cold War that started in 1947 and ended in 1991, it is important to re-state that most African countries had always yearned for left-leaning socialist policies. By the 1970s, most newly independent African countries were committed to achieving national self-determination by redistributing the land to the masses (Murisa & Helliker, 2011: 6–7).

However, towards the late 1970s and early 1980s, there was a paradigm shift to the neoliberalism promoted by the US and UK. The supremacy of markets and states' non-intervention in their operations is the key tenet of neoliberalism. This also led to the popularisation of the "willing buyer willing seller" market-based principle, which is premised on the notion that a land market exists or can be established if land can be bought and sold (Murisa & Helliker, 2011: 6–7). Other policies related to neoliberalism include trade liberalisation, deregulation of national currencies and prices, the commercialisation and privatisation of parastatals and Structural Adjustment Programmes (SAPs). Neoliberal policies had a calamitous impact on Africa's development, and the ten years of SAPs were described as the 'lost decade' (1980s) (Mafeje, 2003: 12–14; Meredith, 2011: 370–377; Murisa & Helliker, 2011).

Under the SAPs, African countries received loans or assistance from the IMF and the WB subject to certain conditions. Mafeje (2003: 13) notes that the three main conditions were: intensification and diversification of farmers' production for export, eliminating price controls on agricultural commodities and removal of subsidies to farms of all sizes. African states were also required to remove food subsidies and reduce expenditure on social services. They were required to remove themselves from the market, especially in terms of production, in order to avoid crowding it out. As a result, SAPs put farmers in a precarious position.

Neoliberalism had three main effects on land reform. The first was that land reform was not as meaningful because of minimal land redistribution and the exorbitant price of land. The second effect was a decline in food security due to a change in land use patterns from basic foods to export crops. Third, there was increased land alienation due to the introduction of foreign direct investment (FDI), leading to land-based conflict. Again, trade liberalisation and the removal or reduction of tariffs meant that local African farmers were now competing with bigger farmers, which led to a rise in imports, weakening the competitive power of African farmers who were no longer subsidised. In contrast, farmers in the Organisation for Economic Co-operation and Development continued to receive generous subsidies (Murisa & Helliker, 2011: 7–8).

The withdrawal of subsidies and minimal post-settlement support should be emphasised because it assists understanding of the future of land reform. In South Africa, subsidies for African farmers are the lowest in the world due to the total liberalisation of the agricultural sector under neoliberal polices such as the Growth, Employment and Redistribution (GEAR) strategy. This exposes African farmers to the vagaries of global competition (Naidoo, 2011: 73; Vink & Kirsten, 2002: 9–10). Mafeje (2003: 12) warned that neoliberal dogma has been popularised as the only viable option since the collapse of so-called Eastern European socialism. It has also led to the commodification of land and the agricultural productivity narrative to avoid redressing historical imbalances in land ownership.

The Curse of Ceasefire Arrangements and Struggling Land Reform

During ceasefire negotiations, the Western powers warned of dire economic and political consequences should neoliberal mechanisms be rejected. Likewise, white farmers did not believe that they had a duty to share their wealth with indigenous people. In the case of Zimbabwe, some white farmers petitioned the international community, especially their former coloniser, the UK, to protect them (Lee & Colvard, 2003: xii–xiii). Likewise, in South Africa, right-wing institutions such as Afriforum and the Institute of Race Relations (IRR) lobbied the US government against "expropriation without compensation", arguing that it would harm the US' economic interests, as well as property rights and the free market (Gerber, 2018; Kgosana, 2018).

In 2000, Robert Mugabe remarked bitterly: 'perhaps we made a mistake by not finishing the war in trenches. We were modest and rushed to Lancaster' (Compagnon, 2011: 167). Despite his brutality towards citizens, as well as a track record of corruption and maladministration, Mugabe recognised that the pre-independence compromises at the Lancaster House Agreement hamstrung Zimbabwe's land reform. His view was that had the liberation movements won the war of independence, they would have been able to shape land reform, rather than be dictated to by the West. However, such nostalgia was wishful and limited thinking because even if Mugabe and Nkomo had won the war, Western governments would probably have destroyed them the same way they destroyed Samora Machel's socialist state and socialist leaders such as Patrice Lumumba, Thomas Sankara, as well as leaders in Latin America. European countries have disproportionate powers to dictate land politics and affairs in Africa. History has shown that successive US governments have always been ready to destroy any left-leaning or socialist government that is not submissive to their interests, whether such a regime is led by a corrupt dictator or a great leader (Perkins, 2005, 2016; Xaba, 2020).

Sam Nujoma, then leader of the ruling South-West Africa People's Organisation (SWAPO) in Namibia, once said that, because of the imperialist conspiracy, the post-independence government was denied an opportunity to embark on effective land reform, as pre-independence compromises entrenched white farmers' property rights (Melber, 2005: 37). In South Africa, some ANC members have expressed regret at some of the compromises made at CODESA which privileged white farmers, especially Section 25 of the Constitution. This does not mean that the ANC had the power to introduce socialist/left-leaning land reform. However, due to pressure from the left-leaning Economic Freedom Fighters (EFF) party, the ruling ANC endorsed "expropriation without compensation" and pledged to review the constitutional provisions on land reform at its December 2017 conference (Merten, 2018; Ntsebeza, 2018).

The main reason for the slow pace of land reform in South Africa is not only white farmers' recalcitrance. There is also evidence of corruption, collusion, red tape and ineptitude in government departments which have increased land prices and slowed reform (High Level Panel, 2017). Besides the impact of neoliberalism, there has been an increasing political capture of land reform, corruption and ineptitude in both Zimbabwe and South Africa (High Level Panel, 2017; Mhlanga, 2016). Given slow progress in market-based land reform, the political and economic elites in these countries as well as Namibia have manipulated and captured land reform, effectively excluding the poor (Cousins, 2016; Lenggenhager & Nghitevelekwa, 2018; Melber, 2005; Mhlanga, 2016).

There is increasing disenchantment with neoliberal land reform in South Africa and growing calls spearheaded by the EFF for the amendment of the Constitution to include "expropriation without compensation" (Xaba, 2021).

The Impact of Land Issues on Society, the Economy and the State

The impact of land conflict on southern African society, politics and the economy has varied, but the main impact has been the *politicisation*, *racialisation* and *elitisation* of the land question. In Zimbabwe, the chaotic process of radical fast-track land reform resulted in the imposition of illegal sanctions by the West, the US and the European Union which nearly collapsed the country's economy.

However, these same countries did not impose sanctions in response to the Gukuraundi atrocities perpetrated by the government in Matabeleland because the Mugabe-led government had submitted to the neoliberal Washington Consensus between 1980 and 1997. Thus, the imposition of sanctions after 2000 was a shrewd attempt by the Western countries, the US and the European Union to create "evidence" that left-leaning land reform is not workable, and an opportunity to publically lynch Mugabe for deviating from the Washington Consensus (Xaba, 2020).

At the same time, the imposition of illegal sanctions has been a perfect excuse for the ZANU PF government to blame all the country's problems on sanctions. Since the post-2000 land reform, the government has entrenched a culture of impunity, maladministration and malfeasance. In any event, the so-called radical land reform largely benefited ZANU PF political elites and supporters, who in most cases, went on to run previously viable farms into the ground (Xaba, 2020). Virtually, every democratic institution in Zimbabwe has been compromised by the ZANU PF elites who are of the view that they are entitled to power, with ever-increasing human rights abuses (Mwonzora & Xaba, 2020; Xaba, 2020).

Therefore, the post-2000 land reform has not transformed agrarian ownership patterns, but has enabled ZANU PF elites to control land apportionment via the state. Powerful political and financial elites continue to grab land. For instance, Professor Jonathan Moyo, a former Cabinet Minister, and Siphosami Malunga, the son of a former freedom fighter argue that individuals linked to the government target certain farms belonging to former members of ZANU PF who have fallen out of favour with the party. Thus, repossessions are a warning not to abandon the party. Other victims include critics of the state and poor rural communities. The *modus operandi* is often to send large groups of young militias or the army to intimidate farm owners or communal areas, or the minister uses his/her powers to repossess the farm.[2]

In June 2021, a news report alleged that a group of senior politicians in Matabeleland North were using the state to grab a farm belonging to Siphosami Malunga, a fierce critic of the government. This is despite the fact that legal jurisprudence bars the government from seizing land from black indigenous Zimbabweans (Gagare, 2021). The farm grabs are

---

[2] This information is based on a presentation by the Institute for Poverty, Land and Agrarian Studies (PLAAS) titled Dispossession and repossession of farmland post fast-track land reform in Zimbabwe, on 24 June 2021. The speakers included former Cabinet Minister Professor Jonathan Moyo; Siphosami Malunga, a human rights defender and son of former freedom fighter Sidney Malunga; and Cynthia Gwenzi, Khanya Noko, Flora Nekatambe, and Phillan Zamchiya from PLAAS. The speakers shared their lived experiences, and a strong theme was that political elites are using state power to appropriate rural land for private gain, leading to further impoverishment of poor communities.

related to wider dispossession of rural land by the state through its conversion to state land for purposes decided by the state. The president through the relevant minister is constitutionally empowered to convert communal land into state land for a specific development (Zamchiya et al., 2021). The Shangaan community in Chiredzi, the Chisumbanje Community in Chipinge, and the Dinde people were evicted to make way for new state-led developments. The irony is that the state is repossessing black people's land and compensating former white farmers. This is contrary to its claims of being Pan-Africanist/anti-colonial/pro-poor (Zamchiya et al., 2021).

Resistance to such state-led development has often been associated with threats by state officials, and arbitrary arrests of activists, which creates an environment of fear.[3] The state has thus become an enabler of powerful individuals and further impoverishment of poor rural communities as they lose their livelihoods and land. Many poor villagers have died from stress, while some committed suicide and women suffered miscarriages after receiving notices of eviction from their ancestral land. Local elites, the middle class, traditional leaders, speculators and those with strong political links to the ruling ZANU PF are the beneficiaries of this exercise (Zamchiya et al., 2021).

Politicisation, racialisation and *elitisisation* of land reform has also been witnessed in South Africa where the debate on land has been captured by politicians, while access to land has become easier for those with money, and those connected to the ruling ANC. The slow pace of land reform has led to *polarisation, racialisation* and *racialisation* of the land debate on even the most technocratic aspects and has resulted in the emergence of populist left-leaning politicians who push for "expropriation without compensation", creating investment uncertainty in the agricultural sector (Akinola, 2019, 2021; Xaba, 2021).

Land has become a rallying cry for decolonisation, and a tool to accuse the ANC of state failure (Kemp, 2020; Kepe & Hall, 2018; Xaba, 2021). Apart from the ceasefire arrangements on land reform, South African politicians and government officials have stalled the reform processes through poor budgeting, corruption, nepotism and collusion with private entities to inflate land prices, which has also constrained land institutions' capacity, and fuelled obsession with market related solutions (High Level

---

[3] Ibid.

Panel, 2017). For example, some ANC cadres have benefited from farm deals for which they did not qualify for (Kemp, 2020).

Akinola (2019: 79–81) also notes that the state has failed to protect farm workers from eviction, despite the existence of enabling legislation. He adds that, apart from maladministration, the major problem confronting the ANC state is the international neoliberal economic order which forces governments to submit to capital and private interests. However, it should be noted that African leaders have also played a part in the failure of land reform. Again, there is no land movement in South Africa, and populist politicians with empty slogans have encouraged land invasions and farm attacks. Furthermore, the land question is not just about farming, but also about the lack of housing in urban areas (Kemp, 2020).

Conclusion

This chapter examined the causes of land conflicts and tensions around land questions, and their impact on society, the economy and the state in southern Africa focusing on Zimbabwe and South Africa. It demonstrated that the tensions around the land question in southern Africa, especially Zimbabwe and South Africa, emanate from ceasefire arrangements which promoted neoliberalism, and the continuity of coloniality in the context of the Cold War (1947–1991). Thus, land conflicts in southern Africa should be contextualised within post-Cold War dynamics, broader geopolitics and African politicians' failure to speedily transfer land to black communities due to corruption, ineptitude, nepotism and other forms of malfeasance.

The imposition of illegal sanctions on Zimbabwe and Trump's stance against land expropriation without compensation is a stuck reminder that the Western powers still fear left-leaning or socialist policies. In this sense, the ceasefire settlements should be understood as a battleground between the Soviet Union, which promoted socialism and communism, and US triumphalism which promoted capitalism and neoliberalism. The granting of negotiated independence, whether to Francophone countries or other colonies, was an act of reshaping coloniality after the destruction of World War II. Thus, little has changed since the colonial era.

The rise of anti-colonialism movements in Africa following World War II highlighted the colonial powers' inability to contain armed liberation struggles across Africa. In southern Africa, the US, the UK and international organisations shrewdly cajoled liberation movements to accept pre-independence agreements with neoliberal compromises that granted political power while maintaining the economy in the hands of the white propertied class. The decline of the Soviet Union left African liberation movements with little choice but to negotiate neoliberal independence packages.

Rather than being shared among peasants, as per the previous socialist orientation of liberation movements in Zimbabwe, Namibia and South Africa, the pre-independence ceasefire arrangements commodified land. Consequently, it had to be bought in a white-controlled market under the "willing buyer, willing seller" principle.

This does not imply that African leaders bear no blame for the lack of meaningful land reform. The evidence shows that land reform has been captured by the elite for personal gain through corrupt collusion and poor support for land reform beneficiaries. I speak of the *politicisation, racialisation* and *elitisation* of the land question because even though land reform in South Africa and Zimbabwe targeted the poor masses; land reform processes have been captured by elites who use the state for accumulation. Nevertheless, there is no doubt that the fall of the Soviet Union, the rise of American triumphalism and neoliberalism, and the ceasefire arrangements' orientation away from socialism and towards neoliberalism, shaped land reform in southern Africa and denied African leaders the opportunity to implement socialist-leaning transformation.

References

Advisory Panel on Land Reform and Agriculture. (2019, May 4). *Final report of the Advisory Panel on Land Reform and Agriculture*. For His Excellency the President of South Africa. Republic of South Africa.

Akinola, A. O. (2019). Farm conflicts and the South African unresolved land question. *Ubuntu, 8*(2), 75–92.

Akinola, A. O. (2021, May 16). We need a new political economy of land reform, not farms without famers and farmers without farms. *Daily Maverick*. https://www.dailymaverick.co.za/article/2021-05-16-we-need-a-new-political-economy-of-land-reform-not-farms-without-farmers-and-farmers-without-farms/

Bratton, M. (2014). *Power politics in Zimbabwe*. Lynne Rienner Publishers, Inc.

Compagnon, D. (2011). *A predictable tragedy: Robert Mugabe and the collapse of Zimbabwe*. University of Pennsylvania Press.

Cooper, R. (2015, August 31). Why African independence was such a disaster. *The Week*. https://theweek.com/articles/574386/why-african-ind ependence-such-disaster

Cousins, B. (2016). *Land reform in South Africa is sinking: Can it be saved?* Council for the advancement of the South African Constitution. Nelson Mandela Foundation. Hanns Seidel Foundation. https://www.nelsonman dela.org/uploads/files//Land__law_and_leadership_-_paper_2.pdf

Cousins, B. (2019, December 8). Global and historical lessons on how land reforms have unfolded. *The Conversation*. https://theconversation.com/glo bal-and-historical-lessons-on-how-land-reforms-have-unfolded-127627

eNCA. (2018, June 7). #TheLandQuestion. Namibia. Part 3. *eNCA*. https:// www.youtube.com/watch?v=JyjtX4GTLl8

Fanon, F. (1963). *The wretched of the earth* (F. Fanon; Preface by J.-P. Sartre; C. Farrington, Trans.). Penguin Books.

Gagare, O. (2021, June 19). CIO big shot behind Malunga farm grab. *NewsHawks*. https://thenewshawks.com/cio-big-shot-behind-malunga-farm-grab/

Gerber, J. (2018, June 20). IRR warns the US about the implications of expropriation without compensation in SA. *News24*. https://m.news24. com/SouthAfrica/News/irr-warns-the-us-about-the-implications-of-exprop riation-without-compensation-in-sa-20180620

Grosfoguel, R. (2007). The epistemic decolonial turn. *Cultural Studies, 21*(2–3), 211–223.

Grosfoguel, R. (2011). Decolonizing post-colonial studies and paradigms of political economy: Transmodernity, decolonial thinking, and global coloniality. *Transmodernity: Journal of Peripheral Cultural Production of the Luso-Hispanic World, 1*(1). https://doi.org/10.5070/T411000004

Hall, R. (2010). Reconciling the past, present and the future: The parameters and practices of land restitution in South Africa. In C. Walker, A. Bohlin, R. Hall & T. Kepe (Eds.), *Land, memory, reconstruction, and justice: Perspectives on land claims in South Africa*. Ohio University Press.

Hamadi, L. (2014). Edward said: The postcolonial theory and the literature of decolonization. *European Scientific Journal, 2*, 39–46.

Hendricks, F., Ntsebeza, L., & Helliker, K. (2013). Land questions in South Africa. In F. Hendricks, L. Ntsebeza, & K. Helliker (Eds.), *The promise of land: Undoing a century of dispossession in South Africa*. Jacana Media.

High Level Panel on The Assessment of Key Legislation and The Acceleration of Fundamental Change. (2017). *Report of the High Level Panel on the assessment of key legislation and the acceleration of fundamental change*. Parliament of South Africa. https://www.parliament.gov.za/storage/app/media/Pages/ 2017/october/High_Level_Panel/HLP_Report/HLP_report.pdf

Jaffre, B. (2018). Who killed Thomas Sankara? In A. Murrey (Ed.), *A certain amount of madness: The life, politics and legacies of Thomas Sankara*. Pluto Press.

Kekana, M. (2018, August 23). Under pressure Donald Trump falls for fake news about South African whites. *Mail and Guardian*. https://mg.co.za/article/2018-08-23-under-pressure-donald-trump-falls-for-fake-news-about-south-african-whites/

Kemp, K. (2020). *Promised land: Exploring South Africa's land conflict*. Penguin Books.

Kepe, T., & Hall, R. (2018). Land redistribution in South Africa: Towards decolonisation or recolonisation? *Politikon, 45*(1), 128–137.

Kgosana, R. (2018, October 30). No evidence of 'white genocide' in SA, say experts. *The Citizen*. https://citizen.co.za/news/south-africa/2029621/no-evidence-of-white-genocide-in-sa-say-experts/?fbclid=IwAR1AcU-Rsom6AiyrPD3q7LaLcrpNiHLB33_enr8CmFXum7OWhPGSBbhKPOg#.W9fotgVmxNw.facebook

Kriger, N. J. (2003). *Guerilla veterans in post-war Zimbabwe: Symbolic and violent politics, 1980–1987*. Cambridge University Press.

Lee, M. C., & Colvard, K. (2003). Introduction. In M. C. Lee & K. Colvard (Eds.), *Unfinished business: The land crisis in southern Africa*. Africa Institute of South Africa.

Lenggenhager, L., & Nghitevelekwa, R. V. (2018, September 26). Why Namibians want fresh impetus behind land reform. *The Conversation*. http://theconversation.com/why-namibians-want-fresh-impetus-behind-land-reform-103379

Mafeje, A. (2003, May). *The Agrarian question, access to land, and peasant responses in sub-Saharan Africa*. Civil Society and Social Movements Programme Paper Number 6. United Nations Research Institute for Social Development.

Mazrui, A. A. (1982). Africa between nationalism and nationhood: A political survey. *Journal of Black Studies, 13*(1), 23–44.

McNamara, F. T. (1989). *France in black Africa*. National Defence University (NDU) Press.

Melber, H. (2005). Land and politics in Namibia (Briefings). *Review of African Political Economy, 103*, 135–204.

Meredith, M. (2011). *The state of Africa: A history of the continent since independence*. Simon and Schuster.

Merten, M. (2018, September 10). Explainer: Everything you want to know (or would rather not have known) about expropriation without compensation. *Daily Maverick*. https://www.dailymaverick.co.za/article/2018-09-10-explainer-everything-you-wanted-to-know-or-would-rather-not-have-known-about-expropriation-without-compensation/

Mhlanga, B. (2016, November 13). Bright Matonga: A classic case of how not to farm. *The Standard*. https://www.thestandard.co.zw/2016/11/13/bright-matonga-classic-case-not-farm/

Moyo, S. (2004, December 17–18). *The land and agrarian question in Zimbabwe*. Paper presented at the Conference on The Agrarian Constraint and Poverty Reduction: Macroeconomic lessons for Africa, Addis Ababa.

Mupambwa, G., & Xaba, M. B. (2019). The land as economy and economy as land: Towards a re-appraisal of the political economy of land repossession in contemporary South Africa. In *Grid-locked African economic sovereignty: Decolonising the neo-imperial socio-economic and legal force-fields in the 21st century*. Langaa RPCIG.

Murisa, T., & Helliker, K. (2011). Contemporary rural realities in Southern Africa. In K. Helliker & T. Murisa (Eds.), *Land struggles and civil society in Southern Africa*. Africa World Press.

Mwonzora, G., & Xaba, M. B. (2020). From the booth to the dock: 2018 elections in Zimbabwe and the elusive search for electoral integrity. *Commonwealth and Comparative Politics, 58*(4), 433–451.

Naidoo, L. (2011). Social mobilization of farm workers and dwellers in the Eastern Cape. In K. Helliker & T. Murisa (Eds.), *Land struggles and civil society in Southern Africa*. Africa World Press.

Nkrumah, K. (1965). *Neo-colonialism: The last stage of imperialism*. Thomas Nelson and Sons.

Nmoma, V. (2008). Son of the soil: Reclaiming the land in Zimbabwe. *Journal of Asian and African Studies, 43*(4), 371–397.

Ntsebeza, L. (2007). Land redistribution in South Africa: The property clause revisited. In L. Ntsebeza & R. Hall (Eds.), *The land question in South Africa: The challenge of transformation and redistribution*. Human Sciences Research Council (HSRC Press).

Ntsebeza, L. (2018, May 3). This land is our land. *Foreign Policy*. https://foreignpolicy.com/2018/05/03/this-land-is-our-land/

Perkins, J. (2005). *Confessions of an economic hitman*. Ebury Press.

Perkins, J. (2016). *The new confessions of an economic hit man: How America really took over the world*. Ebury Press.

Shipway, M. (2008). *Decolonization and its impact: A comparative approach to the end of the colonial empires*. Blackwell Publishing.

Tafira, C. K., & Ndlovu-Gatsheni, S. (2017). Beyond coloniality of markets: Exploring the neglected dimensions of the land question from endogenous African decolonial epistemological perspectives. *Africa Insight, 46*(4), 9–24.

Terreblanche, S. J. S. (2012). *Lost in transformation: South Africa's search for a new future since 1986*. KMM Review Publishing Company.

Venkatachalam, M., & Niang, A. (2017, May 30). France and Africa: Macron's rhetoric shouldn't be confused with reality. *The Conversation*. https://theconversation.com/france-and-africa-macrons-rhetoric-sho uldnt-be-confused-with-reality-77997

Vink, N., & Kirsten, J. (2002). *Pricing behavior in the South African food and agricultural sector.* A report to the National Treasury.

Williams, S. (2021). *White malice: The CIA and the neocolonisation of Africa.* Jacana Media.

Xaba, M. B. (2021). South African land question and the dilemma of land expropriation without compensation: A critical examination. In O. Akinola, I. Kaseeram, & N. N. Jili (Eds.), *The new political economy of land reform in South Africa*. Palgrave Macmillan.

Xaba, M. B. (2020). The Zimbabwe post-2000 'illegal' sanctions. In E. Benyera (Ed.), *Breaking the colonial contract: From oppression to autonomous decolonial futures*. Lexington Books.

Young, C. (2012). *The post-colonial state in Africa: Fifty years of independence, 1960–2010*. The University of Wisconsin Press.

Zamchiya, P., Dhliwayo, O., Gwenzi, C., & Madhuku, C. (2021, June). *The 'silent' dispossession of customary land rights holders for urban development in Zimbabwe*. PLAAS. https://www.plaas.org.za/the-silent-dispossession-of-cus tomary-land-rights-holders-for-urban-development-in-zimbabwe/?fbclid=IwA R2J8b3Zz29_stftq1J6J13E05Tmyz-vKWyNvavr6BHEuoJnDg9mQqhCb1o

CHAPTER 13

The Security Sector in Zimbabwe's Diamond Governance (2006–2015)

Tyanai Masiya

INTRODUCTION

While Zimbabwe is rich in an array of natural resources, the mining sector's contribution to Gross Domestic Product (GDP) has been unimpressive. The mining industry is valued at $5.2 billion, while the platinum group of companies, a major player in the industry, generated about $2.4 billion in 2021 (AllAfrica, 2022). One of its potential cash-cows, the diamond sector, was plagued by poor governance from the mid-2000s and was characterised by corruption, smuggling, opaque licencing and other forms of resource plundering (Sango, 2016). This chapter examines the role of the country's security sector in poor governance of diamond resources in Zimbabwe's Marange alluvial diamond area.

T. Masiya (✉)
School of Public Management and Administration, Faculty of Economic and Management Sciences, University of Pretoria, Pretoria, South Africa
e-mail: tyanai.masiya@up.ac.za

© The Author(s), under exclusive license to Springer Nature Switzerland AG 2023
A. O. Akinola, *Contemporary Issues on Governance, Conflict and Security in Africa*,
https://doi.org/10.1007/978-3-031-29635-2_13

The chapter is based on secondary sources of evidence on diamond governance in Marange between 2006 and 2015. It is important to investigate natural resource governance issues in Zimbabwe and link these to the general situation in Africa, where many rich resource-countries continue to linger in poverty and socio-economic despair. While natural resources could be harnessed to make a significant contribution to development, Zimbabwe's diamond sector suffers from a resource curse. This is a unique case due to multiple actors' contribution to the mismanagement of diamond resources and the overall environment of poor governance in the country. These actors have included the security sector.

The security sector's contribution to poor diamond governance was facilitated by its symbiotic relationship with the Zimbabwe African National Union—Patriotic Front's (ZANU-PF) ruling elite (Maringira & Masiya, 2017). It protected the interests of the ruling elite by helping it to remain in power while it capitalised on its unchallenged status to loot diamond resources.

The Marange diamond fields cover an area of approximately 566.5 km in Mutare District near the border with Mozambique, some 400 km east of Zimbabwe's capital, Harare (GemConnect, 2014). At the time of their discovery, the fields consisted of widespread alluvial diamonds that could be collected using light tools such as shovels and even bare hands. The discovery created hope that the country could become an economic powerhouse. However, the flagship Marange diamond area not only put Zimbabwe on the international map as a potential high diamond producing country but also as a producer of conflict diamonds and a country marked by plunder, in which the security sector was a key participant.

The chapter begins with an introduction, followed by the background and context. The next section focuses on the activities of the security sector in Marange, and it concludes.

Background and Context

Poor governance of natural resources has been a feature of many African countries, including Zimbabwe. The literature suggests that resource-rich and resource-exporting countries suffer disproportionately from bad governance (Makombe, 2016). The African Union (AU) (2009) notes out that despite the continent being rich in natural resources; few of its countries have managed to ensure that extracted resources contribute to national growth and development. Shultz (2005) argues that resource-rich African countries waste this wealth, 'enriching a minority, while corruption and mismanagement leave the majority impoverished'. This contrasts with the assumption that a country with an abundance of natural resources provides economic opportunities for development and prosperity (Tsalik, 2003).

The discovery of the Marange diamond fields coincided with the economic crisis in Zimbabwe; the country's failure to attract foreign aid and foreign direct investment (FDI) and the consequences of economic sanctions imposed on the country. Furthermore, in a bid to resuscitate the economy, Zimbabwe embarked on several economic reforms in the new millennium. These included the Economic Structural Adjustment Programme (ESAP), the Zimbabwe Programme for Economic and Social Transformation (ZIMPREST) and the Zimbabwe Millennium Economic Recovery Programme (ZMERP) However, none of these measures uplifted the economic profile of the fragile country (Besad & Moyo, 2008).

The government's strategies to reverse Zimbabwe's economic decline were negatively impacted by the ruling elite's deliberate mismanagement of the economy to pursue self-serving interests. The black market economy became rampant. Fatton Jnr (1988: 257) contends that, rather than being an indication of institutional weakness and fragility, this is a symptom of the dominance of ruling class interests. It persists because it serves the material and political purposes of the ruling class.

Under the challenging economic circumstances, the ZANU-PF's ruling elite has relied on the security sector[1] to consolidate its power. In order to sustain power, the ruling elite generally rewards the security sector by integrating it into politics and civil governance (Towriss, 2013) and offering it opportunities for personal enrichment. The rewards system extends to the economy, state institutions and executive positions in politics. Indeed, Zimbabwe's major state institutions, parastatals and several departments and ministries have been run by serving or former army generals. At the exit of the self-styled nationalist, Robert Mugabe, his erstwhile deputy, Emmerson Dambudzo Mnangagwa, who has a long-standing relationship with the military as the former Minister of State

---

[1] The security sector refers to Zimbabwe's four security oversight institutions, namely, the army, police, prisons and the Central Intelligence Organisation.

Security and who was in charge of the Central Intelligence Organisation, became president in 2017 through a coup d'etat. He was voted into power in a disputed election in 2018.

Towriss (2013) notes that the earliest example of Zimbabwe's ruling elite attempt at claiming ownership of the security sector's loyalty by offering opportunities for personal enrichment occurred during the country's involvement in the Democratic Republic of Congo's civil war, which gave the Zimbabwe National Army access to the country's valuable natural resources and enabled them to operate as "military entrepreneurs". It is very difficult to separate their professional positions from active political participation. It is in this context that when the Marange alluvial diamonds were discovered, their exploitation was characterised by what can be termed a calculated relationship between the ruling elite and the security forces that resulted in unchecked opaque deals, smuggling and widespread tax evasion.

The German government estimated that African countries lost '$854 billion in cumulative capital flight through tax evasion and avoidance[2] between 1970-2008' (Maradze et al., 2020: 1478). Tax evasion and avoidance have negatively affected all sectors such as security posts at the borders, where under-valuing custom duties have become common practice. It is more rampant in the informal sector, where tax evasion was estimated at between 35 and 55% of total government revenue in the country in 2010 (Maradze et al., 2020: 1480).

The security forces were deployed to the Marange diamond fields at a time when artisanal miners had descended on the fields, resulting in chaotic illegal mining activities. It is estimated that by 2007, more than 35,000 artisanal miners were illegally mining in the area largely due to Zimbabwe's rapid economic deterioration (Masiya & Benkenstein, 2012). It is common for poor people in the country to risk their lives digging in search of gold in a bid to improve their livelihoods. Chifamba (2020) maintains that Zimbabwe has continued to lose money due to gold smuggling into neighbouring countries such as South Africa and nearby countries like Dubai. It was reported that the aviation security

---

[2] Tax evasion constitutes 'illegal practices to escape from paying taxes and/or taxation', while tax avoidance 'is the legal use of tax laws in order to reduce an individual's tax burden by the deliberate omission of income on a tax return, non-payment of taxes owed or an individual not filing a tax return overall to dodge having to pay taxes' (Maradze et al., 2020: 1479).

sector runs a very porous and corrupt system that facilitates smuggling at private airstrips, and national and international airports, resulting in the loss of gold to the value of $100 million per month (Chifamba, 2020).

By the time, the alluvial diamonds were exhausted in Marange, diamonds to the value of at least US$15 billion had been syphoned from the area through opaque licensing deals, smuggling and other forms of corruption arising from the involvement of the security sector, with little received by the state treasury (Nyanagani, 2016).

When the security sector was deployed in the Marange diamond area, a system for dealing in black market diamonds had already been established. Thus, the quest for order was no match for the traditional self-interests of the ruling elite that now incorporated the security sector. Good governance, which includes transparency and accountability in licensing, production, sales and revenue flows as well as recognition of the human and socio-economic rights of communities affected by mining, was systematically undermined.

Zimbabwe's diamond governance problems that put it on the international map of conflict diamonds hit international headlines in 2006/2007 (Masiya & Benkenstein, 2012). It was also during this period that smuggled diamonds were intercepted in the diamond markets and trade routes of India, the United Arab Emirates (UAE), Israel and Lebanon, among others. Gerardy (2011) observes that the Mozambican town of Manica on Zimbabwe's eastern border experienced a boom, with illegal buyers flying in from around the world, snapping up houses and equipping them with tools to examine and weigh diamonds. Illicit diamond deals from Zimbabwe thus turned an ordinarily poor border town into a thriving trade zone.

These issues led to interventions by international bodies such as the World Diamond Council and the Kimberly Process Certification Scheme that are responsible for regulating diamond sales. Zimbabwe also made the headlines as a country not under rebel control that failed to adhere to the Kimberley Process standards guidelines set by the Kimberley Process Certification Scheme. The country not only failed to meet the guidelines but was accused of numerous counts of human rights violations (Human Rights Watch, 2009).

Munemo (2013) argues that a multiplicity of players, including the political elite, the military and police, company executives and officials formed networks that engaged in opaque deals in the diamond sector in a manner that deprived the country of this potential source of revenue. Good governance of diamond resources requires that the state, diamond mining companies and other industry players be transparent in their operations, decisions, or actions as they have a bearing on community interests, national development and sustainable development (Dhliwayo & Mtisi, 2012).

The Security Sector in Marange

According to Kabemba (2010: 1), Zimbabwe's security sector became involved in diamond panning and trade, forming syndicates to pillage and smuggle diamonds in a 'free-for-all and a paradise for illegal diamond smuggling on a scale never seen before in a country not at war. The security involvement militarised and politicised both the extraction and the trade'.

While these activities enriched members of the force rather than contributing to the state purse, it has been argued that the deployment of the security forces in the Marange diamond fields was motivated by the need to protect the elite's interests and enable them to remain in power. Maguwu (2013) asserts that it was also a strategy to grant the security sector access to diamond benefits as the country faced economic collapse and the government was unable to pay the military. Indeed, by 2008, the government was unable to pay any public sector bureaucrats (Human Rights Watch, 2009). Thus, the security forces were allowed to engage in diamond deals to compensate them for supporting the ruling party. The military has never been found wanting when called upon by the ruling party to intimidate the opposition, including civil society organisations.

Police units were the first to enter the fields in 2006. Individual units benefitted in various ways that violated their mandate to restore law and order in the area. The police deployed under an operation code-named *Chikorokoza Chapera* (End to Illegal Panning) got involved in corruption, extortion and diamond smuggling (Munemo, 2013). Police check points were set up along the route to the diamond fields and artisanal miners who wanted to gain access were required to pay a bribe (Human Rights Watch, 2009).

Human Rights Watch notes that the amount paid depended on a number of factors, including the checkpoint's distance from the diamond fields; the amount of time artisanal miners intended to spend in the fields and an increase in the number artisanal miners seeking to try their luck in the fields. The further the checkpoint was from the diamond fields, the smaller the amount, while miners that required more time in the field paid more at the different checkpoints. As the number of artisanal miners entering the fields soared, the incidence and volume of bribes also increased. Access to the field ahead of everyone else therefore depended on a miner's willingness to pay a bribe as well as the amount involved. The bigger the bribe, the better the chances of access. On leaving the fields, the process was repeated. The police are also known to have demanded cigarettes, beer, nuts and sexual favours (Maringira & Masiya, 2016).

As insecurity grew in the fields, criminal gangs attacked artisanal miners and buyers to steal their money and rough diamonds. The police protected those that paid bribes and also secured a larger cut in diamond smuggling (Katsaura, 2010). Syndicates were formed and groups of two to five police officers would escort different groups of artisanal miners to the fields in return for some of the proceeds of their mining activities.

Maringira and Masiya (2016) note that forming syndicates enabled the police to closely monitor and control the artisanal miners. It became easier for the police to gauge how much each group of miners got from the fields. Partnership Africa Canada (2010) states that, as each group of artisanal miners left the fields, they would share their diamonds with the police or simply hand them over to the police to sell, and then share the proceeds with half going to the police group and the other half to the miners' group. The police also encountered buyers at the different checkpoints. Due to the fact that they provided security, buyers preferred to buy from the police than from the artisanal miners where they could encounter criminals. It can thus be concluded that the police deliberately promoted artisanal mining and trading activities in the Marange diamond fields while seeking to profit from them.

As a result of growing syndication by the police, diamond corruption, smuggling and illegal mining grew exponentially, prompting the government to launch an operation code-named *Hakudzokwi Kumunda* (You Will Not Return) (Nyamunda & Mukwambo, 2012). Given that the police were part of the security sector that protected their interests, the ruling elite could not take legal measures against them except in isolated cases such as the arrest of 17 police officers in 2011 (Golan, 2011) and two police officers and a soldier in 2016 (News24, 2016). These cases can be attributed to deals gone sour among senior and junior members of the force.

When the army entered the diamond fields, once again, the purpose was not only to reduce the number of artisanal miners descending on the fields, but also to give soldiers a turn to benefit from diamonds without jeopardising the elite's interests (Maguwu, 2013). Members of the armed forces openly engaged in black market diamond deals. Furthermore, deployment in the area was rotational, presumably for more soldiers to benefit. Army brigades were rotated every two to three months to prevent allegations of favouritism and discontent and to help as many soldiers as possible to supplement their meagre state salaries (Partnership Africa Canada, 2010).

It is also alleged that the military developed a system of forced labour. A roster of villagers (including women and children) from around the fields was developed, and they were required to report for work to dig for diamonds. This led IRIN news to observe that 'soldiers are the new illegal miners' (IRIN, 2009). Unlike the police who only protected their syndicates from potential criminals, the military also operated as violent criminals (Katsaura, 2010). Dressed in civilian clothing, soldiers used the guns issued to them to perform their duties to rob artisanal miners and diamond buyers (Katsaura, 2010). Under the guise of operation *Makazviwanakupi* (Where did you get the property?), they also raided villages and confiscated money, rough diamonds, mobile phones, furniture and clothes for their own benefit. Organised syndicates continued to operate (Mambondiyani, 2011) and soldiers warned them to stay away from the fields when watchdog groups visited.

In addition to illegal activities, the security sector sought to participate in formal mining activities ahead of diamond mining companies in order to continue syphoning off diamonds and gain access to formal international markets. For example, the Zimbabwe Republic Police had a 20% stake in the Gye Nyame diamond mining company (*The Zimbabwe Independent*, 2013). Given the opaque licensing processes, this company became an example of the consequences of shoddy mining deals as it collapsed under a cloudy of controversy over a US$6 million bribe (Murwira, 2013).

The Zimbabwean army also held a 40% stake in Anjin Investments. However, given the predatory instincts of the security sector in Marange, it was alleged that it did not pay revenue due to the state (Marima, 2012). The licensed companies in Marange were mainly from the Zimbabwe Central Intelligence Organisation, the National Army, the Air Force, the National Police and the ruling party's top brass and contributing to the national purse was not a priority (Zvarivadza, 2015). Despite the introduction of formal mining in Marange and the fencing of most of the area, it was alleged that individual members stationed there cut the fences to gain entry to the mining sites and enable illegal artisanal miners to mine (Dhliwayo & Mtisi, 2012).

The security sector's presence was even felt in companies in which it had no stake. According to Swain (2012), security sector interests were evident in the composition of the boards of Canadile (later Marange Resources) and Mbada as well as their export practices. Even after the government introduced formal joint ventures, it was alleged that they continued to engage in large-scale smuggling and illegal auctioning of diamonds from the Marange fields. Companies bypassed the ZMDC and the Minerals Marketing Corporation of Zimbabwe (MMCZ) that were tasked with mining and marketing diamonds, with the result that many diamonds failed to reach government coffers. Illegal diamonds found their way to markets such as India, Belgium, Israel, Lebanon, Russia, South Africa and the UAE.

The cloud of secrecy surrounding the licensing, production, sales and revenue processes is in sharp contrast to what occurs in countries where diamond governance emphasises transparency and accountability. Countries that pursue good diamond governance make information on the diamond trade and the financial records of all companies involved in diamond activities available to the general public upon request; have a clear and specific legal framework that sets licensing, security and control measures and systems to curb illegal mining, smuggling and leakage of rough diamonds; and protect communities' socio-economic rights.

The security sector's involvement in the Marange diamond fields and its impunity were possible because it played a central role in ensuring that the ruling elite remained in power. Thus, it could get away with anything that did not threaten the elite. Indeed, it enabled members of the elite to also engage in illegal diamond activities. They often sent in "runners" who bought and sold the diamonds on the black market on their behalf. It is important to note that politicians, including senior government ministers, were implicated in the illegal extraction, sale and exportation of Marange diamonds. It adds that high-ranking politicians formed syndicates with illegal panners and agents (runners) who acted on their behalf. The runners enjoyed protection from the law and if arrested, politicians would intervene on their behalf with the judiciary and law enforcement agents.

The ruling elite also used the security sector to apply the law selectively to the elite's advantage. For example, most opposition gatherings require prior approval from the police and every year many are banned. In 2016 alone, opposition rallies scheduled for Bulawayo, Harare, Chinhoyi and Zvishavane were banned by the police (Manayiti, 2016; Muvundisi, 2016; Nkala, 2016). However, ZANU-PF is not subjected to the same conditions. Top security leaders regularly declare unflinching support for ZANU-PF and its leadership, from Mugabe to Mnangagwa. They state that they will never be apologetic for supporting the ruling class and argue that worldwide, the security sector has always worked with and protected members of the executive and associated organs. Security sector leaders have thus become political animals that are prepared to abandon professionalism to protect the ruling elite in the ZANU-PF administration (Allison, 2012; Manayiti, 2015).

In turn, retired and serving members in the security sector have been rewarded with public sector appointments. This promotes loyalty and discipline and also offers an attractive retirement package for those in the security service. It has also been noted that, because of the unprofessional relationship between the ruling elite and the security sector, members of the latter have become deeply involved in the country's electoral politics. On the eve of the 2002 presidential elections when for the first time, ZANU-PF faced stiff competition from the Movement for Democratic Change (MDC), the country's security forces through then Defence Forces Commander Vitalis Zvinavashe issued a televised statement that warned citizens against voting for anyone other than the late Mugabe (Machamire, 2015). Since then, the security forces have continued to issue political statements (Politicoscope, 2015). Indeed, the elite has used the security sector's reputation for brutality to ensure compliance and silence any opposition at both personal and party level.

The unholy alliance between the security sector and the ruling elite is not only influenced by the rewards it offers, but is also due to the fact that the security sector has become very powerful and seeks to pursue its self-interests and self-preservation. Indeed, due to the security forces' entrenchment in Zimbabwe's economic system, they are no longer simply loyal but also fear any alternative government. The ruling elite thus preys on the security forces because they have also benefitted immensely from illicit activities such as illegal practices with regard to diamond mining and have grown rich on an entrenched system of political patronage and corruption (Alexander, 2013).

Conclusion

The chapter revisited the question of the resource curse in Zimbabwe and highlighted the convergence between diamond resources and the country's security sector. While the abundant deposits of alluvial diamonds could have turned Zimbabwe's economy around, the plunder that followed the discovery made international headlines due to poor governance of this resource. The exploitation of the Marange diamond fields brought to the fore the corrupt relationship between the security sector and the ruling elite in Zimbabwe. This relationship perpetuated the ruling party's hold on power and enabled the security forces to pursue self-enrichment.

In Marange, the security sector created syndicates and exploited village labour, engaged in diamond smuggling and secured mining rights through opaque and illicit licensing processes. Human rights abuses were also reported. Although international diamond regulating institutions have tried to intervene in order to bring sanity to the diamond sector, the government needs to review legislation on mineral resources governance to improve diamond flows to the formal market as well as revenue flows to the state treasury. It is unconscionable that the cash-strapped Zimbabwean state should continue to lose so much revenue that could be used to fund development initiatives.

References

African Union. (2009). *Africa mining vision*. UNECA Documents and Publishing Unit.

AllAfrica. (2022, February 23). Zimbabwe: 'Zim Halfway towards U.S.$12bn Mining Target'. *The Herald*.

Alexander, J. (2013). Militarisation and state institutions: "Professionals" and "Soldiers" inside the Zimbabwe Prison Service. *Journal of Southern African Studies, 39*(4), 807–828.

Allison, S. (2012). *Zimbabwe's army puts the "general" back in general elections*. http://www.dailymaverick.co.za/article/2012-05-18-zimbabwes-army-puts-the-general-back-in-general-elections/#.VpPkgvl97IU. Accessed 10 December 2016.

Besad, H., & Moyo, N. (2008). *Zimbabwe in crisis: Mugabe's policies and failures* (The Center for International Governance Innovation, Working Paper Number 38).

Chifamba, M. (2020, December 7). Zimbabwe: Losing millions from illicit gold mining trade. *The Africa Report*. https://www.theafricareport.com/53429/zimbabwe-losing-millions-from-illicit-gold-mining-trade/. Accessed 26 October 2021.

Dhliwayo, M., & Mtisi, S. (2012). *Towards a Diamond Act in Zimbabwe*. ZELA.

Fatton, Jr., R. (1988). Bringing the ruling class back in: Class, State, and hegemony in Africa. *Comparative Politics, 20*(3), 253–264.

GemConnect. (2014). *Marange Q1 auctions in Belgium and Dubai earn $99 million*. https://gemkonnect.wordpress.com/2014/04/page/6/. Accessed 2 July 2017.

Gerardy, J. (2011). Zim gem smuggling fuels cross-border dealer hub. *The Mail and Guardian*. https://mg.co.za/article/2010-11-07-zim-gem-smuggling-fuels-crossborder-dealer-hub. Accessed 10 July 2017.

Golan, E. (2011). *Zimbabwe: 17 police officers arrested for illegal diamond trading*. http://www.idexonline.com/FullArticle?Id=28245. Accessed 9 July 2017.

Kabemba, C. (2010). *The Kimberley process and the Chiadzwa diamonds in Zimbabwe: Challenges and effectiveness—Resource governance*. https://za.boell.org/2010/07/08/kimberley-process-and-chiadzwa-diamonds-zimbabwe-challenges-and-effectiveness-resource. Accessed 12 July 2017.

Human Rights Watch. (2009). *Diamonds in the rough: Human rights abuses in the Marange diamond fields of Zimbabwe*. New York. https://www.hrw.org/report/2009/06/26/diamonds-rough/human-rights-abuses-marange-diamond-fields-zimbabwe. Accessed 12 December 2016.

IRIN. (2009, January 20). *Soldiers are the new illegal miners*. http://www.irinnews.org/report/82477/zimbabwe-soldiers-are-the-new-illegal-diamond-miners. Accessed 30 November 2016.

Katsaura, O. (2010). Violence and the political economy of informal diamond mining in Chiadzwa, Zimbabwe. *Journal of Sustainable Development in Africa, 12*, 340–353.

Machamire, F. (2015, October 12). Mujuru warns army generals. *The Daily News*.

Maguwu, F. (2013). Marange diamonds and Zimbabwe's political transition. *Journal of Peacebuilding & Development, 8*(1), 74–78.

Makombe, F. P. (2016). *Governance reforms and national benefits: Problems and prospects in Marange diamond mining in Zimbabwe* (Unpublished thesis). Graduate School of Development Policy and Practice, University of Cape Town.

Mambondiyani, A. (2011). *Illegal diamond mining in Zimbabwe*. https://www.opendemocracy.net/andrew-mambondiyani/illegal-diamond-mining-in-zimbabwe. Accessed 12 October 2016.

Manayiti, O. (2015, October 4). Generals panic over Mujuru. *The Standard*.

Manayiti, O. (2016, February 29). Police ban MDC-T Mbare youth rally. *NewsDay*.
Maradze, T. C., Nyoni, T., & Nyoni, S. P. (2020). Tax evasion and tax avoidance in Harare, Zimbabwe: Empirical evidence from a logit model. *International Journal of Advance Research and Innovative Ideas in Education (IJARIIE)*, 6(6), 1478–1486.
Marima, T. (2012, June 22). Chinese cream off USD200m. *The Independent*.
Maringira, G., & Masiya, T. (2017). When the military become a security and political threat: Zimbabwean army generals in electoral politics. *African Security Review*, 26(4), 399–412. https://doi.org/10.1080/10246029.2017.129 4090
Maringira, G., & Masiya, T. (2016). The security sector and the plunder of Zimbabwe's Chiadzwa alluvial diamonds: "Goat mentality" in practice. *Africa Security Review*, 25(4), 368–377.
Masiya, T., & Benkenstein, A. (2012). *Zimbabwe's Marange diamonds and the need for reform of the Kimberley process*. Governance of Africa Resources Programme, Policy Briefing 43.
Munemo, D. (2013). *Assessing the effectiveness of the Kimberley process in Zimbabwe and the democratic Republic of Congo* (Thesis submitted in partial fulfilment of a Master of Arts). University of the Witwatersrand, South Africa.
Murwira, Z. (2013, September 18). Ex ZMDC Boss in US$6 million scandal. *The Herald*.
Muvundisi, J. (2016, November 19). MDC appeals against rally ban. *Daily News*.
Nkala, S. (2016, November 19). MDC-T sues Chombo, cops over Zvishavane rally ban. *Newsday*.
Nyamunda, T., & Mukwambo, P. (2012). The state and the bloody diamond rush in Chiadzwa: Unpacking the contesting interests in the development of illicit mining and trading, c. 2006–2009, *Journal of Southern African Studies*, 38(1), 145–166.
Nyanagani, K. (2016, May 18). Missing $15 billion diamond revenue exposes Zanu PF: Chimene. *Newsday*.
News24. (2016). *2 cops, soldier, 3 villagers arrested with diamonds in Zim's Chiadzwa fields: Report*. http://www.news24.com/Africa/Zimbabwe/2-cops-soldier-3-villagers-arrested-with-diamonds-in-zims-chiadzwa-fields-rep ort-20160304. Accessed 10 July 2017.
Partnership Africa Canada. (2010). Diamonds and clubs: The militarised control of diamonds and power in Zimbabwe. *Partnership Africa Canada Report June 2010*. http://www.pacweb.org/Documents/diamonds_KP/Zimbabwe-Diamonds_and_clubs-eng-June2010.pdf. Accessed 10 October 2016.

Politicoscope. (2015). *Zimbabwe: Military generals stuck in Mugabe's Zanu PF succession battles*. http://www.politicoscope.com/zimbabwe-military-generals-stuck-in-mugabe-zanu-pf-succession-battles/#sthash.DmcSjvgE.dpuf. Accessed 9 November 2016.

Sango, R. (2016). *Chiadzwa diamond fields: Unprecedented plunder*. http://roape.net/2016/03/11/chiadzwa-diamond-fields-unprecedented-plunder/. Accessed 11 July 2017.

Shultz, J. (2005). *Follow the money: A guide to monitoring budgets and oil and gas revenues*. Central European University Press.

Swain, J. (2012). Robert Mugabe's dirty diamonds. *The Sunday Times Magazine*. http://jonswain.org/articles/articles/articles/Zimdiamonds.html. Retrieved on 18 August 2012.

The Zimbabwe Independent. (2013, October 4). Diamond mining ventures compromise security forces.

Towriss, D. (2013). Buying loyalty: Zimbabwe's Marange diamonds. *Journal of Southern African Studies, 39*(1), 99–117.

Tsalik, S. (2003). Natural resource funds: Case studies in success and failure. In *Caspian oil windfalls: Who will benefit?* Caspian Revenue Watch.

Zvarivadza, T. (2015). *Making the most out of Zimbabwe's Marange diamonds: Leaving a lasting positive legacy for distressed communities*. Conference: 10th International Conference on Mine Closure (MC2015), Vancouver, Canada.

CHAPTER 14

Ethnic Federalism, Exclusionary Self-Determination Rights and Conflict in Ethiopia: Consociational Democracy as an Alternative Approach to Peace and Security

Seyoum Mesfin

INTRODUCTION

Ethnic-based conflicts continue to recur on the African continent. Following decolonisation or internal territorial expansion in the case of Ethiopia, the only country which escaped colonialism in Africa, diverse ethnic communities, both large and small, were grouped within the same political boundaries. This triggered recurring conflict across the continent

---

S. Mesfin (✉)
Center for Federalism and Governance Studies, Addis Ababa University, Addis Ababa, Ethiopia
e-mail: mesfinweg@gmail.com

© The Author(s), under exclusive license to Springer Nature Switzerland AG 2023
A. O. Akinola, *Contemporary Issues on Governance, Conflict and Security in Africa*,
https://doi.org/10.1007/978-3-031-29635-2_14

due to inclusion and exclusion politics, with varying strategies adopted to address the situation.

In the Ethiopian context, ethnicity has been the single most important force behind the state restructuring process since 1991. The Ethiopian People's Revolutionary Democratic Front (EPRDF), an ethnic coalition party that ruled Ethiopia from 1991 to 2018 applied the Stalinist theory of nationalities (Bach, 2014). It held that ethnic groups (which the Ethiopian constitution refers to as 'nations, nationalities, and peoples') were victims of domination and marginalisation in the pre-1991 period and characterised the country as marked by ethnic inequality and discrimination. Indeed, some argued that Ethiopia's government has imprisoned nationalities (Merera, 2003). It has been noted that 'inequality of access [to resources and decision-making powers] has been the primary root cause of conflict throughout the second half of the twentieth century' (Vaughan, 2003b: 6). In its quest to liberate ethnic groups from oppression, the EPRDF implemented a system often dubbed 'ethnic federalism' by scholars that offered them unrestricted autonomy up to the point of secession. The Ethiopian federal system is a pioneer in adopting radical approach on the continent and is also perhaps the most explicit approach to embrace the politics of ethnicity at the global level.

Recognition of a specific ethnic group's affinity with and jurisdiction over an area is a fundamental strategy used by Ethiopian federalism to establish ethnic rights. It declared ethnic groups to be distinct corporate entities with their own language, culture, history and geographical boundaries.[1] Accordingly, the federal system adopts a multilevel governance approach to give expression to ethnic minorities' demands for self-determination and equality. In line with this, the 1995 FDRE constitution established nine regional states (now eleven). Within these major units, an attempt has been made to match and harmonise physical space, an ethnic group, and an administrative unit. Depending on the size of the ethnic groups' regional states, special zones (*Leyu zone*) and special districts (*Leyu woreda*) were demarcated as autonomous and semi-autonomous entities (Bassi, 2014: 52).

Ethiopia has spent nearly three decades building ethnic-based federal democracy that encourages and institutionalises ethnic equality and self-governance (Barata, 2012). Although many ethnic communities

---

[1] See, Article 39(5) of the Federal Democratic Republic of Ethiopia's Constitution.

supported this approach, it went too far by establishing titular administrative entities that exclude other ethnic communities that live in the same administrative unit but are not deemed titular. As a result, this approach resulted in violent clashes at a variety of levels (Asnake, 2013: 43). A notable example is the politics in Yeki *woreda* in the Sheka zone that has been dominated by Sheka elites since 1991. The local political elites in this zone enforce a highly discriminatory governance system that privileges Sheka (also called Shekicho after their language) ethnic groups over other minority groups with no legal basis. At the time of data collection (2013–April 2016) for this chapter and with no changes having occurred until the end of 2021, the dominant Shekicho practised exclusionary politics and controlled all three branches of government. Other communities who share the district, including Amhara, Oromo, Majang and Sheko felt excluded and thus demanded inclusion in the local political, economic and social order. This led to violent, persistent conflicts between 1993 and 2016 that claimed more than 2,500 lives (Vaughan, 2006).

Through unstructured interview and Focus Group Discussion (FGD) in Tapi and Meti, between 2014 and 2016, this chapter explores the implementation of ethnic federalism in Ethiopia by examining the case study of multicultural administrative units in the southwest of the country. Does the system of 'ethnic federalism' meet its promise of promoting inclusive governance and development for majority (whether the majority may be defined in terms of number or influence) rule at the local level? If so, how? If not, why not? Overall, we show that for the past two decades, inclusive governance and development have not been achieved because of one ethnic group's dominance of others. The supremacy of a single ethnic group in ethnic democracies 'is reflected in a control of political decision-making, monopolization of positions in government, and the establishment of a structure of governance favourable to the leading ethnic group' (Scherijver, 2016: 72). This chapter thus identifies opportunities for inclusive governance and socio-economic justice for ethnic minorities to build sustainable peace in Ethiopia.

It proposes 'consociational democracy' as a more responsive governance option that accommodates ethnic-based power-sharing arrangements for minorities in the same political space at the sub-national level. In our view, minority groups' need for inclusive governance and development could be best secured through what Arend Lijphart defines as 'consociational democracy'. This approach could also address the problem of inclusive power-sharing arrangements for ethnic groups occupying the same unit. Federalism in Ethiopia continues to lack a clear power-sharing formula at the local level. Institutionalisation of 'consociational democracy' could realise the constitutionally guaranteed rights of minorities in the country.

The remainder of this chapter is organised as follows: the first section examines the practice of exclusionary politics in the study area and describes the minorities' response, instances of violent conflict, and the government's response. The second part proposes strategies to address the root causes of the conflict. A conclusion is presented in section three, as well as the implications of the Ethiopian experience for other African countries.

Exclusion of 'Non-Titular' Ethnic Communities and Conflict at the Local Level

The Manjo, Majang and Sheko are ethnic groups that share an administrative unit known as Sheka Zone with the Sheka ethnic community. Other ethnic communities that are considered 'highlanders', i.e., Amhara and Oromo, also live in this zone (Seyoum, 2015). Compared to the Sheka ethnic community, the rest are minorities. Outside of Sheka Zone, the Manjo are dispersed across at least ten other administrative units in southern and south-western Ethiopia but are non-titular in all these units (Yoshida, 2013). Apart from settlements on the borders in Sheka Zone, the Majang are titular to the Majang Nationality Zone (MNZ) of Gambella where they are concentrated. The Sheko are also found in the Bench-Maji Zone in Southern Nations, Nationalities, and People's Region (SNNPRS), and Illubabor Zone in the Oromiya Regional States and are titular to Sheko Woreda. They also live in Bench Maji Zone on the common borders.

Researchers have noted that these minorities are not only scattered across different politico-administrative units, but also experience extreme forms of marginalisation and domination by majority ethnic groups in their areas (Seyoum, 2015; Yoshida, 2013). As a dominant group, Sheka exercises 'ownership' in Sheka Zone while those in Bench Sheko Zone suffer marginalisation from the Bench community who are titular in this zone. This situation prevails in all parts of the country where there is ethnic diversity, and reflects what Coakly, in explaining patterns of ethnoterritorial relationships, terms 'locally weak, territorially dispersed groups' (Coakly, 2003: 9) (Fig. 14.1).

14 ETHNIC FEDERALISM, EXCLUSIONARY ... 231

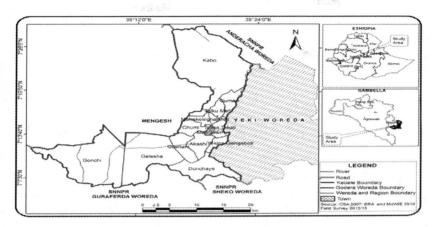

Fig. 14.1 Map of Yeki District and Its Neighbours

As noted previously, this chapter focuses on Yeki *woreda* of Sheka Zone. Sheka is a zone-level administration (middle-level administrative hierarchy) whose titular group is the Sheka ethnic community in southwest Ethiopia. It is divided into three *woredas*: Masha, Yeki and Anderacha. While Anderacha and Masha are exclusive settlements of the Sheka people, the ethnic composition of Yeki is relatively diverse. Yeki is located in the south of Sheka Zone, bordered in the west by the Gambella region, the east by the Keffa Zone, the south by the Bench-Maji Zone and the north by Anderacha district of Sheka Zone (see Fig. 14.1). The *woreda* is part of the south-western rainforest of Ethiopia, which is characterised by fertile soil and adequate rainfall. It is a cash-crop producing area, particularly known for its quality coffee that is one of the major sources of income for the community.

Yeki *woreda* is further divided into 26 *kebeles*,[2] and its capital is Tapi. The *woreda* is home to various ethnic groups,[3] including Sheka, Majang, Manjo, Sheko, Oromo, Amhara and Kefa. However, the Sheka, Majang,

---

[2] These are Abiy 1 and 2 Ersh, Achani, Addis Alem, Alem Beche, Beko Limat, Darimu Depey, Enderise, Feday, Gaylecha, Hberete Feray, Keremeche (Ermich), Komi, Komie Ersha Limat, Kubito, Kukey, Mecha, Selam Sefer, Shaye, Shemerega, Shosha, Shosha Ersha Lima, Shuma, Tsanu, Yeki and Zeneki.

[3] Nonetheless, the area is an exclusively Majang and Sheko settlement starting from Alamo hot land. According to the 2008 Population and Housing Census, there are 22

Manjo and Sheko are considered 'owner nationalities' of the *woreda*, with the Sheka the dominant and de facto primary ethnic community. Since 1991, there has been constant conflict among the 'owner' ethnic groups of Sheka on the one hand, and Majang, Manjo and Sheko on the other over the representation of the latter in the *woreda*'s politics, government and economy. As discussed earlier, Ethiopia's ethnic federalism revolves around the notion of *yikelili balbet*, which means 'owner nationalities'. Among other things, this involves attachment to a place on which rights are based. Where there are multiple owners, contestation arises over who should be the supreme owner.

As noted in the introduction, in federal Ethiopia, ethnicity is the major criterion used to assign owner-nationality and non-owner-nationality status in a given political unit. A political unit 'owned by one group could not be owned by another' (Clapham, 2002: 29). Political representation and territorial administration were reorganised in terms of ethnicity (Vaughan, 2003a). Accordingly, '[a] stratum of the local elite of each ethnic group was encouraged to form an ethnic organisation as a platform for executive office' (Vaughan, 2003a). Ethnic political elites thus use the owner-nationality principle as a matter of political expediency. The notion of owner nationalities gives rise to the issue of access to power and resources in a particular unit. This has prompted debates over owner-nationality-based claims in a given locality and the conflicts that arise from counterclaims. Allocation of benefits among ethnic groups in the same political space is based on owner nationality. The group with owner nationality benefits while the group with outsider status forfeits various benefits and is thus marginalised. The struggle to shift the balance of power among groups creates simmering tension and violent forms of ethnic conflict (Holden, 1966). Such contestation largely plays out in conflict over the control of a given administrative unit. Owner nationality thus plays an important role in the inclusionary and exclusionary currents of entitlement in governance.

Since 1991, people in Yeki *woreda* and those of the same ethnic affiliation living in adjacent areas have been plagued by conflict between Sheka, on the one hand, and Majang, Manjo and Sheko, on the other. The root of the conflict is exclusionary politics and socio-economic injustice. Evidence shows that minority ethnic groups in Yeki have become victims

---

kebeles in Yeki. Of these, 11 are Sheko-inhabited, four are dominated by Majang and four are Shekicho-dominated kebeles.

of local tyranny, with minorities relegated to the margins of governance. The dominant group, the Sheka, adopted exclusionary politics in terms of representation, appointments, budget allocations and the language used in education and administration. It is worth examining the various facets of marginalisation.

The first domain of exclusion is from opportunities in politics and administration. Minorities claim that the Shekicho political elites exclude them from participating in the *woreda* administration. Although the three groups are all original inhabitants of the *woreda*, the name of the zone is drawn from the Shekicho name, Sheka. This has significant implications for ethnic politics in modern Ethiopia as the nomenclature gives the Sheka the right to play a dominant role in the *woreda*. Four pieces of evidence can be cited to support this argument. To start with, until the time of data collection, no Majang had ever served as the head of Yeki *woreda*, with the group falling under the domination of the Shekicho people.

In February 2015, almost all the members of the cabinet of the Yeki *woreda* were Shekicho. The cabinet is the highest decision-making body at this level. Secondly, minorities' representation in the *woreda* council was insignificant. In the 1995 election, the Shekicho were elected in Masha and Tapi *woreda* to represent the local community for the Federal House of People's Representatives (Markos, 2009). Thirdly, staffing patterns in the various civil service institutions do not reflect the *woreda*'s multicultural context. This extends to the *woreda* police; of 121 police, there were only six Sheko and seven Majang (Markos, 2009). According to informants, fluency in the Shekicho language is a precondition for employment. Fourthly, minorities are denied the constitutional right of receiving primary education in their mother tongue, despite persistent demands for such. They receive primary education in Amharic while the Shekicho started education in their language five years earlier. Informants indicated that the Sheko people in Bench-Maji Zone received primary education in their language, as did the Majang in MNZ. Yeki officials stated that a budget had been allocated and preparations had been completed to launch primary education in the mother tongue in Sheko areas (Interview, Tapi, June 2014).

The second domain of marginalisation in Yeki is exclusion from the economy. Members of minority groups complained that although they pay taxes as residents in the *woreda*, they are considered 'outsiders'. Local informants also indicated that there is no infrastructural development in the Yeki *woreda*. A Sheko informant explained: 'Yeki *Woreda* is a very resourceful area. Especially, it is known for its cash crop, i.e., coffee. A considerable amount of tax has been collected every year. However, the entire budget from the *woreda* source and federal subsidy of Yeki *woreda* went to Masha' (Interview with the Sheko Police, June 2014). This was confirmed by a Ministry of Federal Affairs (MoFA) expert in MNZ, who said, 'the Sheko people obtained social services in Dunchayi *kebele* [that were] built for Majang resettled villages' (Interview with Tasew Meti, 2 July 2014).

Due to minorities' complaints, the SNNPRS organised a conference in Tapi in January 2001. Participants included 15 representatives from each of the minority groups, two to three representatives from various ethnic groups in the district, the then President of the SNNPRS (Abate Kisho), the Speaker of the Yeki *woreda* Council and other officials. Among other things, the minorities demanded the establishment of Yeki as a special zone in which Majang-Sheko people will have ownership rights and will be able to establish their own political party, where their children will receive education in their mother tongue, and where there is fair access to development opportunities. They stated that while Masha and Anderacha (Shekicho area) had experienced much development, Yeki had been neglected since 1991. Although Tapi town in Yeki is economically prosperous and generates significant revenue, Masha is more highly developed and enjoys greater benefits. This creates a sense of 'relative deprivation'. Above all, the indigenous communities alleged that the Shekicho's dominance, and despotism, and indigenous people's exclusion from Yeki political processes had intensified even after 1993. The meeting ended without addressing the root causes of the tension. Indeed, in his closing remarks, the then regional President ridiculed the demands of the indigenous Majang and Sheko.[4]

The local government administration (staffed by Shekicho community members) was accused of intimidating and arresting indigenes rather than coming up with tangible solutions to address communities' legitimate demands. In addition, few Majang and Sheko people had access to land for residences in Tapi town. Other studies indicate that following the deadly conflict in 2002 between the Majang-Sheko group and the Shekicho, the Tapi town administration distributed land to the Sheko and Majang in reparation (Markos, 2009: 47). However, this measure

---

[4] See the minutes of the meeting in Tapi, 2014.

was insufficient. The Shekicho also systematically displaced significant numbers of the Majang-Sheko group from their land.

For the past three decades, a considerable number of Majang have been displaced from the Yeki *woreda* and settled in Godere *woreda*, especially in Gelishi and Goshene *kebeles*. Furthermore, the Shekicho leadership appropriated the forestland of the indigenous Majang and Sheko people for commercial farming without the consent of the local community. This land was allocated to so-called migrant Highlanders (who have moved from the highland areas of Ethiopia) and Shekicho people. For instance, the zone leadership recently leased indigenous forestland and farmland to a Shekicho investor in Tsanu and Dunchayi *kebele* of Yeki and Godere *woredas*, respectively. According to Yeki *woreda* officials, this was free land leased with the informed consent of the local community (Interview with Yeki Woreda Cabinet, Tapi, 26 February 2014). However, local people reported that the land was the community's farmland and was leased without their consent (Interview with Debochi, Tapi, 23 June 2014).

According to local people, the Yeki *woreda* first displaced people from the area in the name of a forest reservation, without providing any compensation (Interview with Debochi, Tapi, 23 June 2014). The local community took the case to the Yeki *woreda*, but the *woreda* administrator provided no immediate and proper response (Focus Group Discussion with Sheko and Majang in Tapi, 23 June 2014). Some community representatives who lodged complaints were arrested.

Apart from political and economic exclusion, social and cultural marginalisation and stereotypes have made minority 'black' group vulnerable to being labelled socially inferior and intellectually limited. There are visible physical differences between the Sheka ('the excluders'), the dominant group, and Majang, Manjo and Sheko ('the minorities'), the excluded. While the Sheka have light skin, blonde hair and straight noses, the Manjo, Majang and Sheko generally have dark skin, flat noses and curly hair. According to some informants, the Shekicho consider themselves superior to the minorities in terms of language, culture and colour. Some elderly Majang and Sheko informants from Alamo stated that the Shekicho did not see the Majang as equals and despised their way of life and language. This attitude, they said, is manifest in common sayings of the Shekicho such as '*Beriya*' and '*Shankilla*', which mean 'slave' and 'black'.

To illustrate these points, let us consider the experience of a Majang informant and his family who left Yeki *woreda* due to marginalisation.

He said that his family was stigmatised and lived in subordination to the dominant Shekicho in Yeki *woreda*. For instance, they were treated as second-class citizens in terms of public service delivery and ownership of forestland. His family and relatives decided to abandon their longstanding residence and move to Gelishi *kebele* of Godere district. Several Majang families followed their example. The Manjo have long been discriminated against by the Sheka (Yoshida, 2013). According to Yoshida, they experience social discrimination by the majority groups 'because of their different dietary habits, i.e., eating wild animals and those not ritually slaughtered' (Yoshida, 2013: 4). While one Shekicho informant, aged 64, denied these accusations, on-the-ground praxis shows that such things are an entrenched social tradition. Although the law forbids this kind of discrimination and stigmatisation, the administration does not enforce it.[5] According to Esman, such activities can be categorised as a 'non-formal process of institutionalized stratification' (Esman, 2004: 124).

Due to socio-economic and political marginalisation, Yeki *woreda* has witnessed a cycle of violent conflict since 1991. At least three major conflicts, occurring at roughly ten-year intervals, can be used as an illustration. The first broke out in 1993. The root cause was a dispute over the Sheka ethnic community's domination of Yeki *woreda*. The militant minorities successfully managed to gain control of Tapi town of Yeki for a few days until the Ethiopian military intervened (Sato, 1997: 569). While the military were deployed to restore peace and offer mediation, the conflict turned into a battle between the military and the excluded communities' United Front. Many people on both sides lost their lives and much property was destroyed. About 18 Majang died (Interview, anonymous, Meti, 2013); however, the biggest losses were experienced by the national defence force and the Sheko local community. The Sheko incurred their biggest loss in their confrontation with the military force at Tsanu *kebele*. The United Front killed more than a hundred people who they regarded as political opponents (Sato, 1997: 569). According to informants, about 275 members of the Ethiopian military died, chiefly

---

[5] For instance, the federal and the regional government instructed the Sheka zone administration to use some sort of equal participation and quota system, but the zone did not enforce it. See for example Minutes of the January 2001 Meeting in Tapi.

in the Arogi *kebele* battle. After the conflict, more than 170 Majang, including the then Godere chief administrator, were imprisoned.[6]

Angered by the government response and continued despotism, minorities took the 2001 national election as an opportunity to control Yeki. In March 2001 they established a registered political party, Sheko-Majangir People's Democratic Unity Organization (SMPDUO). The main office was in Yeki, with branch offices in Godere of Gambella and Sheko district of Bench-Maji Zone in SNNPRS (Vaughan, 2003a). A letter of application was sent to the Southern Ethiopia Peoples Democratic Front (SEPDF), which is one of the members of EPRDF representing the SNNPRS (FGD with Majang and Sheko in Tapi, 23 May 2016). However, the SEPDF/EPRDF rejected their application to become a partner in a letter written by the then president of SNNPRS in November 2002.[7] The SMPDUO participated in the 2001 election as an opposition party and won the majority of seats in Yeki and Godere districts. However, the election board declared the SEPDF/EPRDF ruling party the winner.

This alleged election swindle triggered violent conflict for a second time, lasting from 4 to 8 March 2002. Equipped with guns and spears, the United Front under the leadership of a former Derg regime army officer attacked Tapi on 5 March. The death toll was unclear. According to Majang informants, 45 of their people and 100 Sheko were killed, with around 400 Sheko and 494 Majang houses burned down. The Ethiopian Human Rights Commission (EHRC) estimated that 24 people died, six were injured and about 1,177 houses were burned, with 5,800 people displaced (Markos, 2009). The opposition party, the Southern People's Democratic Coalition (SEPDC), put the figure much higher at 1,672 deaths.

According to an eyewitness, 'In *Koricha kebele* alone 1,000 Sheko died' (Interview, Yeki, 2015). Once the conflict had died down, the SNNPRS Police Commission sent an investigative team to Yeki on 14 March. According to Birhanu (cited in Markos, 2009), after a thorough investigation, the Federal High Court found 121 SMPDUO leaders and members and 247 Manjo people guilty of failure to discharge their

---

[6] The Majang-Sheko informants contended that the government only imprisoned members of weak minority groups without due process of law.

[7] Letter from the Region President to the Sheka Zone Administration, 2002.

official responsibilities and inciting and participating in armed conflict. Police and other officials were fired and imprisoned, with some sentenced to life imprisonment. The minority party SMPDUO was outlawed and banned. Informants said that the investigation was biased, unjustified and discriminatory.

The third bloody conflict erupted in 2014 after 12 years of simmering tension and minor incidents. The researchers were conducting fieldwork during this period and witnessed the unfolding conflict. The major cause was a conflict over mining rights in a location bordering the Gambella region. The Tsanu residents, who are Sheko community members requested a mining licence from Sheka Zone after the Sheko people did, but their request was turned down. They then obtained a licence from Majang Zone. Given that Sheka Zone had already granted access to other Shekicho community members, the Shekos were refused access. Conflict broke out and the security guard in charge of the location was killed. This was followed by large-scale conflict in the area. As part of data collection, the researchers attempted to interview the Sheka Zone chief administrator, but were unsuccessful. The Tapi town administration prosecutor Assegai Demesne said that the conflict occurred in the Yeki *kebele* between 30 and 40 kilometres from Tapi town. He explained that people fled to Tapi town and about 129 houses were burnt to the ground. Citing the difficulty of obtaining information due to the remoteness of the area, another informant, Assefa, stated that residents whose houses were burnt sheltered in Tapi town, and that the area enjoyed relative peace thereafter.

The leasing of land in Sheka Zone to an investor further complicated the situation (Interview with Tasew, Meti, 2 July 2014). The Shekicho investor, Getu, also obtained a lease for land in Dunchayi *kebele* (Interview with Demelash, Tapi, 26 February 2014). The Sheko in the area protested to the Yeki *woreda* administration. Local people linked the selling of land to investors to the Shekichoization of their land. No action was taken in response to the Sheko's demand and violent conflict broke out guards employed by the investor killed a Sheko farmer in February 2014. The local community had tried to continue to farm their land FGD with Sheko, Tapi, 24 June 2014), resulting in the killing of the Sheko farmer (Interview with Demelashi and Ms. Kassechi, Tapi, 26 June 2014). In revenge, the family and relatives of the deceased burned down the investor's property, which was estimated to be worth two million Ethiopian Birr.

Thereafter the houses of around nine Sheko families in Gubeta sub-*kebele* were burned by unknown people, but the Shekicho police were implicated. Shekicho officials asserted that a group of Sheko robbers and Dunchayi Majang cooperative members had burned the houses. Officials in Yeki stated, 'The problem is a direct target against the Shekicho' (Interview with Demelashi and Ms. Kassechi, Tapi, 26 June 2014). In August 2014, the entire Gubeta sub-*kebele* of 400 Sheko people was moved to Dunchayi *kebele*. Some of them, especially the men, entered the jungle. Displaced informants told the researcher that about eight women delivered babies in the forest without medical help, proper food or shelter. People in and around the controversial area are moving into Tapi and other areas (Interview with Demelashi and Ms. Kassechi, Tapi, 26 June 2014). The researcher also witnessed some of these incidents. For instance, on 25 June 2014, about seven buses full of people left the area and arrived in Tapi town. Sheko children have stopped going to school.

Yeki *woreda* police and the SNNPRS special force were immediately deployed in the disputed area. They established a temporary police cluster in Tsanu to restore peace and protect the community's property. The MNZ also deployed local militia and a few police in the area. The security forces arrested and intimidated indigenous civilians and political appointees on slim evidence and without following the due process of the law (Interview with Tasew, Meti, 2 July 2014). Every Majang and Sheko was a potential suspect. Shekicho officials intimidated the local community and most Tapi Majang and Sheko officials and experts fled for fear of arrest. The relatives and families of those arrested were afraid to visit them. Tasew, MNZ from MoFA said that the problem arose when Yeki *woreda* officials identified 12 Sheko people as rebels (Interview, anonymous, Meti, 2 July 2014). This led to community members fleeing to Dunchayi and Gelishi *kebele* in MNZ, changing the dynamics of the conflict that had involved the Majang in Guraferda *woreda* and MNZ.

This tension escalated into large-scale violent conflict on 30 June 2014 around Gubeta sub-*kebele* in Tsanu. The immediate cause was the lowering of the federal flag on 29 April 2014 by a Sheko youth called Teka Tama to show his anger and opposition to Tsanu. He and his followers exchanged gunfire with the Yeki *woreda* police and the police retreated to Tapi. The United Front of the minorities attacked the cars belonging to Sheka Zone police. Eyewitness accounts indicated that many people were killed and injured. The researchers saw injured *kebele* militia and the dead body of a highlander in Yeki *kebele*. A significant number of people were displaced not only from Tsanu *kebele* but other areas. Several houses were burned down in and around Mersha Forest in Gingebeti sub-*kebele* on 3 July 2014. The researcher witnessed the displacement of many Highlanders from Gelishi to Meti town between 1 and 5 July 2014 and also saw Majang police patrols moving to Dunchayi via Goshen *kebele*. On 2nd July federal police were deployed in Meti town to control the situation. The aim of the Sheko and Majang joint revolt expanded to 'liberating Yeki *woreda* from the Shekicho domination' (Interview with a Sheko civil servant, Tapi, 7 July 2014). There was very serious fighting between the two groups between 30 June and 7 July 2014.

The conflict claimed the lives of many people, even though contradictory figures were issued by different sources. According to local private newspapers, about 130 houses were burned down. Unconfirmed reports indicated that as many as 35 people were killed and 58 injured. Many people were also displaced. Acting on a request by the Yeki *Woreda* and Sheka Zone, the Federal Police and Ethiopian National Defence Force intervened. The boundary continued to be a conflict hot spot until August 2014 (Interview with a Sheko civil servant, Tapi, 7 July 2014).

The government convened a peace conference in Tapi from 21 to 22 October 2014 under the auspices of Shiferaw, Minister of the MoFA, to address the conflict between the Gambella and SNNPRS neighbouring *woredas*. There was a high level of participation in the forums, with 37,009 people (including 6,567 women) taking part, including 240 religious leaders, elderly people and popular personalities, 1,707 civil servants and 5,767 members of administrative structures. The conference identified 'anti-peace elements', 'narrow-minded people', arrogance, illegal trafficking in weapons, land-related problems, people serving as intermediaries for foreign forces and rent-seeking among the leadership as causes of the conflict. It was also stated that a party of '*yetikure hayilochi abiyot*' (Black People's Revolutionary Party) had been recently established, ostensibly based on 'racial' solidarity between the Majang and the Sheko.[8] About 18 suspects were arrested with the collaboration of the Federal Police and regional police special force of SNNPRS and their case was

---

[8] Interview with Kiros, Conflict and Early warning expert in the MoFA, Addis Ababa, 17 February 2015. However, local informants deny that this party exists. They argue that the government is externalising its shortcomings. According to the researcher's investigation, it is indeed a mere allegation or labelling.

under investigation. In addition, all the people who were displaced and staying in Majang Zone returned to their homes.

Fostering Peace and Security

We observed persistent social, political, and economic injustice in Yeki *woreda*, which is also common in other parts of Ethiopia marked by ethnic complexity. While federalism presented opportunities for autonomy, in reality, some ethnic groups are subjected to degrading socio-economic and political conditions due to the lack of a clear power-sharing formula. This could undermine the very essence and virtue of federalism in Ethiopia. The crisis is due to social and political institutions' failure to meet the needs of the multiple ethnic groups dispersed across the country's administrative areas. Limited in power, authority and control, minority groups have often been politically and socially excluded. Ongoing stigmatisation and exclusion have led to fatal conflicts. Furthermore, when minorities demanded that such imbalances be addressed based on their constitutional rights, they were tortured, arrested and in many instances, forced to flee.

The Shekicho Zone and Yeki *woreda* police, which are staffed largely by the Shekicho, routinely use torture and intimidation to silence the minority indigenous people. In terms of their closure strategy, the situation in Yeki illustrates what Parkin termed 'exclusionary and usurpationary closure' (Parkin, 1983: 45–46). One of the distinguishing features of exclusionary closure is 'the attempt by one group to secure for itself a privileged position at the expense of some other group through processes of subordination', which Parkin refers to metaphorically as 'the use of power downwards' (Parkin, 1983: 45–46). The minorities' response reflects Parkin's notion of 'usurpationary closure', which refers to 'the use of power upwards, by the groups of subordinates created by the exclusionary closure, aimed at winning a greater share of resources, threatening to bite into the privileges of legally defined superiors' (Parkin, 1983: 45–46).

As noted above, the case study of Yeki *woreda* (district), where the Sheka, Majang, Sheko and Manjo occupy the same political space, shows that tyranny at the local level poses a serious challenge to successful inclusive governance and development in federal Ethiopia. Many of the drivers of the conflict are rooted in exclusionary governance and development deficits. In particular, it is clear from this discussion that the dominance of a single ethnic group undermines local institutions' ability to accommodate diversity. In light of these teething troubles of inclusive governance at the local level in the context of divided multiple ethnic minorities, this section highlights the virtues of 'consociational democracy' as a suitable response.

The model of 'consociational democracy' advocated for by Lijphart (2002) and further promoted by the work of McGarry and O'Leary, in combination with federalism, would seem to be an appropriate alternative to address the rights claims of minorities dominated by a different ethnic group. Power-sharing through 'consociational democracy' is important because it enables marginalised minorities to participate in local governance. While it has its limitations, Lijphart's model of 'consociational democracy' seems best able to deal with these troubles, if not to end them.

Consociational democracy is a neglected theory in federal Ethiopia due to the political culture of hegemonic control (Asnake, 2013). Lijphart argues that it is the most effective approach to achieve inclusive governance in a highly divided society given that 'ethnic divisions have replaced the Cold War as the world's most serious source of violent conflict'. Lijphart identifies four key ingredients of power-sharing under consociational democracy, namely, sharing executive power (grand coalitions), group autonomy (segmental authority especially in the areas of education and culture), mutual veto power and proportionality. We strongly believe that power-sharing arrangements, particularly Lijphart's consociational model, could address ethnic groups' demand for inclusive governance. Ethiopia can take advantage of the intrinsic worth of federalism and consociationalism to promote inclusive governance and ensure socio-economic equality.

There are at least three good reasons to adopt consociational democracy at the local level. First, it will enable effective participation of members of minority groups. Scholars point to consociationalism's ability to achieve inclusive politics and accommodate ethnic diversity. In the context of multiple ethnic minorities at the local level, it serves as a tool for inclusion and the protection of minority interests and stable power-sharing. Constitutional arrangements enable executive power-sharing based on a grand coalition and proportional representation of all major groups in both elected and appointed office, as well as cultural autonomy. As noted previously in the context of first-past-the-post elections since 1991, minorities have not been able to secure representation due to their dispersed settlement patterns and dominant groups' manipulation of election processes. This argument is supported by Vaughan:

> Given the ethnic federal arrangements, minority ethnic groups, even numerically small ones, are less marginalized at the national political level than ever previously in Ethiopia's history. However, several occupational or clan minorities within ethnic groups continue to be marginalized, despised, and disadvantaged, their political representation subsumed within the wider ethnic group. Such stigmatized and despised groups (often craftsmen [sic] or hunters) exist amongst many if not all of Ethiopia's ethnic groups and a number have been encouraged by ethnic federalism to petition for separate representation. Since they live mixed amongst other groups they are unlikely ever to secure representation in a "first past the post" electoral system and remain largely excluded from the local socio-political arena. (Vaughan, 2003a)

Indeed, sharing executive power would reverse the disadvantage brought about by absolute domination by a single ethnic group at the local level. This arrangement could be applied through proportionality (Vaughan, 2003a), with political parties from ethnic groups obtaining proportional representation in appointed positions and allocation of resources. Proportionality in the civil service will also address minorities who are underemployed. This could give minorities the right to access socio-economic privileges and *woreda* administrative, policy-making and decision-making processes.

The second reason for the adoption of consociational democracy is to achieve stable democracy and avoid violent conflict. As detailed in Lijphart's classical work *The Politics of Accommodation* (1968), the Netherlands exemplified a polarised society, yet there was stable democracy and elite consensus because constitutional arrangements enable executive power-sharing/a grand coalition minority veto in government and proportional representation of all major groups in elected/appointed office. In similar vein, Stephan Wolff (cited in Asnake, 2013: 120) proposed the idea of regional consociationalism that combines 'territorial autonomy and consociational power-sharing' to address one of the perennial problems of multi-ethnic federations, the conflict between local minorities and local majorities.

The third argument is that consociational democracy facilitates minority protection through a minority veto in government and cultural autonomy. Through the power of veto, matters sensitive to minorities such as land leasing to investors can be addressed. This is imperative because minorities' core values and resources have been challenged by the economic and political choices formulated and enacted by the majority Sheka elites, such as in the allocation of land for investment. In this way, minorities can influence democratic and governance processes via a win-win approach. Some would argue that federalism combined with consociational democracy would promote ethnic fragmentation. However, this overlooks minorities' struggle for adequate inclusive governance. The main advantage of consociational democracy lies in its inclusion of all groups in the political and economic sphere and its preservation of ethnic cultural autonomy.

Concluding Remarks

The dominance of a single ethnic group is heavily implicated in the (re)production of inequalities in the study area. Although ethnic federalism offers an opportunity for inclusive governance along with self-governance for previously marginalised minorities, this has yet to be achieved. This is because it lacks a clear power-sharing formula at the local level among the elites of various ethnic groups in the same political space. As a result, political exclusion and socio-economic injustice have not only created but sustained disadvantaged minority ethnic groups. There has been a high degree of exclusion with one ethnic group (Sheka) attempting to gain an advantage by employing a variety of exclusionary mechanisms against minorities. Minorities are stigmatised and discriminated against; they feel alienated and estranged from their social and political environment; ultimately, they feel powerless. This demonstrates ethnic federalism's inability to institutionally accommodate the concerns of minority communities dominated by the majority ethnic group at the local level. Furthermore, the minorities experience shared misery at the hands of the Sheka elites. As a response to majority dominance and continued misery, they have adopted usurpationary methods ranging from petitions to violence.

While ethnic federalism has created opportunities for minority inclusive governance, evidence from Yeki *woreda* shows that there are some gaps at the local level. The Yeki *woreda* is just one instance of a bigger issue that exists elsewhere in Ethiopia as well as in other federal systems. The ethnic minorities' situation in Yeki is similar to that in Benishangul-Gumuz, Gambella, Somali and other places. Thus, the experience of marginalised groups may explain the contemporary politics of inclusive governance and development at the local level in federal Ethiopia. This has implications for both how inclusive federalism develops and how it is experienced by different ethnic groups at the local level. Political stability in the study area requires dedication to inclusive governance and equitable development that are indispensable in any society. Governance institutions need to be transformed into an inclusive system that responds to the needs of minority groups. The exclusionary domination observed in the study area is a social ill that must be eliminated in federal Ethiopia by democratic power-sharing and equitable development. I argue that the state's commitment to inclusive governance within the framework of federalism remains the main way of addressing these issues. To do so, it must take into account indigenous people's land rights and right to self-determination. It is therefore strongly recommended that power-sharing arrangements, particularly Lijphart's model of consociational democracy, be used to address ethnic groups' demands for inclusive governance.

Acknowledgements This work was supported in part by Open Society Foundations (OSF) and UPEACE Africa. The author would like to thank OSF and UPEACE for their financial support. The opinions expressed herein are the author's own and do not necessarily reflect the views of OSF or UPEACE Africa.

References

Asnake, K. (2013). *Federalism and ethnic conflict in Ethiopia: A comparative regional study*. Routledge.

Assefa, F. (2013). Ethiopia's experiment in accommodating diversity: 20 years balance sheet. *Ethiopian Journal of Federal Studies, 1*(1), 103–153.

Bach, J.-N. (2014). EPRDF's nation-building: Tinkering with convictions and pragmatism. *Cadernos de Estudos Africanos, 27*, 103–126. https://doi.org/10.4000/cea.1501.

Barata, D. (2012). Minority rights, culture, and Ethiopia's "Third Way" to governance. *African Studies Review, 55*(3), 61–80.

Bassi, M. (2014). Federalism and ethnic minorities in Ethiopia: Ideology, territoriality, human rights, policy. *DADA Rivista di Antropologia Postoglobale, 1*, 45–74. https://doi.org/10.5281/zenodo.1168580

Clapham, C. (2002). Controlling space in Ethiopia. In W. James, D. L. Donham, E. Kurimoto & A. Triulzi (Eds.), *Remapping Ethiopia: Socialism and after* (pp. 9–30). James Currey.

Coakly, J. (2003). Introduction. In J. Coakly (Ed.), *The territorial management of ethnic conflict* (pp. 1–22). Frank Casee.

Esman, M. (2004). *An introduction to ethnic conflict*. Polity Press.

FDRE (Federal Democratic Republic of Ethiopia Constitution). *Proclamation No. 1/1995, Proclamation of the Constitution of Federal Democratic Republic of Ethiopia*, Federal *Negarit Gazeta*, 1st year, No. 1, Addis Ababa, 21 August 1995, adopted on 8 December 1994 and entered into force on 21 August 1995.

Holden, M. (1966). Ethnic accommodation in a historical case. *Comparative Studies in Society and History, 8*, 168–180.

Lijphart, A. (1975). *The politics of accommodation: Pluralism and democracy in the Netherlands* (2nd ed.). University of California Press.

Lijphart, A. (2002). The wave of power-sharing democracy. In A. Reynolds (Ed.), *Architecture of democracy: Constitutional design, conflict management, and democracy* (pp. 1–16). Oxford University Press. https://doi.org/10.1093/0199246467.003.0003

Markos, F. (2009). *Ethnic-conflict and its resolution in the Sheka Zone of Southern Nations, nationalities and peoples regional state* (MA Thesis). Addis Ababa University.

Merera, G. (2003). *Ethiopia: Competing ethnic nationalisms and the quest for democracy, 1960–2000*. Shaker Publishing.

Ministry of Federal Affairs (MoFA). (2005). *A study report on the issues of development and good governance challenges and solutions in Majang Zone Gambella regional state* (in Amharic language). MoFA.

Parkin, F. (1983). *Marxism and class theory: A bourgeois critique*. Reprint. Columbia University Press.

Sato, R. (1997). Christianization through villagization: Experiences of social change among the Majangir: Ethiopia in broader perspective. In K. Fukui & E. Kurimoto (Eds.), *Papers of 13th international Ethiopian studies* (Vol. 2, pp. 574–575). Shokado Book Sellers.

Scherijver, F. (2016). Ethnic accommodation in a unitary state. In K. Cordell & S. Wolff (Eds.), *Routledge handbook of ethnic conflict* (2nd ed., pp. 266–274). Routledge.

Seyoum, M. (2015). *Federalism at the margins of the Ethiopian state: The lived experience of the Majang people* (Doctoral dissertation). Addis Ababa University.

SNNPRS. (1996). *Minutes of the SNNPRS and region 12 security committee. Tapi: SNNPRS government* (Unpublished Document in Amharic Language).

SNNPRS. (2001). *Minutes of the conference on the question of the Majang and Sheka people demand on the Yeki woreda* (Unpublished Document in Amharic Language). SNNPRS Government.

SNNPRS. (2002). *Letter of the president of SNNRS to the Sheko-Majangir peoples democratic unity organization* (Unpublished Document in Amharic Language). President of SNNPRS.

Vaughan, S. (2003a). *Ethnicity and power in Ethiopia* (Doctoral dissertation). University of Edinburgh.

Vaughan, S. (2003b). *Structures and relations of power: Ethiopia. SIDA, background documents country strategy 2003b–2007*. SIDA, Department for Africa.

Vaughan, S. (2006). Response to ethnic federalism: Ethiopia's southern region. In D. Turton (Ed.), *Ethnic federalism: The Ethiopian experience in comparative perspective* (pp. 181–207). James Currey.

Yoshida, S. (2013). The struggle against social discrimination: Petitions by the Manjo in the Kafa and Sheka Zones of Southwest Ethiopia. *Nilo-Ethiopian Studies, 18*, 1–19.

CHAPTER 15

Somaliland's Plural Justice System and Its Influence on Peacebuilding and Development

Hamdi I. Abdulahi

BACKGROUND

A plural justice policy has legal, and governance implications for society. In developing countries, non-state justice systems often handle most disputes and have substantial autonomy and authority (Albrecht, 2012). However, the importance of plural justice is rarely recognised. It is estimated that 80% of disputes in many post-conflict countries are handled outside of the state justice system (Albrecht, 2012). Legal pluralism,

---

The chapter is extracted from my PhD research and therefore reflects the context and influence of plural justice at the time of the research period, 2018–2022.

H. I. Abdulahi (✉)
University for Peace, Addis Ababa, Ethiopia
e-mail: habdilahi@doctorate.upeace.org

© The Author(s), under exclusive license to Springer Nature Switzerland AG 2023
A. O. Akinola, *Contemporary Issues on Governance, Conflict and Security in Africa*,
https://doi.org/10.1007/978-3-031-29635-2_15

which refers to the existence of multiple legal systems within a particular population and locality is vital in conflict and post-conflict settings because state institutions are weakened, and the authority to govern is often contested, resulting in the legitimisation of non-state justice mechanisms (Fearon & Laitin, 2004). However, customary justice often has negative implications, including the downgrading of individual rights (Mar & Tamanaha, 2018).

Non-state law is more appealing than state law because it is less complex and rigid, offers quick solutions and does not involve the payment of fees (Bendaña & Chopra, 2013). It has not only played a significant role in delivering justice to individuals and communities in Somaliland but has also influenced the state justice system's decisions. The judiciary and police transfer cases, including criminal cases to a traditional elder who applies customary law and traditional conflict resolution approaches (Bendaña & Chopra, 2013). However, traditional conflict resolution is not suitable to settle disputes involving children, women and vulnerable communities and individuals as it focuses on communal rather than individual justice (Griffiths, 2011).

Despite this, non-state law retains "authority" that 'is derived mainly from the fact that the non-state is law,' and that its authority is defined by its effectiveness rather than its legality (Mar & Tamanaha, 2018). Therefore, it is 'not all about a law' but the articulation between normative systems in a number of interactions between individuals, individuals and institutions, and institutions (Röder, 2012).

The plural legal governance literature covers most of the domains of human behaviour, including property, contracts, family issues, crime, politics, business, human rights and even issues under constitutional and international law, as well as legal history (Mar & Tamanaha, 2018). From the 1990s, research in this field expanded to cover different transnational dimensions of law and legal pluralism (Nollkaemper, 2013). While transnational flows of legal standards and their "localisation" have a rich history, more contemporary transnational flows involve a great diversity of actors, including governmental and non-governmental organisations, multilateral and bilateral donors and foreign and international law firms who offer legal services to organisations and states in post-conflict situations or in developing countries (Schmitz et al., 2012).

These legal services vary from issues concerning good governance and human rights to protection. The changing nature of state power and changes in states' relationships with civil society have resulted in the revitalisation and reinvention of customary and religious authorities in many regions (Eriksen, 2017). These processes are usually a continuation of earlier transformations in colonial and post-colonial, and pre-socialist and socialist legal history (Gebeye, 2017).

The British imposed common law on Somaliland in 1884 and created new civil and criminal courts called District and Protectorate Courts, respectively (Malito, 2017). The criminal courts followed the British Colonial Indian Penal Code (Abou-elyousr et al., 2016). Family matters were heard in the *Qadi*[1] courts which applied Islamic law, while the local population used customary law for cases involving land disputes, water rights and other matters involving the payment of *Diya*[2] (Ganzglass Martin, 1997).

Several legal instruments amalgamated common law and customary law systems, including the 1898 Principal Order-in-Council, which recognised that Somalis' way of life is customary law-based, as well as the 1937 Qadis Court Ordinance and the 1947 Subordinate Court Ordinance which recognised the application of Sharia law to family issues (Battera & Campo, 2001). Sharia law laid the foundations for both state and tradition systems of governance in Somaliland (Gundel, 2006).

Following conflict with Somalia's Siad Barre-led military regime (Bendaña & Chopra, 2013), in 1991, the Somali National Movement, which had governed Somaliland since the collapse of the central state in 1991, unilaterally declared Somaliland to be a sovereign country independent of the Republic of Somalia (Menkhaus, 2006). Ten years later, on 31 May 2001,[3] Somaliland voted to secede from Somalia (Hammond, 2013; Menkhaus, 2006).

Although no state recognises Somaliland's independence, it operates autonomously and has a functional, centralised government (Bendaña & Chopra, 2013). Its current justice system, which reflects its historical development, is pluralistic and is comprised of the state justice system, Sharia and customary law (Bendaña & Chopra, 2013). What continues to distinguish Somaliland from Somalia is its high levels of stability and

---

[1] An Arabic word for judge.
[2] An Arabic word meaning blood compensation.
[3] Forty-one years after British Somaliland became independent and merged with the Somalia Republic.

security. It has been democratically governed since independence and the state and the elders have made concerted efforts to achieve inter-clan and broader reconciliation (Walls, 2014).

Somaliland's Constitution of 2001 provides for a plural justice order in which Sharia is the paramount law: 'The laws of the nation shall be grounded on and shall not be contrary to Sharia'.[4] Formal justice, and customary, and Sharia orders are operative within this framework. It is estimated that about 80% of judicial services are supplied by customary law, while customary justice services are mainly concentrated in urban centres (Horizon Institute, 2018).

As shown in Table 15.1, Somaliland's judiciary has not undergone any changes since 2009. This is largely due to the political environment. No concerted efforts have been made to address the inadequate legal and policy frameworks and poorly performing state justice institutions. There is little or no civilian oversight, and few mechanisms to hold these institutions to account. The main reason is that the state is more interested in maintaining the support of its key constituencies (primarily clan-based) than in improving the delivery of legal services.

The judiciary is an independent organ of Somaliland's government, which is mandated to interpret laws, settle disputes and adjudicate court cases. It consists of courts and the Attorney-General's office and is under the administrative authority of the High Judicial Council, while the Ministry of Justice is also responsible for the implementation of this council's administrative decisions.

Traditional leaders also exert influence within Somaliland communities. After the collapse of the Somalian government in 1991 and the clan conflicts that continued for the next six years, the elders in Somaliland played a critical role in building peace (Ridout, 2012). The customary-based clan reconciliation process was a multi-phase process and from that time and following the adoption of the constitution in 2000, Somaliland established active formal and traditional governance structures that are slowly gaining public legitimacy and trust.

Somaliland also has a history of consensus-based informal governance by traditional leaders and elders that rests on a system of clans, and sub-clans (Mohamed, 2009). Its traditional dispute settlement system remains

---

[4] Article 5. See, https://aceproject.org/ero-en/regions/africa/SO/somaliland-constitution-2001/view.

Table 15.1 The development of Somaliland's justice system (1991–2021)

Stage	Features
1991–2000	**Establishment** • This post-independence period witnessed successful stabilisation of the country led by its political leadership and elders. Reconciliation was achieved among the clans, providing a stable foundation for state-building • The military regime's draconian legislation was repealed and the focus was on rebuilding judicial institutions and developing a constitution • It was firmly believed that international recognition would be achieved
2001–2012	**Formalisation** • Following a constitutional referendum in which 97% of voters pledged their support, a constitution was enacted setting out rights and separation of powers with an independent judiciary • With external assistance, particularly from the United Nations Development Programme (UNDP), state institutions and civil society legal aid organisations were established and strengthened • Significant effort was put into training judges and prosecutors • New legislation was introduced including the Organization of the Judiciary Act (2003) and Juvenile Justice Law (2007) • Belief in the possibility of international recognition continued following successful municipal (2002), presidential (2003) and parliamentary elections (2005), and an African Union Fact Finding Mission (2005)

(continued)

Table 15.1 (continued)

Stage	Features
2012–2021	**Stagnation** • Progress in state service delivery slowed and stagnated as the state focused on international recognition and opposition to Somaliland's independence. Dissenters' views were repressed, including in the media • The Office of the Attorney General established a specialist Gender-based Violence (GBV) Unit to deal with GBV cases and appointed female prosecutors • Efforts to strengthen the justice sector became more fragmentary, with less will on the part of the state and citizens to address glaring weaknesses in judicial institutions, the legal framework and service delivery standards, and in the critical need to improve intra-government coordination and accountability • Supported by international donors, pilot projects for case management systems for the judiciary were developed but were not replicated beyond Hargeisa • Key formal judicial institutions remain under-resourced, their staff lack training and little progress has been made in expanding their services to rural areas • The National Development Plan II (2017–2021) embraces a human rights approach and identifies a range of justice concerns, but has no comprehensive plan to address them

Source Interview with legal advisor in Hargeisa

Table 15.2 Main actors in the local plural justice system

State justice	Sharia justice	Customary justice
Police	Sharia Arbitration Centres (SAC) headed by Sheiks	Traditional clan leaders (Elders)
Prosecutorial service		
Courts		
Lawyers		
Custodial service		

Source Interview with legal advisor in Hargeisa

the most trusted provider of conflict mediation, prevention, and negotiation (Menkhaus, 2006). However, the formal governance and traditional peacebuilding and conflict resolution systems need to be linked to draw on their respective strengths and to ensure that Somaliland continues to develop as a peaceful state (Menkhaus, 2006).

Many elders remain suspicious of (or hostile to) the formal legal system and its normative focus on individual rights-based justice, regarding it as a threat to the status of *Xeer*. However, some regard themselves as having a shared interest with state institutions in maintaining peaceful coexistence between and within communities (Walls, 2009). Increased collaboration between the customary and state justice systems has emerged in several regions. For example, in the Togdheer region, elders are significantly involved in the state formation process and argue for a more institutionalised role within the state justice system (Walls, 2009). See Table 15.2 for more information on the main actors in the plural justice system.

The plural justice system consists of justice service providers, national, regional and local government authorities and communities.

The Dynamics and Narratives of Plural Justice Systems in Post-conflict Contexts

Several post-conflict societies such as Somaliland, Namibia, East Timor, Kenya and Sudan have fairly functional customary law institutions. Such orders tend to enjoy public confidence despite having practically no budget, as they offer prompt and accessible dispute resolution (Wardak, 2012).

In pre-colonial Africa, the justice framework was solely based on religion and the customary system, informed by culture and norms (Ruppel & Ruppel-Schlichting, 2011). Colonisation introduced state laws that resulted in a more plural legal order in many countries. European colonial occupation significantly altered African legal, political, social and economic governance and institutional structures (Fenrich et al., 2011). For example, the English common law system introduced by the British contributed to the existence of several legal systems within former colonies like Nigeria, Malawi, Namibia, South Africa, Uganda and Ghana (Obatusin, 2018).

Legal pluralism in these countries involves multiple legal systems where the law of a former colonial authority exists alongside religious and customary-based systems (Ruppel & Ruppel-Schlichting, 2011). The justice system thus bases its legal rules and institutions on two or more normative orders. This is true in every African country (Obatusin, 2018) whose primary sources of law include indigenous African customary orders, Sharia, and colonial imported legal systems (Grenfell, 2006).

While Africa's state justice mechanisms stem from the former colonial powers' legal customs, the customary justice system is based on norms and values passed down from generation to generation as customary law (Cubitt, 2014). This mechanism, which operates alongside the formal system in some African countries, deals with a wide range of issues. Ndulo (2011) notes that, the fact that it is accessible at community level and uses local languages makes it more popular than other normative orders.

Several scholars have promoted the creation of plural justice mechanisms by combining state and non-state justice systems. Clark and Stephens advocate for a grounded approach tailored to local needs and prospects that focuses on reducing injustice rather than seeking to achieve an ideal form of justice. The authors propose five key steps to strengthen plural justice systems, namely, (1) understanding the political and policy context of plural orders; (2) analysing their strengths and weaknesses; (3) identifying entry points to strengthen hybrid justice systems; (4) assessing opportunities for engagement; and (5) long-term commitment to implementation.

Customary justice systems have been in existence since time immemorial in Africa (Derrer, 2012). Although colonialism tended to reject the notion of a plural order, some approaches pointed to a degree of accommodation (Shinwari, 2015). For example, in Somaliland, the British respected the authority of customary leaders to administer local customary law (Gebeye, 2019). The colonisers played a role in empowering some customary leaders and disempowering others, which reduced the influence of customary law (Danish Institute for Human Rights, 2012). The policy was to defer to customary leaders with regard to clan-related issues; however, clan chiefs who collaborated with the colonial authorities' roles were strengthened, while those who resisted colonial authority were deposed (Danish Institute for Human Rights, 2012).

Finally, it is worth noting that, while a single state justice system was tested in a few post-conflict African states, this was found to be challenging in the majority of cases. However, in Rwanda, there has been some success in using the customary system to promote post-conflict reconciliation, while clan conflict resolution mechanisms remain operational in Somaliland. As noted previously, with the collapse of the central Somalia government and the re-birth of Somaliland, the customary system regained public legitimacy and trust and its traditional dispute settlement system is the most trusted provider of conflict mediation, prevention and negotiation (Menkhaus, 2006).

SOMALILAND'S PLURAL JUSTICE ORDERS IN PRACTICE

Somaliland's customary system was one of the main tools employed to facilitate clan reconciliation. The process was led by elders who later continued to address community disputes using the customary system. Prior to the arrival of the British in Somaliland, the people were governed by customary laws and the Sharia system Kulow (2018). Members of the Somaliland Lawyers Association (SOLLA) in Hargeisa indicated in an interview that:

> The earliest justice regulations applied in Somaliland go way back to early Muslim influence through trade relations along the coast of Berbera, Maydh, Hiis, and Zaila. The development of a legal system for justice governance throughout Somaliland resulted in contests between the clan and pertinent opposing social and political interests. These conflicting interests were manifested by colonial policy on one hand, and the Somali clan based system on the other. British efforts to eliminate customary justice failed, leading to the creation of a plural justice order that endures to the present.

Indeed, as witnessed in many parts of Africa, the legal and institutional frameworks for justice governance increasingly took root in the Somaliland territories due to colonial influence (Menkhaus, 2006). The British colonists insisted on the use of the English legal system in Somaliland. However, they were confronted by (a) the need to adapt and work with pre-existing Somali customary systems, and (b) demands by traditional leaders that both the customary system and the Sharia legal system be preserved (Hart et al., 2010). The judicial system fell short of equal access to justice. Instead, state law was applied as a tool for social and political control, which is not founded on reason or the common good (Kulow, 2018).

State law was built on colonial policy to legalise what I would argue was an affront to justice. Rawls conceptualised justice as a guarantee that no arbitrary distinction is made between people in assigning fundamental rights and duties. Justice in Somaliland draws from three dominant legal traditions that have coexisted, competed and evolved throughout history (Bendaña & Chopra, 2013). A traditional leader in Hargeisa observed:

> Before colonial rule, a combination of *Xeer* and Sharia coexisted across the communities and clans; then, colonial authorities introduced their legal systems. The first pre-independence Constitution adopted in 1958 included the principle that the parties to a dispute could agree on whether to resolve their case through customary law, Sharia, or the state codified law. Somali customary law dominated the pre-colonial legal system; this was a clan-based system where individuals were characterised as clan members and were loyal to their clan leaders.

Customary justice has traditionally been used in Somaliland to govern relations among clans and sub-clans through the delivery of justice that primarily aims to manage conflict and maintain peace (Bendaña & Chopra, 2013). Firmly rooted in the notion of collective responsibility, it focuses less on the rights of individuals than ensuring rights-based justice (Kulow, 2018). As an expression of a value system, *Xeer* reflects clans' priorities and strengths; therefore, it is not designed to provide equal protection to minority clans. People without clan protection (for example, the Gabooye[5] community) have a significantly lower chance of successfully resorting to *Xeer* for protection of their rights and interests. The traditional leader in Hargeisa indicated that

> a clan is first and foremost a category of social organisation that anchors individual and group identity. In other words, not only does it divide Somalis into different clans, but each clan into further sub-clan segments, each of which harks back to one common male ancestor. The sub-clan segments themselves comprise further sub-groups up to the most basic unit that is responsible for compensating a victim's kin (blood compensation) in case their member commits murder.

In other words, compensation, retaliation and distribution of compensatory payments are collective. Under *Xeer*, the parties involved choose retaliation or negotiations for compensation. To avoid retaliation, the principle that collective liability outweighs individual responsibility is often applied (Bendaña & Chopra, 2013).

The clan system is important in regulating, protecting and adjudicating cases over land-based resources. For example, the traditional leader added that:

> the nomadic pastoralists in Somaliland rely on selected water sources as crucial bases from which to access pastures during the drought period. This imperative elevated the question of territorial control and, ultimately, clan homelands. In some cases, the elders in Sallahley district introduced protocol for the usage of wells and safe passage had to be regulated among host clans, highly mobile herders, and their clans, [resulting in] ... flexible contractual agreements; this was specifically for the drought period. In this case, *Xeer* became necessary. These clans tend to be more open to the adoption of new arrivals, and their members' allegiance to their clans was traditionally equalled by their allegiance to their location of residence.

Rather than a single cohesive and universally applicable code, a large part of Somali customary law consists of bilateral or multilateral contracts entered into by clan groups in a particular locality. Unlike foundational constitutions, *Xeer* represents a convention of legal practice among

---

[5] Groups of people known collectively as *Gabooye* that have traditionally been considered distinct and lower-caste groups, and are also referred to by the derogatory moniker "Midgan".

Somali clans that is based on collective responsibility and compensation rather than individual punishment—a common feature of most customary justice systems (Bendaña & Chopra, 2013).

Customary and Islamic practices are intertwined, with elements of Sharia filling gaps in customary Somali regulation, while *Xeer* offers particular provisions in relation to specific issues. Sharia thus operates at a more general level. *Xeer*, which predates Sharia, is composed largely of Somali terms and concepts, and is thus truly indigenous to the Somali community. It was established that *Xeer* continues to be the dominant system in Somaliland, governing social relationships, disputes and crimes (LAW, 2015, 56). Taking into account preference for the implementation of Sharia law across society, it can be argued that these systems compete, but sometimes operate interchangeably, offering various legal tools. Elders are central to the process by which *Xeer* is negotiated, agreed upon and applied. They are usually selected by male clan members based on their reputation for fairness, rhetorical aptitude, knowledge of Sharia, *Xeer* precedence and a commitment to supporting their communities. Others inherit their positions.

This is an exclusively male position, with elders often being selected to sit on both ad hoc and permanent councils (*Guurti*). The differentiation among elders in part responds to the exigencies of more centralised political systems, and in part, corresponds to the policies of colonial and subsequent military administrations. The traditional leader in Hargeisa commented that:

> At the highest political level, elders represent the legacy of past Somali sultanates, operating under the title of *Sultan,* and second level leadership which operates under the title of *Boqor* or *Akil*. These elders are influential in political decisions, where they represent their entire clan, including all sub-clans, even if they may be at odds with one another. The *Aqil* operate between communities and government in Somaliland; they were instituted by British colonial administrators and installed for political reasons by the military government during the latter half of the twentieth century. Their primary duties which are the main source of legitimacy are the application of *Xeer Guud* (general customary laws) and *Xeer Gaar ah* (specific customary laws) when disputes arise, to prevent their escalation into violence, or to halt violence once erupted. The *Xeer* comprises two different types of law, *Xeer Guud* that is applied to common issues and procedures such as blood compensation, and *Xeer Gaar ah* that stipulates appropriate compensation and handling of a range of violations, which are

negotiated by clan elders. The application of the specific one is always between two sub-clans whereas the general one applies to the wider clan.

Rather than advancing that state institutions have failed completely, scholars describe the current situation as one of 'hybrid political orders'. This discursive shift stems from acknowledgement that rather than an absence of the rule of law, Somaliland now operates in a pluralistic legal and justice landscape. This approach sidesteps the previously common depiction of customary justice as "traditional" and recognises that this system follows highly formalised processes, which Western observers long disregarded on the basis that *Xeer* did not exist in written form and was not aligned with international human rights norms.

A former member of parliament (MP) in Somaliland indicated that:

> Following independence from the British colonies in 1960, a series of laws structuring the Somalia judiciary and legal system were adopted, including the 1962 Law on the Organization of the Judiciary, along with criminal, civil and procedures codes. The 1960 Somali legal system combined elements from the Italian and British legal traditions, including the civil code copied from Egypt, elements of the Italian commercial code, the criminal code from Italy, and criminal procedure from the Indian system practiced in the British colony.

The MP explained that the criminal and procedure codes of 1963 indicate that Sharia was only allowed for matters concerning family, inheritance and minor civil disputes, while Somali *Xeer* was accepted as a legitimate option for the settlement of clan disputes. The post-colonial state system was rarely applied outside the main urban areas, where *Xeer* and Sharia continued to dominate (Kenny et al., 2019). Within the state system, legal practitioners continued to follow the system applied prior to independence, namely common law in the former British Somaliland and civil and penal codes in the former Italian territory (Kenny et al., 2019).

The failure to integrate these sources of law contributes to conflicts over the applicable law, procedure and jurisdiction. In an interview, a former Somaliland Solicitor-General in Hargeisa confirmed that:

> After the 1969 coup that brought Major General Siyad Barre to power, the Somali legal and judicial system was transformed to reflect the regime ideology of scientific socialism. The Supreme Revolutionary Council (SRC) of 1969 effectively nullified the independence of the judiciary by

temporarily abolishing the Constitution and courts, establishing a national security court with jurisdiction over all offences under the Somali penal code with a prioritisation of crimes against the State and public order, and restricting the functions and jurisdictions of the courts that remained.

He added that the SRC obliterated "tribalism" and key elements of *Xeer*, including rights to tribal land, water and grazing rights. By 1972, all land not owned by a group recognised as legitimate by the SRC was nationalised. In 1973, a draft civil code was introduced that included drastic changes to the laws of inheritance, personal contracts, water grazing rights and clan-based responsibility for payment of damages that had previously been provided for under Sharia and Somali customary law.

The Somaliland Constitution (2000)[6] recognises Sharia as the ultimate source of law and the guiding principle of governance.[7] It also recognises state law and custom (*Xeer*), although they are deemed secondary in authority, and only valid to the extent that they do not contradict Sharia principles. In practice, this means that judges have to navigate and juggle between *Xeer*, statute and Sharia to determine which rules apply in different contexts. This poses a significant challenge when judges lack a sound understanding of *Shafi'i*[8] jurisprudence and the principles underlying the application of the primary and secondary sources (*ijtihad*).

Although the Somaliland Constitution explicitly states that the laws of the nation shall be based on, and not contravene, Islamic Sharia (Article 5), its application to deliver clear and predictable justice can be a challenge. One of the Sheikhs at the Hargeisa SAC stated that:

> One of the reasons is the lack of knowledge of Shari'ah jurisprudence among formal, informal, and religious justice actors. This limited knowledge can be attributed to the years of conflict in the country where local universities ... ground to a halt and have not yet regained their

---

[6] Available at http://www.somalilandlaw.com/Somaliland_Constitution_Text_only_Eng_IJSLL.pdf

[7] Article 5: Religion (1) Islam is the religion of the Somaliland state, and the promotion of any religion in the territory of Somaliland, other than Islam, is prohibited. (2) The laws of the nation shall be grounded on and shall not be contrary to Islamic Sharia. (3) The state shall promote religious tenets (religious affairs) and shall fulfill Sharia principles and discourage immoral acts and reprehensible behavior. (4) The calendar shall be the Islamic Calendar based on the hijra, and the Gregorian calendar.

[8] One of the four schools of Islamic law in Sunni Islam.

capacity to deliver rigorous high-quality legal education. The knowledge and experience [of] ... justice practitioners who received their religious education in other countries with different jurisprudences than *Shafi'I* complicates matters. This contributes to further confusion around the applicable Shari'ah principles.

The Sheik added that, despite its formal supremacy, Sharia coexists, and is often applied in combination, with *Xeer* norms. Especially in the absence of strong religious scholarship, this means that the different justice actors' understanding of Sharia is strongly influenced by *Xeer* norms. As a result, some rules and practices in the two systems are in agreement, but some practices upheld by *Xeer* contradict the principles enshrined in Sharia.

There are a variety of reasons why people resort to *Xeer* or *Sharia* mechanisms instead of the regular courts when seeking justice. Based on interviews with numerous traditional leaders and regional court judges, one of the primary reasons is that citizens perceive customary law and *Sharia* mechanisms as less time-consuming with more simple and straightforward protocols and procedures than the formal court system. Lawyers in Hargeisa also noted that such informal mechanisms tend to reach and enforce judgements more quickly than the formal justice system and to resolve cases more efficiently. The reason is that they have fewer procedural safeguards. While efficiency is an important consideration, in some cases, procedural safeguards should be prioritised to protect the rights of vulnerable parties and ensure the accuracy of judgements.

The costs associated with opening a case is another important reason why people tend to prefer to seek justice through informal mechanisms. In most cases, no fees or payments are required to initiate or continue litigation. This makes these mechanisms an attractive option for those that lack the means to pay legal and court fees. However, as noted by the Director of Hargeisa University Legal Aid Clinic, this should not prevent someone from approaching the courts:

> Legal assistance should be provided to indigent parties. While there is no comprehensive legal aid scheme in place in Somaliland, work has been done to address this justice gap. For example, Oxfam partnered with the Legal Aid Clinic, a national legal services organisation based at the University of Hargeisa to implement *Danyare Kalkaal*, a two-year programme funded by a European Union grant, which helps communities in Somaliland to access legal services fairly and in a cost-effective manner.

For centuries, Somalis used *Xeer* to resolve their disputes, and they resorted to this system when the government system collapsed in 1991. *Xeer* thus provided stability in the intervening years. In part because of this history, interviewees from lawyers' associations stated that informal justice mechanisms have more legitimacy and credibility among the public, as well as being better adapted to the cultural needs and sensitivities of many (except for women, minority groups and migrants). A Director-General at the Ministry of Justice noted that:

> People in Somaliland, like anywhere else, are attached to their traditional customs and values, and feel more comfortable solving problems in a manner which comports with those traditional customs and values. This includes better accessibility for the average Somali man, who is generally the head of his household and would handle any disputes engaged in by close relatives. He does not need any special education or qualifications to access informal justice mechanisms, as opposed to the formal court system where qualified legal representation is necessary. ... [However, these mechanisms] systematically exclude Somali women. Therefore, while an informal justice mechanism might be culturally better suited to Somalis, this ... should not be placed above the protection of the fundamental rights of women or vulnerable groups.

Nonetheless, traditional leaders, Sheiks, regional court judges and lawyers that were interviewed acknowledged the weaknesses of *Xeer* in resolving some types of disputes. For example, *Xeer* judgements do not have the force of law, or government endorsement, unless the use of *Xeer* in the particular case has been certified by the court before the parties concluded the final agreement. In addition, Somali culture is changing, especially in major cities such as Hargeisa. Returnees from the diaspora have more experience of a formal justice system and prefer to use it to resolve disputes. Returnees also endorse societal changes, including the abandonment of *Xeer* and the adoption of formal systems of justice like those they experienced during their time abroad, and increased participation of women in the justice sector.

RESOLVING RESOURCE-BASED DISPUTES

The security situation in Somaliland essentially depends on maintaining friendly and productive inter-clan relations. As explained by a traditional leader, the peacekeeping processes between clans depend on *Xeer* in the form of agreements between clan elders to apprehend criminal elements who threaten the peace. *Xeer* generally governs the distribution of resources between clans in rural areas. Moreover, he noted that where public institutions are weak, such as in rural areas, people depend much more on *Xeer* and *Sharia*. Thus informal mechanisms shape the security situation in rural areas to a much greater extent than in the major cities. In this way, *Xeer* is seen as the most important mechanism to resolve land and resource disputes, and thus maintain peace and stability in Somaliland.

A traditional leader in Hargeisa explained that *Xeer* evolved as the primary means to settle disputes over land and other resources. Beyond the rural areas, many urban land disputes continue to be resolved through *Xeer*, and land usage in urban centres is administered by committees of traditional elders. Increasingly, however, urban dwellers are referring land disputes to Land Dispute Tribunals (LDT) and the formal courts. According to an LDT committee member in Hargeisa, this special tribunal was created by an act of parliament to enforce statutory law governing land ownership. However, it seems to mainly handle land disputes in urban and peri-urban areas around Hargeisa, and it is not clear how well it functions.

Consultations between elders, Sheiks, the judiciary, and representatives of various government ministries, such as the Ministry of Justice, should be organised to discuss ways to strengthen trust and cooperation between these multiple actors and create relevant and useful links between the two systems. A regional court judge noted that:

> Gradually, Somaliland justice stakeholders are coming to grips with the challenges of contextualising the place of customary justice, Sharia courts, and the merits and demerits of adopting a state justice system. At the centre of this choice should be how Somaliland's legal system can protect individual rights and promote human rights. Adherence to Sharia law and loyalty to one's clan are highly valued in practice. Both govern the private and collective life of clan members in particular and Somaliland in general, and these values would not be easily changed by bringing in new polices and laws.

A traditional leader in Hargeisa commented:

> The traditional justice system mainly focuses on clan norms of land tenure and use of water. Livestock and grazing land are preserved by the clan, and

communal access to pasture and water is the norm. Any attempt to codify customary justice and laws is not only challenging, but might also be risky as it may to eliminate flexibility.

A lawyer in Hargeisa indicated that,

> there is widespread mistrust of the judiciary due to a lack of judicial impartiality, external interference, and abuse of power by judges for political influence. Radical reform of customary and Sharia institutions would fail to bring about satisfactory justice. Moreover, such reform could lead to unpremeditated harmful consequences such as damaging the fabric of traditional society and leading to unnecessary litigation and violence.

This is consistent with Sage (2005) and Maru's (2008) findings. The lawyer added that,

> customary justice needs to be reformed gradually to bring it in line with the constitution and human rights laws. An example of the incompatibility of Sharia legal practices, the customary justice and state justice system is collective criminal responsibility; the three [differ] ... in establishing [the] age for criminal responsibilities.

Moreover, as observed by the Director-General in the Somaliland Ministry of Justice, designing and implementing justice reforms require significant capacity and resources, and in particular a strong Ministry of Justice, parliament, judiciary and police organs, all of which Somaliland lacks. He added that, while international development support has encouraged justice reform, such reform should embrace the goals of Somaliland's peace building and community policy strategies and processes and protection of constitutionally guaranteed individual rights. He was of the view that the customary justice system will continue to play a vital role in Somaliland's rural areas for some years to come as the country still needs to extend state justice institutions to all regions and districts.

A former MP in Somaliland noted that,

> there are two ways of reorganising the justice system in Somaliland; amendment of the constitution to provide clarity on article 5,[9] its scope and limitation and the Judicial Council should be mandated to carry out the re-establishment and reform of the justice system. Harmonisation and integration of the different justice systems should include inclusive consultation and strong political commitment from all ... stakeholders including [the] Shira Arbitration Centre, the independent sheiks, the judiciary, the Ministry of Justice, parliament, the police, prisons, the lawyers' association, local traditional institutions, universities and civil society organisations.

As a first step, the consultations could focus on state recognition of decisions by customary justice mechanisms and their enforcement with the help of governmental institutions. The relationship between customary dispute settlement and state courts needs to be placed within the context of Somaliland's fledgling court system and its ongoing efforts to become more reliable and accessible across the country.

As the state courts mature and deliver more high-quality decisions, the question will be whether they should be able to apply *Xeer* norms; function as an appeal court for decisions made by the customary dispute settlement system; and decide whether a *Xeer* norm or practice contravenes Sharia or national law. A unified judiciary vested with all judicial powers requires that all laws (Sharia, common, civil and customary) are applied. A Supreme Court judge remarked:

> A unified judiciary that has the power to adjudicate all cases regardless of the system, will encourage judges to learn all the different justice systems, legal systems and laws so as to deliver better justice service for the Somaliland society. This approach will avoid jurisdictional conflict, and enhance uniformity of decisions to avoid contradictory decisions and conflicts of laws. It eases the review and application of laws as any review will reflect the delivery of a justice service that is substantively uniform and procedurally harmonised.

This is in line with Maru's (2008) recommendations.

---

[9] Article 5 sub (2) The laws of the nation shall be grounded on and shall not be contrary to Islamic Sharia.

Conclusion

Three justice systems (state, Sharia and customary) currently operate in Somaliland. As a developing country on a pathway out of fragility, one of the challenges is the high cost of state justice services, composed of police, prosecutors, courts, prisons and legal aid services. As a result, these services are often confined to urban centres. Outside of urban centres, customary justice systems predominate. However, these are also not free from challenges. Customary systems struggle to provide redress in fast-urbanising, demographically changing environments with a high volume of complex disputes, such as over land, calling for technical capacity that non-state actors lack. Similarly, while customary systems play an effective role in preventing communal conflict, when it comes to handling disputes involving women and minority groups, they frequently do so in a way that undermines their rights. The limited presence of formal justice systems in many parts of Somaliland means that it is difficult for the state to intervene to safeguard these rights.

There is significant value in assisting providers of informal and traditional services and fostering links between them and formal state provision. Previous interventions by the international community have mainly involved ad hoc state justice institutions with a focus on policy and legal support, training, equipment, and infrastructure. There is no overall agreement on which approaches could be effectively coordinated, or collective consideration of lessons learned. This has led to duplication and confusion as well as a tendency to repeat interventions without clarity on their effectiveness. Moreover, the state justice system is marked by irregularities, high costs and delays in the adjudication of cases, mainly due to rigid, complex and outdated laws.

Arguably, international interventions have perpetuated the colonial legacy, where state police mainly focused on protecting the elite in the main urban centres, marginalising the poor in rural areas. No strategies have been proposed to create a sustainable model for national service delivery, or even a path towards this goal. It is thus not surprising that interventions have seemed to lack coherence, vision or relevance. Indeed, so far they have shown no signs of providing any sustainable alternative to the informal arrangements on which most Somaliland citizens depend, if that was their aim.

Socio-demographic differences in knowledge levels were found to be less statistically prominent. For instance, respondents who opted for the state justice system had either secondary or post-secondary certificates, whereas the majority of those that chose the non-state justice system, had primary or no formal education. These findings raise both theoretical and politically relevant questions such as: "why do justice users prefer the non-state justice system? Could this be attributed to context, knowledge, and understanding of the practitioners?" An analysis of the factors that influence the choice of a justice system by the users provided answers.

The systemic discrimination in customary justice experienced by women, minority clans, and internally displaced communities is rooted in Somaliland's patriarchal clan-based social order. It manifests in several ways and is often compounded for those belonging to more than one of these social groups. Firstly, customary law prohibits these groups' full enjoyment of their individual rights as defined in the Somaliland Constitution, in the relevant international human rights instruments that Somaliland has adopted, and Sharia prescripts that promote individual and women's rights. For instance, it restricts women's rights to own land, and tolerates the theft of their land inheritance and abuse such as forced marriage. Secondly, given that the customary legal system is directed at dispute resolution through restitution and compensation between clans and sub-clans based on legal agreements (*xeer*), rather than individual justice and punishment of individual perpetrators, female survivors of gender-based violence often receive little or no compensation, and the perpetrators are not directly held to account. Thirdly, the structural discrimination experienced by minority clans often stems from the protection they may have to seek from majority clans which comes at a material cost and often subordinates their legal rights to those of the majority clan. Fourthly, internally displaced people's vulnerability to discrimination frequently stems from their lack of *xeer* with surrounding host clans. Without the rights and protection a *xeer* affords, they rarely receive fair justice in disputes with their host communities. Despite Somaliland law and Sharia explicitly proscribing many of these discriminatory customary practices, the prevalence of customary law and the deep-rooted social norms and practices underpinning them have successfully resisted their abolition.

Sheiks and Sharia law judges are the leading opinion shapers whose advice is frequently sought, followed by traditional clan leaders and lawyers. Religious and clan leaders are often approached on issues regarding family matters, while a lawyer's opinion is often sought in criminal cases. Several factors determine the choice of justice options, including the outcome, physical accessibility, type of case, enforcement capacity and external influence such as a clan or a family member.

In conclusion, numerous factors erode public confidence in the state justice system. There is a need for a unified judiciary with the power to adjudicate all cases regardless of the system. This will encourage judges to learn about all the different justice and legal systems, and laws so as to deliver improved justice to Somaliland society. It will avoid jurisdictional conflict and enhance uniformity to avoid contradictory decisions and conflicts of law. A unified approach will ease the review and application of laws as any review will reflect delivery of justice that is substantively uniform and procedurally harmonised.

REFERENCES

Abou-elyousr, K., Islamic, S., & Union, C. (2016). *Understanding the Somalia justice systems challenges and the way forward.* https://www.academia.edu/32137861/Comparative_Analysis_of_the_Somali_Justice_Systems_Sharia_Law_Statuary_Laws_and_Customary_Law_Xeer_

Albrecht, P. A. (2012). *Foundational hybridity and its reproduction: Security sector reform in Sierra Leone.* Copenhagen Business School (CBS).

Battera, F., & Campo, A. (2001). The evolution and integration of different legal systems in the Horn of Africa: The case of Somaliland. *Global Jurist Topics, 1*(1), 1–38.

Bendaña, A., & Chopra, T. (2013). Women's rights, state-centric rule of law, and legal pluralism in Somaliland. *Hague Journal on the Rule of Law, 5,* 44–73.

Cubitt, C. (2014). An introduction to governance in Africa. *Governance in Africa, 1,* 1–9.

Danish Institute for Human Rights. (2012). *Informal justice systems: Charting a course for human rights-based engagement.* UNDP, UNICEF and UN Women. https://www.unwomen.org/sites/default/files/Headquarters/Attachments/Sections/Library/Publications/2013/1/Informal-Justice-Systems-Charting-a-Course-for-Human-Rights-Based-Engagement.pdf

Derrer, N. (2012). *The role of civil society in good governance as part of international development cooperation case study Uganda.* https://www.semanticscholar.org/paper/The-role-of-civil-society-in-good-governance-as-of-Derrer/e0b77073ecb77eb892d140ed926e2a68d58871e9.

Eriksen, E. O. (2017). *Three conceptions of global political justice* (GLOBUS Research Papers 1/2016), pp. 1–27.

Fearon, J. D., & Laitin, D. D. (2004). Neotrusteeship and the problem of weak states. *International Security, 28,* 5–43.

Fenrich, J., Galizzi, P., & Higgins, T. (Eds.). (2011). *The future of African customary law.* Cambridge University Press.
Ganzglass Martin, R. (1997). The restoration of the Somali justice system. In W. Clarke & J. Herbst (Eds.), *Learning from Somalia: The lessons of armed humanitarian intervention.* Westview.
Gebeye, B. A. (2017). Legal theory in Africa: Between legal centralism and legal pluralism. *Queen Mary Law Journal,* 27–48. https://www.academia.edu/ 34195081/Legal_Theory_in_Africa_Between_Legal_Centralism_and_Legal_ Pluralism
Gebeye, B. A. (2019). The Janus face of legal pluralism for the rule of law promotion in sub-Saharan Africa. *Canadian Journal of African Studies, 53*(2), 337–353.
Grenfell, L. A. (2006). Legal pluralism and the rule of law in Timor Leste. *Leiden Journal of International Law, 19*(2), 305–337.
Griffiths, A. (2011). Pursuing legal pluralism: The power of paradigms in a global world. *Journal of Legal Pluralism and Unofficial Law, 43*(64), 173–202.
Gundel, J. (2006). *The predicament of the Oday: The role of traditional structures in security, rights, law and development in Somalia.* DRC.
Hammond, L. (2013). Somalia rising; Things are starting to change for the world's longest failed state. *Journal of Eastern African Studies, 7*(1), 183–193.
Hart, B., & Muhyadin, S. (2010). Integrating principles and practices of customary law, conflict transformation, and restorative justice in Somaliland. *Africa Peace and Conflict Journal, 3*(2), 1–18.
Horizon Institute. (2018). *Seeking justice for rape in Somaliland.* https://www. thehorizoninstitute.org/usr/documents/publications/document_url/15/ horizon-institute-s-report-on-prosecution-of-rape-cases-in-somaliland-march-2018.pdf
Kenny, L., Koshin, H., Sulaiman, M., & Cislaghi, B. (2019). Adolescent-led marriage in Somaliland and Puntland: A surprising interaction of agency and social norms. *Journal of Adolescence, 72,* 101–111. https://doi.org/10.1016/ j.adolescence.2019.02.009
Kulow, M. (2018). *Silent cry of Somali customary law "Xeer".* International Conference on Social Science, Humanities and Education. https://www.dpu blication.com/wp-content/uploads/2018/12/ICSHE-2-V-202.pdf, p. 114.
LAW. (2015). *Legal Aid Providers Supporting GBV Survivors in Somalia.* https://www.legalactionworldwide.org/gender-equality-gbv/report-legal-aid-providers-supporting-gender-based-violence-survivors-in-somalia/
Le Sage, A (2005). *Stateless justice in Somalia: Formal and informal rule of law initiatives.* Henry Dunant Centre for Humanitarian Dialogue.

Malito, D. (2017). *Neutral in favour of whom? The UN intervention in Somalia and the Somaliland peace process.* https://booksc.org/book/637 46218/c83c06

Mar, M., & Tamanaha, B. (2018). Understanding legal pluralism: Past to present, local to global. *Legal Theory and Social Sciences*, 447–483.

Maru, M. T. (2008). The future of Somalia's legal system and its contribution to peace and development. *Journal of Peacebuilding & Development*, 4(1), 1–15.

Menkhaus, K. (2006). Governance without government in Somalia spoilers, state building, and the politics of coping. *International Security*, 31(3), 74–106.

Mohamed, F. H. (2009). *Research guide to the Somaliland legal system.* Hauser Global Law School Programme.

Ndulo, M. (2011). African customary law, customs, and women's rights. *Indiana Journal of Global Legal Studies*, 18(1), 87–120.

Nollkaemper, A. (2013). *Normative pluralism and international law: Exploring global governance.* Cambridge University Press.

Obatusin, S. C. (2018). Customary law principles as a tool for human rights advocacy: Innovating Nigerian customary practices using lessons from Ugandan and South African courts. *Columbia Journal of Transnational Law*, 56, 636–679.

Ridout, T. A. (2012). Building peace and the state in Somaliland: The factors of success. *The Journal of the Middle East and Africa*, 3(2), 136–156.

Röder, T. J. (2012). *Informal justice systems: Challenges and perspectives* (58th ed.). Innovations in Rule of Law.

Ruppel, O. C., & Ruppel-Schlichting, K. (2011). Legal and judicial pluralism in Namibia and beyond: A modern approach to African legal architecture? *Journal of Legal Pluralism and Unofficial Law*, 43(64), 33–63.

Schmitz, C., Matyok, T., Sloan, L., & James, C. (2012). The relationship between social work and environmental sustainability: Implications for interdisciplinary practice. *International Journal of Social Welfare*, 21(3), 278–286.

Shinwari, A. N. (2015). *Understanding the informal justice system: Opportunities and possibilities for legal pluralism in Pakistan.* Community Appraisal and Monitoring Programme: CAMP.

Walls, M. (2009). The emergence of a Somali state: Building peace from civil war in Somaliland. *African Affairs*, 108(432), 371–389.

Walls, M. (2014). *Statebuilding in the Somali Horn: Compromise, competition and representation.* Available at https://www.africaresearchinstitute.org/new site/publications/statebuilding-somali-horn/

Wardak, A. (2012). State and non-state justice systems in Afghanistan: The need for synergy. *University of Pennsylvania Journal of International Economic Law*, 33(5), 1305–1324.

CHAPTER 16

Exploring the Impact of Women's Organisations in Peacebuilding in South Sudan: Post-independence Progress

Tolulope Adeogun, Obianuju E. Okeke-Uzodike, and Abidemi A. Isola

INTRODUCTION

South Sudan gained its independence on 11 July 2011 and, unfortunately, since then there have been repeated episodes of war. This continual conflict has affected the large population of South Sudan, especially women and children. There have been numerous unsuccessful peace processes that have been conducted without the participation of women, and this has led to speculation that they have failed largely because women

---

T. Adeogun (✉) · O. E. Okeke-Uzodike
Durban University of Technology, Durban, South Africa
e-mail: tfor9@yahoo.com

A. A. Isola
Babcock University, Ilishan-Remo, Nigeria

© The Author(s), under exclusive license to Springer Nature Switzerland AG 2023
A. O. Akinola, *Contemporary Issues on Governance, Conflict and Security in Africa,*
https://doi.org/10.1007/978-3-031-29635-2_16

have not been involved. This is of major concern to women and women's organisations in South Sudan, who want to seek lasting solutions to the unending war, and they are clamouring for meaningful inclusion in the formal peace processes, which are anchored by both national and international bodies, especially the United Nations.

In light of this continual conflict and failed peace, explorative research was carried out in Juba, South Sudan in 2013, via interviews with grassroots women, women's organisations and scholars, using a qualitative methodology approach. This research was conducted in order to document the gender-sensitive challenges militating against actualising sustainable peace in South Sudan. The study utilised unstructured interviews, involving 28 participants, including men and women, to interrogate conflict management and the peacebuilding processes through a gender lens to effect changes to the peace processes in relation to women and their children. Purposive and snowball sampling technic were also utilised to interview specific stakeholders and to locate other stakeholders that were known to the respondents. Data analysis revealed that only a few women had been included in the decision-making and peace processes. However, this chapter, which involved a systematic review of recent literature, reveals the progressive efforts of women's organisations in peacebuilding and their inclusion in decision-making in South Sudan, post-independence (2014–2021), compared to the findings of the above explorative research done in 2013. This clearly illustrates women's impactful progress in peacebuilding in South Sudan.

Conflict in South Sudan: Background and Context

Historically, South Sudan cannot be discussed without a reference to Sudan. Before South Sudan gained independence from Sudan in 2011, it was the southern part of the nation, comprising 30% of the larger population of Sudan, mostly animists and Christians. After Sudan gained independence from Britain in 1956, it experienced 50 years of war; history reveals that there has been only one peaceful period of 11 years (Frontline, 2005). Discord that has fuelled these decades of war has ranged from religious conflicts (between the Muslims of the North and the animists/Christians of the South) and fierce competition for lands between farmers and herders in Darfur, to terrorist attacks speculated to be aided by the al-Bashir regime (Frontline, 2005). The southern part of the nation continuously felt cheated and neglected and this eventually led to its independence on 11 July 2011.

Despite decades of war, Sudanese women (from both the North and South) have been actively involved in peacebuilding, especially at the grassroots level through mediation, awareness creation and workshops, to mention a few initiatives. During the second civil war (1983–2005), the then leader of the Sudan People's Liberation Movement (SPLM), the late Dr. John Garang, formally created a women's wing of the resistance movement, which was recruited into the army with the help of the women's Battalion, which was formed in 1984 (Adeogun, 2015). This women's wing of the SPLM, through the secretariat for Women, Gender and Child Welfare and the Department for Women's Affairs (later renamed 'Family Affairs'), helped to create awareness among women through workshops and conferences from 1994 onwards (Faria, 2011). Although, this could have been a way of getting women involved in the struggle because, according to the interviews, after peace was restored in South Sudan, there have been fewer campaigns (Adeogun, 2015).

Furthermore, in the context of grassroots participation, after independence and from the onset of war, South Sudanese women began forming formal groups such as the Central Equatorial Women Association, Voice for Change, St Monica Women's Association and human right associations like the South Sudan Human Rights Society for Advocacy, to transform the society. However, since they were not allowed to participate in decision-making, they started to meet to influence policies, either directly or indirectly (Adeogun, 2015). The reasons given for women's exclusion from decision-making during this early post-independence period and war are as follows: first, women are not educated—the level of literacy among women was low (Mlambo & Kapingura, 2019); second, girls and women are treated like properties that can be bought and sold; for instance, South Sudanese girls are often married off at the tender age of nine years, with an exorbitant dowry (Sefa-Nyarko, 2016). Nonetheless, these women refused to keep quiet, and they formed groups because they felt that they were victims of war more than the general society and they also felt that the conflicts could be handled in a non-violent way (Adeogun, 2015).

Despite the grassroot breakthrough for South Sudanese women, the unstructured interviews undertaken in 2013 revealed the invisibility of women in peace processes, or at any decision-making level, which they felt had grossly affected the peacebuilding progress in the country. Women make up approximately 48% (or nearly half) of the population (Gender in brief, 2020; Kumalo & Roddy-Mullineaux, 2019) so if they are excluded from peace processes and decision-making, the outcome could never be fair. In other words, ineffective and inadequate representation of these women in decision-making negatively impacts their interests. It also implies that the bottom-up approach to women's peacebuilding cannot be effective if they are not well represented at the decision-making levels. The 2013 study revealed that although 25% female representation in the peace processes was ratified in the Comprehensive Peace Agreement of 2005, this was never implemented (Edward, 2011), so most of the women's representatives were excluded. This chapter explores whether women's organisations have had any impact on sustainable peacebuilding in South Sudan since 2013.

Theorising Women's Organisation and Peacebuilding

Molyneux (1985), a sociologist who focuses on women's movements, theorised about women's organisation and came up with three focus areas: women's interests; strategic gender interests; and practical gender interests. For the purpose of this study, only the strategic gender interests and the practical gender interests will be examined. According to Molyneux (1985), strategic gender interests are those that women (or men) may develop by virtue of their social positioning through gender attributes. That is, they can be derived deductively from the analysis of women's subordination and from the formulation of alternative or more satisfactory arrangements to the existing ones. These may include the abolition of the gendered division of labour and the alleviation of the burden of domestic labour and childcare, the removal of institutionalised forms of discrimination and the attainment of political equality. In the case of women in South Sudan, the removal of institutionalised forms of discrimination and the attainment of political equality are needed most, as this is the strategic gender interest that would usher in all of their other practical needs.

Practical gender interests, on the other hand, are those that emerge from factors that directly affect women in a particular location rather than external interventions, that is, interests that are usually a response to an immediate perceived need, such as education, empowerment, shelter, women/girl child protection. However, unless the strategic interests of South Sudanese women, such as their effective representation in peace processes and decision-making (at all levels) are met, their practical interests such as education, sustainable peace and the eradication of poverty and girls' early marriage, cannot be achieved.

JUSTIFICATION FOR SOUTH SUDANESE WOMEN'S PARTICIPATION IN PEACE PROCESSES

Historically, women's organisations in South Sudan were involved in peacebuilding and engaged in the work of reconciliation, dialogue and affirmative action at grassroots level to help restore peace to their country. For example, Awut Deng, one of the founders of the Sudan Women's association in Nairobi in 1993, helped to develop and coordinate the New Sudan Council of Churches (NSCC) by using a 'people-to-people' peace process, which led to the signing of the Wunlit Peace Agreement in 1999 (Faria, 2011). Another instance of the role of women in peacebuilding can be seen in Julia Aker Duany, who together with her husband Wal, started a group called South Sudanese Friends International (SSFI) in the Upper Nile, in 1994. Inter-ethnic warfare over fishing and grazing areas had broken out and this was making life unbearable for the women in this area. After all efforts had failed, Julia Duany began to tell the village women to urge their husbands, fathers and brothers to stop fighting (Duany, 2001). To everyone's surprise this worked, and the women discovered that they had an underlying influence that was powerful enough to move an entire community towards reconciliation (Duany, 2001). They discovered that when they stopped reacting like helpless victims, they could become agents for change and their circumstances in the community began to improve (Duany, 2001). However, women's involvement has been more visible at the grassroots level, where informal peace processes take place, but their effective representation in formal peace processes had been rhetorical. Knowing that the invisibility of women in formal peace processes will hamper the peacebuilding efforts at the grassroots, women started agitating for 35% quota in informal peace processes.

War impacts women differently from men; for example, women lose sons and husbands to war, and this suddenly make them the breadwinner of the family—a position they are mostly ill-equipped for as a result of less education and the sources of income. Therefore, women cannot be represented effectively by men alone, because only those who wear shoes know where they pinch. Women are generally seen as the peace brokers in the family and society at large, and women's involvement in informal peacebuilding in South Sudan backs this up. In other words, bringing women on board would expose peace processes to equality and wholesomeness, which would positively affect their outcome and lead to positive and long-lasting results.

Women's inclusion in peace processes is also supported by United Nations' Security Council resolutions on women and peace, UNSRC 1325 (2000), UNSCR 1888 (2009) and UNSCR 1889 (2009), which serve as the legal ground on which women can claim their right to participate effectively in peace processes and sustainable peacebuilding (Kizito, 2017).

Women and Peacebuilding Post-independence, Prior to 2013

The involvement of women's organisations in conflict management and peacebuilding processes can ensure sustainable peace in post-conflict zones, if they are substantively represented in decision-making. Their skills and methods of peacebuilding, which they used at grassroots level, can be brought to the table in formal peace negotiations. According to Molyneux (2002), the bottom-up approach demands greater attention to grassroots issues, more sensitive policy instruments, and changes in the nature of state–society relations. In other words, skills used in grassroots peacebuilding can positively influence policymaking at the formal peace processes.

The unstructured interviews conducted in 2013 with twelve (12) key informants showed that some of the reasons for the continuing exclusion of women in conflict management and peacebuilding processes included a lack of education, a lack of adequate finance, the patriarchal nature of the society, and incompetence on the part of women's organisations. Literacy levels among South Sudanese women are low, for instance, in 2008 the literacy rate was 19.19% for females compared to 34.84% for males (South Sudan Literacy rate, 2018), and this has been used to keep women subordinate to men. However, when the conflict exploded in mid-December 2013, women organisations were able to lobby the Government of South Sudan to include women in the peace negotiations, which took place in Addis Ababa in 2014. Although there were only three women delegates at this peace negotiation, they were able to make their voice their opinions, such as speaking up against President Kiir's ethnicism and the means to ensure an effective ceasefire (Van der Wolf, 2014). This is encouraging—but more needs to be done.

Although selected women organisations in South Sudan have been able to document the demands from women at the grassroots, the participants in the study disclosed that South Sudan's patriarchal culture and norms hinder women from participating in empowerment training, politics and public activities, and have limited the effectiveness of women's organisations in peacebuilding. Decision-makers at all levels in South Sudan are men, and this has not changed over the years. Women who venture into politics and stand for election are called names, sometimes humiliated and election results have even been rigged to exclude them. In support of this claim, Godia (2009) asserts that it is common in South Sudan to compare women in politics to prostitutes, and this discourages many women from getting involved in politics. In addition, men who do not want their family name associated with this negative perception discourage their wives, sisters and daughters from participating in politics.

Participants in the 2013 study disclosed that factors such as a lack of family law and insufficient policy instruments play a part in negating the efforts of women organisations in peacebuilding processes. They revealed that South Sudan did not have family laws that sanction and discourage rape, divorce, wife battering and forced or early marriages. When issues such as these are reported to the officials in women's organisations, little can be done in the absence of adequate legal instruments. The South Sudanese Government, through the Ministry of Justice, has only recently begun to work on this.

Other important findings in this study that support Molyneux's theory on strategic needs aiding practical needs include:

The Post-conflict Status of Women in South Sudan

As a result of the long war, many South Sudanese women acquired leadership positions at the local level, such as family heads, household chiefs and breadwinners. This prepared them for leadership positions in their newly independent nation. Many of them were also indirectly involved in peacebuilding activities by influencing their husbands, brothers and sons who were policymakers into taking risks during the war to resolve the causes of the conflict.

The Socio-Cultural Status of Women in South Sudan

The study found that South Sudanese women are more involved in peacebuilding at the grassroots level than at the decision-making level, which meant that they were stereotyped and there was a belief that women could only be effective peacebuilders at the grassroots level. For example, the peace processes that took place in South Sudan in 2013 excluded women from fully participating effectively despite the constitutional guarantee of their participation. The study identified the patriarchal system that characterises South Sudan as the major cause. This includes the entrenchment of male domination and the violent oppression of females in every facet of life, from the family unit to the economic, political, social and religious sectors of the state.

Women's Literacy Status in South Sudan

The study showed that for women, processes of disempowerment and subordination begin in childhood. For example, a girl child is denied education because of early marriage and various other factors embedded in the entrenched patriarchal cultures of South Sudan. From independence to 2013, little effort was made to improve the education of girls and women. This lack of education provided the alibi for their exclusion from the peace processes. It has become clear that if women are not directly involved in peace processes in post-conflict zones, there is an increased likelihood that war will reoccur.

A Needs Assessment of Women in South Sudan

The study showed that South Sudanese women have the following practical needs: entrepreneurship training, loan facilities, education of young people and adult education and the creation of awareness on women's rights at the grassroots level. Their strategic interests include their involvement in conflict management and peacebuilding processes; achieving the 30% representation of women at all levels of government; and negating discrimination in any form against women.

Women's Organisations in Peace Empowerment

The women's organisations in the study strategised their activities in line with their own particular programmes of each organisation, in relation to the empowerment of women, by involving the men and youth in the society. To some extent, they were able to challenge an entrenched system of patriarchy which militates against women's participation in public advocacy and training programmes. Their efforts are creating opportunities for women to participate, directly or indirectly, in a series of peacebuilding roles in post-conflict South Sudan. They are able to perform various roles in mediation, reconciliation and creating awareness of women's rights, especially at the grassroots level. They also organise meetings, workshops and conferences to sensitise women and the society on peacebuilding. In addition, they use these meetings as platforms to empower women economically, socially and politically. The study uncovered how deeply patriarchy had eaten into the political, social and economic system of the country.

Government's Response to Women Organisations

The study also revealed that the government permits women to register their organisations, hold advocacy conferences, workshops and meetings. This was used to create awareness of women's right in order to get more women on board in decision-making. There was direct participation of female stakeholders in gender-sensitive policy decisions and policy instruments for achieving sustainable peace in South Sudan. The women's organisations were able to influence government policies in post-conflict zones by demanding the implementation of a constitutional provision that guarantees a 25% quota of women in government. This percentage has since increased to 35%. However, this legal instrument has yet to be implemented at all levels. The lack of implementation indicates that while there is evidence of the ability of women's organisations to modify engrained socio-cultural attitudes and to influence government, they are yet to produce widespread results on the ground.

Summarily, the unstructured interview sessions findings revealed the exclusion of women from peacebuilding either intentionally or by a pose of gender neutrality; a situation whereby women's needs are not separated from that of men and policies are implemented under the same influence. Also, the findings revealed the major practical needs of women in South Sudan, which is education, as very low. This is one of the major reasons for the slow progress in promoting women's inclusion in peace processes. Furthermore, it was concluded that women were excluded majorly from peace processes prior to independence, and post-independence 2013 because of many challenges that were overwhelming, and also that at the time frame of this interview, South Sudan was still young and battling with instability in all its ramification.

Women's Organisations and Peacebuilding in South Sudan Since 2013

Since 2013, some progress has been made. In the 2015 peace agreement, the Agreement of Resolution of the Conflict in South Sudan (ARCSS), women made up 15% of the delegates sent for negotiation, which led to its ratification in August. Initially, before the peace agreement was signed, not a single woman was chosen by the Intergovernmental Authority on Development (IGAD) for the negotiation. It was only after women's organisations fought against this exclusion, that six women were chosen to be part of the 18-member delegation (Pelham, 2020). Although 15% is an increase in women's representation in peace processes, this is slow progress, which raises concerns about women's inclusion in formal peacebuilding.

After the peace agreement of 2015, groups of women came up with a seven-point agenda to make women's voices matter in peace agreement. This included a 25% quota for women's inclusion in peace agreements, institutions and government bodies, and women should be able to contest the remaining 75% of positions; an end to sexual violence and the punishment of perpetrators; consultation with women on security reform; a 30% quota of women in all institutions; freedom of expression; the implementation of a cease fire; and the translation of agreements so that they can be understood by the general public (Kezie-Nwoha & Were, 2018).

Mai (2015) stated why women's inclusion in peacebuilding is essential: firstly, history recorded South Sudanese women's experiences and skills in peacebuilding in the past years; secondly, their support healing and reconciliation skills displayed at the grassroot also proves their competency; thirdly, the war impact women's life differently much more than their male counterparts, hence their strategic needs in peace processes are quite different; lastly, South Sudanese women have both national rights and the support of United Nations Security Council (UNSCR) 1325 to participate in peacebuilding at any level. All the aforementioned points reveal why South Sudanese women should be involved in peacebuilding. However, up till 2015, women were still struggling to meet up with the 25% quota representation in South Sudan. Mai (2015) blamed this poor representation on the patriarchal nature of South Sudanese society and customary laws, which prevent women from active participation in the public sphere.

Despite the August 2015 peace agreement, the war continued in South Sudan, and actually surged in July 2016 due to disagreement between the Sudan People's Liberation Movement/Army (SPLM/A) and Sudan People's Liberation Movement/Army in Opposition (SPLM/A-IO). This resulted in hundreds of thousands of killings and displacements of people (Pelham, 2020).

In December 2017, IGAD resumed peace talks, supported by the United Nations (UN), the African Union (AU) and Troika (the US, Norway and the UK) and this led to the Revitalised Agreement of Resolution of the Conflict in South Sudan (R-ARCSS), which was signed in September 2018. On this occasion, women made up 25% of the negotiating team. Although this is a record of women representation in peace processes around the globe, it is still not sufficient (Pelham, 2020). This is substantiated by Kumalo and Roddy-Mullineaux (2019), who believe that although women's representation has increased numerically in peace processes, their influence is not tangible enough because they are still not allowed to hold key positions such as heads of committees.

South Sudanese women's groups are also having an indirect impact on formal peace processes. For instance, in 2017 numerous women's group held a peaceful march throughout Juba (the capital of South Sudan) to protest sexual violence, displacement, the killing of local citizens and many other issues (CMI Brief, 2018). It was after this exercise that the peace agreement of 2018 was signed with the involvement of a higher percentage of South Sudanese women.

As mentioned earlier, low literacy levels among South Sudanese women have affected their status and denied them many rights. However, more recently the government, together with the United Nations International Children's Emergency Fund (UNICEF), Plan International and the local organisation called Girls Education South Sudan (GESS) are strategising to eradicate the anomalies in educating the girl child (Thelwell, 2019). Strategies such as teaching via radio, and changing perceptions on the importance of educating girls through radio programmes, theatre and public debates are very effective in changing their perspectives and enhancing their civil education (Mott Mc Donald, 2022). According to Mott Mc Donald (2022), girls' education is beginning to take shape: for instance, GESS had recorded 6,000 girls whose families were receiving payments so that they could stay in school, while 2,824 schools were also received grants to build a conducive learning environment. This progress in girls' education will impact both present and future women and South Sudan as a nation.

Conclusion

Women's active involvement in both formal and informal peacebuilding had been legislated by the UNSCR of 1325 (2000), 1888 (2009), 1889 (2009), but despite this, South Sudanese women still had to lobby for effective and substantive representation in peacebuilding, especially formal peace processes where decisions are made and agreement are signed on their behalf, with any contribution from them. Women made up 48% of the population of South Sudan, so it is blatantly unfair for almost half of the population to be invisible when peace agreement are negotiated and signed.

Furthermore, literature shows that when women are actively involved in peace processes, the agreement reached endures for a longer period than the ones negotiated by men only. This has been evident in South Sudan. Since the progressive visibility of women at the negotiation tables, relapses of war have receded.

Much improvement has taken place since the interview sessions in 2013. South Sudan became independent in 2011, so the analysis of women's involvement in peacebuilding was too soon after independence as the country was too young and had many issues to deal with then. It was discovered that South Sudanese women had shifted focus and were no longer satisfied with being involved only in grassroots peacebuilding. They demanded a 35% quota in the decision-making arena, especially in peace processes, which would produce positive results in the long run. Women comprised 25% of the 2018 negotiation team after women's organisations had lobbied for it. This was a huge increment and bodes well for women's representation in the future.

Another important development is the increased agitation for girls' education supported by the government, UNICEF and GESS. It is obvious that the low literacy level of women in South Sudan posed a greater challenge than anything else in their pursuit of inclusion in decision-making and peace processes. Lastly, the study revealed that as women's strategic interests are met, their practical needs are also being met. For instance, as more women are represented in the decision-making arena, girls' education has been impacted positively and there are more girls in schools now than in the early years of independence.

REFERENCES

Adeogun, T. J. (2015). *Exploring the impact of women's organizations in peacebuilding in Africa: A case study of women's organizations in South Sudan*, submitted in partial fulfilment of the requirements for the degree of doctor of philosophy (Political science) in College of Humanities, School of Social Sciences, University of KwaZulu-Natal, Pietermaritzburg.

Duany, J. A. (2001). *A gender specific approach to peace building in Sudan*, by SSFI.

Edward, J. K. (2011, September 7). Women and political participation in South Sudan. *Sudan Tribune*. https://www.sudantribune.com/article39608/. Accessed 12 October 2022.

Frontline/World. (2005). *Sudan: The quick and the terrible facts and stats*. PBS. https://www.pbs.org/frontlineworld/stories/sudan/facts.html. Accessed 12 October 2022.

Faria, C. (2011). Gendering war and peace in South Sudan: The Ellison and emergence of women. *The Association of Concerned Africa Scholars* (ACAS), Bulletin no.86

Gender in brief. (2020). https://www.care.org. Accessed 22 September 2022.

Godia, J. (2009). Sudan balancing the delicate political act. *South Sudan women's Agenda*. Gems News, Issue No 1.

Kezie-Nwoha, H., & Were, J. (2018). Women's informal peace efforts: Grassroots activism in South Sudan. *CMI Brief No. 7*, 1–6.

Kizito, S. (2017). South Sudan's 2015 peace agreement and women's participation. *African Conflict and Peacebuilding Review, 7*(1), 80. https://doi.org/10.2979/africonfpeacrevi.7.1.06. Accessed 12 October 2022.

Kumalo, L., & Roddy-Mullineaux, C. (2019). *Sustaining peace: Harnessing the power of South Sudanese women*. ISSAfrica.org. https://issafrica.org/research/east-africa-report/sustaining-peace-harnessing-the-power-of-south-sudanese-women. Accessed 12 October 2022.

Mai, N. J. H. (2015). *The role of women in peace-building in South Sudan*. The Consortium on Gender, Security and Human Rights. https://genderandsecurity.org/projects-resources/research/role-women-peace-building-south-sudan. Accessed 12 October 2022.

Mlambo, C., & Kapingura, F. (2019). Factors influencing women political participation: The case of the SADC region. *Cogent Social Sciences, 5*(1681048), 1–13.

Molyneux, M. (1985). Mobilization without emancipation? Women's interests, the state and revolution in Nicaragua. *Feminist Studies, 11*(2), 227–254.

Mott Mc Donald. (2022). *Helping keep the peace after the war*. https://www.mottmac.com/views/helping-to-keep-the-peace-after-the-war. Accessed 11 May 2023.

Pelham, S. (2020). *Born to Lead: Recommendations on increasing women's participation in South Sudan's peace processes*. Oxfam. https://doi.org/10.21201/2020.5518. Accessed 12 October 2022.

Sefa-Nyarko, C. (2016). Civil war in South Sudan: Is it a reflection of historical secessionist and natural resource wars in greater Sudan? *African Security, 9*(3), 188–210.

South Sudan Literacy Rate. (2018). https://countryeconomy.com/SouthSudan. Accessed 12 October 2022.

Thelwell, K. (2019). *Top 10 facts about girls' education in South Sudan*. The Borgen Project. https://borgenproject.org/top-10-facts-about-girls-education-in-south-sudan/. Accessed 12 October 2022.

Van der Wolf, M. (2014). *Women take a role in South Sudan peace talk*. VOA News. https://www.voanews.com/sudan-peace-talks/183155. Accessed 12 October 2022.

CHAPTER 17

Gender-Based Violence in South Africa: The Second Pandemic?

Nompumelelo Ndawonde

INTRODUCTION

Post-apartheid South Africa is plagued by high levels of violent and hate-driven crime, including pervasive gender-based violence (GBV). More than 2,100 cases of GBV were reported from April to August 2020 while at least 902 women were murdered from October to December 2021 and 11,315 rape cases were reported, an average of 123 per day (Nyoka, 2022; SAPS, 2020: 4). Violence against women is eroding the social fabric (Gouws, 2016: 400), with South Africa cited as the most dangerous place in the world (World Population Review (WPR), 2020). South African President, Cyril Ramaphosa has described GBV as the "second pandemic" after COVID-19 (Crabtree, 2020). According to the World Population Review, in 2022 South Africa was ranked as the country with the fourth

---

N. Ndawonde (✉)
Institute for Pan-African Thought and Conversation,
University of Johannesburg, Johannesburg, South Africa
e-mail: nndawonde@uj.ac.za

highest number of rape cases in the world after Botswana, Australia and Lesotho. In 2019, 42,289 incidents of rape were reported per 100,000 citizens (WPW, 2022). It is thus no surprise that the country has been dubbed the "rape capital of the world" (Interpol, 2020). These figures do not include rape incidents that go unreported. Femicide[1] is also a major issue, with the South African Police Service (SAPS) noting that a woman is murdered every three hours in South Africa (Crabtree, 2020).

In a presidential address in June 2020, Ramaphosa named the most recent victims of GBV:

> We will speak for Tshegofatso Pule, Naledi Phangindawo, Nompumelelo Tshaka, Nomfazi Gabada, Nwabisa Mgwandela, Altecia Kortjie and Lindelwa Peni, all young women who were killed by men. We will speak for the 89-year-old grandmother who was killed in an old age home in Queenstown, the 79-year-old grandmother who was killed in Brakpan and the elderly woman who was raped in KwaSwayimane in KwaZulu-Natal. (Ellis, 2020)

In response to the ongoing scourge of GBV, South African women, men and non-binary people called for a *#TotalShutdown* in August 2018. Many protests followed, often triggered by the killing of a woman, such as the *#AmINext movement* of 2019 following the deaths of Uyinene Mrwetyana, Jess Hess and Leighandre Jegels at the hands of men (Lyster, 2019). In 2020, the South African Government adopted the Gender-based Violence and Femicide National Strategic Plan (GBVF-NSP) with a budget of R21 billion. While GBV occurs in all societies, the high rate of its occurrence in South Africa is a cause for major concern. What are its underlying causes and why is it so prevalent? This chapter argues that GBV in South Africa is a dynamic, multi-layered phenomenon, whose underlying causes are located in the intersection of race, gender, sexual orientation and gender identity and expression. It thus presents a holistic overview of GBV. The chapter begins with an introduction. Section two

---

[1] According to the World Health Organisation (WHO), femicide refers to the intentional murder of women simply because they are women or due to their gender or biological makeup which makes them different from men. A broader definition includes any killing of women or girls. The different types of femicide include intimate femicide, murders in the name of "honour", dowry-related femicide, and non-intimate femicide. Femicide also refers to the killing of women by an intimate male partner, see Brodie (2019) and World Health Organisation (2012).

defines GBV and discusses its causes. Section three presents the masculinities approach and social norms theory, and the fourth section historicises GBV in South Africa. Section five examines the roles played by non-state actors in addressing GBV. Lastly, the chapter focuses on GBV as a human rights violation and presents recommendations and a conclusion.

Defining GBV

According to the United Nations High Commissioner for Refugees (UNHCR), GBV refers to harmful acts directed at an individual based on their gender. It is rooted in gender inequality, the abuse of power and harmful norms (UNHCR, 2022). The term has also been wrongly equated with that of violence against women (VAW), a sub-category of GBV, which refers to women's sexual, physical and emotional abuse. It commonly manifests in the form of intimate partner violence and sexual violence (Centre for the Study of Violence and Reconciliation, 2016: 4; World Health Organization, 2012). In the South African context, the term GBV is largely associated with physical and sexual violence towards women, although it extends beyond this. There are many different forms of GBV, including manipulation, coercion, "honour" crimes, female genital mutilation and child marriage (UNHCR, 2022). The terminology used to describe victims of GBV is often exclusionary and "othering" to cis men and non-binary and trans bodies.

Non-binary and trans bodies have long experienced erasure from the definition of *womanxhood*, as many still subscribe to the view that trans women are not "women". Sex and gender are interrelated albeit different, with the former referring to biological anatomy and the latter identity. The danger in the misuse of these terms is that when one speaks of cases of femicide, GBV and VAW, trans and non-binary bodies are excluded from the conversation, reporting and ultimately from any intervention. It is important to consider the "intersectionality" of GBV, and how race, class and sexual orientation create the risk of many experiencing oppression, discrimination and any form of GBV. However, this chapter focuses on men's abuse of women, including physical attacks, leading to death.

While men also experience GBV, women are most often the target (Brodie, 2019). Indeed, the number of women killed as a result of this scourge in South Africa can be compared to the casualties that occur in a war zone (Thabela-Chimboza, Abrahams & Chigona, 2020: 2). Omari (2013) noted that 55,000 violent sexual crimes against women were reported annually while the SAPS estimated that, a female was raped every 36 seconds. Crime Statistics for the financial year 2018/2019 show that 179,683 contact crimes were committed against women, of which 82,728 were cases of common assault and 54,142 assault with the intent to cause bodily harm. Furthermore, 2,771 women were murdered, with a further 3,445 attempted murders and 36,597 cases of sexual offences against women were reported. This broad category includes rape, attempted rape, sexual assault and contact sexual offences (Leburu-Masigo & Kgadima, 2020: 16619).

Accurate statistics are difficult to obtain as most incidents of GBV are not reported (Machisa et al., 2011). However, it is evident from recent headlines from South Africa's news outlets such as Twitter, Facebook, newspapers, television channels, and various social media channels that most cases of GBV are perpetrated by men against women. Most of the roughly 20,000 murders reported each year in South Africa are of men killing women and children. Crime statistics (2019/2020) show that 16% of the victims were murdered by a boyfriend or girlfriend, 10 per cent by a family member, 4% by a spouse and 2% by a former boyfriend or girlfriend (Crime Stats, 2020). Studies have shown that one in five women in South Africa experiences rape or sexual violence during their lifetime. It is estimated that underaged children are the victims in 15% of these cases (Brodie, 2019). The SAPS noted that 41% of rapes reported in 2019 involved children. Rape includes gang rape (Jewkes, 2012) and statistics show that most men who rape do so for the first time as teenagers or in their mid-20s (Jewkes et al., 2010). The majority of GBV incidents take place in townships or informal settlements (Mpunzi, 2020).

Causes of GBV

The causes of GBV within the South African context vary. Hamber (2010: 81) argues that men are experiencing a 'calamity of masculinity' and are increasingly confused and uncertain because of women's assault on 'male bastions of power' and growing 'social and cultural disapproval of traditional displays of masculinity'. Moreover, poverty, unemployment and economic dependency create the conditions in which women become victims of GBV (Yesufu, 2022: 95). Within an African context, traditional beliefs on *lobola* or bride price where the groom's family offers a payment to the bride's family including cattle and money are among the causes of GBV (Kim & Motsei, 2002: 1247) as men seem to think that the one that pays *lobola* has power over the bride. In general, traditional beliefs support GBV and sexual abuse (Jewkes et al., 2007: 48). Sociocultural factors such as patriarchy and male dominance exclude women from economic and other opportunities (Yesufu, 2022: 96). Thobejane (2019: 61) also notes that some women who are abused tend to be treated differently by others. Changes in gender roles, and abuse of alcohol (and other substances), which are closely linked to unemployment, contribute to GBV (Strebel et al., 2006: 526), as do traumatic life events, depression and unequal power in sexual relationships. Machisa's (2018: 9) study found that the latter as well as binge drinking resulted in intimate partner violence over a 12-month period in South Africa. In addition, normalisation of sexual power relations and sexual harassment, derogatory name-calling using terms such as "slut", "sket", "slag", and "poof", "queer" and "faggot" could also result in GBV (Strebel et al., 2006: 526).

The Masculinities Approach and Social Norms Theory

The masculinities approach to GBV seeks to challenge harmful male norms, gender dynamics and unequal power relations in society, particularly those that increase the likelihood of men's perpetuation of violence against women and children. Understanding the intersectionality[2] of masculinities and femininities in a patriarchal gender order and how patriarchal masculinities sustain gender inequality is imperative in understanding GBV, particularly in South Africa. Hegemonic masculinity is:

> a configuration of gender practice that embodies, guarantees, and legitimises hierarchical relations between men and women and among men... as a social construct, the model of masculinity that is regarded as ideal will therefore vary considerably across different national, institutional, and interpersonal locations... a particular form of masculinity is understood only in relation to a certain form of femininity and to nonhegemonic (subordinate) masculinities. (Carrigan et al., 1985)

---

[2] Intersectionality 'refers to the idea that people have multiple identities and that people experience and perform/live within multiple, intersecting, and concurrent positions of privileges and oppressions' (Patton et al., 2010: 270). It enables an understanding of how race, gender, sexual orientation as well as gender identity and expression intersect in GBV.

In the South African context, hegemonic masculinity is sustained in several institutions, namely, the family, government, media and corporations. As will be discussed, in such institutions men benefit most from a "patriarchal dividend", which rewards the existing patriarchal society that serves and upholds men's needs.

According to Perrin et al. (2019: 2–12), social norms can be conceptualised in two ways: '1) an individual's beliefs about what others typically do in a given situation (i.e., descriptive norm); and 2) their beliefs about what others expect them to do in a given situation (i.e., injunctive norm)'. Social norms in patriarchal and hegemonic masculine societies clearly outline the formulation of the masculine and the feminine, with masculinity being associated with strength and dominance, while femininity speaks to weakness and submissiveness. Masculine norms perpetuate GBV, while feminine norms perpetuate underreporting of GBV. In the context of GBV, social norms such 'as sexual purity, family honor, and men's authority over women and children in the family' all put women and children at risk of violence (Perrin et al., 2019: 2–12). Unfortunately, these toxic descriptive and injunctive social norms and the patriarchal dividend have excluded cis men from discussions around GBV, including male victims who have often opted to remain silent for fear of being shamed, ridiculed or emasculated.

Historicising GBV in South Africa

Apartheid South Africa

Gender-based violence is a longstanding issue in South Africa. Under the apartheid regime the state was a hostile space for women and cultural norms perpetuated violence against women and disenfranchised black women (Manicom, 1992). The racial hierarchy, a key building block of apartheid, facilitated gender inequality and the subordination of women, with black women most at risk due to socio-economic factors that placed them in unsafe spaces that lacked support services (Andrews, 1999: 430). Patriarchal legal structures such as non-recognition of customary marriages and black women's lack of rights meant that, 'women were under the perpetual tutelage of a male, whether their father, husband, or even a son… these laws operated to deprive them of rights to rent or buy their own homes, to custody of their children, to an education, or a living' (Andrews, 1999: 430).

Apartheid left women vulnerable to violence in public and private spaces. *The Weekly Mail and Guardian* newspaper now known as *The Mail & Guardian* reported high levels of rape in Johannesburg and Soweto in 1991 (432). Furthermore, African laws and customs were protected by the Bantustan system, where 'the chiefs were frequently the apartheid government's surrogate' (434). Traditional law clashed with calls for gender equality and feminist movements were accused of "breaking" down or undermining African culture and traditions. The apartheid militarist government was authoritarian to its core, 'underpinned by an ideology which viewed black women as loose and licentious' (Hassim, 2006). In response to the oppressive apartheid system "Jackrolling" and "Modelling" became prominent in the townships during the 1980s. "Jackrolling" refers to the gang rape of young women, mainly schoolgirls in the township of Soweto, which remains prevalent today. It has now become a trend among some Soweto youth with the aim being to impregnate every woman under the age of 26 in the township in order to 'earn respect in public places which enhances the perpetrator's status' (Manicom, 1992). Women suspected of being informers for the apartheid government were made to walk the streets naked in what was coined "Modelling" (WITS Vuvuzela, 2012).

Black men also experienced GBV in many forms during the apartheid era. Rape, unlawful imprisonment, torture and death were all forms of GBV used against black men, in particular those rallying against the racist government. The Truth and Reconciliation Commission (TRC) that was established with the aim of encouraging perpetrators of human rights violations during apartheid to confess and undergo rehabilitation, uncovered the depths of the violence inflicted on black male bodies (Campbell, 2000: 48). At the time, these crimes were not characterised as a form of GBV, despite being directed at black males and the fact that the intersectionality of race and gender made black men more vulnerable and susceptible to such abuse.

The TRC failed to acknowledge the implications of these human rights violations not just at the individual level but at the social and economic levels. This culture of violence and its implications for the black male psyche remain evident today. The lack of acknowledgement that the abuse experienced by men is a form of GBV persists, furthering dividing the experiences of women and children from that of men and in some cases, young boys. This is exacerbated by harmful hegemonic masculinity and the social norms discussed previously.

Post-Apartheid South Africa

Violence and discrimination against women have continued in the democratic South Africa. While the post-apartheid state has sought to alleviate women's burden of domestic care through social welfare measures, such as grants, it is trapped in the global neoliberal capitalist order that creates precarious working and living conditions for those who are not in formal employment (Gouws, 2016: 403). Post-apartheid social and labour reforms were based on the premise that men are breadwinners and were confined to a small group of wage earners that excluded women, rural workers and casual employees (Barchiesi, 2011: 14). Post-apartheid South Africa thus failed to prioritise women's needs, especially around GBV. High unemployment rates propel people into a growing underclass, many of whom are women (Gouws, 2016: 403).

Nazneen et al. (2019: 13) also note that female activists face numerous challenges including limited funding and human resources, traditional and cultural restrictions and a lack of effective monitoring and evaluation systems within government to implement policies in relation to GBV and gender equality. Mile (2020) points out that such challenges are due to the prevalence of crime in general, which is associated with the legacies of colonialism and apartheid. Colpitts (2018: 427) also argues that the gender relations and constructions of masculinity embedded in South Africa by colonialism and apartheid render it difficult to implement legislation on GBV. However, the post-apartheid government has worked closely with women and various organisations to ensure that legislation is in place to protect women and children (Nazneen et al., 2019: 108).

The South African government has enacted several pieces of legislation, including the Constitution; the Children's Act No. 38 of 2005; Prevention of and Treatment for Substance Abuse Act No 70. of 2008; Child Justice Act No. 75 of 2008; Protection from Harassment Act No. 17 of 2011; and the Domestic Violence Act No. 116 of 1998. Its most recent response was the National Strategic Plan on Gender-based Violence and Femicide. As a result of this plan, in January 2022, President Ramaphosa signed the following bills into law: (i) the Criminal Law (Sexual Offences and Related Matters) Amendment Bill; (ii) Criminal and Related Matters Amendment Bill and (iii) the Domestic Violence Amendment Bill. The ten-year plan, which aims to ensure 'human dignity and healing, safety, freedom and equality in our lifetime' (GBVF-NSP, 2020) received government funding of R21 billion. It highlights the following six pillars (National Strategic Plan on Gender Based Violence and Femicide, 2021: 66–79):

1. Pillar 1: Accountability, Coordination and Leadership
2. Pillar 2: Prevention and Rebuilding Social Cohesion
3. Pillar 3: Justice, Safety and Protection
4. Pillar 4: Response, Care, Support and Healing
5. Pillar 5: Economic Power
6. Pillar 6: Research and Information Management

Several strategies and implementation modalities have been adopted to support these pillars. A total of R200 million has been received in donations from the private sector, various institutions and government. Based on proposals received by the Gender-Based Violence and Femicide Response, R69 million was granted to 110 high-impact community-based organisations (CBOs) in the first tranche (GBVF Response Fund, 2022). The funding was allocated to organisations focused on pillars two and three[3] of the GBVF-NSP, particularly those in rural and informal areas, and 'as many as 6.1 million women, 383,000 children, 76,700 people living with disabilities, and 51,000 youth will benefit from the coordinated programmes and strategies' (GBVF Response Fund, 2022). According to the chairperson of the board of the GBVF, Ms Judy Dlamini, the challenges in addressing GBV are largely due to under-reporting and thus the lack of accurate data and statistics (Dlamini, 2021).

Despite these efforts, many are critical of the government's intervention. According to Kwezilomso Mbandazayo, women's rights and gender justice programme manager for Oxfam South Africa:

> The state consistently wants to depoliticise the issue of gender-based violence—there is no real interest in getting to the actual causes and the things that enable domestic violence to continue...Women are always painted as victims but are never empowered or afforded the agency to take control of their own revolt—the focus is always on someone needing to "save" you ... This narrative of being protected takes away from the fact that someone is perpetrating, and it's the perpetration that needs to stop. (Oxfam, 2022)

---

[3] Pillar 2: Prevention and Rebuilding Social Cohesion; Pillar Three: Justice, Safety and Protection. See https://www.justice.gov.za/vg/gbv/NSP-GBVF-FINAL-DOC-04-05.pdf.

Closer examination of government legislation against GBV reveals that prevention is at the forefront, while the "causes and motivations" are ignored. How can GBV be eradicated when the causal factors are not addressed? De-politicising GBV absolves the government from addressing the deep-rooted issues of patriarchy, toxic masculinity and the role of African culture in GBV. African culture is capable of devaluing women, girls and victims of GBV through the normalisation of abuse, or regarding GBV as accidental while ignoring sexism and promoting aggressive or toxic masculinity. Hence, some men use African culture to exonerate, excuse and deny the impact of their behaviour, creating barriers to services and resources for access to justice. The legislation frames GBV as a "woman and children issue". This legislation could have been used as an opportunity to re-educate society at large on what GBV is, how it manifests through seemingly harmless behaviour, and the importance of observing early warning signs and reporting.

Notwithstanding this legislation, cases of GBV and femicide continue to rise in South Africa. In November 2020, during *#16DaysofActivism*, an annual international campaign dedicated to challenging violence against women and children, several women and children perished at the hands of men.[4] The COVID-19 pandemic highlighted the degree to which women are at risk of GBV. Valeria Manzini (2021) notes that cases of GBV increased from March 2020 when the South African government adopted one of the world's longest and strictest lockdowns in response to COVID-19. Prior to the pandemic, femicide in South Africa was already five times higher than the global average and the death rate resulting from interpersonal violence against females was the fourth highest out of 183 countries listed by the World Health Organisation in 2016.

The evidence suggests that cases of violence against women are increasing. In 2019/2020, there was an average increase of 146 sexual offences and 116 rape cases per day compared to 2018/2019. The government's GBV and Femicide Command Centre, which supports victims of GBV recorded more than 120,000 victims in the first three weeks of the lockdown. Researchers from the School of Governance at the

---

[4] See Nkanjeni, U. (2020). 16 days of activism: Five shocking cases that took place over this period in the past two years. *Times Live*. Available at: https://www.timeslive.co.za/news/south-africa/2020-11-30-16-days-of-activism-five-shocking-cases-that-took-place-over-this-period-in-the-past-two-years/ (accessed 12 February 2022).

University of the Witwatersrand note that the lockdown measures forced women to stay home, leaving them vulnerable to domestic abuse. They also prevented women from accessing support structures. Furthermore, as Dlamini noted, 'There are so many needs right now. For example, when it comes to Covid-19, people poured billions into the Covid-19 Solidarity Fund because... guess what? It's affecting everyone, it's a global challenge' (Mafolo, 2021).

Cases of GBV are often dismissed by the South African police who perceive this as a private family issue, rather than a crime that should be tried in a court of law. This discourages women from reporting to the police. The stigma associated with sexual violence also contributes to underreporting of GBV cases.

ROLES OF NON-STATE ACTORS: ACTIVIST GROUPS

Activism has become a significant tool in addressing GBV in South Africa. Growing frustration with government institutions, particularly the police and the judiciary's failure to intervene has prompted ordinary citizens and civil society groups to speak out and take action.

The People Against Suffering, Oppression and Poverty (PASSOP), a grassroots non-profit organisation in Cape Town, focuses on the rights of refugees, immigrants, and asylum seekers. It also implements projects on gender rights, and support for disabled children and LGBTQ. Instagram pages such as Women for Change, another non-profit organisation advocating for protection of women and children's rights, have also been effective in the media war to combat GBV. With about 38,900 followers and 1,061 posts, the platform is dedicated to memorialising victims of GBV by recounting their experiences to ensure that they are never forgotten, using hashtags such as *#SayHerName*, *#EnoughIsEnough* and *#AmINext*. One such post, dated 21 February 2022, reads:

> Charlene Naiker, 38 and her two children, Chazlyn 2, and Ainzlee, 14 were gunned down at their home in Chatsworth, on 11 February. Both children died within 24 hours and Charlene died in hospital, two days after the children's funeral service. Three armed men approached their home and opened fire on the mother and children. Fly high Angel, we will fight for your justice! #womenforchange #sayhername #EnoughisEnough #aminext #waronwomen. (@WomenforChangesa, 2022)

The page provides education and helpful resources on GBV and features a petition urging the South African government to prioritise GBV policies and programmes (Women for Change, 2022).

Other non-state actors that address GBV include People Opposing Women Abuse (POWA) which provides referral services and shelter to women experiencing domestic violence and the Saartjie Baartman Centre for Women and Children (SBCWC) that caters for women and children who are survivors of abuse and offers legal assistance to victims of violence, shelter and on-the-job training (*Police Magazine*, 2020: 4). The Frida Hartley Shelter provides shelter to homeless women and children who survived GBV and other trauma, while FAMSA (Families South Africa) offers counselling and education on domestic violence and trauma to help improve marriages and families. Organisations such as the TEARS Foundation, the Trauma Centre and Thuthuxela Care Centres provide access to crisis intervention, violence prevention and reduction of secondary victimisation, as well as information on GBV (*Police Magazine*, 2020: 4).

The Role of the Media in Publicising GBV

The media has a significant contribution to make in reporting GBV. Although it is necessary to publicise this scourge, there is an unsettling air of sensationalism in reporting and consumption of such news. News channels are in constant competition with one another to break the story first, present the most shocking headline and release the most gruesome facts (Ndawonde, 2022). Details of the violence and the manner of death, as well as the face of the perpetrator and the victim are at the forefront of news reporting, while genuine acknowledgement of the tragic loss of a promising life is downplayed. While it is important to document these cases to raise public awareness, it is important to draw the line between public awareness and public spectacle.

Consider the case of Tshegofatso Pule, a 28-year-old woman who, along with her unborn child, was found hanging from a tree in Roodepoort, on 4 June 2020 (Bhengu, 2020). The key details that people know and remember are how she died, where she was found and who has been charged with her murder. People are familiar with the accused's mask-wearing face, his daily court outfit (a tailored suit), and his relationship with Pule (a married man) and his mistress. Not much has been said about Pule or the life she lived before her untimely death as these details do not attract sales or garner much interest (Ndawonde, 2022). She is simply branded as a victim.

Similarly, convicted murderer Sandile Mantsoe, who was responsible for the death of his girlfriend Karabo Mokoena, was reportedly a church-going and God-fearing man who had done well for himself in Forex trading (Ndawonde, 2022). Other stories published in the media about victims of GBV that run along the same lines include those on Mangosuthu University of Technology student Zolile Khumalo who was shot in the head and chest by her former boyfriend who confessed to the crime on Facebook, Gloria Sekome shot by her boyfriend, Phumeza Pepeta shot by her former husband (Bhekisisa Centre for Health Journalism, 2021) and Asithandile "Kwasa" Zozo who was murdered by her lover after ending the abusive relationship.

The approach adopted by the media desensitises the reader, dehumanises the victim and shows a total lack of empathy. Unless the latest murder or assault is more gruesome than the former, it is simply not newsworthy. Furthermore, problematic language used in the reporting perpetuates harmful gender norms and stereotypes and heterosexual dominance, and upholds damaging patriarchal attitudes.

Readers are often not cautioned that the article may contain triggers, exposing them to disturbing content without their consent. This has likely contributed to underreporting of GBV cases, as people's image of what GBV looks like and who it affects has been streamlined to the extent that those who do not fit into the standard mould fall between the cracks. By its very definition, GBV is a harmful act that is directed at an individual based on their gender. A child who is forced into an arranged marriage, a female who must endure genital mutilation, junior employees being subjected to unwanted sexual advances by their superior, hate crimes targeting trans or non-binary bodies, including men who endure sexual assault in prison, are all manifestations of GBV.

Sadly, many of these stories go un-reported and thus un-heard, often due to fear of judgement or stigma. For some, reluctance to report is motivated by the valid fear of becoming a headline, with their ordeal plastered all over the news for national consumption. Cis men are reluctant to report for fear of judgement and not fitting the traditional social norm of what a man should be. The stories of victims who have died are told without their consent in the name of public awareness.

GBV as a Human Rights Violation

GBV should be seen as abuse of human rights. This accounts for several human rights bodies supporting the quest to eradicate it. For instance, Lawyers for Human Rights (LHR), which focuses on human rights advocacy and is a constitutional watchdog for the disadvantaged, provides free legal services to victims of human rights abuses. The organisation approaches GBV and discrimination from a systemic perspective, and take on cases, projects, and activities that promote access to information for women and girls about how the justice system works; and assists in preventing GBV and discrimination while advocating for ongoing availability of support services for victims of violence and discrimination. Lawyers for Human Rights also promotes collaboration among government role-players and them and civil society for improved implementation of important laws and policies and access to well-functioning complaints mechanisms within South Africa (Lawyers for Human Rights, 2022).

The Centre for Human Rights at the University of Pretoria focuses on human rights education (Lawyers for Human Rights, 2022), and research and education on issues such as the rights of women; people living with HIV; indigenous people; and other vulnerable groups in South Africa and Africa at large (Lawyers for Human Rights, 2022). The Dullah Omar Institute for Constitutional Law, Governance, and Human Rights at the University of the Western Cape publishes books, articles and reports on criminal justice reform and women's rights (Dullah Omar Institute, 2022).

The Foundation for Human Rights (FHR) supports civil society organisations (CSOs) and social movements that are working to prevent and eliminate GBV in South Africa. It focuses on addressing discrimination through constitutional rights awareness, enhanced access to justice and participatory democracy. Through its various programmes, the FHR recognises that despite advances at the level of law and policy, women in South Africa continue to be marginalised. Most South Africans living in poverty are black women who are also disproportionally affected by various forms of discrimination. These are linked to patriarchy, culture and GBV (Foundation for Human Rights, 2020).

The FHR mainstreams gender in all its programmes and also supports initiatives addressing GBV and women's inequality. It has been involved in advocacy and mobilisation, including the 2019 *#SandtonShutDown* campaign as well as mass protests aimed at encouraging the private sector to fund interventions to address GBV in communities (Sonke Gender Justice, 2022). It has also been involved in capacity building initiatives such as workshops and training on the legal and medical aspects of combating GBV. Non-governmental organisation, Sonke Gender Justice draws on a human rights framework to create the change necessary for men and boys, women and children to enjoy equitable, healthy and happy relationships that contribute to the development of a just and democratic society.

All these human rights institutions in South Africa including the Human Rights Institute of South Africa (HURISA) seek to address issues around GBV that affect communities. While their efforts are laudable, many challenges remain, calling for a review of strategies.

Conclusion

This chapter examined GBV in South Africa through historical and contemporary lenses. It explored the root causes of GBV and highlighted state and non-state actors' interventions to address this scourge. However, GBV remains a pressing issue in South Africa, and the number of people killed and victimised increases everyday. What needs to be done going forward?

Some actors have called for government fiscal intervention through gender budgeting and greater efforts by civil society organisations to build strong advocacy and awareness. While gender budgeting may be effective, implementation is a key issue. The GBVF-NSP community-based organisations could assist in ensuring that funding reaches grassroots levels.

However, the most pressing issue is the harmful social norms on masculinity and femininity that persist in South Africa. Transformation of minds is required to eradicate these norms. This calls for transformation of the rhetoric the government uses regarding GBV. By re-conceptualising the way we speak about GBV, highlighting the root causes before rushing to implement preventative measures, we can begin to unpack why the issue is so rampant and devise an effective legislative and policy framework to tackle it. Preventative efforts are effective, but the greater need is to address the root causes. Toxic masculinity needs to be challenged from primary school level to the corporate office. Naming and shaming and creating an offenders' list may help but is not enough if men still believe they have the right to women's bodies, irrespective of the circumstances and women's resistance to such. Harsher punishment may be helpful, but it has been proven that consequences are not sufficient to curb the scourge of GBV in South Africa.

How do we create transformation of the mind? The decolonisation of African minds advocated for by several African scholars can be applied to GBV. It is recommended that government-led, activist-supported dialogues be convened to facilitate conversations on the harmful cultural practices and social norms that are pervasive in South Africa. Given the male-dominated socio-economic and political environments and leadership structure, it is uncertain how much support an "anti-patriarchal" agenda will garner. Furthermore, there is a need for re-education on GBV, as most associate it solely with the rape and murder of children. This may be helpful in encouraging others to report their experiences, including "less" sensational cases such as coercion, harassment, and manipulation, which often lead to more physical forms of GBV. Addressing this issue will require more than government intervention and activism.

The media has a responsibility to report on GBV fairly and less provocatively or sensationally, respecting the rights and dignity of victims and accepting that all degrees of GBV are newsworthy. Due to South Africa's unique nature and the major socio-economic disparities, the country has a digital divide. Online activism which increases the visibility and power of marginalised groups is critical. South Africa is one of the few nations in Africa whose citizens enjoy freedom of speech, offering great potential for online activism. These strategies should prove helpful in destigmatising GBV, which is a positive step in dismantling longstanding oppressive beliefs and norms that have only served to divide society. Without a concerted effort by all, GBV will continue to haunt South Africa.

References

Andrews, P. (1999). *Violence against women in South Africa: The role of culture and the limitations of the law.* CUNY School of Law. https://academicworks.cuny.edu/cgi/viewcontent.cgi?referer=&httpsredir=1&article=1274&context=cl_pubs. Accessed 24 February 2022.

Barchiesi, F. (2011). *Precarious liberation—Workers, the state and contested citizenship in postapartheid South Africa.* SUNY Press.

Bhekisisa Centre for Health Journalism. (2021). *#SayHerName: The faces of South Africa's femicide epidemic.* https://www.news24.com/news24/SouthAfrica/News/sayhername-the-faces-of-south-africas-femicide-epidemic-202 10414. Accessed on 4 May 2022.
Bhengu, C. (2020). *Pregnant & hung from a tree—Here's what we know about the murder of Tshegofatso Pule.* https://www.timeslive.co.za/news/south-africa/2020-06-10-pregnant--hung-from-a-tree-heres-what-we-know-about-the-murder-of-tshegofatso-pule/. Accessed on 4 May 2022.
Brodie, N. R. (2019). *Using mixed-method approaches to provide new insights into media coverage of femicide.* University of Witwatersrand. https://hdl.handle.net/10539/29294
Campbell, P. J. (2000). *The Truth and Reconciliation Commission (TRC): Human Rights and State Transitions—The South Africa Model.* https://asq.africa.ufl.edu/files/ASQ-Vol-4-Issue-3-Campbell.pdf. Accessed on 3 May 2022.
Carrigan, T., Connell, B., & Lee, J. (1985). *Towards a new sociology of masculinity.* https://www.jstor.org. Accessed on 3 May 2022.
Centre for the Study of Violence and Reconciliation. (2016). *Gender-based violence (GBV) in South Africa: A brief review.* https://www.csvr.org.za/pdf/Gender%20Based%20Violence%20in%20South%20Africa%20-%20A%20Brief%20Review.pdf. Accessed 11 May 2023.
Colpitts, E. (2018). *Engaging men and boys to prevent gender-based violence in South Africa: Possibilities, tensions and debates.* https://doi.org/10.1080/02255189.2018.1491393. Accessed on 4 May 2022.
Crabtree, J. (2020). *South Africa's other pandemic: Femicide rate spikes as coronavirus lockdown lifts.* https://news.cgtn.com/news/2020-06-20/South-Africa-s-femicide-rate-spikes-as-coronavirus-lockdown-lifts-RskMmKKcus/index.html. Accessed on 3 May 2022.
Dlamini, H. J. (2021). Gender-based violence, twin pandemic to COVID-19. *Symposium: COVID-19, Globalization, Health Disparities and Social Policy, 47*(4–5), 583–590.
Dullah Omar Institute. (2022). https://dullahomarinstitute.org.za/. Accessed 20 February 2022.
Ellis, E. (2020). *Gender-based violence is South Africa's second pandemic, says Ramaphosa. Daily Maverick.* https://www.dailymaverick.co.za/article/2020-06-18-gender-based-violence-is-south-africas-second-pandemic-says-ramaphosa/. Accessed 10 February 2020.
Foundation for Human Rights. (2020). *Gender-based violence.* https://www.fhr.org.za/seja-programme/gender-based-violence/. Accessed 10 February 2022.

GBVF-NSP. (2020). *Human dignity and healing, safety, freedom & equality in our lifetime*. https://www.justice.gov.za/vg/gbv/NSP-GBVF-FINAL-DOC-04-05.pdf. Accessed 23 February 2022.

GBVF Response Fund. (2022). *GBVF Response Fund accelerates fight against gender-based violence and femicide through appointment of 110 grant partners*. https://gbvfresponsefund1.org/press-release/gbvf-response-fund1-accelerates-fight-against-gender-based-violence-and-femicide-through-appointment-of-110-grant-partners/. Accessed 18 February 2022.

Gouws, A. (2016). Women's activism around gender-based violence in South Africa: Recognition, redistribution and representation. *Review of African Political Economy, 43*(149), 400–415.

Hamber, B. (2010). Masculinity and transition: Crisis or confusion in South Africa? *Journal of Peacebuilding & Development, 5*, 75–88.

Hassim, S. (2006). *Women's organization and democracy in South Africa—Contesting authority*. UKZN Press.

Interpol. (2020). *Development of a nationally accessible assistance and support network for victims of rape and sexual abuse*. https://www.tears.co.za/wp-content/uploads/2020/07/presentation.pdf. Accessed on 4 May 2022.

Jewkes, R. (2012). *Streamlining: Understanding gang rape in South Africa*. Middlesex University.

Jewkes, R., Nduna, M., Levin, J., Jama, N., Dunkle, K., Wood, K., Koss, M., Puren, A., & Duvvury, N. (2007). *Evaluation of stepping stones: A gender transformative HIV prevention intervention*. The Communication Initiative Network. https://www.comminit.com/content/evaluation-stepping-stones-gender-transformative-hiv-prevention-intervention. Accessed 11 May 2023.

Jewkes, R., Sikweyiya, Y., Morrell, R., & Dunkle, K. (2010). Why, when and how men rape? Understanding rape perpetration in South Africa. *South African Crime Quarterly, 34*, 23–31.

Kim, J., & Motsei, M. (2002). "Women enjoy punishment": Attitudes and experiences of gender-based violence among PHC nurses in rural South Africa. *Social Science & Medicine, 54*(8), 1243–1254.

Lawyers for Human Rights. (2022). *We use the law as a positive instrument for change for our clients, and in the public interest*. https://www.lhr.org.za/. Accessed 10 February 2022.

Leburu-Masigo, G. E., & Kgadima, N. P. (2020). Gender-based violence during the Covid-19 pandemic in South Africa: Guidelines for social work practice. *Gender & Behaviour, 18*(4), 16618–16628.

Lyster, R. (2019). *The New Yorker*. https://www.newyorker.com/news/newsdesk/the-death-of-uyinene-mrwetyana-and-the-rise-of-south-africas-aminextmovement. Accessed 3 May 2022.

Machisa, M., Christofides, N., Machisa, R. et al. (2018). Social support factors associated with psychological resilience among women survivors of intimate partner violence in Gauteng, South Africa. *Global Health Action, 11*(1491114), 1–9.

Machisa, M., Jewkes, R., Morna Lowe, C., & Rama, K. (2011). *The war at home: The gauteng GBV indicators research study*. Gender Links and the South African Medical Research Council.

Mafolo, K. (2021). Gender-based violence and Femicide response fund to disburse R69m to 110 organisations. *Daily Maverick*. https://www.dailymaverick.co.za/article/2021-12-10-gender-based-violence-and-femicide-response-fund-to-disburse-r69m-to-110-organisations/. Accessed 22 February 2022.

Manicom, L. (1992). Ruling relations: Rethinking state and gender in South African history. *Journal of African History, 33*, 441–465.

Manzini, V. (2021). *Global risks insights: Know your world*. https://globalriskinsights.com/2021/03/south-africas-secondary-pandemic-a-crisis-of-gender-based-violence/. Accessed on 3 May 2022.

Mile, K. (2020). *Gender based violence: A South African plague*. https://www.researchgate.net/publication/344748162_Gender_Based_Violence_A_South_African_Plague. Accessed on 4 May 2022.

Mpunzi, Z. (2020). These are SA's 30 gender-based violence hotspots. *Times Live*. Johannesburg (p. 1). https://www.timeslive.co.za/news/south-africa/2020-09-22-these-are-sas-30-gender-based-violence-hotspots/

National Strategic Plan on Gender-Based Violence and Femicide. (2021). https://www.justice.gov.za/vg/gbv/NSP-GBVF-FINAL-DOC-04-05.pdf. Accessed on 4 May 2022.

Nazneen, S., Hickey, S., Sifaki, E. et al. (2019). *Negotiating gender equity in the Global South: The politics of domestic violence policy*. Francis and Taylor Group.

Ndawonde, N. (2022). *Public awareness or public spectacle?* https://www.iol.co.za/news/politics/opinion/public-awareness-or-public-spectacle-67f1ed88-5d7b-434c-8131-f03589d690fb. Accessed on 3 May 2022.

Nkanjeni, U. (2020). 16 Days of Activism: Five shocking cases that took place over this period in the past two years. *Times Live*. https://www.timeslive.co.za/news/south-africa/2020-11-30-16-days-of-activism-five-shocking-cases-that-took-place-over-this-period-in-the-past-two-years/. Accessed 12 February 2022.

Nyoka, N. (2022). Talking about Gender Based Violence is not enough. *New Frame*. https://www.newframe.com/talking-about-gender-based-violence-is-not-enough/. Accessed 3 May 2022.

Omari, S. (2013). *Women in South Africa are living in a war zone*. Women's Media Centre. Cape Town. https://www.womensmediacenter.com/women-under-siege/women-in-south-africa-are-living-in-a-war-zone

Oxfam. (2022). *Five women activists doing important work to end gender violence.* https://www.oxfam.org.za/five-women-activists-doing-important-work-to-end-gender-violence/. Accessed 10 February 2022.

Patton, L. D., Shahjahan, R. A., & OseiKofi, N. (2010). Introduction to the emergent approaches to diversity and social justice in higher education special. *Equity & Excellence in Education, 43*(3), 265–278.

Perrin, N., Marsh, M., & Clough, A. (2019). Social norms and beliefs about gender-based violence scale: A measure for use with gender-based violence prevention programs in low-resource and humanitarian settings. *Confl Health, 13*(6). https://conflictandhealth.biomedcentral.com/articles/10.1186/s13031-019-0189-x#citeas. Accessed 20 February 2022.

Police Magazine. (2020). *Stop gender-based violence and femicide.* https://www.saps.gov.za/resource_centre/publications/police_mag/pol_aug_2020_final.pdf. Accessed 23 February 2023.

Sonke Gender Justice. (2022). *Stop gender violence: A national campaign.* https://genderjustice.org.za/project/policy-development-advocacy/stop-gender-violence-national-campaign/. Accessed 20 February 2022.

South African Police. (2020). *Stop gender-based violence and femicide.* https://www.saps.gov.za/resource_centre/publications/police_mag/pol_aug_2020_final.pdf

Strebel, A., et al. (2006). Social constructions of gender roles, gender-based violence and HIV/AIDS in two communities of the Western Cape, South Africa. *Journal of Social Aspects of HIV/AIDS, 3*(3), 516–528.

Thabela-Chimboza, T., Abrahams, A., & Chigona, W. (2020). ICIS 2020 India: Social media movements of# GBV in South Africa.

The Gender-based Violence and Femicide National Strategic Plan. (2020). https://www.justice.gov.za/vg/gbv/NSP-GBVF-FINAL-DOC-04-05.pdf. Accessed 23 February 2022.

Thobejane, T. (2019). Effects of gender-based violence towards young females: The case of Vhufuli village in Thohoyandou, Limpopo Province, South Africa. *Journal of Reviews of Global Economics, 8*, 53–62.

United Nations High Commissioner for Refugees. (2022). *Gender-based violence.* https://www.unhcr.org/gender-based-violence.html. Accessed on 20 February 2022

Women for Change (@womenforchangesa). (2022, February 21). https://www.instagram.com/womenforchangesa/?hl=en

Women for Change. (2022). https://womenforchange.co.za/. Accessed on 20 February 2022.

World Health Organisation. (2012). *Understanding and addressing violence against women.* https://apps.who.int/iris/bitstream/handle/10665/77421/WHO_RHR_12.38_eng.pdf. Accessed 20 February 2022.

World Health Organisation. (2021). *Violence against women.* https://www.who.int/news-room/fact-sheets/detail/violence-against-women. Accessed on 25 February 2022.

World Population Review (WPR). (2020). *Crime rate by country 2020.* World Population Review, WPR2020. https://worldpopulationreview.com/country-rankings/crime-rate-by-country. Accessed on 4 May 2022.

World Population Review. (2022). *Rape statistics by country 2022.* https://worldpopulationreview.com/country-rankings/rape-statistics-by-country. Accessed 12 February 2022.

Wits Vuvuzela. (2012). *Jackrolling becomes more prevalent.* https://witsvuvuzela.com/2012/06/22/child-rape-by-youth/. Accessed on 23 February 2022.

Yesufu, S. (2022). The scourge of gender-based violence (GBV) on women plaguing South Africa. *Social and Humanities, 1,* 96–100.

CHAPTER 18

A Reflection on Gender-Based Violence in Nigeria

Bolanle Oluwakemi Eniola and Joseph I. Aremo

INTRODUCTION

The phenomenon of gender-based violence (GBV)[1] has been recognised since the eighteenth century, with the first official reference to femicide in British legal discourse upon the publication of John Wharton's *Law Lexicon*. This form of violence violates the victim's human rights, particularly the right to life, equality, dignity, freedom and security of the person, health and reproductive autonomy. Due to the common belief that GBV

[1] Gender-based violence refers to violence directed against an individual or group on the basis of their gender or a form of violence that unduly affects persons of a particular gender.

B. O. Eniola (✉)
Faculty of Law, Ekiti State University, Ado Ekiti, Nigeria
e-mail: bolanle.eniola@eksu.edu.ng

J. I. Aremo
Faculty of Law, Elizade University, Ilara-Mokin, Nigeria
e-mail: joseph.aremo@elizadeuniversity.edu.ng

© The Author(s), under exclusive license to Springer Nature Switzerland AG 2023
A. O. Akinola, *Contemporary Issues on Governance, Conflict and Security in Africa*,
https://doi.org/10.1007/978-3-031-29635-2_18

only affects women, the term is often used interchangeably with that of Violence Against Women (VAW). However, GBV and VAW are not the same. The Declaration on the Elimination of Violence against Women (1993) defines violence against women as a sub-category of GBV. It describes it as 'any act of gender-based violence that results in physical, sexual or psychological harm or suffering to women, including threats of such acts, coercion or arbitrary deprivations of liberty, whether occurring in private or public life'.[2] This understanding shows that the scope of GBV is wider than that of VAW. Based on the belief that GBV and VAW are synonymous, most investigations have regarded men as the perpetrators of GBV. Indeed, some authors have noted that it originates from power imbalances between men and women, and serves to maintain them among both groups and individuals at the personal, household, community and state levels (Hoare, 2007; Terry, 2007: xiii).

In reality, GBV is not age- or gender-specific, as children are victims of some forms of GBV and not all women are subservient to men. Women may participate in enforcing gender hierarchies and may consequently perpetrate GBV (Baldasare, 2012: 2). Gender-based violence against men could be physical (like slapping or hitting a man), emotional, (such as insults or name-calling), sexual abuse or denying fathers access to their children (Durham, 2022). Young men have also been falsely harassed, punished and even killed for alleged offences because of their gender (Sahara Reporter, 2021; Ukpong, 2020).

Thus, GBV affects men, women, girls, boys and humanity at large, although it mostly affects women and girls (European Institute for Gender Equality, 2022). While it is pervasive, it is the least visible human rights violation in the world and is hence a major human rights concern. This is particularly true of Africa because some African cultural practices condone GBV.

While Nigeria's constitution does not explicitly protect citizens against GBV, some of its provisions can be inferred to afford such protection. This is couched in the fundamental human rights that the constitution guarantees including, among others, the right to life, dignity, personal liberty, health and the right to private and family life. However, these

---

[2] See Article 1, Declaration on the Elimination of Violence against Women, UN General Assembly Resolution 48/104 of 20th December 1993 Available at https://un.org/en/genocideprevention/documents/atrocity-crimes/Doc.21_declaration%20vaw.pdf.

rights are not enforceable.[3] Nigeria has also adopted a national legal framework aimed at combating GBV. This includes the Child Rights Act and criminal and penal codes. The Violence Against Persons Prohibition (VAPP) Act was enacted in 2015 specifically to deal with GBV. Some of the federation's states have also enacted laws in a bid to curb GBV in the areas under their jurisdiction.

However, despite these efforts, the prevalence of GBV remains high. According to the Global Database on Violence against Women, 22.3% of women in Nigeria experience lifetime physical and/or sexual intimate partner violence, while 43.4% of young girls are victims of child marriage and 19.5% of young girls are victims of female genital mutilation (FGM)/cutting (UN Women, 2022). Usigbe (2022) found that 28% of Nigerian women aged 25–29 had experienced some form of physical violence since the age of 15, with 15% of women experiencing such violence within the 12 months preceding the survey. The study further revealed that 44% of divorced, separated or widowed women had experienced violence since age the age of 15, and that 25% of married women or those living with their partners had done so (Usigbe, 2022). Against this background, this chapter engages the discourse and reality of GBV in Nigeria, and examines the legal framework, particularly its adequacy and effectiveness in curbing GBV. It explores the impact of GBV on victims' human rights, and offers sustainable recommendations to combat the tide of GBV in the country.

GBV: Concept, Nature and Scope

According to the United Nations High Commission for Refugees (UNHCR), GBV refers to harmful acts directed at an individual based on their gender. It is rooted in gender inequality, the abuse of power and harmful norms. Gender-based violence can include sexual, physical, mental and economic harm inflicted on a specific gender in public or in private. It also includes threats of violence, coercion and manipulation (UNHCR, 2022). This can take many forms such as intimate partner

---

[3] See Chapter 4 of the Constitution of the Federal Republic of Nigeria, 1999, and Sects. 17(3) and 33(1).

violence (sexual, physical or emotional), sexual violence, child marriage, FGM and so-called honour crimes,[4] and non-intimate partner violence.

Explicit forms of GBV include sexual violence, which includes sexual harassment, intimidation, abuse, assault and rape, while implicit GBV includes marital rape, forced prostitution, sexual abuse of female children, sexual harassment, trafficking in women, wife battery, FGM, widowhood practices, child and forced marriage and appropriation of property.

Theoretical Framework

This chapter employs the lenses of the Social Learning Theory (SLT) and Liberal Feminism to shed light on GBV. The SLT postulated by Bandura (1977: 9) holds that people learn behavioural patterns from others around them. It is anchored on the notion that learning occurs through social observation and subsequent imitation of modelled behaviour. People learn by observing the actions of others and the resultant consequences (Sherry & Lyons, 2012). By doing so, they learn to imitate others' behaviour and thus reap the rewards, or they learn not to imitate a particular action and thereby avoid disagreeable consequences (Sherry & Lyons, 2012).

The SLT thus assumes that the social environment causes people to behave in certain ways (Mshelia, 2021: 675). Mshelia (2021) notes that modelling of parental behaviour may be relevant in understanding VAW; it is generally believed that a man who witnessed violence against women (VAW) during childhood is more likely to perpetuate it than one who did not. The SLT suggests that early exposure to violence causes children to condone the use of interpersonal violence and thus increases the likelihood of them engaging in it. Gender-based violence against women by intimate male partners. For instance, Nigerian Gospel Singer Osinachi Nwachukwu was reported to have suffered several violent attacks at the hands of her husband and died as a result of the ill treatment (Sahara Reporter, 2022). This often occurs in the presence of children; this influences such children's perceptions of women and how they should be treated in a relationship. That is, children tend to mimic their parents'

---

[4] These are acts of violence, usually murder, committed by a male member of a family against a female member who is perceived in line with their culture, to have brought dishonour to the family.

behaviour; when their father abuses their mother, they are likely to perpetrate such behaviour later in life. Bandura's SLT thus demonstrates the link between learning processes and interpersonal and intergenerational violence.

Other factors such as culture, religious practices and women's low status also account for violence against them. A theory on violence that is gender blind and lacks a feminist lens inevitably results in the presentation of the dominant patriarchal perspective. A feminist perspective provides a deeper understanding by analysing how violence is connected to and embedded in, patriarchal structures of power (Cockburn, 2004). As Cockburn (2004: 28) argues, 'gender power shapes the dynamic of every interaction'. Gender norms thus shape and are shaped by power structures; the positioning of human subjects within these structures is central to feminist theory (Cockburn, 2004: 29).

Violence is inherently linked to power and arguably, no act of violence occurs without intersecting with gender. However, feminism interrogates gender-specific violence within the confines of the male–female binary (Heyes, 2013: 201). Using Nigeria as a case study of a patriarchal society, males are regarded as the dominant group with females as their subordinates. This is a major feature of a traditional society (Makama, 2013: 105). It is a set of social relations with a material base which enables men to dominate women. In most cases, women are prevented from acquiring formal education, mistreated and perpetually kept as house help; the average Nigerian woman is seen as an object that is available for prostitution, forced marriage and street hawking, and as an instrument of trafficking and a misfit in society (Makama, 2013).

This patriarchal society fosters belief in men's entitlement to women's services, obedience, loyalty and subservience. In exercising their culturally given authority in relationships, men seek to control women through a variety of means which foster psychological, physical and mental violence, among other forms (Mshelia, 2021: 676). Furthermore, there is increasing evidence to suggest that marital violence revolves around cultural definitions of appropriate sex roles and partners' expectations of each other's roles, particularly those related to wifely obedience and domestic services (Mshelia, 2021). Women's failure to satisfy their partners' expectations of their roles often results in violence against them. As noted by Rakovec-Felser (2014: 64), when a man needs support, he often does not have the kind of social network that a woman enjoys. He might also be afraid that if he was to report his wife to the police, they would not take his allegations seriously. Women's economic dependence on their husbands is also encouraged by cultural and religious beliefs that regard men as the breadwinners in their families.

Feminist theory has been criticised on the grounds that it exaggerates male power and implies that all men exercise the same degree of authority over women. Nonetheless, it offers the most relevant explanatory and predictive basis in light of VAW in Nigeria and beyond. As Bailey rightly noted, it has been instrumental in driving significant legal, educational and policy initiatives of women's rights movements which have improved the plight of women in diverse contexts (Bailey, 2016: 669).

The Reality of GBV in Nigeria

Gender-based violence is on the rise in Nigeria, with women and girls experiencing harmful practices like child marriage, FGM and sexual and domestic violence. According to the United Nations' Population Fund (UNFPA), three in 10 Nigerian girls have experienced physical violence by the age of 15, while a Thomson Reuters Foundation Survey ranked Nigeria the ninth most dangerous country for women in 2018 (Okunola, 2021). Equally, the United Nations' Children's Fund (UNICEF) states that one in four Nigerian girls and 10% of boys have been victims of sexual violence and the country also has the largest number of child brides in Africa (UNCEF, 2017). One in four girls and women (27%) aged 15–49 have undergone FGM, and the country has the third-highest number of women and girls who have undergone FGM worldwide (UNCEF, 2017).

There have been many cases of sexual violence and 11,200 rape cases were reported in 2020 (Amnesty International, 2021). According to this Amnesty report, Hamira a five-year-old was drugged and raped by her neighbour in April 2020 and May 2021, while Uwaila Omozuwa a 22-year-old student was raped and killed in a church in Benin. Barakat Bello, an 18-year-old student was raped during a robbery in her home in Ibadan. She was butchered with a machete by her rapist and died on 1 June 2020. Favour Okechukwu an 11-year-old girl was gang-raped to death in Ejigbo Lagos State. These and many other cases totalling 11,200 were reported in 2020. In June 2020, the Nigeria Governors Forum declared a state of emergency on GBV, while the federal government established the Ministerial Gender-Based Violence Management Committee. During the same period, the Senate (the upper arm of the National Legislature) approved the Sexual Harassment Bill, and the National Human Rights Commission, the Nigerian police and the National Agency for the Prohibition of Trafficking in Persons (NAPTIP) signed an agreement to formally join forces to combat GBV.[5] However, there has been a steady increase in reports of GBV in different parts of the country (Adedigba, 2022).

GBV AS A HUMAN RIGHTS VIOLATION

Gender-based violence is one of the most severe and widespread human rights violations. Despite the legal framework in Nigeria on the protection of citizen's against GBV, it continues to rear its ugly head. Gender-based violence systematically undermines the victim's autonomy and self-esteem, violating their right to dignity. It can lead to injury, illness and death. Presently, there are a number of murder cases in Nigerian courts which occurred as a result of GBV. One of them is the murder of Bamise Ayanwola. A bus driver, Andrew Ominikoro, allegedly raped her to death. The husband of a popular gospel singer who died recently is also on trial for her murder. Exposure to GBV increases health risks for girls and women, including the increased likelihood of early sexual debut, forced and unprotected sex, exposure to sexually transmitted diseases, unwanted pregnancies and mental illness.

As noted previously, GBV violates a number of human rights. The practices that give rise to GBV include but are not limited to virginity testing, FGM, widowhood practices, early/forced marriage, marital rape, rape, sexual harassment, wife battery, sexual abuse of female children and property appropriation. This section presents a brief overview on selected practices that give rise to GBV.

Virginity testing has been recognised as GBV because young girls are coerced to undergo this examination to assess their virtue, honour or social value (WHO, 2018). The main aim is to promote sexual purity in marriage. In Nigeria, a young girl is expected to be chaste until she marries (Eniola & Mubangizi, 2017: 10). Although virginity testing is not a known cultural practice in Nigeria and as such is not peculiar to any region, parents engage in this gynaecological examination to determine the sexual status of their girl-child and to instil the culture of sexual purity. This test has been extended to the educational sector. In 2013,

---

[5] For more information, see https://naptip.gov.ng/.

a school principal allegedly conducted virginity testing on her students in Ogun State of Nigeria (Adedeji, 2013). Virginity testing is a form of GBV as only the female gender is subjected to it. It reinforces women's inequality and a stereotyped view of female morality as it is attached to sexual purity. Virginity testing inhibits a number of women's human rights such as the right to human dignity, equality, health and reproductive autonomy, among others. Female genital mutilation is another form of GBV that is practised in Nigeria. It infringes women's human rights such as the right to life, human dignity, equality and health.

Equally, widowhood practices constitute a form of GBV. Such practices are restricted to women that are subjected to demeaning activities such as depriving them of their freedom of movement, forbidding them to eat certain food, being forced to sleep with the corpse of the deceased and depriving them of personal hygiene, among other things. While the mourning period and the nature of the activities vary from one ethnic group to another, they are inhumane (Durojaye, 2013: 179). Consequently, widowhood practices violate the right to life, equality, human dignity, freedom and security of the person, health and reproductive autonomy, among others.

Sexual violence such as marital rape, rape, sexual harassment and sexual assault are forms of GBV that infringe on women's human rights. Sexual violence is often due to social norms and practices that are based on patriarchal beliefs that men are entitled to women's bodies. For example, married women may experience sexual violence at the hands of their husbands due to the cultural practice of bride price (Eniola & Aremo, 2020: 28). This is the consideration in the form of money or goods given by the groom's family to the bride's family during customary marriage. While it legitimises the marriage (Eniola & Aremo, 2020: 28), some consider it as a 'purchase' (Enemo, 2008: 35). Rape and sexual assault are perpetrated by both intimate partners and strangers. Sexual violence in whatever form is degrading and humiliating and invariably violates the victim's right to life, dignity and bodily autonomy, among other things.[6]

Women are also subjected to economic violence such as appropriation of property. Some are forced out of their homes by their in-laws following

---

[6] See Sections 33, 34 and 42 of the 1999 Constitution of the Federal Republic of Nigeria as Amended, Sexual violence is also prohibited by the Penal Code Act, the Criminal Code Act, the Child Rights Act and the Violence Against Persons (Prohibition) Act.

the death of their husbands or by the husband in the case of divorce. This invariably renders them destitute. While property appropriation is a form of GBV, the perpetrators are not always men, with mothers- and sisters-in-law sometimes the culprits. In whatever form, it denies women their right to decent shelter, livelihoods and self-esteem (Izumi, 2007: 22). Equally, a lack of economic empowerment may make women susceptible to violence.

Legal Frameworks on GBV

Nigeria has signed and ratified some international instruments that protect its citizens from GBV. The 1945 Universal Declaration of Human Rights formed the basis for number of subsequent instruments that pertain to GBV, such as the International Covenant on Economic, Social and Cultural Rights (ICESCR); the CEDAW (1979); the Convention on the Rights of the Child; the Declaration on the Elimination of Violence against Women adopted by the UN General Assembly in 1993; the Vienna Declaration emanating from the World Conference on Human Rights; and the Platform for Action issued by the United Nations Fourth World Conference on Women in Beijing.

At the continental level, the African Charter on Human and Peoples' Rights; the Protocol to the African Charter on Human and Peoples' Rights on the Rights of Women in Africa; the Convention Governing the Specific Aspects of Refugee Problems in Africa; the African Charter on the Rights and Welfare of the Child; the Protocol on the Statute of the African Court of Justice and Human Rights; and the African Union Solemn Declaration on Gender Equality in Africa seek to eliminate GBV.

However, Nigeria operates a dualistic system in terms of treaty ratification. For a treaty assented to by the government to be applicable in the country, it must subsequently be ratified by the National Assembly.[7] Some of the treaties on GBV assented to by Nigeria are yet to be domesticated and as such they cannot be applied in cases of GBV.[8] The Constitution further requires that treaties on matters that are on the concurrent legislative list must be reenacted by states' Houses of Assembly before they can

---

[7] See Section 12 of the Constitution of the Federal Republic of Nigeria as amended.

[8] The treaties include the International Covenant on Economic, Social and Cultural Rights, the Convention of the Elimination of all forms of Discrimination against Women and the Protocol to the African Charter on Human and People's Rights, among others.

be applicable in such states. This creates geographical disparities in the application of laws on GBV. For example, some states have reenacted the Child Rights Act into law, while others are yet to do so.

In addition to the constitutional provisions on fundamental human rights which protect citizens against GBV, Nigeria has national legislative and legal frameworks. Among others, they include the Child Rights Act, criminal and penal codes and the Violence Against Persons Prohibition (VAPP) Act. The VAAP Act was enacted in 2015 specifically to address GBV. It expanded the scope of the offence of rape, but is silent on the issue of consent. Issues of this nature are on the concurrent list,[9] and as noted above, states are expected to reenact these laws in order for them to operate in their respective states. Prior to the enactment of the VAPP, Lagos (Lagos State Protection against Domestic Violence Law, 2007) and Ekiti States (Ekiti State Gender Based Violence Prohibition Law, 2011) adopted laws on domestic violence and the prohibition of GBV.

Although gender advocates consider this as a major milestone alongside the introduction of sex offenders' registers in Ekiti and Lagos States, they cite the paucity of funds as a major hindrance to effective operationalisation of these laws (Fadare, 2022). Other states of the federation have enacted laws that prohibit some forms of GBV such as widowhood practices, FGM and child marriage among others. Currently, 30 of the 36 states of the federation have enacted comprehensive laws that prohibit GBV in their States (Fayemi, 2021), including Adamawa, Anambra, Bauchi, Bayelsa, Ondo, Delta, Ebonyi, Kaduna, Plateau and Rivers, among others (VAPP TRACKER, 2015). The anti-GBV law, Violence Against Person's Prohibition Act (VAPP) of Nigeria, which was passed in 2015 has been domesticated by 30 of the States (VAPP TRACKER, 2015).

GBV AND LEGAL CONSTRAINTS IN NIGERIA

As noted, in Nigeria, ratification and signing of an international treaty does not translate to attainment of the rights recognised by such

---

[9] These issues fall under the concurrent list, which is the jurisdiction of both States and the national government.

treaties.[10] Even though Nigeria now has a national law that protects citizens against GBV, it is not wholly effective due to the fact that issues of this nature are on the concurrent legislative list. Thus, despite that VAAP Act having been enacted by the National Assembly, any state of the federation that wants its provisions to be operational in the state must reenact its provisions to become part of state laws. Hence, these laws cannot be uniformly enforced in Nigeria.

Most of the laws on GBV in Nigeria are inadequate or their scope is limited based on the undue burden of proof placed on victims. Some of these laws are gender-biased. Furthermore, Section 55 (1) (d) of the penal code which is applicable in the northern part of the country provides that:

> nothing is an offence which does not amount to infliction of grievous hurt upon any person and which is done by …(d) a husband for the purpose of correcting his wife. Such husband and wife being subject to any routine law or custom on which such correction is recognized as lawful.

These provisions contradict the constitution that guarantees the right to dignity of all Nigerian citizens.

Other laws, particularly those pertaining to matrimonial cases, circumscribe women's ability to leave violent relationships. For instance, one of the grounds for dissolution of marriage under the Matrimonial Causes Act, Section 15 (2)(c) and 16 (1) (e) of 2004 is that the marriage has broken down irretrievably, that is, the respondent has behaved in such a way that the petitioner cannot reasonably be expected to live with the respondent.

To satisfy this condition, the petitioner has to satisfy the court that since the marriage and within a period of one year immediately preceding the date of the petition, the respondent has been convicted of:

i. having attempted to murder or unlawfully kill the petitioner.
ii. having committed an offence involving the intentional inflicting of grievous harm or grievous hurt on the petitioner.

The implication is that the onus is on the petitioner to first secure a conviction against the respondent for attempting to kill her or inflict harm

---

[10] See Section 12 of the Constitution of the Federal Republic of Nigeria, 1999 (as amended).

on her, failing which she will not be able to leave the relationship. This is a serious legal constraint for women that are victims of domestic violence. Many women lose their lives before getting out of such marriages because of this cumbersome legal constraint.

Section 221 of the Criminal Code Act that addresses the defilement of girls under the age of 16 provides that:

> any person who has or attempts to have unlawful carnal knowledge of a girl being above thirteen years and under sixteen years of age is guilty of a misdemeanor and is liable to imprisonment for two years with or without whipping. It is a defense to a charge in this section to prove that the accused person believes on reasonable grounds that the girl was above sixteen years. A prosecution for any offence in this section must begin within two months after the offence is committed. Any person cannot be convicted of any offence in this section upon the uncorroborated testimony of the witness.

The time frame set for the commencement of prosecution (within two months of commission of the offence) is likely to make it difficult for the victim to obtain justice. This section also requires that the victim's evidence must be corroborated, which might be difficult to achieve given the nature of the crime. Finally, it is easy for a victim to appear older than her age.

With regard to rape and sexual assault, Section 179(5) of the Evidence Act provides that: 'a person shall not be convicted of the offences mentioned in paragraphs (h) and (j) of Section 51 or Sections 218, 22, 223 and 224 of the criminal code upon the uncorroborated evidence of one witness'. Such provisions are obstacles to victims in obtaining justice.

Lessons from South Africa

South Africa is one of the African countries that is being ravaged by the scourge of GBV. South Africa and Nigeria are regional powers in terms of political and economic development. While they have different political histories, they are both democratic states which affirm the supremacy of their constitutions as the *grundnorm*.[11] They are also signatories to a

---

[11] Section 2 of the Constitution of the Republic of South Africa, 1996, and Section 1(1) of the Constitution of the Federal Republic of Nigeria, 1999.

number of international and regional treaties on GBV and have adopted frameworks to protect their citizens from GBV.

South Africa's measures to combat GBV are unique due to its more developed constitutional, legislative and institutional approach. The Bill of Rights in the country's constitution guarantees a number of rights that seek to protect citizens against GBV, particularly the right to bodily and psychological integrity.[12,13] Chapter 9 of the constitution also provides for the establishment of state institutions to support constitutional democracy, including the South African Human Rights Commission, and the Commission for Gender Equality.[14]

Other laws also protect the rights of South African citizens against GBV,[15] some of which were recently amended to improve protection and bring justice to victims of GBV. These include the Criminal Procedure Amendment Act, Criminal Law (Sexual Offences and related matters) Act and the Domestic Violence Amendment Act No. 14, 2021.

The amendments to these laws broadened the scope of GBV by introducing the offence of sexual intimidation. The scope of the National Register for Sex Offenders (NRSO) has also been broadened to include the particulars of all sex offenders. The list of people to be protected has been expanded, as well as the length of time a sexual offender's particulars must remain in the register. The Criminal Law and Related Matters Amendment Act made changes to the Magistrate Courts Acts to provide for the appointment of intermediaries and for evidence to be given through intermediaries. Evidence can also be given using an audio-visual link. The Criminal Procedure Act, 1977, the Criminal Law Amendment Act, 1997 and the Superior Courts Act, 2013 were also amended to promote flexibility in the administration of justice.

The Domestic Violence Amendment Bill amended the Domestic Violence Act of 1998 by including a new definition of controlling and coercive behaviour. It also expanded the definition of domestic violence, removed binary terms and uses gender-neutral terminology. The scope of the Act has been expanded to include harms that could come about

---

[12] Sections 12(2).

[13] See Chapter 2 of the Constitution of the Republic of South Africa, 1996.

[14] Sections 184, and 187 of the Constitution of the Republic of South Africa, 1996.

[15] See, Domestic Violence Act 116 of 1998, Children's Act 38 of 2005 and Criminal Law (Sexual Offences and Related Matters) Act 32 of 2007, among others.

through the use of electronic communication. Finally, protection orders against domestic violence can now be applied for online. All these developments strengthen the fight against GBV.

Conclusion

This chapter examined the concept, nature and scope of GBV in Nigeria through the lenses of the social learning theory and liberal feminism. Learning through observation, and cultural and religious practices play a major role in GBV in Nigeria, which remains a persistent challenge despite the country's legal framework. The chapter noted that legal constraints to combating GBV include Nigeria's dualistic approach to domestication of treaties, geographical disparities in the application of laws on GBV due to Nigeria's federal system, inadequate laws on GBV and the undue burden of proof imposed on its victims.

The chapter highlighted South Africa's approach to addressing GBV from which Nigeria can learn a number of lessons. One is that Nigeria must muster the political will to domesticate international treaties on GBV. Furthermore, national legislation pertaining to GBV should be amended to ensure that its provisions adequately protect citizens from GBV. Where their rights are infringed, adequate provision should be made for victims to obtain justice.

Reforms within the political structure are also required to foster equal opportunities for males and females in every sphere. Women should become equal partners in development through increased participation and an improved share of resources, employment and income so as to improve their living conditions.

While religious beliefs and cultural values cannot be disregarded, the government should ensure that they are not used to perpetuate GBV. Religious leaders should be sensitised, while female church leaders should be encouraged to help younger women to obtain justice and not to try to cover up the issue though prayer. Furthermore, there is a need to interrogate how the social construction of men as authority figures has been used to subject women to abuse across the different religious traditions. At a broader level, the international community should engage in ongoing advocacy and monitoring to encourage governments worldwide to protect the human rights, health and well-being of all their citizens and promote positive development.

REFERENCES

Adedeji, D. K. (2013, January 22). Ogun orders psychiatric test on virginity test principal. *Premium Times*. https://premiumtimesng.com/regional/ssouthwest/116457-ogun-orders-psychiartric-test-on-virginity-test-principal.html. Accessed on 19 July 2022.

Adedigba, A. (2022). *Nigeria struggling to combat gender-based violence. Despite Laws*. https://humanglemedia.com/nigeria-strugling-to-combat-gender-based-violence-despite-laws-govt-promises/. Accessed on 19 July 2022.

Amnesty International. (2021). *Nigeria: Failure to tackle rape crisis emboldens perpetrators and silences survivors*. www.amnesty.org/en/latest/news/2021/11/nigeria-failure-to-tackle-rape-crisis-emboldens-perpetrators-and-silences-survivors/. Accessed on 5 April 2022.

Bailey, E. L. (2016). Feminism, liberal. *The Wiley Blackwell encyclopedia of gender and sexuality studies* (pp. 669–671). Wiley.

Baldasare, A. (2012). *Gender-based violence: Focus on Africa*. Sai from vision to results. https://sai-dc.com/wp-content/uploads/2014/05/GBV-Literature-Review.pdf

Bandura, A. (1977). *Social learning theory*. General Learning Press.

Cockburn, C. (2004). The continuum of violence: A gender perspective on war and peace. In W. Giles & J. Hyndman (Eds.), *Sites of violence: Gender and conflict zones* (pp. 29–30). University of California Press.

Durham, S. (2022). *Hidden suffering: Gender Based Violence (GBV) against boys and men*. The South African College of Applied Psychology. https://www.sacap.edu.za/blog/applied-psychology/hidden-suffering-gender-based-violence-gbv-against-boys-and-men. Accessed on 29 January 2022.

Durojaye, E. (2013). 'Woman, but not human': Widowhood practices and human rights violations in Nigeria. *International Journal of Law, Policy and Family, 27*(2), 176–196.

Enemo, I. (2008). Legal implications of "bride price" or "dowry" on women's human rights in Nigeria. In J. N. Ezeilo & J. F. Alumanah (Eds.), *Bride price and the implications for women's rights in Nigeria* (pp. 23–40). Women Aid Collective.

Eniola, B., & Aremo, J. (2020). Bride price and sexual and reproductive rights of women: A case study of South Africa and Nigeria. *Journal of Law, Policy and Globalization, 96*, 26–33.

Eniola, B., & Mubangizi, J. (2017). The legal frameworks for the protection of women's reproductive health rights in South Africa and Nigeria: Some comparative lessons. *Journal of Social Welfare and Human Rights, 5*(2), 1–12.

European Institute for Gender Equality. (2022). *What is gender-based violence?* https://eige.europa.eu/gender-based-violence/what-is-gender-based-violence. Accessed on 29 January 2022.

Fadare, T. (2022). *CSW66: How Nigeria can record more successes on Gender-based issues with VAPP law*. https://www.premiumtimesng.com/news/more-news/517531-csw66-how-nigeria-can-record-more-successes-on-gender-based-issues-with-vapp-law.html. Accessed on 25 July 2022.

Fayemi, K. (2021). *30 States in Nigeria enact laws prohibiting gender-based violence*. http://businessday.ng/news/article/30-states-in-nigeria-enact-laws-prohibiting-gender-based-violence-fayemi/. Accessed on 5 April 2022.

Heyes, C. (2013). Feminist solidarity after queer theory: The case of transgender. In S Stryker & A. Z. Aizura (Eds.), *The transgender studies reader* (Vol. 2). Routledge.

Hoare, J. (2007). *Gender based violence*. Oxfam.

Izumi, K. (2007). Gender- based violence and property grabbing in Africa: A denial of women's liberty and security. In G. Terry & J. Haore (Eds.), *Gender-based violence*. Oxfam GB.

Makama, G. (2013). Patriarchy and gender inequality in Nigeria: The way forward. *European Scientific Journal, 9*(17), 101–110.

Mshelia, I. H. (2021). Gender based violence and violence against women in Nigeria: A sociological analysis. *International Journal of Research and Innovation in Social Science, V*(VIII), 674–683.

Okunola, A. (2021). *Everything you need to know about the law that could reduce gender-based violence in Nigeria*. https://www.globalcitizen.org/en/content/everything-you-need-to-know-vapp-Nigeria/

Rakovec-Felser, Z. (2014). Domestic violence and abuse in intimate relationships from public health perspective. *Health Psychology Research, 2*(1821), 62–67.

Sahara Reporter. (2021, December 6). *It's now crime to be in fine cars, look good—Imo residents laments rising police harassment*. https://twitter.com/SaharaReporters/status/146795884655147008. Accessed on 29 January 2022.

Sahara Reporters. (2022, April 9). *How Nigerian gospel artist, Osinachi Nwachukwu, died from domestic violence, was brutalised by husband—friends*. https://saharareporters.com/2022/04/09/how-nigerian-gospel-artist-osinachi-nwachukwu-died-domestic-violence-was-brutalised. Accessed 8 April 2022.

Sherry, D., & Lyons, S. (2012) *Social learning theory*. https://www.researchgate.net/publication/302350884_Social_Learning_Theory. Accessed 8 April 2022.

Terry, G. (2007). Introduction. In G. Terry & J. Haore (Eds.), *Gender-based violence*. Oxfam GB.

Ukpong, C. (2020, February 26). Speaker condemns police harassment of young Nigerians. *Premium Times*.

UN Women. (2022). *Global database on violence against women: Nigeria*. https://evaw-global-database.unwomen.org/fr/countries/africa/nigeria. Accessed on 7 July 2022.

UNHCR (2022). *Gender-based violence.* https://unhcr.org/gender-based-violence.html#:~:text= Accessed on 19 July 2022.

UNICEF. (2017). *Child protection: Nigeria.* https://www.unicef.org/nigeria/child-protection. Accessed 19 July 2022.

Usigbe, L. (2022). *Nigerian women say 'no' to gender-based violence.* https://un.org/africarenewal/news/Nigerian-women-say-'no'-gender-based-violence. Accessed on 7 July 2022.

VAPP TRACKER. (2015). *The Violence Against Person's Prohibition Act (VAPP) of Nigeria.* https://www.partnersnigeria.org/vapp-tracker/. Accessed on 25 April 2022.

WHO. (2018). *Eliminating virginity testing: An interagency statement.* https://who.int/news/item/17-10-2018-united-nations-agencies-call-for-ban-on-virginity-testing. Accessed on 19 July 2022.

CHAPTER 19

Food Security as a New Frontier of War: A Geo-Historical Perspective of Food Security and Armed Conflict in Sub-Saharan Africa

Malaika Lesego Samora Mahlatsi

INTRODUCTION

The post-independence epoch in sub-Saharan Africa has been defined by numerous episodes of armed conflict. Across all regions within the sphere of the African Union (AU), particularly sub-Saharan Africa, it has been one of the key factors informing instability and socio-economic struggle. The causes and nature of this conflict are varied, with some instances reflecting a fragmented and militarised political system. Recent studies indicate that armed conflict in sub-Saharan Africa is characterised by

M. L. S. Mahlatsi (✉)
Institute for Pan-African Thought and Conversation,

University of Johannesburg, Johannesburg, South Africa
e-mail: malaikawaazania@gmail.com

© The Author(s), under exclusive license to Springer Nature Switzerland AG 2023
A. O. Akinola, *Contemporary Issues on Governance, Conflict and Security in Africa*,
https://doi.org/10.1007/978-3-031-29635-2_19

the centrality of non-state actors arising from the fracturing of armed groupings (Cilliers, 2015). Importantly, it is also informed by particular historical contexts. Previous studies have largely focused on factors such as colonial legacies, militarisation and military cultures, ethnicity, religious clashes, political frailties including regime consolidation, and competition for ownership and control of natural resources. Indeed, the mineral resource-conflict nexus has been the focus of attention in studies on conflict in sub-Saharan Africa, particularly in countries such as Nigeria, South Africa and The Republic of Congo (Congo DRC). This is informed by the reality that access to and control of mineral resources and land is a fundamental underlying issue in many of the region's protracted conflicts that has impacted on national as well as regional peace and security.

Abiodun Alao's *Natural Resources and Conflict in Africa: The Tragedy of Endowment* provides the most comprehensive account of the link between natural resources and violent conflict in Africa (Alao, 2015). As with most studies of this nature, the focus is largely on conflict over oil in Nigeria, mineral resources in Congo DRC and Sierra Leone, land in Zimbabwe and water in the Horn of Africa. This necessary focus on mineral resources and water as a major source of conflict has overshadowed the emergence of food security as a new frontier of war. In common with many studies on the link between natural resources and conflict, food is not given centrality in the analysis, and is treated as nothing more than a footnote in the broader discussion. This is partly due to the widely held belief that food security is a by-product rather than a source of conflict (Mahlatsi, 2022b). Based on an analysis of the geo-histories of some contemporary conflicts in sub-Saharan Africa, this chapter contends that food security is in fact, both a source and a result of conflict. With regard to the former, it demonstrates how the cocoa pod was at the centre of the civil war in Ivory Coast at the turn of the twenty-first century and how hunger in the Sahel region has triggered violent conflict and instability. The chapter also attributes growing and increasingly violent anti-immigrant sentiment in South Africa to rising levels of urban hunger, while the convergence between food and conflict is illustrated by the food insecurity suffered in Ethiopia as a result of conflict. The chapter concludes that just as the eruption of armed conflict over mineral resources in a country has significant implications for stability in neighbouring countries due to the spillover effects, so too does armed conflict arising from food insecurity. Hunger alleviation is thus crucial to the mitigation and resolution of conflict in the sub-Saharan African region.

Understanding Food Security

Prior to the World Food Summit in November 1996, various definitions of food security were employed in public policy. Food security as a concept originated in the mid-1970s as a result of discussions around international problems at a time of the global food crisis. At this time, it largely focused on food supply problems, specifically that of 'assuring the availability and to some degree the price stability of basic foodstuffs at the international and national level' (Clay, 2002). In addition, issues of hunger and famine were extensively examined. As a result, the 1974 World Food Summit defined food security as the 'availability at all times of adequate world food supplies of basic foodstuffs to sustain a steady expansion of food consumption and to offset fluctuations in production and prices' (United Nations, 1975). Recognising the lack of focus on vulnerable people securing access to available supplies, this economistic definition was altered and in 1983, the Food and Agriculture Organisation of the United Nations (FAO) expanded it to include 'ensuring that all people at all times have both physical and economic access to the basic food that they need' (FAO, 1983).

In 1986, the World Bank released the highly influential report on *Poverty and Hunger*, which analysed the temporal dynamics of food security. It analysed the important distinction between chronic and transitory food insecurity. According to the report, chronic food insecurity is associated with structural poverty and low incomes, while transitory food security is linked to periods of intensified pressure caused by conflict, natural disasters or economic collapse (World Bank, 1986). By the mid-1990s, food security was recognised as a significant concern and its scope was expanded to incorporate both food safety and nutritional balance. By the early 2000s, its definition had been refined to 'a situation that exists when all people, at all times, have physical, social and economic access to sufficient, safe and nutritious food that meets their dietary needs and food preferences for an active and healthy life' (FAO, 2002). This is the most accepted definition, and this chapter adopts this conceptualisation in its data presentation and analysis.

According to Jorari (2012), there are four dimensions or indicators of food security, namely, food availability, access, utilisation and stability. Food availability refers to the presence of food, which may be sourced from the markets or through one's own production. Food access is ensured when 'all households and all individuals within those households have sufficient resources to obtain appropriate foods for a nutritious diet' (Jorari, 2012: 13). This is dependent on the resources available to a household, which include, in the main, capital and labour. Knowledge is also an important resource in terms of food access as constantly changing activities correlate with evolving knowledge systems around agricultural production (Anderson, 2015). However, it is important to note that the availability of capital to purchase food does not translate to food security. This can be seen in Egypt where there is relatively high per capita income and low unemployment, but a crisis of reliance on imported food (Sulkin, 2020) that renders the country's food supply susceptible to market volatility. Egypt thus suffers growing rates of hunger and malnutrition despite being the world's biggest producer of wheat. The socio-economic, policy and the physical environments have an impact on food access.

With regard to the latter, Ringler et al.'s (2010) study on the impact of climate change on food security in sub-Saharan Africa contends that climatic conditions, which include changes in precipitation, are having a direct impact on soil arability and yield, as well as other geographic factors. Social environments such as conflict also disrupt food production and pose a serious threat to food access for households in conflict area (Jorari, 2012: 13). For example, in many parts of northern Nigeria that has been described as the 'food basket' of the country, Boko Haram terrorism has driven away farmers, creating food shortages. The policy environment might also impede households' capacity to access food. This can be seen in the post-apartheid dispensation in South Africa. The government's failure to develop and implement effective land and agrarian reform has led to systematic de-agrarianisation, which is a driver of food insecurity (Hall, 2011; Mahlatsi, 2017).

The dimension of food utilisation has two interlinked aspects: biological and socio-economic. The biological aspect focuses on the individual level of food security and refers to the individual's ability to consume food and convert it into energy. Utilisation is dependent on a nutritious diet and a healthy environment, as well as access to clean drinking water and sanitation, which play a role in the prevention of communicable and other diseases. The fourth and last dimension, food stability, refers to the length of time food security persists, and is defined through the distinction between chronic food insecurity and transitionary food insecurity (Jorari, 2012: 15). Chronic food insecurity, which captures the inability to meet food needs on an ongoing basis, is differentiated from transitionary food insecurity where the inability to meet food needs is temporary, often due to climatic conditions such as floods or drought, or in cases of civil conflict, although in the last-mentioned context food insecurity challenges might persist for a much longer period of time (Brück & d'Errico, 2019).

Food Security and the Question of Power

The food regime is an important component of food security. Contemporary food regime analysis, whose foundation was laid by Harriet Friedman and Phillip McMichael's essay, *Agriculture and the State System: The rise and decline of national agricultures, 1870 to the present*, is centred on the Marxist notion that unequal distribution of power and resources creates global food regimes. The authors state that 'the notion of food regime links international relations of food production and consumption to forms of accumulation broadly distinguishing periods of capitalist accumulation' (Friedman & McMichael, 1989: 95). International relations of food production and consumption have always been skewed against developing nations, who throughout history have carried the burden of producing food which neither consume nor can afford to purchase. This had a negative effect on their food production as the African agricultural economy was moved from food-based to cash-crop production. A clear example is the production of chocolate, which although not a basic food commodity, lays bare the extent of the capitalist accumulation to which Friedman and McMichael refer.

Chocolate is derived from the cacao bean, more than 70% of which is cultivated in West Africa, particularly in the Ivory Coast and Ghana (Diakate, 2020). According to Pecorelli (2020), while the chocolate industry generates about $100 billion in annual profits, farmers that grow the cacao bean receive only 6% of the revenue while manufacturers net 35% and retailers receive 44%. Significantly, the manufacturers are predominantly based in Western Europe, with a few in the United States of America and China. Pecorelli goes on to argue that 'the average annual income from cocoa cultivation is approximately $1000 per farm, translating to about $2.70 per day. This figure is meant to be divided amongst the workers of the farm, which can be as many as a dozen. In order to avoid splitting the profits, some farmers use enslaved children for labour' (Pecorelli, 2020). This assertion is corroborated by the latest *Cocoa Barometer*, a biennial report compiled by a global consortium of civil society organisations that include the European Federation of Food and Oxfam, which states that a shocking 1.5 million child labourers work in the cocoa fields in West Africa (Fountain & Huetz-Adams, 2020).

Cacao production in West Africa has been the source of violent conflict in the region. In the post-independence era, the Ivory Coast (officially regarded as the Republic of Côte d'Ivoire) was a relatively stable and economically prosperous country with a strong agricultural sector. This stability was especially pronounced in a region that has historically been characterised by civil wars and economic decline. However, at the end of the twentieth century, the Ivory Coast was plunged into a civil war that largely centred around land. In 2004, hundreds of people were killed in cocoa plantations. Carroll (2004) contends that there are overlapping micro-conflicts across much of the cocoa belt between indigenous farmers and settlers from the north, as well as neighbouring countries, including Mali and Burkina Faso. The question of property rights in the Ivory Coast is intrinsically linked to the production of cocoa. The declining availability of virgin forests and cocoa plantations led to an increase in the cost of labour on cocoa plantations, the result of which was ethno-regional division among those selling their labour, leading to an all-out civil war (Woods, 2003).

Violent Conflict as a Source of Hunger: The Case of Ethiopia

The East African nation of Ethiopia faces one of the highest levels of food insecurity in the world, with the 2020 Global Hunger Index ranking it at 92 in terms of the hungriest countries on earth. Ethiopia has experienced numerous cycles of famine, defined as 'severe and prolonged hunger in a substantial proportion of the population of a region or country, resulting in widespread and acute malnutrition and death by starvation and disease' (Hasell & Roser, 2022: 1). The first documented famine in Ethiopia occurred in the first half of the ninth century and the most recent is currently taking place in the Tigray region to the north of the country, where there is an ongoing civil war. Famines in Ethiopia have claimed the lives of millions of people. According to Bahru (1991), the 1958 famine in Tigray claimed the lives of more than 100,000 people, while the 1973 famine that began in the Amhara region and spread throughout the northern provinces of the country claimed twice that number. The worst documented famine in Ethiopian history in terms of mortality rates occurred between 1984 and 1985 in the Tigray region. According to Gill (2010), it claimed the lives of 1.2 million people. It also created a huge humanitarian crisis, with 2.5 million people displaced and nearly half a million seeking refuge in neighbouring countries (Giorgis, 1989). In January 2021, the Famine Early Warning Systems Network declared a phase 3 crisis and phase 4 emergency in Tigray based on the number of deaths resulting from starvation and acute food insecurity in the region due to the ongoing war. The Ethiopian Red Cross Society corroborated this analysis, confirming that 80% of the population in the war-torn region was cut off from humanitarian aid, and that this could lead to the deaths of tens of thousands of people over and above those who have already perished (AFP, 2021).

Throughout history, the food insecurity crisis in Ethiopia has been the result of both environmental factors and conflict. In the case of the devastating 1984–1985 famine, these two factors intersected in catastrophic ways. According to a 1985 study commissioned by Cultural Survival, which is the first in-depth research on the systemic factors that resulted in the Ethiopian famine, environmental factors that included drought, critically low rainfall and the infestation of army worms that destroyed crops in the Tigray region and other parts of northern Ethiopia were compounded by military policy. Regarding the latter, the report states:

> Army worms can destroy a crop overnight, but the long-term stripping of the region's productive assets by the Ethiopian military was no less debilitating. Ninety-five percent of the famine victims who fled to the Sudan before the end of 1984 reported that in their villages the Ethiopian army had burned crops in the fields and grain they had harvested. The army, they said, never stole the grain, it simply destroyed it. (Holcomb et al., 1985)

Vestal (1985) also notes that the famine in Ethiopia was caused by various socio-political, economic and environmental factors, characterising it as a 'crisis of many dimensions'.

Asfaw (2015) posits that the successive famines in Ethiopia had a direct relationship with the constitutional priorities of the government of the time. Based on an analysis of the country's 1955, 1987 and 1994 constitutions, to some degree, famines in Ethiopia have been caused or exacerbated by the lack of a constitutional mandate to prioritise food security. Asfaw further argues that, like their predecessors who drafted the previous constitution, Ethiopian legislators who drafted the 1987 constitution laid the constitutional foundation for hunger by, among other things, 'failing to translate already declared source of death from its preamble page into an article, clearly stipulating freedom from hunger/right to adequate food as the fundamental rights of the body' (Asfaw, 2015: 45). According to the World Food Programme (2010), another factor that has contributed to current food insecurity in the country was the 2008/9 global financial crisis that led to rising food and fuel prices. Ethiopia is a highly underdeveloped country, ranked 171 out of 182 countries in the Human Development Index (United Development Programme, 2009) and with a poverty rate of 30% (World Bank, 2011). While some progress has been made in reducing poverty, the lack of structural change has resulted in persistent underdevelopment, extreme poverty and hunger (World Bank, 2015). The result is Ethiopia's continued reliance on food aid from the World Bank and the United Nations. From 1994 to 2003, these two agencies mobilised emergency relief food aid for more than five million Ethiopians—a practice that continues in some regions of the country such as Tigray where communities currently rely completely on humanitarian relief from aid agencies (AFP, 2021).

Hunger as a Source of Violent Conflict: The Case of the Sahel Region

The Sahel region has experienced growing levels of political and social instability due to a myriad of factors that include political instability and ecological disasters. Prolonged and severe drought and floods in Mali, Niger and Burkina Faso have resulted in massive population displacement. According to Action Against Hunger (2022), more than 3.2 million people have been displaced in these three countries alone. The international aid organisation has sounded the alarm on the exponentially rising levels of food insecurity in the Sahel region, where more than 27 million people per annum were deemed food insecure between 2019 and 2022. Action Against Hunger estimates that hunger will increase by 50% by mid-2022 in Mali, Niger, and Burkina Faso, plunging more than eight million people into a severe food security crisis. In the rest of the Sahel region, an estimated 16 million people could suffer from extreme hunger (Action Against Hunger, 2022).

The social instability resulting from hunger in Niger can be traced to growing extremism in Nigeria. According to the United Nations

High Commissioner for Refugees (UNHCR, 2015), as of 2015, at least 135,000 Nigerians had fled to neighbouring Cameroon, Chad and Niger to escape Boko Haram's reign of terror. Prior to the spillover of terrorism to several Sahel countries, they had all been struggling with the influx of refugees, owing in great part to their own economic limitations. Niger is ranked last in the UN Human Development Index (2019) while Chad is fourth from last, indicating the extent of their extreme poverty. The burden of refugees has placed a great strain on the limited food resources in the region. This is especially the case for Niger which already faced a drought-induced food security crisis in the Diffa; the region that took in almost 90,000 Nigerian refugees (Reuters, 2014). At the time of accepting these refugees, half a million inhabitants of Diffa, nearly a quarter of them children, were already facing acute food shortages.

In Burkina Faso, food is increasingly being used as a weapon of war. According to Mednick (2020), extremists in the country are targeting farmers' agricultural produce and land. Crops are intentionally left to rot in the fields and granaries as more than a million people have been displaced by the unarmed groups. There are also indications that food is being used as a political tactic to turn the population against the government. Christian Poonwah (cited in Mednick, 2020), the director of Safer Access Consulting, an international security company in Ouagadougou, the capital of Burkina Faso, notes that increasing violence is a mechanism for extremists to cut off the country's food supply in order to facilitate riots and protests against the state. He contends that this is why extremists are targeting the largest cereal-producing region in the country for their crop torching campaign. This same tactic has been used by extremists in Niger where farms and food banks have been set ablaze, threatening the supply of food across the entire country (Mosadomi, 2021).

The situation in the Sahel region corroborates Bora et al.'s (2011) conclusion that food insecurity is both the source of conflict and the cause of instability. Competition for food brings about instability and conflict between locals and refugees who often have to share very limited food resources. In sub-Saharan Africa, the crisis, trifecta of conflict, climate change and the COVID-19 pandemic, has been particularly devastating in the Sahel. All these factors are at the heart of the food security crisis that threatens to tear the region asunder. The waves of military incursions into politics in countries such as Mali, Burkina Faso and Guinea will aggravate the food crisis, particularly due to the sanctions imposed on these countries by the regional supranational organisation, the Economic Community of West African States (ECOWAS).

THE URBAN FOOD SECURITY CRISIS AND SOCIAL INSTABILITY IN SOUTH AFRICA

Xenophobic conflict, manifesting as Afrophobic[1] violence, has been a feature of the post-apartheid dispensation in South Africa. Since the dawn of democracy, relations between South Africans and immigrants from the continent have been greatly strained. It can be reasonably argued that 'anti-immigrant sentiment is not only strong; it is extremely widespread and cuts across virtually every socio-economic and demographic group' (Danso & McDonald in Nyamnjoh, 2006: 38). While several theories have sought to explain the etymology of this conflict, competition for resources is one of the most enduring. According to Crush (2008), the material motivations of xenophobic violence are rooted in the idea that foreign nationals are taking jobs from locals, thereby posing a threat to their capacity for livelihood generation. Viewed in light of the reality that most foreign nationals in South Africa are employed in exploitative industries and have precarious jobs (Mahlatsi, 2022a), this argument is debatable and is being used to mask the 'reinvention of difference' (Hassim et al., 2008) that underpins Afrophobic sentiments in South Africa. Yet it is at the centre of the argument posed by the popular *Operation Dudula*, an anti-immigrant movement with branches across Gauteng province. According to Myeni (2022), *Operation Dudula* is a splinter group from a faction in the *Put South Africans First movement*, an organisation that first popularised and renewed anti-immigrant campaigns on social media before finding expression on the ground.

It is no accident of history that such a movement is more popular in the most industrial province in South Africa, Gauteng, which is the nerve-centre of the country's economy. Unemployment and food insecurity are particularly pronounced in this province and its unemployment rate stood at 37% in 2021 (Evans, 2022). The country's macro-economic policies are not changing socio-economic realities for the working-class majority. Many citizens' standard of living continues to deteriorate and the poor are

---

[1] Afrophobia refers to hatred and intolerance for peoples of Africa and the African diaspora.

being forced to the margins of existence. Millions of South Africans are food insecure especially in urban areas. According to the South African Cities Network, in 2015, the national prevalence of households at risk of hunger in the country's cities was 28% in 2015, while 26% were experiencing hunger. The equivalent figures in urban informal areas were 32% and 36%, respectively. The numbers have been increasing exponentially. Statistics SA's (2019) study, *Towards measuring the extent of food security in South Africa: An examination of hunger and food inadequacy*, posits that almost two-thirds of the households that are vulnerable to hunger reside in urban areas.

The relationship between growing levels of Afrophobic violence and hunger in urban South Africa is illustrated by deepening anti-immigrant sentiment that has become especially pronounced in the era of COVID-19. Mahlatsi's (2022b) study on the pandemic's impact on urban food security contends that with more than three million people having lost their jobs in 2020, hunger has become a feature of urban existence and is pushing the growing mass of the unemployed to the brink. Bonti-Ankomah (2001) argues that food security has two components, namely the ability to be self-sufficient in food production through own production and access to markets and the ability to purchase food items. The growing levels of unemployment due to the COVID-19 pandemic mean that households that already have limited land for subsistence farming are also now confronted with the inability to purchase food items due to limited or no income. Bonti-Ankomah's argument that 'the threats to food security...interact with such factors as market and access to credit, the availability and sustainability of technology, the terms of trade, pricing policies and other idiosyncratic factors to threaten food supply' (2001: 2) has significant implications for future realities of urban food security and conflict in South Africa.

Conclusion

Discourse on the resolution of conflict in sub-Saharan Africa is largely focused on de-militarisation. This is evidenced by initiatives such as 'Silencing the guns', a commitment by African heads of state to create a conducive environment for development on the continent by silencing illegal weapons as a means of promoting peace. While such initiatives are crucial, hunger alleviation must be factored in as a key strategy for the prevention and mitigation of violent conflict and instability. This is especially important as countries begin to recover from the COVID-19 pandemic that decimated national economies and battered public social infrastructure across the sub-Saharan region. Discussions on ways to create a 'post-pandemic economy' that does not prioritise equitable access to nutritional food for all people at all times set the parameters for failure. The reality is that food security is a new frontier of war and a source of conflict in many countries across sub-Saharan Africa. This chapter illustrated the ways in which conflict and other factors such as climate change converge to create and reproduce food insecurity. The inability of African governments and broader civil society to centre food security in peace and security strategies is a fatal flaw that may lead to increasing conflict with long-lasting repercussions for national economies and people. The cases of Ethiopia and Nigeria, highlighted in this chapter underscore this argument.

The history and reality of food security in Africa is complex and layered, as are the factors driving it. Food insecurity on the continent is rarely driven by a single factor. The Sahel region is an apt demonstration of how ecological, political, environmental and socio-economic factors converge to create the perfect storm for hunger. In South Africa and Namibia, food insecurity is driven by factors both historical and contemporary. These include landlessness as a result of dispossession by colonial regimes, as well as the failure of legislation in the post-independence and post-apartheid epochs. In Zimbabwe, political and economic instability converge with ecological factors to drive food insecurity, while in Mozambique, conflict and environmental factors are at the centre of the hunger crisis. For this reason, the resolution of food insecurity must be multidimensional. The starting point is the resolution of landlessness, particularly in countries such as South Africa and Namibia where unequal land ownership patterns are a significant factor in the failure to deal with the agrarian question. Progressive land and agrarian reform anchored on equitable redistribution is also important. Linked to this, particularly in the case of smallholder farmers, must be technical and material assistance on the part of the state and the private sector. This will assist smallholder farmers not only with increased productivity, but with access to markets, ensuring that food security is achieved alongside other critical developmental goals. Finally, conflict resolution is fundamental to alleviation of hunger on the continent. This chapter has demonstrated that failure to prevent armed conflict is the foundation on which food insecurity is built.

REFERENCES

Action Against Hunger. (2022). *Hunger triggers violence and instability in the Sahel*. [Online] Available at: https://www.actionagainsthunger.org/story/hunger-triggers-violence-and-instability-sahel. Accessed 4 March 2022.

Alao, A. (2015). *Natural resources and conflict in Africa: The tragedy of endowment*. University of Rochester Press.

AFP. (2021). Ethiopian Red Cross says 80 percent of Tigray cut off from aid. *France24*. [Online] Available at: https://www.france24.com/en/live-news/20210210-ethiopian-red-cross-says-80-percent-of-tigray-cut-off-from-aid. Accessed 24 March 2021.

Anderson, M. (2015). The role of knowledge in building food security resilience across food system domains. *Journal of Environmental Studies and Sciences*, 5(4), 543–559.

Asfaw, T. (2015). *The society of Hunger Ethiopia Government (1930–2014) and famine: The importance of constitution* (Masters dissertation). University of Windsor: Department of Sociology, Anthropology and Criminology.

Bahru, Z. (1991). *A history of modern Ethiopia: 1855–1974*. James Currey.

Bonti-Ankomah, S. (2001). *Addressing food insecurity in South Africa*. Paper presented at the SARPN conference on Land Reform and Poverty Alleviation in Southern Africa. Pretoria.

Bora, S., Ceccacci, I., Delgado, C., & Townsend, R. (2011). *Food security and conflict* (World Development Report), World Bank. [Online] Available at: https://web.worldbank.org/archive/website01306/web/pdf/wdr%20background%20paper_bora%20et%20al4dbd.pdf?keepThis=true&TB_iframe=true&height=600&width=800. Accessed 20 February 2022.

Brück, T., & d'Errico, M. (2019). Food security and violent conflict: Introduction to the special issue. *World Development*, 117, 167–171.

Carroll, R. (2004). Chocolate war erupts in Ivory Coast. *The Guardian*. [Online] Available at: https://www.theguardian.com/world/2004/may/14/rorycarroll. Accessed 20 February 2022.

Cilliers, J. (2015). Future (im)perfect: Mapping conflict, violence and extremism in Africa. ISS Paper 287. *Institute for Security Studies*. [Online] Available at: https://issafrica.s3.amazonaws.com/site/uploads/Paper287-1.pdf. Accessed 25 February 2022.

Clay, E. (2002). *Food security: concept and measurements* (Conference Paper for FAO Expert Consultation on Trade and Food Security: Conceptualizing the Linkages, Rome, 11–12 July 2002). Overseas Development Institute.

Diakite, S. (2020). Addressing challenges in West African cocoa farming. *Rainforest Alliance*. [Online] Available at: https://www.rainforest-alliance.org/insights/addressing-the-challenges-in-west-africa-cocoa-farming/. Accessed 10 June 2022.

Evans, J. (2022). Unemployment in Gauteng 'at its worst', (another) war room established, Makhura announces. *Daily Maverick*. [Online] Available at: https://www.dailymaverick.co.za/article/2022-02-21-unemployment-in-gauteng-at-its-worst-another-war-room-established-makhura-announces/#:~:text=Unemployment%20Statistics%20SA%E2%80%99s%20third-quarter%202021%20Labour%20Force%20Survey,to%2044.9%25%20under%20the%20expanded%20unemployment%20rate%20definition. Accessed 11 June 2022.

FAO. (1983). *World food security: A reappraisal of the concepts and approaches*. Director General's Report.

FAO. (2002). *The state of food insecurity in the world 2001* (pp. 4–7). Rome.

Fountain, A. C., & Huetz-Adams, F. (2020). *Cocoa barometer 2020* (Online). Available at https://voicenetwork.cc/wp-content/uploads/2022/12/Cocoa-Barometer-2022.pdf. Acccessed 09 May 2023.

Friedman, H., & McMicheal, P. (1989). Agriculture and the state system: The rise and decline of national agricultures, 1870 to the present. *Sociologica Ruralis, 29*(2), 93–117.

Gill, P. (2010). *Famine and foreigners: Ethiopia since live aid*. Oxford University Press.

Giorgis, D. (1989). *Red tears: War, famine, and revolution in Ethiopia*. Red Sea Press.

Hall, R. (2011). Revisiting unresolved questions: Land, food and agriculture. *Transformation, 75*, 81–94.

Hasell, J., & Roser, M. Famines. Our World in Data. [Online] Available at: https://ourworldindata.org/famines. Accessed 13 June 2022.

Hassim, S., Kupe, T., & Worby, E. (Eds.). (2008). *Go home or die here: Xenophobia and the reinvention of difference in South Africa*. Wits University Press.

Holcomb, W., Clay, J., & Bonnie, K. (1985). The politics of famine in Ethiopia. *Cultural Survival Quarterly Magazine: Identity and Education, 9*(2), 44–58.

Jorari, A. (2012). *Pacific food security framework for action: Food security indicators*. PowerPoint presentation: 1–22.

Mahlatsi, M. L. S. (2017). *Peasants revolt: Analysing the role of the democratic state in the struggle for land and environmental justice in Xolobeni, Eastern Cape* (Honours dissertation). Department of Geography. Rhodes University.

Mahlatsi, M. L. S. (2022a). *Gentrification and the displacement of vulnerable communities in the post-apartheid city: A case study of the Maboneng Precinct and Braamfontein, Johannesburg* (Masters dissertation). Department of Town and Regional Planning. University of Johannesburg.

Mahlatsi, M. L. S. (2022b). *The impact of the COVID-19 pandemic on urban food security in South Africa: An analysis of the City of Ekurhuleni Metropolitan Municipality Central Food Bank* (Masters dissertation). Department of Public Administration. Tshwane University of Technology.

Mednick, S. (2020). Conflict and coronavirus spark a hunger crisis in Burkina Faso. *The New Humanitarian*. [Online]. Available at: https://www.thenew humanitarian.org/2020/08/19/conflict-and-coronavirus-spark-hunger-cri sis-burkina-faso. Accessed 9 March 2022.

Mosadomi, W. (2021). Unrelenting bandits burn down Niger farms, threaten food supply. *Vanguard*. [Online] Available at: https://www.vanguardngr. com/2021/11/declaration-as-terrorists-unrelenting-bandits-burn-down-niger-farms-threaten-food-supply/ (accessed 07 March 2022).

Myeni, T. (2022). What is Operation Dudula, South Africa's anti-migration vigilante? *Al Jazeera*. [Online] Available at: https://www.aljazeera.com/features/2022/4/8/what-is-operation-dudula-s-africas-anti-immigration-vig ilante. Accessed 20 June 2022.

Nyamnjoh, F. (2006). *Insiders and outsiders: Citizenship and Xenophobia in contemporary Southern Africa*. CODESRIA Books.

Pecorelli, S. (2020). The hidden ingredient in chocolate: Africa's child slaves. *Charged Affairs*. https://chargedaffairs.org/the-hidden-ingredient-in-chocol ate-africas-child-slaves/. accessed 23 November 2020.

Reuters. (2014). Niger Seeks Aid After Poor Harvest, Influx of Boko Haram Refugees. *VOA*. [Online] Available at: https://www.voanews.com/a/niger-seeks-aid-after-poor-harvest-influx-of-boko-haram-refugees/2554718.html. Accessed 7 March 2022.

Ringler, C., Zhu, T., Cai, X., Coo, J., & Wang, D. (2010). *Climate change impacts on food security in Sub-Saharan Africa insights from comprehensive climate change scenarios* (IFPRI Discussion Paper 01042).

South African Cities Network. (2015). *A study on current and future realities for urban food security in South Africa*. South Africa.

Sulkin, M. (2020). Understanding hunger in Egypt. *The Borgen Project*. [Online] Available at: https://borgenproject.org/hunger-in-egypt/ (10/06/2022).

UNHCR. (2015). *More than 7000 flee to western Chad to escape attacks on key town in Nigeria*. [Online] Available at: https://www.unhcr.org/54afb6dc9. html. Accessed 6 March 2022.

United Nations. (1975). *Report of the World Food Conference, Rome 5–16*.

Vestal, T. M. (1985). Famine in Ethiopia: Crisis of many dimensions. *Africa Today, 32*(4), 7–28.

Woods, D. (2003). The tragedy of the cocoa pod: Rent-seeking, land and ethnic conflict in Ivory Coast. *The Journal of Modern African Studies, 41*(4), 641–655.

World Bank. (1986). *Poverty and hunger: Issues and options for food security in developing countries*.

World Bank. (2015). *Ethiopia Poverty Assessment 2014*. World Bank. [Online] Available at: https://openknowledge.worldbank.org/handle/10986/21323. Accessed 23 August 2020.

CHAPTER 20

IGAD and the Quest for Economic and Security Regionalism

Mohamed Farah Hersi

INTRODUCTION

This chapter focuses on the Inter-Governmental Authority for Drought and Development (IGADD) established in 1986, and its successor, the Inter-Governmental Authority for Development (IGAD) that was formed in 1996. Several individuals, causes and structural changes within and beyond IGADD/IGAD's geopolitical and economic environment shaped these regional institutions' development. The chapter begins with the formation of IGADD, focusing on its goals, contributions and the historical factors and players that led to its formation. It examines the political actors and circumstances that prompted member states to establish a regional intergovernmental authority to address the challenges affecting livelihoods in the Horn of Africa.

M. F. Hersi (✉)
Director of the Academy for Peace and Development, Hargeisa, Somaliland
e-mail: mohammed.herssi@gmail.com

The discussion then turns to IGAD's evolution from an organisation focused on strategies to mitigate drought to a regional economic community (REC) recognised by the African Union (AU). The political actors and factors that impacted its revitalisation, reformulation and transformation are dissected, and its challenges and constraints since 1996 are discussed, including its mandate to enhance regional integration in the Horn of Africa. Through open-ended interviews with regional key actors, this chapter assesses the role of IGAD in enhancing the economic prosperity and security of the Horn of Africa.

IGADD's Formation

Despite their vast natural resources, countries in the Horn of Africa remain among the poorest in the world (IGAD, 2016). With a population of 226 million and a land area of 5.2 million km^2, the region's per capita income is substantially lower than the sub-Saharan African average of USD 1,624 (IGAD, 2016). Around 80 per cent of the territory is classed as arid and semi-arid (ASALs), with more than 40 per cent of this being unproductive (IGAD, 2016). In 2011, its member states' aggregate GDP stood at $167 billion, significantly less than Egypt's GDP of $232 billion (Byiers, 2016).

IGADD was founded in response to the catastrophic drought and famine that afflicted the Horn of Africa. While internal factors favoured the establishment of a cross-regional body, external circumstances and actors prevented the region's countries from forming a regional organisation to manage the impact of droughts and avert famine. Each of these nations was involved in a war with another, either directly or indirectly. Border disputes between Ethiopia and Somalia erupted in 1964 and 1977. Kenya and Uganda experienced similar issues, as did Sudan and Ethiopia (Interview, 2019). Furthermore, the region's terrain renders it difficult for a regional intergovernmental authority to address issues relating to famine and drought.

IGADD was created as a top-down, United Nations (UN)-led regional agency to address natural disasters, desertification and environmental degradation. It was first suggested by the UN General Assembly[1] and

---

[1] The UN General Assembly passed Resolution 35/90 in 1980 that urged the drought-stricken countries of Djibouti, Sudan, Somalia and Kenya to form an intergovernmental entity. It mandated the organisation to coordinate and support countries' efforts to address

was supported by a number of foreign countries. Due to the level of enmity among prospective member countries, the five original member states only agreed to the proposal after five years of deliberations (Weldesellassie, 2001). In contrast to the situation in Europe, regionalism in Africa, particularly in the Horn of Africa, has proven challenging as it poses a threat to state sovereignty. The fragile nature of African state structures is a further complication. According to Clapham:

> In Europe, regionalism was founded on strong nation-states, each of which had a government capable of defending its borders, controlling its territory, exerting a monopoly on the legitimate use of force, and providing security and community to all of its residents. Many African countries lack this unique blend of state-building characteristics. Rather than encouraging successful forms of regionalism, state fragility has served to strengthen Africa's political leaders' loyalty to legal sovereignty and zealous defense of statehood. (Clapham, 2017)

As dictated by the UN agenda, IGADD's scope was limited to drought, famine, food security and desertification. While other African RECs debated regional concerns such as economic integration and regional security, due to internal and external constraints, IGADD focused solely on non-political issues. As Healy (2009) notes, 'The organization's name didn't imply any political aspirations for broader regional integration. IGADD's goals were limited to functional coordination in the areas of environmental protection, food security, and natural resource management'.

IGADD received financial support from the international community from its inception. Member states did not pay their dues on a regular basis (Interview, 2019) and it remained a donor-driven regional organisation. It is estimated that 98 per cent of IGADD's funding was provided by donors (Interview, 2019). Financial constraints and a lack of political support from member countries resulted in the organisation being unable to carry out its five-year plan from 1992 to 1996. Furthermore, it suffered

---

drought and other natural catastrophes, as well as medium- and long-term recovery and rehabilitation (UN General Assembly Resolution 35/90 of 1980). Other UN resolutions that extend aid to drought-stricken countries in the Horn of Africa are included in Resolution 35/90. UN Resolution 35/91 stated that UN member nations should assist Ethiopia.

from limited technical capacity, with few employees and limited funding (Weldesellassie, 2001).

IGADD's top-down approach to regionalism hampered its ability to fulfil its mission. Scholars observe that it and its successor, IGAD, were primarily driven by external players. 'The perception has been that IGAD and regionalism were not so much a necessary step for the regimes of the Horn as the realization of an agenda encouraged from outside of multiple levels of the international community', writes Woodward (2013: 142). Mengisteab and Bereketeab assert that, 'If regional integration is to be meaningful, durable, and democratic, the existing top-down process of regional integration must be supplemented by a bottom-up process' (Mengisteab & Bereketeab, 2012: 175).

Despite a lack of financial and human resources, IGADD promoted inter-state discussion during its first decade (1986–1996). The forum discussed matters of inter-state national interest, security and economics at the summit of the Heads of State and Government. IGADD was also involved in conflict resolution and mediation (Interview, 2019).

Revitalisation of IGADD

In the 1990s, the Horn of Africa's changing regional dynamics and IGADD's lack of progress called for a re-energised, re-configured and revived regional intergovernmental authority. In early 1995, IGADD member nations met in Addis Ababa, Ethiopia, for consultative meetings to debate the organisation's future as well as the possibility of its transformation from a drought-focused to a regional integration instrument. The Assembly of Heads of State and Government convened an emergency summit on 18 April 1995 that released a declaration declaring its intention to extend IGADD's mandate and renew collaboration among member governments (IGAD, 1996). The Heads of State and Government signed a Letter of Instrument in March 1996 to rename IGADD 'the Intergovernmental Authority on Development' (IGAD, 1996). Eritrea, which legally seceded from Ethiopia in 1993 and was accepted as a member of IGAD during the fourth Summit of Heads of State and Government in Addis Ababa became the sixth member state (Megisteab & Bereketeab, 2012).

Despite its drought-focused mandate, IGADD was involved in regional security and economic development (IGAD, 2016). IGAD's new mandate included cooperation among member states. Article 13A of the

Agreement Establishing the Intergovernmental Authority on Development lists areas in which member nations can collaborate (IGAD, 1996). IGAD's main goal is regional integration and cooperation, with a focus on economic and security issues. These two aspects of regional integration are the subject of this chapter.

Actors, Factors and Incentives in IGAD's Transformation

IGAD's new mandate emphasises regional integration (with a focus on economic and security issues). The transition from a drought-focused and famine-control regional agency to an economic and security integration authority was influenced by internal and external factors, incentives and actors. IGAD has been reshaped and restructured by the following important factors and players:

The Post-Cold War International Security Order

The end of superpower rivalry altered global security arrangements, making regional actors responsible for their regions' security and establishing a new security order in which regional actors (primarily states) play a critical role (Al-Effendi, 2009). There is no space for unipolarity in post-Cold War security dynamics. Buzan and Woever propose three analytical frameworks to characterise the post-Cold War security order, namely, neorealist, globalist and regionalist, all of which address the challenges confronting the post-bipolar security system (Buzan & Woever, 1998).

The neorealist and regionalist perspectives both reflect the unipolar system in international security agreements. This study adopts a neorealist and regionalist approach to the IGAD region's security regime before and after the restructuring of the organisation in 1996. 'In the post-Cold War, the regional level stands more clearly on its own as the locus of conflict and cooperation for nations, and as the level of study for scholars attempting to explore current security issues' (Lake & Morgan, 2010: 6–7).

The regionalist view of global security is based on the premise that the breakdown of the bipolar system reduces global power concentration. In the post-Cold War international system, the greatest of the great powers have become lite powers (Buzan & Segal, 1996). That is, their national dynamics require attention, causing them to avoid military engagement and strategic rivalry in problematic areas of the world. This allows regional governments and societies to determine their military and political connections with less interference from the big powers than in the past (Buzan & Woever, 1998). The Regional Security Complex Theory (RSCT) developed by Buzan and Woever was influenced by the post-Cold War international security system's regionalist approach.

The fall of the Soviet Union and the internal dynamics of the countries in the Horn of Africa drastically reshaped the regional political structure in the late 1980s and early 1990s. Internally driven regime change ousted Ethiopia's Mengistu and Somalia's Siyad Barre, paving the way for Eritrea's ultimate independence following agreements between the Tigray Peoples' Liberation Front (TPLF) and the Eritrean Peoples' Liberation Front (EPLF). With the total collapse of Somalia, Somaliland unilaterally declared the dissolution of the 1960 union between the two countries and became a de facto independent state. Uganda and Sudan both installed new governments, while Kenya remained one of the most stable countries in the Horn of Africa (Interview, 2019). These internal and external factors prompted IGAD to revise its mandate in line with shifting regional and global dynamics in the direction of regional security and economic integration. Thanks to the United States (US)-led unipolar system in place at the time, IGAD was transformed to play a role in regional security and economic integration. For example, since 1996, it has played a crucial role in mediation processes in Sudan and Somalia.

The United States' Post-Cold War Security Strategy in the Horn of Africa

Superpower rivalries during the Cold War and the Arab–Israeli conflict influenced the US' strategic interests in the Horn of Africa, determining its policy in the region. According to Haste Bereket Selassie (1984), the following factors impacted US-Horn of Africa relations:

a. The need to protect the supply of oil from the Persian Gulf transiting through the sea routes off the Horn of Africa from disruption.
b. America's wartime backing for Israel.
c. The increasing Soviet/Cuban presence in Ethiopia from the end of the Ethio-Somali conflict in 1977.

d. Restricting Russian access to the Arabian Sea.
e. The increased presence of American submarines carrying nuclear weapons within striking distance of significant areas of the Union of Soviet Socialist Republics (USSR).

The US' approach has changed fundamentally since the end of the Cold War and the Arab–Israeli conflict. Radical extremists have arisen that represent a worldwide and regional menace. Al-Qaeda, a pro-jihadi extreme Islamist group founded by Osama Bin Laden, was established in Sudan with the assistance of former dictator Omar Hassan Ahmad al-Bashir (Rabasa, 2009). According to Rabasa (2009), 'East Africa (together with Yemen, which is part of the same geopolitical region) has been a central theatre of al-Qaeda operations' since the mid-1990s. The US held that militant Islamists took advantage of Africa's weak governance to establish bases in Somalia, Kenya, Sudan, Yemen and Ethiopia (Rabasa, 2009).

IGAD's revitalisation strategy has influenced the region's evolving geopolitical dynamics, particularly the US' anti-radicalisation strategies in East Africa. The US backed IGAD's revitalisation in order to create a regional entity that would complement its counter-terrorism operations. Some speculate that the US lobbied for IGAD's new role in order to isolate Sudan due to its ties to Al-Qaeda. Furthermore, IGAD's revitalisation was sparked by Eritrea and Ethiopia, the US' two primary allies at the time (Interview, 2019).

The Ethiopian-Eritrean Alliance

Following Ethiopia's absorption of Eritrea in 1962, nationalist movements such as the EPLF and the TPLF were founded in Cairo, Egypt, with the goal of achieving Eritrea's independence. The Eritrean liberation organisation finally overcame Ethiopian soldiers in 1991, after a 30-year struggle. Ethiopia granted Eritrea independence with the approval of the TPLF, which came to power after military rule was deposed (Interview, 2009). In 1991, Western governments, especially the US, considered Ethiopia and Eritrea as new, emerging democratic republics in a region racked by war and conflict for more than three decades (Interview, 2019). Melez, Ethiopia's late Prime Minister, and Eritrean President Isaias shared a common vision for the region. Ethiopia positioned itself as the new regional force in the IGAD zone following the collapse of Somalia, Ethiopia's primary adversary. Ethiopia and Eritrea were the primary actors in IGAD's revitalisation effort due to Somalia's absence, Djibouti's limited participation in regional diplomacy and Uganda and Kenya's lack of engagement.

Kenya and Uganda had fewer political incentives to participate in the IGAD transition because they were focused on the East African Community (EAC) (interview, 2019). However, they were concerned that the growing fallout from the Sudanese crisis and the clash between the South Sudan Liberation Movement (SPLM/A) and the Khartoum administration could spill over into their countries. Both nations were directly impacted by the Sudanese crisis, and thus felt that it was important to work with IGAD to address regional issues such as peacekeeping and coordinated regional security measures (Woodward, 2013).

Challenges and Issues Confronting IGAD's Regional Integration Initiatives

IGAD has experienced significant obstacles as a regional intergovernmental authority, limiting its activities and scope. These include the effects of multi-membership, donor dependency, intra-and inter-state conflicts in the region, the lack of a hegemon and Ethiopia's narrow view on regional integration in IGAD.

Multi-Membership of RECs

Horn of Africa countries' overlapping participation in several RECs is a perplexing issue (ECA, 2016). Most IGAD member nations are also members of one or more African RECs; it is estimated that 95 per cent of members of one REC belong to another one, with economic interests and loyalty to the Abuja Treaty following closely behind. In a poll conducted by the UN Economic Commission for Africa (ECA), half the countries cited strategic and political reasons for joining different RECs (ECA, 2016). Together with Burundi, Rwanda and Tanzania, Kenya, South Sudan and Uganda belong to the EAC, which is one of the most successful RECs in terms of economic cooperation and integration (ECA, 2016). The Common Market for Eastern and Southern Africa (COMESA) includes Djibouti, Ethiopia, Eritrea, Kenya, Sudan, South Sudan and Uganda. Somalia was re-admitted on 19 July 2018 at a summit of Heads of State and Government in Lusaka, Zambia

(African Legal Network, 2018) and COMESA now has a total of 21 member states. Djibouti and Eritrea are also members of the Community of Sahel-Saharan States (CEN-SAD) (Table 20.1).

Multi-membership of RECs has resulted in (a) low levels of financial contributions, (b) the implementation of conflicting programmes, (c) poor programme implementation and (d) poor attendance of meetings (ECA, 2016). All these issues have undermined IGAD's performance. Due to the fact that IGAD has failed to accomplish the intended regional economic unification, Uganda and Kenya are more economically dependent on the EAC than IGAD. The former has a better track record than IGAD and attracts more members from Central and Eastern Africa. However, Uganda and Kenya have relied on IGAD in terms of regional security cooperation, with a focus on containing the spillover of the conflict in Somalia and Sudan (Interview, 2019).

Variable geometry is a possible explanation for the numerous memberships. This approach to integration allows member states of a regional body to be flexible and choose different speeds at which to cooperate in different areas (Nagar, 2016). As noted by the ECA, it allows members to collaborate on a variety of issues while recognising that some countries move more quickly than others. The EAC is a model for this approach in East Africa. It has successfully implemented free trade agreements and

Table 20.1 IGAD member states' multi-membership of RECs

IGAD	EAC	CEN-SAD	COMESA	ECCAS	UMA	SADC	ECOWAS
Djibouti	Kenya	Djibouti	Djibouti				
Somalia	Uganda	Eritrea	Eritrea				
Ethiopia	South Sudan		Ethiopia				
Eritrea			Kenya				
South Sudan			Uganda				
Sudan			Sudan				
Kenya			Somalia				
Uganda			South Sudan				

Africa Regional Integration Index Report, United Nations Economic Commission for Africa, 2016.
Note ECCAS—Economic Community of Central African States; UMA—The Arab Maghreb Union; ECOWAS—Economic Community of West African States; SADC—Southern African Development Community

customs unions and is currently working to develop market integration. However, IGAD has been unable to adopt free trade agreements and customs unions, and is currently implementing market integration (ECA, 2016).

The term "spaghetti bowl" was coined by Bhagwati to describe the lack of a regional integration framework and the fragmentation brought about by multi-membership (Nagar, 2016). Leape and Thomas argue that '...in spite of their political appeal...[m]any schemes were designed without taking into account members' divergent interests and conflicting obligations stemming from overlapping [multiple] memberships of different regional arrangements; without considering the feasibility of implementation for participating countries; and without assessing members' incentives to comply and participate'.

Due to the fact that IGAD lags behind in terms of African regional integration, its members have applied to join other RECs. COMESA and the EAC are the organisations of choice for the majority of IGAD member states (Interview, 2019). While, as noted previously, IGAD has achieved significant progress in the areas of security and peacekeeping due to external players' incentives and interests, economic integration has not proceeded as envisaged, leaving the region considerably behind its continental peers (Interview, 2019). Somalia applied for membership of the EAC in 2013, but a decision has not yet been taken. South Sudan joined the EAC in 2016, making it the third IGAD member state to do so since the organisation's creation in 1999. South Sudan was admitted to COMESA in the same year (Trade Mark East Africa, 2016). All IGAD's members are currently members of COMESA, with South Sudan being the final one to join. COMESA offers a model for effective regional integration and the spirit and goals of its founding treaty are respected by IGAD (IGAD, 1996). As a result, IGAD and COMESA signed a Memorandum of Understanding solidifying their collaboration (COMESA, 2018).

COMESA was established in Uganda in 1993 to replace the Preferential Trade Area, which was established in 1981. On 8 December 1994, its member states adopted a treaty empowering COMESA to achieve the status of regional economic bloc (Makonnen & Haleiiujah, 2014). COMESA's main goals are: (a) to establish and maintain a full free trade area (FTA) that guarantees the free movement of goods and services produced within COMESA and eliminates all tariffs and non-tariff barriers; (b) to establish and maintain a customs union in which goods and services imported from non-COMESA countries will be subject to a single agreed-upon tariff (Common External Tariff) in all COMESA member states; and (c) to promote free movement of capital and investment (COMESA in Brief, 2018).

Countries that have not joined the COMESA FTA since its inception in 2000 have imposed tariff reductions on COMESA members. As of 2017, 16 COMESA members were enrolled in FTA programmes. Ethiopia, Eritrea, South Sudan and Eswatini are the four countries that have yet to join the FTA process (Interview, 2019). Commerce between COMESA countries increased by 7 per cent as a result of the FTA's operationalisation (COMESA, 2018). Ethiopia, a COMESA member, has yet to sign the FTA agreement. However, the country has been active in the leadership of the trading bloc with its late Prime Minister, Meles Zenawi elected as chair of COMESA in 2002 (Makonnen & Haleiiujah, 2014). Countries such as Ethiopia have cited the following issues as reasons for not joining the COMESA FTA:

a. Loss of government revenue: Customs duties/import tariffs on COMESA goods will result in a loss of revenue by all participating governments. Governments may be able to recoup this by adopting alternative taxation mechanisms (for example, VAT or sales taxes).
b. Job losses and increasing development imbalances: Some countries will benefit more from the agreements than others. Ethiopia's analysis of the ramifications of FTA membership concludes that 'although trade liberalization would result in welfare improvements, it would also result in job losses, revenue decrease, and de-industrialization' (Makonnen & Haleiiujah, 2014). Furthermore, Ethiopia's economic nationalism and policies on state-controlled markets obstruct the implementation of a COMESA and IGAD FTA.

Financial Dependence

As noted previously, external players, primarily the West and the UN influenced the formation of IGADD and IGAD. These initiatives were funded by donors that supported African regionalism for their own economic and security purposes. Internal circumstances and actors have hampered regionalism in Africa, particularly in the IGAD zone. Furthermore, scholars have questioned IGAD's level of ownership of regional integration, asserting that this should be a bottom-up, IGAD-driven process (El-Effendi, 2013). Instead, external donor organisations and institutions have charted the paths along which IGAD regionalism programmes are implemented. Indeed, it would seem that donors are more dedicated to such programmes than African governments (Interview, 2019).

Donors have funded the majority of RECs in Africa. As one of RECs recognised by the AU, IGAD has received funding from a variety of sources. The majority of its regional cooperation, security, peacekeeping and migration programmes have been funded by donors. The average IGAD annual budget is estimated to be around $115 million, with member states only contributing 10 per cent of this amount (Byiers, 2016). Given that peace and security are IGAD's top priorities, the security sector receives half the annual budget. Payment of the subscription fee varies between member states, with Ethiopia and Kenya both on time with their payments (Byiers, 2016). Uganda has not paid its annual dues for the past ten years (Interview, 2019). Given that donors fund 90% of IGAD's budget, the organisation will always be more accountable to them than to its member nations (Interview, 2019).

IGAD's regional cooperation and integration process under donor control has a number of flaws. Firstly, member states are hesitant to fully commit to a process dominated by external actors. Secondly, financial dependence results in a lack of long-term viability (Interview, 2019). Indigenous, IGAD-led, internally financed regional integration initiatives in the Horn of Africa have the potential to achieve successful integration.

Ethiopia's Power Game

Ethiopia continues to be IGAD's major powerhouse for the following reasons: Sudan, Somalia and South Sudan have been afflicted by political upheaval for many years; Eritrea is no longer part of IGAD; Djibouti is a member of many African RECs; and Kenya and Uganda are focused on the EAC. Ethiopia's significant role in IGAD is due to a number of factors. Firstly, Ethiopia is Africa's second most populous country and has the fastest expanding economy after Nigeria (World Bank, 2017). Following Eritrea's independence in 1993, Ethiopia became the world's largest landlocked country (Byiers, 2016). It is a large, diversified country with a landmass of more than one million km^2 bordering all IGAD member states except Uganda, and a population of 108 million, accounting for 40 per cent of IGAD's total population (World Bank, 2017). It is forecast that its population will exceed 150 million in 2035, with a population growth rate of 2.5 per cent.

Secondly, Ethiopia's GDP has grown at a rate of 10.5 per cent per annum for the past two decades, making it one of Africa's fastest-growing economies (World Bank, 2017). Its economic development relies on access to IGAD coastal nations' ports. Thirdly, Ethiopia has been a reliable partner of the AU, the UN and the US in the fight against terrorism in the Horn of Africa, as well as a key player in peacekeeping missions. Its former Prime Minister remarked, 'What is good for Ethiopia is good for the region' (Woodward, 2013). Byiers notes that Ethiopia has demonstrated its influence on regional organisations through 'conflict prevention, deploying thousands of Ethiopian UN peacekeepers to the Abyei border region between Sudan and South Sudan; conflict management, hosting mediation efforts for the South Sudanese civil war; and combating terrorism, continuing military action against Somalia's Al-Shabab. It houses the bulk, if not all, of the IGAD's security-related specialized institutions' (Byiers, 2016).

Ethiopia's regional status has been hotly debated by academics and policymakers. Similarly, its involvement in regional integration has been questioned due to perceptions that its goal is to dethrone Kenya as the region's most powerful economy (Healy, 2009). There is no doubt that Ethiopia plays a crucial role in the IGAD region. However, it could serve as enabler of developing regional integration or a stumbling block to seamless, stable and balanced regional cooperation in IGAD. As a regional governance tool, IGAD reflects the power balance among its member nations, with Ethiopia and Kenya its two most powerful players. Ethiopia controls its decision-making process, while Kenya participated in peace processes in Sudan and Somalia in 2005 and 2004.

The core-building blocks for emerging regionalism in the IGAD region have been economic development and security. Ethiopia's internal economic and political systems (a state-controlled economy, revolutionary democracy and developmental state model of political and economic governance) have had a profoundly negative impact on regional integration programmes. IGAD-led regional economic integration proposals were downplayed by Ethiopia for fear that they would challenge its protectionist approach to industrialisation.

With regard to regional security efforts, Ethiopia's foreign policy was modified following the attempted assassination of Egypt's former president, Hosni Mubarak, in Addis Ababa in 1995. Previously it focused on upholding the security, territorial integrity and sovereignty of the Ethiopian state, complemented by its non-interference doctrine (Prunier & Ficquet, 2015). Furthermore, Ethiopia suspected that the Sudanese government was behind the attempted assassination of President Bashir (Prunier & Ficquet, 2015). This led to a shift in policy from non-interference to non-tolerance. Ethiopia became embroiled in Sudan's civil war, which resulted in South Sudan's independence in 2011. It also intervened in one of the Horn of Africa's longest civil wars in Somalia in 2006. This was accomplished by defeating Al-Shabab, an extremist terrorist group. As a security-oriented country, Ethiopia has played a key role in regional security through the IGAD security framework.

Lack of a Regional Hegemon

The term "hegemony", which is derived from the Greek word "hegemonic" refers to one element in a system's dominance of others (Yilmaz, 2010). According to Antonia Gramsci (cited in Yilmaz, 2010), power is not just dependent on force, but can also be depending on consent. Hegemony signifies the status of the most powerful country in the international system or the position of a dominant state in a particular region. Gramsci adds that hegemony is coercive cooperation that combines social and political surveillance, force and consent. However, Bates focuses on Gramsci's initial thesis, claiming that the key premise of the concept of "hegemony" is that 'man [sic] is not dominated solely by force, but also by ideas' (Bates, 1975).

The concept of "hegemony", which is opposed by most international relations theorists that subscribe to neorealism and historical materialism, remains a contentious theoretical issue (Bates, 1975). While both schools of thought agree that hegemony is not a historical accident but a social phenomenon that emanates from a social situation, they disagree on the circumstances under which the notion is applicable. For example, realism claims that hegemony arises from chaotic international relations that necessitate the use of force to bring about world order. Historical materialism believes that hegemony can be traced back to a mode of production that serves a specific class, and that there is an economically dominant state system that is served by modes of production. Order is brought to the world system when other states imitate the dominant state's behaviour and expectations that are consistent with its demands.

Despite the ongoing debate, the importance of the hegemonic state in the international system and regional affairs cannot be denied. Scholars and policymakers continue to discuss and analyse the role of hegemony in regional politics. Iyob notes that the colonial legacy impacts on regional hegemonic powers (Iyob, 1993) and that regional hegemony is an artefact of post-colonial international and regional regimes (Iyob, 1993). She compares South Africa and Libya (which have hegemonic strength and influence) to Ethiopia (which does not), and notes that, 'The concept of regional hegemony is particularly important in understanding the role of institutionalized legitimacy conferred or denied to certain nations'. In wars that threaten the terms of order envisioned by any regional power, the need for diplomatic capacity is clear. Libya and South Africa's hegemonic claims were never realised since neither gained regional legitimacy, and their hegemonic ambitions were in direct conflict with regional norms. However, Ethiopia was able to sustain armed combat for many years without being sanctioned by international or regional organisations due to the legitimacy and diplomatic capability conferred by hegemonic supremacy (Iyob, 1993: 4). Operationalisation of the concept of "hegemony" in the IGAD region is hotly debated. Regional hegemony is determined by: (a) post-colonial international and regional orders, (b) the post-Cold-War global security system and (c) the war on terror.

The British colonial authorities assisted Ethiopia to move from the main highlands to the lowlands, occupying a vast swath of land that is today known as the new Ethiopia. Ethiopia subjugated various ethnic groups that would later become part of modern Ethiopia during this imperial assault. With the help of the British, Ethiopia conquered the largest ethnic groups in Ethiopia including the Oromos, Somalis, Afars and other groups and nationalities. This illustrates how international assistance and influence helped to create and consolidate regional hegemons.

Nigeria and South Africa play crucial hegemonic roles in the regional orders of SADC and ECOWAS in West and Southern Africa, respectively. While Ethiopia has this status in IGAD, it has been unable to achieve the status of a regional hegemonic force. It does not have the same clout in the region as that enjoyed by Nigeria and South Africa in West and Southern Africa, respectively. Furthermore, IGAD does not operate within a unipolar system, but a tripolar system. Several countries have claimed leadership in this region, including Sudan, Kenya and Ethiopia.

Scholars express different opinions on Ethiopia's regional hegemony. Comarin asserts that, 'Ethiopia intends to play hegemon over one of the planet's poorest regions—the Horn of Africa'. Verhoeven argues that 'Ethiopia could be a future African hegemon' (Le Gouriellec, 2018), while Herbst predicted that, 'There would be four African countries to operate as hegemons, Nigeria, South Africa, the Democratic Republic of the Congo, and Ethiopia'. He added that Ethiopia is 'too impoverished and too internally divided to genuinely perform the position of regional hegemon' (cited in Le Gouriellec, 2018).

Thus, despite Ethiopia's large population, economic prosperity and military strength, protracted conflict within the IGAD region as well as its geopolitical and strategic value to regional powers and superpowers, make it difficult for the country to become a regional hegemon (Table 20.2).

The global powers have exerted considerable influence in the IGAD region which has been ravaged by intra- and inter-state conflict for the past three decades and characterised by regional and global aspirations for territorial dominance. Muslim-majority countries (Qatar, the United Arab Emirates, Saudi Arabia, Turkey and Iran) have used their clout to impose their influence. Israel also regards the region as a strategic asset because it includes the Red Sea, the Gulf of Aden and the Bab al Manden Strait. All of these countries have established relationships with IGAD member states, while China, Russia, India and the US have also secured their stake. In the past two decades, China has invested more in the region than any other global power.

Table 20.2 Profile of IGAD member states

State	Territory (km^2)	Population (million)	GDP (US$ billion)	Military expenditure ($ million)	Troops
Ethiopia	1,127,127	105	80.56	1,344,020	138,000
Somalia	637,657	14.74	7.369	Na	16,000
Djibouti	23,000	956,985	1.845	138,320,000	10,000
Sudan	1,861,484	40.53	117.5	5,020,420,000	109,000
South Sudan	619,745	12.58	2.904	2,187,093	Not available
Kenya	580,367	49.7	74.94	2,291,800,000	24,000
Eritrea	117,598	4.475	2.680	460,698,000	300,000
Uganda	241,037	42.86	25.89	400,000	45,000

Source Danish Institute for International Studies, 2009

While the Horn of Africa's multipolar nature has created a non-hegemonic power structure in the past five decades, successful regional integration requires a hegemon to provide political leadership that steers regionalism. Unlike ECOWAS and SADC, where Nigeria and South Africa, respectively, play an important role in the integration process as political leaders, the IGAD region lacks such leadership and hence fails to function as a substantial regional integration bloc (Interview, 2019). 'South Africa's hegemonic power impact in the area is anchored on its claim to be projecting Africa's voice and interests at major global economic forums and groups, and in its efficacy as Africa's single player in BRICs (Brazil, Russia, India and China) and the G20' (Ogunnubi & Amao, 2016).

IGAD's Role in Regional Security and Economic Integration: A New Agenda

By incorporating new functions, IGAD's revitalisation fundamentally changed the nature of its mandate. Regional integration is one of the pillars of its new mandate, while regional security and economic integration are its major focus. In terms of the former, IGAD has intervened in Sudan and Somalia, two of the region's most conflict-ridden countries. IGADD participated in Sudan's 1993 peace and reconciliation conferences despite not having been assigned a clear mandate to undertake such work. Despite the region's political environment during the Cold Wat, it succeeded in healing relations between the two main regional rivals—Ethiopia and Somalia—by building a regional co-operative framework to tackle contentious issues (El-Effendi, 2013).

Regional security, conflict and peacemaking are at the core of IGAD's regional cooperative framework and the organisation has adopted an interventionist stance. Following the collapse of military rule in Somalia in 1991, the UN and US took responsibility for the peacemaking process, and IGAD shifted its focus to Sudan where conflict has raged between the Arab-Muslim north and the African indigenous-Christian south since 1955 (El-Effendi, 2019).

Since its transformation, IGAD has been actively involved in regional peacekeeping. It has been hailed for dealing with intra- and inter-state disputes in the Sudan peace process. However, IGAD's failure to halt Somalia's intra-state civil war and to engage Ethio-Eritreans in 1998 have been labelled as failures. While IGAD has also prioritised regional economic integration, little progress has been made in this regard. The establishment of an FTA is the first step in establishing a regional market, and IGAD member states have not adopted the protocol for doing so.

Conclusion

This chapter examined the major players and factors in the founding of IGADD and its metamorphosis to IGAD. External players and circumstances rather than the region's internal dynamics resulted in the establishment of IGAD. It and its predecessor are regarded as top-down, donor-driven and geopolitically motivated regional intergovernmental organisations, with serious consequences for long-term viability, neutrality and ownership, as well as peace processes.

While many saw IGAD's re-formation as the creation of a new regional organisation to deal with the Horn of Africa's severe challenges, it remains weak despite its massive donor-led initiatives in conflict and peacebuilding in Somalia and Sudan. The Abuja Treaty and Lagos Plan of Action call for vibrant RECs that promote regional integration; however, IGAD has been unable to fulfil this goal due to the restrictions and challenges outlined in this chapter. The first phase of market integration, the establishment of a FTA has yet to be achieved.

IGAD has played a critical role in regional security, having actively led and, in some circumstances, participated in the Sudanese and Somalia peace processes. The Comprehensive Peace Agreement reached by the parties to the Sudanese conflict in 2005 led to the establishment of Africa's youngest state, the Republic of South Sudan. However, IGAD has failed to secure long-term political stability in Somalia.

As an REC that is recognised by the AU, IGAD is important in many respects. Changes are, however, required. Its economic integration programmes should be overhauled. Given the recent changes in this region, IGAD should take responsibility for the integration process rather than delegating it to member states' national administrations. A regional agenda driven by member states may not result in a robust, integrated regional economy and security; thus, policy with regard to the Horn of Africa should emanate from IGAD.

References

Bates, T. R. (1975). Gramcsi and the theory of hegemony. *Journal of the History of Ideas, 36*(2), 351-366.
Buzan, B., & Segal, G. (1996). The rise of "lite" powers: A strategy for the postmodern state. *World Policy Journal, 13*(3), 1-10.
Buzan, B., & Woever, O. (1998). *Security: A new framework for analysis*. Lynne Rienner.
Byiers, B. (2016). *Understanding ECONOMIC INTEGRATION AND PEACE AND SECURITY in IGAD*. ECDPM.
Clapham, C. (2017). *The horn of Africa: State transformation and decay*. Oxford University Press.
COMESA in Brief. (2018). *Growing together, for prosperity*. COMESA.
El-Affendi, A. (2009). The perils of regionalism: Regional integration as a source of instability in the Horn of Africa. *Journal of Intervention and State Building, 3*, 1-20.
Healy, S. (2009). *Peacemaking on the mist of war: An assessment of IGAD's contribution to regional security*. Royal Institute of International Affairs.
Inter-Governmental Authority and Development. (1996). *Establishing agreement of IGAD in 1996*. Assembly of Head of State and Government.
Inter-governmental authority for development. (2016). *IGAD State of the Region*. IGAD.
Iyob, R. (1993). Regional hegemony: Domination and resistance in the horn of Africa. *Journal of Modern African Studies, 31*(2), 257-276.
Lake, D., & Morgan, P. (2010). *Regional orders: Building security in new world*. Pennsylvania State University Press.
Le Gouriellec, S. (2018). Regional power and contested hierarchy: Ethiopia and imperfect hegemon in the horn of Africa. *Journal of International Affairs, 94*(5), 1059-1075.
Makonnen, T., & Haleiiujah, L. (2014). *Ethiopia regional integration and the COMESA free trade area*, Occasional Paper, 198 South African Institute of International Affairs.
Mengisteab, K., & Bereketean, R. (2012). *Regional integration, identity and citizenship in the greater horn of Africa*. James Curry.
Nagar, D. (2016). *The politics and economics of regional integration in Africa: A comparative study of COMESA and SADC, 1980-2015*. University of the Witwatersrand.
Ogunnubi, O., & Amao, O. B. (2016). *South Africa's Emerging 'soft power' influence in Africa and its Impending Limitations: Will the Giant be able to Weather the Storm?* University of Zululand.
Prunier, G., & Fiquet, E. (2015). *Understanding contemporary Ethiopia: Monarchy, revolution and the legacy of meles Zenawi*. C. Hurst and Co. Publishers.

Rabasa, A. (2009). *Al-Qaeda in east Africa*. RAND.
Selassie, H. B. (1984). The American dilemma on the horn. *Journal of Modern African Studies*, 22(2), 249–272.
Trade Mark East Africa. (2016). News Article on COMESA membership. Available online at https://www.busiweek.com/trademark-east-africa-comesa-open
Weldesellassie, I. (2001). IGAD as an International Organization, its institutional development and short-comings. *Journal of Africa Law*, 55(1), 262–312.
Woodward, P. (2013). *The IGAD and regional relations in the horn of Africa: The horn of Africa intra-state and inter-state conflicts and security*. Pluto Press.
World Bank. (2017). *The inescapable manufacturing service nexus: Exploring the potential distribution service*. World Bank.
Yilmaz, S. (2010). *State, power and hegemon*. Centre for Promoting Ideas.

Index

A
African agricultural economy, 331
African culture, 293, 296
African Union Mission in Somalia (AMISOM), 177, 178
Afrophobic, 336, 337
Ahlu Sunnah Wal Jammah (ASWJ), 110, 111, 113, 114, 118–120
Al-Qaeda, 109, 111, 114
Al-Qaeda in the Islamic Maghreb (AQIM), 128–130, 133, 134
Al-Shabaab, 6, 7, 177, 178, 185
Anti-colonialism movements, 195, 206
Artisanal miners, 216, 218–221
Attractive retirement package, 222

B
Biafra war, 34
Boko Haram/ISWAP, 9, 109–118, 120, 126, 128, 131–133
Bottom-up approach, 276, 278
Bourgoutié, 58, 61, 64
Bride price, 290, 316

C
Capacity, 77
Cattle ranching project, 40
Ceasefire arrangements, 192, 195, 197, 202, 205–207
Chronic food insecurity, 329, 330
Clans, 180, 182–185
Climate change, 12, 13, 33–37, 39, 41–47, 53–55, 57–64
Cold War, 127, 192, 194, 195, 200, 206
Colonial boundaries, 22, 23
Colonialism, 192–195, 200
Colonial police, 73, 74
Colonial structural configuration, 19
Common Market for Eastern and Southern Africa (COMESA), 350–353
Comprehensive Peace Agreement of 2005, 276

Conflict, 17–19, 21, 23
Conflict in Africa, 17–19, 21, 23, 30
Consensus-based informal governance, 252
Consociational democracy, 229, 230, 242–245
Consolidation of power, 162
Conventional democratic system, 160
Corruption, 55, 58, 60, 62, 64, 74, 75, 77, 79, 83–85, 138, 178, 188
COVID-19, 5, 335, 337, 338
Criminal Code Act, 316, 320
Curriculum change, 96
Customary-based clan, 252
Customary justice, 250, 252, 255, 257, 258, 261, 265–267, 269
Customary justice system, 256, 260, 266, 268

D
Decision-makers, 279
Decolonisation, 26, 27, 93, 94, 96
Democracy, 149, 151, 153–156, 159, 160, 163
Democratic government, 76
Democratisation in Africa, 142
Desertification, 34, 36, 37, 41–43, 45, 46
Development thesis, 150
Diamond governance, 214, 217, 221
Drought, 34, 36, 37, 39, 42, 43, 45, 46

E
Economic Community of West African States (ECOWAS), 134, 140, 141, 153–156
Ecosystem, 53, 55–57, 64
Election management body, 164, 171

Elections, 159–161, 164–167, 169–171
Elements of human security, 137
Environmental degradation, 34
Ethiopia's regional status, 355
Ethiopian federal system, 228
Ethiopian People's Revolutionary Democratic Front (EPRDF), 228, 237
Ethnic-based conflict, 227
Ethnic federalism, 228, 229, 232, 243, 244
Ethnic groups, 228–232, 234, 241–245
Ethnic politics, 233
Exclusion, 228, 230, 233–235, 241, 244
Expropriation without compensation, 192–194, 196, 197, 199, 202, 203, 205, 206

F
Famine Early Warning Systems Network, 333
Famines, 332, 333
Fanon, Frantz, 17, 20, 25–30
Farmer-herders conflict, 34, 38, 42, 45, 46
Farming communities, 40, 41, 44, 45
Fast-track land reform, 196, 203
Fees Must Fall (FMF), 5, 6, 91–101, 103–106
Femicide, 288, 289, 294–296
Femininity, 291, 292, 301
Feminist perspective, 313
Feminist theory, 313, 314
Food access, 329, 330
Food aid, 334
Food insecurity, 139, 141
Food regime, 331
Food security, 328–331, 333–335, 337, 338

INDEX

Forced labour, 220
Free education, 94, 100, 105
Free trade area (FTA), 352, 353, 360
Fulani herders, 34, 35, 37, 38, 40, 41, 44, 45, 47

G

G-5 Sahel Force, 129
Galkayo, 179–188
Gang rape, 290, 293
Gender-based violence (GBV), 11, 12, 287, 288, 291, 292, 295, 309–312, 314–322
Gender norms, 313
Gender roles, 291
Girls' education, 284, 285
Global powers, 358
Good governance, 217, 218
Governance, 70, 72, 74, 75, 85
Grazing Bill, 37
Guardian perspective, 151

H

Hegemonic masculinity, 291–293
Hegemonic state, 357
Hegemony, 40, 356, 357
Highly Indebted Poor Countries (HIPC), 176, 178
Horn of Africa, 343–346, 348, 350, 354–356, 358–360
Humanitarian crisis, 333
Humanitarian responses, 139
Hunger, 328–330, 332, 334, 337, 338
Hunger alleviation, 328, 337
Hybrid political orders, 261

I

Illegal diamonds, 221
Illegal mining, 216, 219, 221
Inclusive governance, 229, 241, 242, 244, 245
Independent media, 168
Independent National Electoral Commission (INEC), 164
Inner Niger Delta, 53–64
Insecurity, 179, 180, 184, 186–188
Institutionalized stratification, 236
Inter-clan hostility, 182
Inter-Governmental Authority for Development (IGAD), 175, 282, 283, 343, 344, 346–360
International conflict, 18
Intersectionality, 289, 291, 293
Islamic State in the Greater Sahara (ISGS), 128, 130, 133, 136, 137

J

Judiciary, 250, 252–254, 261, 265–267, 270

L

Lancaster House Agreement, 197, 198, 202
Land conflict, 192, 194, 203, 206
Landlessness, 338
Law enforcement, 75, 82, 84, 85
Legal pluralism, 249, 250, 256
Legitimacy, 72, 75, 77, 85
Liberal feminism, 312, 322
Liberation movements, 192, 194, 195, 197, 198, 200, 202, 207
Literacy levels, 278, 283, 284
Local tyranny, 233
Low human development, 129, 142

M

Majeerteen, 183, 184
Makerere Student Guild, 92
Mamdani, Mahmood, 17, 22–25, 27–30
Marange diamond fields, 214–216, 218, 219, 221, 223
Marginalisation, 228, 230, 233, 235, 236
Masculine norm, 292
Masculinities, 289–292, 294, 296, 301
Mass media, 160, 162
Mbembe, Achille, 20
Media, 160–162, 166–171
Media independence, 168
Migration of herders, 41, 44, 60
Military coup, 9, 10, 147–149, 151–156
Military *coup d'états*, 148
Military entrepreneurs, 216
Military intervention, 147–156
Mineral resource-conflict nexus, 328
Minority ethnic groups, 232, 243, 244
Modern policing, 73
Mopti region, 53, 56, 58, 60–63
Movement for Democratic Change (MDC), 222

N

Nature of the Nigerian state, 164
Neoliberal policies, 196, 201
Nigeria Governors Forum, 314
Nigerian police force, 74
Non-state law, 250
Northern nomads, 40

O

Opération Barkhane, 135
Operation Dudula, 336
Opération Sérval, 134
Owner nationality, 232

P

Patriarchal cultures, 280
Patriarchal dividend, 292
Patriarchal legal structures, 292
Patriarchal society, 313
Patriarchy, 291, 296, 300
Peace agreement of 2015, 282
Peacebuilding, 274–284
Plural justice, 249, 252, 255–257
Plural legal governance, 250
Police brutality, 5
Police corruption, 74, 75, 79, 84
Political ecology, 54
Political economy framework, 161
Political process models, 102
Politicisation of disputes, 42, 44
Poor governance, 56, 62
Post-Cold War, 347, 348
Post-Cold War dynamics, 192, 206
Post-colonial African states, 11
Post-structural political ecology, 54, 55
Practical gender interests, 276
Prebendalism, 163

Q

Qadi, 251

R

Race, 19, 23–25, 27
Radical extremists, 349
Rape, 287, 288, 290, 293, 296, 302
Rebellion, 182, 183
Refugees, 335
Regional cooperation, 354, 355
Regional hegemony, 357
Regional integration, 11

Resource conflicts, 13
Resource curse, 8
Resource mobilisation theory, 100, 101, 105
Resurgence of military coups, 148, 154–156
Ruling elite, 214–217, 219, 221–223
Runners, 221

S
Sahel, 125–143
Scramble for Africa, 21
Security perspective, 177
Security sector, 213–223
Sex roles, 313
Sexual offences, 290, 296
Sexual power relations, 291
Sexual violence, 312, 314, 316
Shariᶜah, 8
Sharia Law, 251, 260, 269
Silencing the guns, 337
Social contract of the state, 71
Social environment, 312
Social impact, 115, 120
Social instability, 334, 336
Social Learning Theory (SLT), 312, 313, 322
Social media, 93, 95, 100, 101, 103
Social movement, 93, 99, 101
Social movement theory, 92, 99, 100, 105, 106
Soldiers, 220
Somaliland Constitution, 262, 269
Somaliland Lawyers Association (SOLLA), 257
Spaghetti bowl, 352
Special Anti-Robbery Squad (SARS), 5, 80
State fragility, 10
Strategic gender interests, 276
Structural violence, 132, 135, 142

Student movement, 91–93, 100, 104, 105
Student protest movements, 92
Sultanate, 181, 182
Superpower rivalry, 347
Syndicates, 218–221, 223

T
Tax evasion, 216
Telecommunication firms, 177
Terrorism, 2, 3, 7, 9, 10, 14
Terrorism in Africa, 110, 111
Terrorist group, 6, 9
Terrorist organisations, 111
Torture, 76, 78, 79, 82, 85
Traditional conflict resolution, 250
Traditional leaders, 252, 258, 263, 264
Traditional security threats, 180, 184
Truth and Reconciliation Commission (TRC), 64
Tuareg, 128, 129

V
Violence Against Persons Prohibition (VAPP), 311, 318
Violence Against Women (VAW), 287, 289, 291, 292, 296, 310–312, 314, 317
Violent extremism, 113
Virginity testing, 315, 316

W
Widowhood practices, 312, 315, 316, 318
Women's economic dependence, 314
Women's inclusion, 278, 282
Women's organisations, 274, 276–279, 281, 282, 284
Wunlit Peace Agreement, 277

X
Xenophobia, 2, 3, 10, 11, 14, 29
Xenophobic conflict, 336

Y
Yeki *woreda*, 229, 231–236, 238–241, 244
Youth, 2, 4, 5, 7, 14

Printed in the United States
by Baker & Taylor Publisher Services